INDIA ABROAD

INDIA ABROAD

DIASPORIC CULTURES OF
POSTWAR AMERICA AND ENGLAND

Sandhya Shukla

PRINCETON UNIVERSITY PRESS   PRINCETON AND OXFORD

PUBLISHED BY PRINCETON UNIVERSITY PRESS, 41 WILLIAM STREET,

PRINCETON, NEW JERSEY 08540

IN THE UNITED KINGDOM: PRINCETON UNIVERSITY PRESS,

3 MARKET PLACE, WOODSTOCK, OXFORDSHIRE OX20 1SY

LIBRARY OF CONGRESS CATALOGING-IN-PUBLICATION DATA

SHUKLA, SANDHYA RAJENDRA.

INDIA ABROAD : DIASPORIC CULTURES OF POSTWAR AMERICA

AND ENGLAND / SANDHYA SHUKLA.

P.   C.M.

INCLUDES BIBLIOGRAPHICAL REFERENCES AND INDEX.

ISBN: 0-691-09266-4 (ALK. PAPER) — ISBN 0-691-09267-2 (PBK. : ALK. PAPER)

1. EAST INDIANS—UNITED STATES. 2. EAST INDIANS—ENGLAND.

3. EAST INDIANS—FOREIGN COUNTRIES. I. TITLE.

E184.E2 S58 2002

305.891'4041 '09045—DC21   2002035550

BRITISH LIBRARY CATALOGING-IN-PUBLICATION DATA IS AVAILABLE

THIS BOOK HAS BEEN COMPOSED IN SABON

PRINTED ON ACID-FREE PAPER. ∞

WWW.PUPRESS.PRINCETON.EDU

PRINTED IN THE UNITED STATES OF AMERICA

1 3 5 7 9 10 8 6 4 2

For My Parents
and
For Tom

CONTENTS

INDIA ABROAD

INTRODUCTION

GEOGRAPHIES OF INDIANNESS

IN A "MILLENNIUM SUPPLEMENT," the August 1999 issue of *National Geographic* featured a set of articles on globalization. On the cover was a photograph of two Indian women: one dressed in a traditional sari, gold jewelry, and flowers and the other, her daughter, clad in a vinyl bodysuit (see fig. 1), with the title "Global Culture." The same photograph also appeared inside the magazine, with a caption that read, in part, "SOPHISTICATED LADIES. They're well-off, well educated, widely traveled, fluent in several languages. . . . The global marketplace for goods, information, and style is their corner store."[1] Though the women were apparently "Indian," the picture's significance was described by the magazine's editors in more global terms: "Goods move. People move. Ideas move. And cultures change." We are in a new moment, suggests a magazine that has served as a prime vehicle for middlebrow cultural representation, and that moment can be read through a chaotic Indianness.

Lest difference get out of control, readers in the United States have *National Geographic* to help order their perceptions.[2] Remarking on the millennium theme, the editor confessed some anxiety about the growing association between globalization and cultural homogenization, while adding: "But for the moment, at least, it is still arresting to see the juxtaposition of different societies, as men in Shanghai carry around a life-size Michael Jordan cutout or a Los Angeles artisan applies Old World henna designs to a woman's hand."[3] And indeed, a kind of ironic, tongue-in-cheek detachment is the mood of the images in *National Geographic* that suggest difference. Hong Kong action star Michelle Yeoh is suspended from a rope in front of the famous Hollywood sign in southern California in an image appearing aside the title "A World Together." In another photograph, with a caption noting the significant population of Thai peoples in Los Angeles, a large group of fully robed Buddhist monks eats breakfast at a Denny's restaurant amid seeming nonchalance from other diners.

About a third of the photographs accompanying the *National Geographic* series feature some kind of Indianness. This fact, along with the decision to frame the issue with the image of the Indian mother and daughter, certainly prompts us to consider the central role of Indianness in the broader production of interpenetrating globalism, where nationalities come into direct contact and yet remain highly discrete. An overly polar-

Figure 1.   The National Geographic of India on the move
(copyright Joe McNally).

ized sense of the traditional and the modern, unsurprisingly, is signaled by the cover, in images—familiar and shocking—of exotic femininity. Heightened ironies are signaled by the appearance of Coca-Cola signs, tubes of Colgate brand toothpaste, and an inflatable American astronaut amid Mumbai's shack houses, small villages, and a Bangalore shopping mall. Juxtaposition here is a visual strategy that gives America the mark of commercial modernity, and India and other non-European nations cultural (and economic) difference; the penetrations of east by west, as well as of west by east, retain some measure of contrast. Still, the photos hint at the possibility of a national Indianness being reinvented *through* commodity capitalism that can illuminate the governing theme of goods and people moving, cultures changing. Dislocations and reconstructions of India in a global context begin to expand the field of representational possibilities, even beyond the categories of "here" and "there" in which the magazine traffics.

India on the move and Indianness remade are central concerns of this book. While *National Geographic* cannot help but exhibit residual interest in the project of identifying where the nation and its cultures are, *India Abroad* seeks to thoroughly disturb that sensibility by explaining how migrant cultures express global belonging in multiple national spheres.[4] Echoing a major Indian immigrant newspaper in New York, I use the title

"India Abroad" to evoke a mobile and dynamic nation that takes shape in spaces far removed from a territorial state. India, this book's "national geographic" is thus not a precise location of homeland, nor a singular motivating impulse, but instead a heterogeneous imaginary that draws energy from historical formations of colonialism and postcolonialism, discourses of diversity, and exercises of bureaucratic power.

Like all nations, India is freighted as much with metaphorical possibility as with geopolitical presence. Secure, now, in the insight that the nation has always been under production, scholars in South Asian studies have been able to develop sophisticated analyses of complex social formations and cultures of resistance.[5] Since work on immigrants has needed to overcome the fixation on lands of settlement as defining its object, and studies of diaspora have taken nation to mean homeland, there has been a great deal of emphasis on how Indian migrants develop relationships with the Indian nation-state.[6] But some of the constructedness, the fictiveness, of nation in cultures of migration can be lost when Indians are too thoroughly linked with their country of origin. Certainly associations between Indians and the Indian state abound, in transnational capital flows, in political movements, and in social relations, but the argument I make here is that the excesses of "India" in the space of Indian diaspora suggest more than long-distance nationalism. I suggest that it is through a broadly symbolic India that Indians can see themselves not only as national subjects of a modern world, but also as citizens of postwar United States and England—nations that themselves are undergoing processes of reconstruction. As India is built abroad in what we might see as the "contact zones"[7] of migrant cultures in unstable first-world spaces, a new set of discourses for citizenship and subjectivity are created. Ultimately a different sensibility of how one can live in a multicultural space is performed not only for Indians, but also for other American and British peoples.

There are 1.7 million people in the United States today who claim Indian descent.[8] While the number itself is significant, even more striking is how recently the migrations that created this heterogeneous population took place: largely after 1965, when the Immigration and Naturalization Act was passed to create less racially discriminatory standards for entry. England's Indian population is close to 1 million, a huge portion of which is attributable to migrations after the mid-1950s; at 1.9 percent of the population, it represents the largest ethnic minority.[9] The Indian immigrant, in both the United States and England, is a presence in daily life, in urban and suburban residential communities, in business and education, and even in politics. The postwar period, of roughly fifty years, in which Indianness has become locally visible and recognized, has been one of quite dramatic transformations in the world: massive movements of peoples, the unfolding consequences of colonialism and postcolonialism, new forms of diversity in all nation-states, and transitions from largely industrial to largely service-based global economies. In and through each shift, a specific form of Indianness comes into focus, and it is this book's task to explore the variety of possibilities therein.

The "Indian diaspora" discussed here is simultaneously a concept and a set of social formations. In allowing us to consider how migrant peoples negotiate life amid tremendous social, cultural, and political change, by building the "imagined communities" of nations, by creating identities, and by expressing themselves as multiply constituted, diaspora invokes, always with qualification, ways of life—community, culture, and society. The term diaspora also conveys an affective experience in a world of nations, through its proposition of global belonging as a means of self- and group representation. Yet neither globality nor diaspora should be interpreted to mean the absence of location. The Indian diaspora of this book is read very much through its locatedness, in space and time, however shifting the coordinates provided by the many movements of Indians across Asia, the Americas, Africa, and Europe. To narrow the inquiry of this book, I identify the United States and England as primary foci of the Indian diaspora. Importantly, however, other formations of Indianness— say, in the Caribbean or East Africa—do not fall out of sight, but instead become incorporated as secondary and related possibilities. As a conceptual space of negotiation, the Indian diaspora allows us to challenge the dichotomization of the global and the local, to address, in Michael Hardt and Antonio Negri's words, "the social machines that create and recreate the identities and differences that are understood as the local."[10] So while the United States and England may be sites for expressions of locality, they are cross-cut, always, by forces from other worlds, only one of which is an imagining of India.

We turn, then, to the Indian diaspora to interpret what is simultaneously global and local. In that move, there is no compulsion to make specific claims to the territory of the Indian nation-state, nor remain exclusively within the social fields of the United States or England. Instead, this book develops a sphere of representation that traverses other boundaries, too, of east and west, and of first and third worlds. Diaspora then provides a different kind of "field" site from those of past anthropological preoccupations. Situated within and across a range of nations, Indian diasporic lives come to embody a set of disconnections between place, culture, and identity.[11] Necessarily, then, in both subject matter and methodology, this book reworks and revises a classic premise of ethnography: that visiting and observing a place yields primary meanings about people, their experiences, and their cultures. While the material in this book suggests that some insights do emerge from traditional understandings of place and community, it also proposes that a whole range of life experiences, imaginative inclinations, and psychic investments lie outside observed geographical boundaries. Indianness, here, emerges in forms much grander and more dispersed than the neighborhood or workplace, such that there can be no necessary correspondence between its expressions and its locales.[12] The shape of "community" itself, in the architecture of consumption of an entrepreneurial space like Jackson Heights in New York, or the international political interests of peoples in Southall, London, grants those places rather diverse meanings.

When place is recast as the global arena, cultural practices of migration assume interesting new shapes. The news of India and the diaspora found in the U.S.-based *India Abroad* or the British *Asian Times* is a collection of stories that address publics with material interests in the subcontinent, needs for group identity in urban and suburban areas of settlement, and longings for a homeland. An entrepreneurial community's production of itself as a "Little India" and a British Indian reggae star's naming of himself as "Apache Indian" suggest that the very language of a national imaginary diversely negotiates spaces of social invention. How, in such thick occasions, can we confidently distinguish the material from the symbolic or, for that matter, experience from fiction? As Indian migrants abundantly produce readings of the condition of their shifting locality, processing their physical and imaginative movement, they develop a set of discourses that can reveal something special about diaspora. The textual materials create the rather unbounded "field" or "archive" of representation. Reading across modes of expression, as well as through physical sites, I suggest, is to get closer to diasporic life.

Analyzing the Indian diaspora formed by migrations enables us to discuss territorial fantasy in new ways. The fact that this study focuses on Indianness outside of India may yield findings different even from those of subcontinental critics of nationalism, who have been keen to demonstrate the historicity of nation-building in terms of British colonial and postcolonial histories and literatures but have for obvious reasons been less interested in countries outside the colonial circuitry, like the United States. Yet the participation of other national-cultural ideologies, such as those of "America," as well as "England," in the lives of migrants may shift our understandings of what constitutes India. Within many national identities, the stable meanings of "America" and "England" remain uninterrogated. But by looking at how migrant discourses have created India abroad, we can challenge the assumed centrality of "America" and "England" in the lives of peoples who inhabit the spaces of the United States and Britain. Negotiating the divides between nations and national affiliations, Indian diaspora can illuminate the instability of the places where we all stand.

Indian Diasporas and Multicultural Identities
of Race, Nation, and Ethnicity

Handmaiden to the processes of globalization, through time, are discourses of multiculturalism. Multiculturalism has also been a necessary ideology for playing out the logic of capitalism. While many debates on the topic emphasize the highly contemporary nature of incorporating a concept of diversity into North American and European national imaginaries, the Indian diaspora encourages us to rethink that conventional wisdom. It may not have been before the 1960s and 1970s that policymakers in England and the United States began to engage in public soul-searching to conceive of their nations and cultures as constituted by difference, but recent Indian arrivals were coolly (or perhaps hotly) familiar with heterogeneity. India was always and already a fragile whole of many cultures, religions, languages, and regional groups, well before Jawaharlal Nehru's popularization of the motto "unity in diversity."[13] And the British empire, one prominent example of globalism, employed ideologies of unhomogenized multiplicity to establish sovereignty over its totality. This colonial discourse constructed "India" as a land of many peoples, with racial typologies to match.

In discussions of confronting difference in the United States and England, particularly through formations of Indian diaspora, it is essential to see the field in which identities are being articulated as one of comparative multiculturalisms, rather than simply national(ist) frameworks for diversity. Though certainly not all models for diverse societies, past or present, are the same, there are important influences that help to shape all frameworks for multiplicity. And the Indian diaspora is a space where possibilities of a heterogeneous Britain, United States, and India meet. Any singular sense of identification will always be undermined by the plural forms that build Indianness, though its appearance as Indian may suggest otherwise.

Central to all those frameworks for pluralistic societies is what Immanuel Wallerstein has called the construction of peoplehood.[14] This process of construction, from the structural-ideological forces with which Wallerstein is preoccupied, as well as from movements that emerge from below, results in fluid and entangled discourses of "race," "nation," and "ethnicity." The tremendously powerful lived and particularized experience of any one of these categories as a form of identity or community can often obscure the integrated nature of the development of all three. Etienne Balibar has approached this difficult problematic with a special clarity, asking: "How are individuals nationalized or, in other words, socialized in the dominant form of national belonging?"[15] In dissolving the distinctions between "real" and "imaginary" communities, and "individual" and "collective" identities, Balibar is able to capture how all sorts of identifications are historically produced and felt. His notion of "fictive ethnicity," for populations "represented in the past or in the future *as if* they formed a natural community . . . an identity of origins, culture and interests which transcends individuals and social conditions,"[16] is particularly evocative as a way to think about the Indianness explored in this book. The fictional nature of that formation lies not so much in its falsity as in its constructedness, what Balibar calls "fabrication." In the chapters to follow, I closely consider the contours of constructed Indianness in a variety of diasporic modes.

National belonging may underlie Indianness, but that organizing principle becomes more heterogeneous as it maps onto other forms of identification in diaspora and even becomes a newly constitutive category of other national frameworks, like America or England. Here we return to the scheme of the multicultural. To be part of the place (and myth) of America has increasingly entailed belonging to a minority group that hails from *another* nation, and possessing discrete and ethnic origins.[17] How those origins are cast has a great deal to do with the specificities of the construction of race or ethnicity, and the development of a group with reference to nationalities like American or English. A preliminary question we must ask is whether the very state of diaspora, between and across nations, may trouble or at least make more complex the framework of multiculturalism. Diasporic cultures continually translate a set of differences into something new, yet those differences often appear within discourses of origins or other hierarchical social orderings. And the geopolitical forces of nationalism may constrain the field of social formation and the depth of possible critique.

Looking comparatively at the development of Indian diaspora in England and the United States allows us to consider multiculturalism as a set of specifically national projects that are articulated to broader global conceptions of difference and diversity. Indian migrants to Britain entered into a social landscape in which there were already referents, in the experiences of colonialism, for their "blackness," "Asianness," or, more simply, "otherness." While this kind of *racial* subjectification had a history, it gained a new life in the postcolonial era, in which identificatory categories emerged through conflicts over the space in the British nation-state that migrants could occupy in terms of socioeconomic position, residential arrangements, and political representation. Of course, the England of destination was hardly in any simple terms "white," as a range of peoples had undergone individual and group transformations in order to uneasily occupy positions there; the presence of Irish, Scottish, Jewish, West Indian, and African peoples compelled continual deliberations on the nature of what made a British citizen and why. Mirroring local instability in

Britain itself were the effects of Englishmen going abroad and returning home. It is in the midst of all these complicated forces that Indian migrants have lived race. Being "black" or "Asian" has been an uncertain and historically contingent vocation, one formed through needs for solidarity with other peoples who are coming to terms with the issue of belonging, as well as by the force of desires for group autonomy. Violence by the British state and by its self-designated patriots oftentimes prescribed narrower terms in which the process of identity formation could take place.

Ethnicity, too, has been an important language of identity for Indian migrants in England. In efforts to distinguish themselves from Afro-Caribbean migrants, and also to downplay their own racialization, Indians have mobilized ethnicity by adopting "Indian" as a primary self-descriptor. There are other more liberatory and representational effects of this mode of identification, as Stuart Hall has remarked: "The term ethnicity acknowledges the place of history, language and culture in the construction of subjectivity and identity, as well as the fact that all discourse is placed, positioned, situated, and all knowledge is contextual."[18] Hall has argued that "new ethnicities" can be decoupled from more conservative notions of the British state, like "Englishness," and, in effect, become crucial (and politically progressive) points of departure for developing important identities for migrant groups and others who are seen as different. Supporting these more oppositional understandings is the rehearsing of political-economic opposition to colonial power through commitments to being "Indian" that are embedded in certain discourses of ethnicity.

In the United States, the frames of racial and ethnic formation are unique and have mediated the creation of Indian diasporic cultures in ways that differ somewhat from the corresponding processes in Britain. The national-historical project of "America," in which immigration is posited as central to the building of the country, and an ideological formation of race, based on the legacies of African slavery and shifting to accommodate and mark new forms of difference and alterity, together provide the story of ethnicity and shape the social worlds into which Indians enter as immigrants. After coming in large numbers to the United States after 1965, Indian subjects became interpellated by "third-world migration" (and the subset of "Asian American") as a category that disrupted the black/white binary of race and challenged popular Americanist notions of ethnicity as assimilability.

Through the period of significant migration, Indian Americans have also moved from invisibility to visibility.[19] Categorical representation was important in this shift, and immigrants struggled through the 1970s to be allotted the category "Asian Indian" in the U.S. census. More recently there have been other kinds of indicators of presence, in popular culture, when, for example, a television show like *The Simpsons* has an Indian character.[20] And in the year 2000, at the dawn of the new millennium, President Bill Clinton gave as one reason for his trip to South Asia the growing importance of its immigrant communities in the United States. Clinton also rhetorically installed these groups in a sequence of other ascendant ethnics, particularly Irish and Jewish Americans: "I think one of the reasons we've been able to play a meaningful role in Northern Ireland is we have so many Irish Americans here. I think one of the reasons we've been able to play a meaningful role in the Middle East is we have a lot of Jewish Americans and a lot of Arab Americans. I think we forget that among all the some-200 ethnic groups that we have in our country, Indian Americans and Pakistani Americans have been among the most successful in terms of education level and income level. They have worked and succeeded stunningly well in the United States."[21] Clinton's is a rich text that can be mined by Indian Americans seeking teleologies of success and visibility, and also by those who might want to see the expanded possibilities of multiculturalist models for membership, in which nations abroad are always a part of the interests of domestic migrant groups.

Indeed, while race and ethnicity are often understood within national arrangements, they have reference points and related formations within a more diasporic circuitry of capital, ideas, and communities. Indians' connections to each other and to places that traverse the boundaries of countries of settlement are often formulated in languages that straddle conceptual categories of race, ethnicity, and nation. In fact, Indianness itself can become a language of either race or nation, particularly when we consider how it may express a set of identifications that have emerged out of colonialism and anticolonialism. In this vein, I would suggest that third-worldism and nonalignment, too, as programs of both individual nation-states and whole regions, can be interpreted as discourses that racially subjectivize their citizens both at home and abroad. Here again, in the multiplicity of languages and histories that impress upon the formation of the Indian diasporic subject and his or her cultures, is the production of globality in the local and of locality in the global.[22] Considering the Indian diaspora in this fashion may revise the concept of postcolonial,[23] as Indian migrants bring to various contexts concerns born of the dynamics of British imperial rule, or fantasies of escaping these dynamics in the "new lands" of America.

Private longings to be Indian are always tied up with a concern about what that means in public terms. This is why symptoms of visibility, such as Clinton's reference to Indian Americans, or the recent population figures of the U.S. census, or the naming of curry as a national British cuisine, can seem so significant.[24] The contemporary moment, of course, has been worked toward, historically, as some sense of Indianness has been created through a range of integrated national and cosmopolitan possibilities.

Membership in a diaspora, forged through migration, profoundly shapes what it means to be a subject, just as the process of becoming part of any constructed community, religious, national, or familial, does. But the very state of multiplicity, of being "abroad," and of being a particular kind of national, I would suggest, has specific implications for individual and collective identity. Even if an ambivalence that already existed comes to the fore or is newly articulated, the affective dimension of being Indian is changed by diaspora and by being located in and through multiple processes of racialization, ethnicization, and nationalization. There may be surprising results, say, when the dreams of assimilation into America fuse with Indian anticolonialism. There are various ways to apprehend identity and subjectivity, many of which this book engages in the chapters to follow, but it seems important at the outset to grant to the concept of identity and even its collective expression, "identity politics," their proper complexity and power. In terms of being able to organize sympathies and solidarities, many forms of identity, in language, race, ethnicity, religion, and nation, do more than reify difference. Indeed, they can negotiate, through consolation and alienation, the multiple structures of lived experience for those who migrate.

From Immigrant to Diaspora

What Indian diaspora confronts in this moment, what it has always confronted, is a simultaneous nationalism and internationalism. The nonresident Indian, popularly called an NRI, is a diasporic figure who illumines the surprising complementarity of those two spheres of operation. In occupying a category created by the Indian government in the 1970s to repatriate investment from abroad, this migrant is lexically bestowed with a relationship to India and receives benefits that would not normally be available to those living outside the nation-state, such as the right to own property within its borders, as well as the affirmation of political loyalties to what is perceived as an originary place. He gains meaning from his state of being *abroad*, and yet he is interpellated as an Indian national. It is precisely the NRI's citizenship in and of the world, and all the influences that inhere therein, that have made him both a powerful preoccupation of the Indian nation-state, and also a site of anxiety for those concerned with a purer relationship to homeland.

Physical mobility, psychic life in many spaces at once, and flows of capital—that which appears in exaggerated form in the case of the NRI—is one enactment of that presumptive breakdown between "first" and "third" worlds. While it is true that migrancy, and increasingly transnational cultures and economies, might seem to compress the distance between a poor country like India and a wealthy one like the United States, it is worth making explicit the incredibly class-specific rendition of bridging areas of the world with vastly divergent histories. And while the exploration undertaken here shall be of largely middle-class migrations, *difference* and even inequality—of economy, politics, and power—remain central to the social and conceptual constructions that take place. Diaspora in this way becomes a space not to flatten difference, to make everything seem equal, but a site in which to comprehend the negotiations structured by difference. Becoming Indian in the United States or England is a consequence simultaneously of the ease of mobility and the difficulties of being other in a place that still in some basic way is cast as "first world."

It is through unequal international relations, with economic, cultural, and political manifestations, that migration is now taken to be a given. The older categories of immigration, of making permanent moves to one nation from another, have less and less purchase in a world in which mobility is no longer unidirectional, if it ever was. And the Indian diaspora represents some of those changes, too, particularly when placed within rubrics of academic fields like immigration history or transnational studies. Classic immigrant history paradigms, worked out within the subfield of U.S. history, have posited that people leave one country for another and in the process relinquish an attachment to the homeland in favor of new identities in a foreign country. This first generation, the story goes, begins the process of integration and eventually assimilation, which successive generations complete as they become nationals with diverse origins. Oscar Handlin's 1951 book *The Uprooted*[25] may be seen as a perfect encapsulation of this developmentalist narrative. Properly criticized for being overly embedded in nationalist mythologies of "America" and primarily evidenced in the experiences of southern and eastern European immigrants, who could, in a sense, "become white,"[26] this assimilation-based model for immigration has been superseded by more complicated approaches to the study of peoples from Asia, Latin America, Africa, and Europe who have settled in the United States, and who have retained important connections to their countries of origin.[27] Many historians and sociologists have demonstrated how the process of racialization, particularly for post-1965 immigrants from the third world, punctures the teleology of "becoming American," and challenges the divide between studies of racial minorities and immigrants. Yet this very careful work may still be haunted by the terms in which it operates: namely, that of *immigration*, and, to some extent, "America." Immigration remains in its most essential meaning a one-way process, from one country into another; the framework of the United States as destination significantly shapes the way that the homeland is constructed, as necessarily a political and/or cultural space with fewer resources. It can be difficult to develop in this language a sense of the continuous movements back and forth of many and varied groups of peoples.[28]

These are the claims of recent scholars of transnationalism.[29] Finding limitations in the language of immigration of the kind noted above, anthropologists Nina Glick Schiller, Linda Basch, and Cristina Szanton Blanc defined transnationalism as "the processes by which immigrants forge and sustain multi-stranded social relations that link together their societies of origin and settlement."[30] Part of their important project seems to be to highlight national formation; they wrote: "by living their lives across borders, transmigrants find themselves confronted with and engaged in the nation building processes of two or more nation-states."[31]

India Abroad exists, partly, in the space that scholars of transnationalism have opened up in their critiques of immigration as a category and in their emphasis on social networks embedded in the logics of multiple national formations. But given this book's accent on the various levels of cultural signification and translation, it takes issue with distinctions that are often made, between "observable social action" and "subjective intentionality" in the phenomenon of transnationalism.[32] Like many other scholars explicitly concerned with cultural production, I find it very difficult, indeed impossible, to separate the work of the imagination from the everyday cross-border activities of migrants; nor does it seem useful for what I see occurring in the Indian diaspora, to draw single, univocal, or unilinear causality between those associated spheres of activity. On some level, then, this book will necessarily enter into debates on the limits of empiricism by questioning models of the relationship between material worlds and subjectivity.

In the postwar world, assimilation is not necessarily on the mind of all Indians in the United States or Britain. Nor is an undifferentiated nationality always the standard for other American or British subjects. Beginning in the 1970s, an all-inclusive mass culture, even for Americans who might not identify themselves as ethnic, began to wane, due in no small part to enormous population changes as well as to shifts in capitalist production. People increasingly consumed difference, and it was becoming untenable that being "American" or even "British" meant identifying with a homogeneous majority group. In that context, an India open to the world could become a different sort of ideal of the postwar era, too. Even earlier, in 1950, Indian Prime Minister Jawaharlal Nehru articulated a developmentalist vision of multiple nations and cultures: "One can see each nation and each separate civilization developing its own culture that had its roots in generations hundreds and thousands of years ago. . . . That conception is affected by other conceptions and one sees action and interaction between these varying conceptions. There is, I suppose, no culture in the world which is absolutely pristine, pure and unaffected by any other culture."[33] Within global nations migration and diaspora must necessarily take on alternative meanings. If migration describes movements of peoples and ideas that have constituted subjects in the eyes of the law, and those subjects that are still situated with reference to particular nations, then diaspora conjures forth a form of belonging that is global. In the postwar world, particular forms of migration—postcolonial and national—have produced many diasporas. Those diasporas are coeval with multicultures; sometimes they are compatible and sometimes they are contradictory, and it is one task of this book to carefully explore those possibilities.

Diaspora is where constructed nationalisms come into contact. While there is no singly more evocative term for this process than Benedict Anderson's "imagined communities," it is also Partha Chatterjee's critiques of Anderson's fixation on nationalism as a political movement, and its proposition of the derivative nature of anticolonial nationalisms of the third world, that have been essential to rethinking nationalist cultures of India.[34] Building on the very important work of these two theorists, I would suggest further that diaspora may give a new cast to discussions of nationalism. In the state of diaspora, we can see the languages of anticolonialism, capitalism, and postcolonialism blend into a real feeling for nations, one that does not only reproduce the state or have it as an endpoint. Like Chatterjee, I want to suggest that the nations of diaspora are heterogeneous, composed of many and often contradictory fragments. Though there is support in some Indian diasporas for the fundamentalist Bharatiya Janata Party (BJP), there are other important ways to be national abroad, with a variety of political implications. And while my focus here will be a diasporic Indianness that is inevitably linked with some idea of nation, there are moments of that construction where nationalism is not the primary consequence of complex forms of identification. I do not want to reduce diaspora to long-distance nationalism.[35] Because, as I hope this book makes eminently clear, diaspora is not only about homeland or nation-state formation; it also signifies a more densely constituted sense of place and identity.

Created out of a sentiment of progress and modernity, the Indian diaspora of this book particularly courts a quasi-postmodern multiplicity, of nations, communities, and expressive modes. In this way, perhaps, it might be distinguishable from Jewish or black diasporas, which are very much premised on a rehearsal of originary forms of suffering and persecution that have created dispersals, and that construct a compensatory nation. Many have argued for reserving the term diaspora itself for the sense of forced dispersion that is recalled in modern notions of Jewishness or blackness, or for groups like Armenians.[36] My own answer to these dilemmas is that, first, the very question of compulsion in scattering is difficult to ascertain, particularly as many migrants have seen few economic possibilities—possibilities that would constitute a form of survival—in underdeveloped economies like that of India, or those in Latin America or Africa. Second, diaspora, like any other generalized theoretical category, only gains meaning from its cultural and historical specificity, that specificity which necessarily produces contrasts among, say, Jewish, Chinese, or Indian cases. And third, diaspora should be seen not as reflecting a singular state of being, or as having a reference to one nation or historical experience, but instead as constructing a space to negotiate many identifications.

This book's discussions produce a diaspora that is lateral but differentiated. This is to follow from James Clifford's position on the breadth of the concept, in which "decentered, lateral connections may be as important as those formed around a teleology of origin/return. And a shared ongoing history of displacement, suffering, adaptation or resistance may be as important as the projection of a single origin."[37] Principles of coherence and division are always present in the construction of an object as wide-reaching as "Indian diaspora," which seeks to conceptually encompass Indian cultures abroad from the 1950s to the present day, across three nations. As Avtar Brah has quite precisely distinguished: "The *concept* of diaspora concerns the historically variable forms of *relationality* within and between diasporic formations." She notes further that "diaspora specifies a matrix of economic, political and cultural inter-relationships which construct the commonality between the various components of a dispersed group [and] delineates a field of identifications where 'imagined communities' are forged within and out of a confluence of narratives."[38] What our exploration of diaspora shall contribute to Clifford's and Brah's formulations is the tremendous impulse to multiple nationality that Indianness abroad has made visible. And nationality, too, takes many forms, as New York and London offer particular possibilities for diasporic culture, the general contours of which are outlined in the chapters to follow. The tension between those specific, and deeply located, occasions, and the more general meanings for a formation, is the very tension of diaspora.

The Special Relationship of India and Her Diaspora

Amitav Ghosh has written of an "epic relationship" between India and her diaspora.[39] I read in this term and in much of his work an emphasis on the tremendously historical and imaginative nature of diasporic belonging. When, for instance, Ghosh travels to Egypt as an anthropologist-historian to track down the details of the life of a twelfth-century Indian slave in the book *In an Antique Land*,[40] he is surprised to find himself received as "the Indian doctor," who comes to stand in for all the contradictory cultural and political attributes of a national (and Hindu-inflected) Indianness: cremation, sacralization of cows, progress, and modernity. An intellectual journey into the tremendously hybrid and mobile cultures of the period and context in which the Indian slave and his Tunisian-Jewish merchant patron lived proceeds alongside Ghosh's own more modern (early 1980s) experiences of traveling in a world where nations and their borders are very important. The historical identifications among modern nations, too, are embedded in contemporary affective dimensions of social relationships. An Egyptian villager is conscious of that background, as Ghosh recalls his introduction: "It was their duty to welcome me into their midst and make me feel at home because of the long traditions of friendship between India and Egypt."[41] Here and throughout the narrative Ghosh intimates that Indian subjects are made by India, both by being read as Indian and experiencing the world through that sensibility of nation, in the past and in the present. Yet nation cannot be confined to its purported origins; he has, after all, gone to Egypt to unearth the story of an Indian slave. All sorts of crossings take place to trouble easy correspondences between subject, nation, and territory.

The Indian nation has been the work of history. British colonialism could only draw the boundaries of its field of operation by creating presumed coherences, of making India a distinct place to be ruled. And consequently, the powerful memory of British colonialism, and its role in the relationships between peoples and countries, has cleaved together many formations of Indian diaspora. While in the pre-independence years, the experience of being colonized functioned as a kind of trauma[42] to construct Indian social and political space more directly, in later years we can see how British political rule has been transmuted into, on the one hand, a residual economic force for migrants, and, on the other, a cultural memory to undergird constructions of community. The recovery of British industry following the Second World War brought Indian immigrants to London, to a place they recognized on a range of levels; postwar fiction abounds with immigrant characters who profess recognition of the physical and social space of England well before their arrival on the country's shores.[43] As Britain implemented more restrictive entry requirements, and the United States passed the Immigration and Naturalization Act (1965) to facilitate the immigration of many more third-world migrants, Indians looked to the United States as an opportunity for class mobility and as an alternative to submersion in Britain's post-imperial economy. The intense third-worldist and, more recently, economic nationalisms of India that underwrote movement in the past and in the future exist in relation to "the West" and to Britain, particularly, as representative of first-world forces originating in imperial systems.

To call the Indian diasporas of the post-1947 period "postcolonial," then, signifies a great deal more than chronology. It suggests that these migrant formations emerge from links through time and connections across the span of a former empire. The processing of colonialism and its aftermath occurs on a variety of levels throughout Indian diasporas, in economies, politics, and culture. Underscoring relationships to British rule frames the cultures of Indians abroad historically and also embeds them in a global framework. Postcolonialism, in this case, is a form of transnationalism that emphasizes the complex multinational narratives of the past that produce group identities, and perhaps makes India appear in less stable form. British colonialism is one historical plot, among many, that has organized the constructions of India and the Indian diaspora, and foregrounding that is to create a very particular narrative of formation, of what I will call modern Indianness.[44] This subjectivity results when diaspora is linked to an impermanent India, in past, present, and future, dated in some sense to postcolonialism and its effects, that older notion of empire, and as well to the newer sort of transnational sovereignty that Hardt and Negri speak of in their more contemporary concept of empire.[45] And yet one might imagine that the Indianness of the twelfth-century slave that Amitav Ghosh set out to find in modern Egypt could of course be related to its more contemporary renditions.

Just as constitutive of Indian diaspora's meaning for our exploration are other nations, the United States and England. Herein we might not only unmoor nationality, but also interrogate the locatability of the nation. This book poses the question of whether the temporal and spatial juxtapositions that construct the Indian diaspora might enable us to rethink origin. India is not fixed, it is in formation, just as other nations are, and when some of those processes of formation occur in the space of diaspora, directional coordinates become ever less clear. This year the largest newspaper of the Indian diaspora, *India Abroad*, operating since its 1970 inception in New York, was bought out by Rediff.com, a company based in Bombay that began to oversee the production of news for Indians abroad. For this occasion, and many more of Indian migrant cultures, where the processes of becoming national are multidirectional, we can no longer locate the source or the product of Indianness. Questioning origin thus necessitates a rethinking of time and space of Indianness. Where does India come from, and when did it begin, are queries that are overcome by a quality of nationality that is constantly in formation, and one that recalls the past in its expressions, lives in the present time, and makes claims on the future. In the case of the newspaper, "India, abroad" is made in Bombay and transmitted to other nations where India, too, lives. Utterly central to the NRI's understanding of himself and the world, in another and related example, is the Indian nation-state's development, in a continuing dialogue with the effects of British colonialism.

India and Indianness, then, have no limits, particularly if we imagine those two possibilities as taking shape through postwar diaspora.[46] Even as boundaries seem to be policed, most notably around religion, region, language, and caste, the public discourse for the Indian nation is one of porousness and inclusivity. This in fact is the constitutive contradiction of all formations of Indianness. At once Indianness seems not to respect geographic boundaries of the nation-state, taking shape in North America, the Caribbean, Britain, or Africa with amazing force and not existing fully within a singular temporality of the colonial or postcolonial, while nonetheless being constituted through an imaginary that seems to have an obviously national referent, of India. We can read this dilemma as shaped by its specific historical juncture, in which not only is India actively and wildly multicultural, but so too are all nations. What nation is not in the midst of developing a discourse of diversity, even as that diversity may be violently and possibly fatally contested? One can project a great many possibilities, without coherence, onto national spaces like "India." This ability for projection, I would argue, and not any necessary connection between the nation and her peoples, is why India's relationship with an Indian diaspora is so special. It is also why India, even in its hybridity, can become a ready sign for globalism, as was the case for the *National Geographic* issue on global culture. What is important to underscore here is that diaspora does not exist in the borderlands of the nation, but within and through central spaces of several nations.

What It Means to Be Indian

Recently the Indian government decided to distribute "People of Indian Origin" cards to enable Indians abroad to travel to India and own property there without visas and thus without formal citizenship.[47] Here the state imagined an abiding sense of identification with a place outside that which was literally inhabited. But it was reminded that people often intercede in and disrupt the seamless narratives that are devised. The uncertainty with which such a proposal has been received by Indians in the Caribbean who favor the principle but suggest that the $1000 price tag is unrealistic for populations that are not nearly as well-off as their counterparts in the United States and United Kingdom provides a check not only on the assumptions of the Indian state about emigrant wealth and success, but also on the presumed ease that accompanies ideas of crossing national space. Diaspora, as hybrid cultures, or as a kind of third space between "home" and "new" lands, discloses ambivalence alongside desire, the depth of which can only be understood through the porous and differently weighted histories of nations.[48]

This book focuses on the Indian diaspora, rather than the South Asian diaspora, as its subject of inquiry. There are a number of reasons for this choice. Most prominently, any category will enact exclusions, and reaching too widely across very distinct national processes would very simply produce more of them. As it is, Indianness submerges regional and religious identities, like being Sikh or being Muslim, that have their own autonomous diasporas. The second concern has to do with the historical juncture of the postcolonial and postwar periods, in which the nation-state of India has been formulated distinctly from other national projects, like Pakistan, Sri Lanka, or Bangladesh. Because I am interested in certain dominant postcolonial processes of nation-making, I concentrate on India as the broader discourse for diaspora. Recent and numerous works on the topic have made other choices, to good effect.[49] It also needs to be stated at the outset that the languages of India and Indianness, despite their apparent heterogeneity, often take a Hindu rather than a Muslim orientation. And because of this character of development of postcolonial nationalisms of the subcontinent, it is true that a pan-Islamic diaspora has engaged Muslims from India far more readily than diasporic Indianness, both differently and similarly perhaps from nationality in the context of the Indian nation-state.[50]

In closely gazing simultaneously at the United States and England, this book is necessarily interested in comparison and conjuncture. As symbols of the "first world" and as formerly colonial powers, England and the United States, each in its own way and together, elaborate how a global system has been shaped by power struggles between nations and by differential access to resources for members of national citizenries. While migration in the postwar era has shaken the ease with which exclusivist ideas of British and U.S. nationality are transmitted globally, it has also provided justification for rearticulations of "Englishness" and "what it means to be American" that undergird xenophobic, anti-immigrant trends in both countries. Movements to break down the borders of nationalist ideology, as evidenced in the proliferation of racial and ethnic identities and the continual movements of Indian migrants, face formidable but interesting obstacles in the two hyper-national spaces of Britain and the United States. To add to Benedict Anderson's point in his recent work that nations are best understood comparatively,[51] I would suggest that there is a special insight to be gained when they are experienced in multiple fashion, in the synchronous time of which he has written. The Indian diaspora, I suggest, is an exemplary space in which to contemplate the comparison and multiplication of nations. This book, then, does more than provide a dual case study, comparing migrant cultures in the United

States and England. It also suggests that India and Indianness can be seen more vividly, more clearly, when we place those topics in comparative nations, across time and space. The very heterogeneity that emerges through that interpretive process is what is constitutive of India. Comparisons, then, are not just the obvious ones, between the United States and England, but also between and among India and the United States, India and England, and are cross-cut by class and race.[52] These comparisons give us a sense of cosmopolitanism even as they illuminate nationality.

A major argument of *India Abroad* can be found in its structure. If no one modality can explain how nation and nationality get constructed abroad, no one genre can fully express diasporic life. The chapters, then, are an unfolding, through various kinds of sites, of the content and form of Indianness abroad, that Indianness that I suggest remakes India.[53] Nationality and the nation may have autonomous trajectories, but their overlap, in which the state of the nation is simultaneously that of the identificatory self and the group, has a special draw on the diasporic imagination explored here, through the cultures of migrants in the United States and England. However, the very lack of distinction between India and Indianness, and its presumption of homogeneity, can be very difficult to sustain, and in fact is consistently challenged. This tension forms part of the background of diverse understandings of a site of diasporic culture.

In each *site* of the diaspora, "being Indian" has acquired a particular set of meanings. These sites—history, place, literature, news, and generation—all present unique frames for densely constituting Indian subjectivity. These sites have (crossable) boundaries of time and space, and they exist very much in relation to one another, so that history may be the means by which place is practiced, and fictions of the self enable a generation to see itself as "new." Resulting from this arrangement is a kind of geography of Indianness, mapped through multiple and de-essentialized vectors of identity formation.

The first chapter, "Histories and Nations," interprets a multilayered set of historical narratives of India and Indian migration to the United States and England as a way to think about the development of postwar Indianness, in terms both of its representation in a wider public sphere and the powerful impulse toward nationality. The desire for unity and the experiences of multiplicity that are illuminated in these stories underscore how an imagined India becomes highly invested with emotional value, and also remains contested. Chapter 2, "Little Indias, Places for Indian Diasporas," takes as its subject two instances of "Indian community," Southall, London, and Jackson Heights, New York, to explore how Indianness has come to be associated with diverse castings of place, through the parameters of race and class. One argument here is that the porousness of these nations within nations—"Little Indias"—symptomatize the difficulties in holding diaspora to a constancy of origin or content. The third chapter, "Affiliations and Ascendancy of Diasporic Literature," inquires into diverse representational fictions, in the space of the novel, the autobiography, and the letter, as modes for rethinking the vexed nature of belonging, to India, to America, and to England. Specific texts here are read as bringing into sharper focus temporal and spatial forms of diaspora. Chapter 4, "India in Print, India Abroad," explores various instances of migrant print culture in the United States and Britain that have created a heterogeneous public sphere for imagining India and negotiating the confluence of spatial identifications. The fifth chapter, "Generations of Indian Diaspora," considers alternative logics of diaspora, in music, cinema, and youth political associations, and takes "generation" as a form of processing cultural change.

In each chapter's rendering of diasporic culture, the ways that people describe their lives, the communities they create, and the work that represents their experiences are situated within a plethora of imagined places: at home, nearer to places of settlement, and abroad, linked in a sustained way to others in the diaspora and, most of all, to India. Movements between specific instances and the broader and more general formation mirror what I contend is basic to Indian migrancy: the persistent motion between community life in the city of settlement and an idea of homeland, and between identifications with national (American, English, Indian) institutions and cosmopolitan formations. Strategies of identification that may on the surface seem contradictory flow into one another, sometimes astonishingly, without the archetypal conflict that underwrites the problematic of "immigrant identity." Indian immigrants vote Democratic or Republican as U.S. citizens and concurrently invest in India, because they intend to return to the homeland for their retirement. This is to say that for Indians in the diaspora, as well as other "native" and migrant citizens, the local and the global become highly compressed within a lifetime. So it is that the cultures described in this book are both particular of a place and time, New York City of the 1980s, for example, and also general in, say, the community of nonresident Indians that is appealed to as a transnational formation.

The relational aspects of a range of texts and experiences, which include historical narratives, cultural organizations, autobiography and fiction, musical performance and films, are of paramount importance in this critical ethnography. My method emerges from a space that Arjun Appadurai has opened up to rethink questions of research within anthropology. He notes: "Where lives are being imagined partly in and through realisms that must be in one way or another official or large-scale in their inspiration, then the ethnographer needs to find new ways to represent the links between the imagination and social life. . . . Ethnography must redefine itself as that practice of representation that illuminates the power of large-scale, imagined life possibilities over specific life trajectories."[54] In my own attempt to find and read Indianness, what Appadurai might call the "ethnoscape" of this project, I spent several months in both London and New York, speaking to a wide variety of people, participating in cultural events, and assembling historical sources and other written texts. My position therein was ambivalent—connected to certain qualities of Indianness, diverging from others—much as an ethnographer's or critic's relationship to her topic is always mediated by some set of identifications. The mark of subjectivity can be everywhere felt in a project that has some claims to the contemporary. And even the act of placing different kinds of materials, the proliferation of stories, into a dialogue has resulted in its own discourse, the writing of this book.

While I certainly do not intend my interdisciplinary method here to be authoritative, I do believe that it sheds a particular kind of light on the conditions of the production of diaspora, a concept and set of formations that have imagination at their core. Here I hope to do more than simply juxtapose history, literature, and anthropology, and instead inquire into the importance of textuality in varied productions of culture. What might it mean for us to understand diasporic modes of belonging, ways of becoming Indian, even experiences of physical movement, as created through a relationship to a story of the nation that is to be made a spectacle of in a cultural festival, for example? Beginning to answer this question might yield more intriguing ways to think about moving among different disciplines and their associated methodologies. In creating a deliberation of postwar Indian migration through the use of categories that do not often share conceptual terrain, such as "postcolonial," "diasporic," "transnational," "migrant," and even "American," I ask readers to think differently about the models for subjectivity themselves, and to take them out of their confined spaces of literary criticism, the social sciences, history, and ethnic studies.

An important category of studies of migration has been the post-1965 period, precisely because of the profound transformations in the types of immigrants who arrived in the United States after the Immigration and Naturalization Act. But while the year 1965 signifies something special for the context of the United States, it does not have the same purchase on the experiences of the British populace or other societies that experienced large influxes of peoples in the postwar years. Too historically specific a period, and too Americanist in its focus, "post-65" may not be the most helpful organizing principle for world migrations like those from India. And so this book invites the interrogation of what would happen if we were to look at other dates, in nonfoundational fashion. What about taking Indian independence in 1947 as one reference point in the making of migrant subjectivity? Reframing the trajectory in this and other ways may envelop from the outset memories of colonialism and the realities and possibilities of postcolonialism as structuring migrant culture.

What evolves, too, most especially from where I stand as a U.S.-based scholar, is a discussion of how America is transformed when globalization is really taken seriously.[55] Bringing other histories, of India, of Britain, to bear on the study of U.S. communities invariably breaks down national borders in unexpected ways, in terms of geography, affiliation and allegiance, and cultural possibilities. Thus I believe that the consequences of my arguments about Indian diasporic cultures, through ethnographic analysis that is as much about reading as it is about observing, can contribute to transforming the field of American studies.[56] Perhaps in that move, we can challenge the presumptive cultural power of American empire, too. That this book's exploration of the Indian diaspora might also serve as another model for globalizing cultures should not be seen as incongruous with its local interventions, particularly in the United States, but also in Britain.[57]

The Indian diaspora ultimately challenges immigration as a category, much as many other Asian and third-world migrants have, by rearranging the coordinates of departure and return. Aihwa Ong has wonderfully described the process by which Chinese abroad have maintained a range of affiliations as "flexible citizenship," or "the cultural logics of capitalist accumulation, travel and displacement that induce subjects to respond fluidly and opportunistically to changing political-economic conditions."[58] Yet while it is possible to make the argument that a number of postwar immigrant groups in the United States and England share such characteristics, it is also important to retain the specificity of the Indian example, to attend to the ways that Indian nationalism is distinct from other Asian diasporic nationalisms, due to the conditions of the development of the Indian nation-state. While this is largely to avoid the generalizing tendencies of the categories of "Asian" or even "third world" migrants, the project to draw out particularity is one that gives rise to making transnationalism, like its constituent part of nationalism, more historically contingent.[59] Recalling the amazing persistence of Indian cultures in so many places in the world may also help to grant diasporic subjects themselves some agency within global forces.

And so the diasporic subjectivity of Indianness also interrogates the boundaries of two academic spaces that have remained somewhat autonomous from one another: area studies and ethnic studies. Indian migrant subjects increasingly inspire questioning about what is "Asian" in the identity category "Asian American."[60] Clearly, Indianness engenders topics of colonialism and postcolonialism, and alternative possibilities for racialization, within an interdisciplinary field like Asian American studies; and linking formations of Indian community across the United States, England, and India suggests the very flexibility of identity categories that Asian American studies has been founded upon. So too does the field of South Asian studies require some retooling when India and Indianness are formulated not in the subcontinental area that has been designated by U.S. government and funding agencies, but *abroad*, even in those groups' backyards, in North America. Different interpretive options emerge when "South Asia" or "Asian American" are newly constituted and dislocated, and perhaps too when they are put into some kind of dialogue.

Paul Gilroy has described black diasporic cultures as a "changing same," in which the expression of blackness occurs not only with conscious regard to what has come before, but also through the irruptions of the modern world that impel the creation of something new.[61] I find this to be a very useful way of framing an approach to the Indian diaspora, as reproducing itself through intensified investments in Indianness, and as simultaneously challenging the discourses of the postcolonial and the ethnic, in its ability to continually transform itself. If the tenacity of Indianness around the world helps to mitigate the paranoia about the homogenization of culture in a transnational era, it may also conceal the shifts and variations that occur when cultures move, in which the idea of change itself may need revision so as not to always be about time or nation.

The global India of *National Geographic* is not unrelated to an India of years past: somewhat exotic, hybrid, and faraway. Yet present time and space give the representativeness of this new India a rather different edge, related as it must be to the Indianness that increasingly lives in the west. While the magazine may seek to gaze forward and backward without an overly elaborated sense of time and space, this book is very much invested in the temporal-spatial coordinates of the national geographic of diaspora. Though to many India may appear to be consigned to the subcontinent, migrants continue to construct that nation in places where they have come to rest, all over the United States, England, the Caribbean, Africa, and elsewhere. And their own senses of how they are a part of that nation are multiply shaped, by other nations and peoples with whom they have deep affinity and from which they might experience alienation. If India exists in various forms, and has multifarious origins, its diaspora can provide many points of access into global belonging, too, a global belonging that a range of national subjects might desire, when, for example, contemporary American culture celebrates a film or a fashion that is especially marked by being "Indian." In this sense, India via its diaspora is as much a part of a first-world sensibility as it is from the subcontinent. The achievement of diaspora here, then, is also the achievement of globalization, in which Indianness is neither a dominant nor a subsidiary formation. Diaspora captures the many and contradictory relationships that are a sign of the future, though they continue to draw on the past. The difficulties and pleasures and, yes, necessities of that form of belonging underlie the concerns of this book.

ONE

HISTORIES AND NATIONS

> This is indeed India! The land of dreams
> and romance, . . . of tigers and
> elephants. . . . The country of a hundred
> nations and a hundred tongues, cradle of
> human race, birthplace of human speech,
> mother of history, grandmother of legends,
> great grandmother of tradition.
> —Mark Twain

THESE WORDS appeared on a *New York Times* advertising supplement for the 1991 Cultural Festival of India.[1] Without leaving their homes, *New York Times* readers toured India as they flipped through a promotional brochure filled with pictures of waterfalls, tigers, and the Himalayas. The legitimacy of this travel in the North American cultural marketplace emerged both from the evocation of the prototypical American writer Mark Twain and the assemblage of exotic sights presumed to compose India. Final authentication of this consumption came not from booking a flight to Bombay, but from embarking on a voyage to Edison, New Jersey, to witness a spectacularized representation of Indian culture. Where is India? one might ask. Though the opening quote from Twain for the Cultural Festival promotion exudes a sense of confidence about location—that "this" is India—the reading (and festival) experience may render the referent somewhat indistinct.

From July 12 to August 11, 1991, Bochasanwasi Shree Akshar Purushottam Swaminarayan Sanstha, or BAPS, a Hindu sect with U.S. headquarters in Queens, New York, sponsored a Cultural Festival of India. The $35 million, thirty-day extravaganza featured dance and musical performances, educational workshops, shopping displays, and a food bazaar, among other things. Edison, New Jersey, once an industrial working-class town with large white ethnic populations (Italian and Irish), has more recently developed a significant contingent of middle-class migrant Indians. In fact Indians, over the years, had grown to be the largest Asian American group in the state of New Jersey.[2] In a context of such a rapidly changing racial landscape, the town of Edison served as an important symbolic backdrop for the project of imparting nation to Indians "imagining community" in the diaspora and in the United States.

Six years earlier, from July 15 to August 18, 1985, BAPS arranged a Cultural Festival of India in London, advertised on buses around the city with the lines, "The local tandoori can't give you the true taste of India" and "A Passage to India, Climb aboard a No. 29."[3] For this event, the Swaminarayan collectivity chose the grounds of Alexandra Palace, a certain symbol of the decline of the British empire, to create a vision of India, not now as a jewel in the colonial crown, but instead as a force in the lives of migrants and their children. These British Indians for whom the address was made, like their counterparts in the United States, were navigating the complexities of citizenship that entailed undergoing particular processes of racialization and struggling to develop responsive discourses for group identity.

These Cultural Festivals of India, like so many cultural productions of migrants, constructed nations in places far away from the nation-state of India—places with rather imprecise, though deliberated, geographical coordinates and in moments at once transhistorical and indexed to concerns of the contemporary. The uses of that deeply paradoxical formation is part of what this chapter seeks to unravel. An image of India in the festivals took shape through an "invention of tradition," to use the wonderful phrasing of Eric Hobsbawm and Terence Ranger,[4] a history of nation that could be mobilized for the diaspora's negotiations of past and present. Despite the fact that the stated goal of this particular event was to bring participants, imaginatively, to India, migrants were the audience. Though those United States and British citizens may have lived in complex worlds of ethnic and racial subjectification, the festivals insisted that a particular rendition of India occupy central stage in the formation of identity. Revealing the magnitude of the work that went into producing the conjunctures of India and the diaspora is the fact that BAPS transported by sea huge, "authentic" pieces of forty-foot high display structures from India for both events, and then assembled them at the festival sites. This physical transplantation prepared the ground for discursive importations, as cacophonous stories were massaged into shape to create a history of India that could be read and thus made real for migrants in Alexandra Palace and a county college campus in Edison.

The festivals rightly presumed that a portable history of India was essential to Indianness in diaspora. But in their production of India as a closed entity, they missed a central experience of diaspora, that migration has thoroughly complicated ideas about history and nation. If in diaspora Indianness has become disaggregated, in a sense disintegrated, and has needed force to rebuild, that energy has come from the heterogeneity that constituted diaspora: multiple histories and multiple nations. Diaspora does not simply reproduce India but in fact translates India through alternative languages of time and place and through movement itself. The India in diaspora that has emerged has been inextricably linked to Indianness abroad.

The connection between nation and identity, over time, is the underlying logic for alternative stories to the one the Cultural Festivals tell.

History, I suggest in this chapter, is a site in which to rethink what it means to be Indian in the diaspora. Of course there is no singular history, but a set of stories about the past that operate autonomously or in concert with one another. As Paul Veyne has put it: "History with a capital H . . . does not exist. There only exists 'histories of. . . .' "[5] Stories, or in Veyne's words, "plots"[6] about Indianness have varied trajectories; some emanate from a mythical "homeland," while others emerge through formations dispersed across state boundaries; in all cases, however, the nation cannot remain rooted to a place. A collection of repercussions and projections in and through a notion of India forms a representational archive that diasporic subjects draw on in their productions of culture. This analeptic and proleptic force of history, too, is what can make diaspora comprehensible within narrative. While at first glance the travails of Punjabi factory workers in 1950s London and the financial successes of southern Indian software engineers in California's Silicon Valley in the 1990s may appear incongruous, both experiences represent facets of a cultural world that peoples from India publicly and privately inhabit. And the different periods for these events that become formative for a present-oriented sensibility highlight the complicated nature of time for diaspora. As an alibi for individuals to identify with one another and create communities, a historical Indianness is constantly being adapted and reworked. What results is a densely constituted subjectivity that might be read in a variety of locations provided by stories of the past and present.

From a transnational history that spans the continents of North America, Europe, Asia, and Africa, there emerges a particular kind of heterogeneity based not only on the local interests of a group of people, but also in the notion of India that is being created. Unraveling the process of becoming Indian in the diaspora is to imagine what India, as nation, as state, or as culture, has signified to migrants, and how that India has been articulated with other national formations, like "America." If critically interpreting the importation of categories of origin effectively pulls apart India, looking at the cultures of those who affiliate with a homeland puts India back together again, in altogether different form. Though Indian emigrants come to live in England and the United States, their worlds bear more than traces of nationalities that are formed outside these host countries. Casting one plot of Indian diasporic subjectivity, however heuristically, as "becoming Indian" rather than "becoming American" or "becoming British," through the histories of migrants' movements, allows us to conceive of peoplehood, place, and origin more imaginatively than teleological notions of immigration have previously allowed. This is to say that first-world states do not constitute a conceptual endpoint for the imagination of migrants themselves.

While the United States and Britain cannot fully contain the cultures of migration, they never lose their importance as lands of settlement and as national formations. Indeed, they provide locations for diaspora—locations that are crucial to map in order to comprehend the generated experience of Indianness. Just as a history of migration is a history of nations, the histories of India that migrants reimagine are also histories of multiple nations. A central quality of diasporic Indianness, then, is its discursive arrangement in transnational space, ordered not by a line from one point to another, but by a circularity of movements.

Distinct ideas of Indian migration emerge through rhetorics of time, too. The periodization of shared experiences reveals the nature of political and cultural ideologies, precisely because the choices in how to begin or end a story resound in the manner in which we view these communities, and in how they understand themselves as communities. In this respect, dates will be important for this chapter, both for what they invoke as familiar ways of thinking about India and migration, and for the experiences that they might decenter in established teleologies of diaspora. Formative instances for Indian movements around the world include 1947, the date of Indian independence from colonial rule, and 1965, the year that immigration regulations for Indians were relaxed in the United States. Wading through local and trans-local meanings for particular moments deepens our understanding of group consolidation and citizenship.

In any story, there are a range of textual presences and absences that periodically interrupt the flow. So too in a production of histories, about India, and Indianness, we must encounter seams that cut through not only different renderings of the subject, but often competing claims about its meaning. That is an experience that this chapter seeks to recreate in its juxtaposition of stories of nation and culture—those of the Cultural Festivals of India and those of migration. Though the festivals consign the nation to narrative closure, migration opens that up by indicating that nation is excessive in diaspora. But this is not to suggest that either textual strategy constitutes a true history. The Cultural Festivals of India, both in London and Edison, are able to animate readings of diasporic subjectivity precisely because the hyperbolic constructions of "India" occur multiply, too, through dialogues with each of the following: the British empire and the physical and political movements it generated, ghost immigrant populations in deindustrialized New Jersey, resident Indians in a variety of places, and ideologies of multiculturalism during globalization. Situated within the synchronous developments of late capitalism and the new nationalisms of migrant diasporas, and the framework of colonialism/postcolonialism, the Cultural Festivals dissolved boundaries between the local

Figure 2. Peacock Archway (courtesy BAPS).

and the global, as well as between the past and the present, and were able to represent some experience of the world that was very real to its participants.[7] They thus serve as a useful touchstone for thinking through histories of migration, and, finally, diasporic Indianness.

Peoples of India in the World

To many, India remains little more than an abstraction. Making India real was the intricate feat that the creators of the Cultural Festivals accomplished through the display of material products like food, musical recordings, dancers, and calculators.[8] But the brilliance of the gesture lay in the festivals' concurrent ability to retain the broader imaginative possibilities of India as an integrated whole, in a world where nations and cultures are deeply fragmented. The extravagance of the festival signified the magnitude of such ideological work.

The entry of the festival was framed by two archways, the Mayur Dwar (Peacock Archway) and the Gaj Dwar (Elephant Archway) (see figs. 2 and 3). The huge (30–40 feet high) ornate pieces built in India and transported to the West served a number of purposes; the peacock and the elephant are among the most colorful and exotic animals found in India and have historically appeared in prosaic western images of India. That these animals are really quite common in India seems not to be the point, for they became rare or wondrous in their new setting.

On meticulously organized grounds, a set of exhibits and performances immediately followed the welcome brigade. The participants were invited to peruse a series of handicraft booths (tie-dye, paper pulp objects, stone carvings, brass work) in the part of the fair entitled "India Village," decorated with a banner that read, "Experience rural India." Actual craftspeople, direct from India, were producing the pieces in each of the booths;

Figure 3. Elephant Archway (courtesy BAPS).

the public was invited to watch the process as well as periodically participate in the activities. Quite unlike the real Indian village, nothing was
for sale in these booths, nor were visitors ever directly addressed. This
particular experience of India was about presenting what is old, what is
quaint, and finally what is authentic. What is made by hand is a compelling trope for antiquity, and also for nationalist struggles in the third
world. In fact, the handloom was the prevailing Gandhian metaphor for
all that was untouched by or resistant to (modern) colonialism and imperialism. And it stood in stark contrast to the stalls for Indian American
businesses, many of which specialized in electronics products.[9]

Though the festivals did not directly reference British colonialism or, in
fact, national independence, they certainly performed a response to that set
of historical experiences. In these festivals the creation of a collective set of
(invented) traditions was the means to root an authentic idea of Indianness,
just as it was for an earlier period of nationalism. An intertwining of culture
and nation here, just as in India, could not be anything but overwrought,
precisely because it was so difficult to achieve for such complex and chaotic
entities; the exorbitant physical presentation was one symptom of such
anxiety. Because the Indianness they sought to create required a fixed reference point, the festivals gave India an invented stability.

Among peoples of the Indian diaspora, fixity has acquired a special
status as desired object because of the intensely *unsettling* experiences of

migration; yet migrations themselves can be utilized to interrogate the limits of stable nations. The movements of Indians around the world began well before colonialism and through colonialism acquired the shape that is familiar to us today.[10] Among other things, colonialism determined a sense of connections between India (and its peoples) and England (and its cultures). The colonial state governed from within as well as from without, or abroad, and achieved its work through intimate relationships with local Indian elites and local peoples. England was very real indeed to a wide variety of Indians who had come in contact with the English language, with stories and representations of England, and with English men and women.[11] Migration out of India was not always a particularly culturally disruptive act; the relationship between the colony and the empire had long established the grounds for a kind of movement that forms what we might call an early history, to anchor on one side the developing narrative on diasporic Indian communities extending into the present. This set of experiences constitutes a story that the festivals did not tell, and one that later "histories of Indian immigration" also will not tell.

Fundamental to any form of colonialism is the movement of people, capital, and governing bodies, and occupying center stage within the British variety is the Indian worker-immigrant. As a solution to impending labor shortages in sugar production and other agricultural activities produced by the abolition of African slavery in 1834,[12] indentured labor became a niche for peoples from India who faced high population density and few employment opportunities at home. Between 1830 and 1920, a large proportion of Indians living abroad served as indentured labor in Mauritius, Malaya, Burma, Ceylon, Réunion, Jamaica, Trinidad, Martinique, British Guiana, Natal, and elsewhere.[13] The decline and eventual abolition of this system occurred through a growing awareness of the exploitation inherent in arrangements that were only marginally freely chosen,[14] in the plantation colonies themselves, in Britain, and in India. In the rise of the concept of Indian emigration, as a response to these thorny issues, it is possible to see the confluence of the forces of British liberalism and the desire of moving subjects to define their life trajectories. Reflected as well in the produced shift from the category of workers-in-transit to immigrants in the sugar colonies is the acknowledged failure of the British government to protect its citizens abroad in the face of the inexorable need for cheap labor by profit-driven planters. Indian communities all over the British colonies, from Trinidad to Fiji, evidenced the twinned, if not contradictory, impulses of autonomous development and sustained relationships to the British imperial administration.[15]

In the seat of the empire, in England itself, such issues were, perhaps, more complexly drawn. Some of the first Indians to become noticeable as a population to the English in the late 1700s were those of a veritable underclass of laborers.[16] Indian sailors, or lascars, who had worked on British ships transporting goods, were a matter of great debate among the British public.[17] After being paid minuscule wages and undergoing severe maltreatment on the ships, many of these men, from mostly poor families in India, escaped the hold of the foremen by foregoing their return passage home (and further abuse during the journey) and settling in London; many ended up residing in London simply due to the inability or unwillingness of companies to honor the second part of the agreement.[18] Left in a new city with few financial resources or skills translatable to the local economy, lascars grouped together in the poorest areas of London in boarding houses supplied either by various social reform groups or by the East India Company, which assumed responsibility for the disastrous handling of the situation by ships that were in some form or another in their employ.

Indian women and some men who had made the passage from India to serve English families as nannies, valets, and household servants became part of the British cityscape by the mid-1800s. The distinction between domestic "household" labor and the "hard" labor of slavery was to be partially negotiated on the axis of gender, as Indian women had a particular role in the production of imperial communities; their subsequent presence in England would be framed, from this moment on, by understandings of feminized domesticity. Recently discharged from their duties, some of the nannies, or ayahs, were organized into homes and later dispatched to other jobs in Britain for passage to India and to other places in the empire.[19]

Lascars, however, lived a more publicly immiserated existence and became the subjects of studies and reports that linked ethnic origin or race (being "Asiatic" or "Oriental") with social and cultural vices.[20] The history of British social reform in the nineteenth century took shape partly around the issue of how to address the situation of poor Indians in London. In a classic 1873 study entitled *The Asiatic in England*, Joseph Salter, a missionary, described his social work among lascar communities, and in particular his efforts to bring them to a Christian home. "Asians," he noted, "have an aversion to the Union[,] for eating and drinking are part of their religion, and they would rather huddle twenty or thirty together in a small house, where they can cook and eat and drink and smoke, a la mode Orientale, amid the fumes of opium and joggree."[21] These images of sailors and other poor Indian men in London also buttressed the colonial project, though in rather different ways from stories about exceptional Indians. An anecdote about visiting the residence halls of lascars illustrates the correspondence: "On one occasion, I was requested to accompany two friends . . . one, an officer in the Bengal Army, the other, a gentleman about to proceed to India in the Civil Service. Both acknowledged that much they had seen was harrowing to their feelings and exceeded all belief; the younger of the two . . . felt most deeply the sickening and degrading scenes he had witnessed."[22] Effectively, the British presence in India was justified by defining the deficiencies of the Other. If these poor Indians in England needed someone to take care of them, surely those in the subcontinent required instruction and governance from abroad.

Indians were also drawn to North America. There, newly developing fishing industries, railroads, and agriculture demanded substantial cheap labor just as the largely agricultural regions of Punjab were experiencing drought and famine that forced many to leave in search of work in the late 1800s. Large numbers of Sikh soldiers who had served in the British army also began to look for alternatives to colonial service or subsistence farming. At the same time, migrating to North America began to acquire the aura of opportunity throughout India, as a counterpart to supporting the colonial administration; this was also true throughout Asia more generally, as the continuous move of Chinese, Japanese, and Korean workers abroad to expanding agricultural plantations in the U.S. west evidences.

Simultaneous with the onset of Indian immigration to the United States was an engagement with India and things Indian, though here not through the formal apparatuses of colonialism, but instead through a kind of cultural exchange. Beginning in early colonial times, and through the early 1900s, small numbers of Indians passed through North America for academic, business, and religious purposes. The significance of India (and hence Indians) as a site of spirituality for Americans began in the middle to late 1800s and continues unabated to this day. Various scholars have uncovered the intellectual commerce between religious trends in India and elite U.S. philosophical circles in writings by people like Henry David Thoreau and Ralph Waldo Emerson; theosophical movements established doctrinal links between Buddhism and Brahmanism, and the category of "Boston Brahmin" emerged from this sociocultural formation.[23] Giving further weight to the continuous circuits of "Indian" and "American" intellectual developments was the fact that Mohandas Gandhi was said to have been influenced by Thoreau, and Gandhi's writings and ideas are widely known to have inspired Martin Luther King, Jr.[24] An important marker of this early period was the visit of Swami Vivekananda to the 1893 Chicago World's Fair, to give a talk at the World's Parliament of Religions. Indians were not the only ones on the move; India, too, was traveling.

In the early 1900s, a number of Indians went to the state of Washington to do a variety of manual labor; they formed a small community in the town of Bellingham. Like the Chinese and Japanese before them, Indians—viciously referred to as "rag-heads"—were typed as racial Others taking jobs from white workers. Employers had indeed used recent immigrants as cheaper labor at a time when unions were fighting to ensure fair wages and work conditions, and those same unions excluded nonwhites.[25] A complex set of factors formed the context in which Indians became the target of intense and, to some extent, organized anger.

One of the most dramatic instances of concerted action against Indian workers was in 1907, when hundreds of white workers in Bellingham stormed makeshift Indian residences, stoned Indian workers, and successfully orchestrated the non-involvement of local police. Despite the weak attempts at reconciliation by town officials after the attacks, local action against Indian labor had persuaded residents and employers that it was extremely volatile to have Indians, and foreigners more generally, present. The lasting meaning of these events for Indians lay in the highly racialized subjectivities that were foisted upon laboring immigrants, very much in contrast to the ideologies of ascendancy and agency that United States national mythologies had assumed for them back home. The contradictions of these stories remain unresolved to this day.

In California, issues of race and labor had both a specific and seminal importance for Indians and other immigrants. Mostly Punjabi Sikh Indians moved to California from India itself and also down from northern sites where they had encountered intense discrimination, to work in a variety of occupations. California-bound Indians found a burgeoning agricultural economy that was in great need of cheap labor; the skills of Indian peasants corresponded well to the occupational demands of the area's farming expansion. Fulfilling the same symbolic functions as other Chinese, Japanese, Korean, and Filipino workers, Indians too were part of the "Asian problem," and Punjabi Sikhs, Indian Muslims, and others were all considered to constitute a "Hindu Invasion."[26] The Indian presence in California also became part of a continuous story of Asian workers taking "native" white workers' jobs. Organizations like the Asiatic Exclusion League, which had been formed by anti-Chinese and anti-Japanese activists, now broadened their xenophobic address to encompass Indians entering California and other places in the West.

Work, in indentured or free labor systems, in North America and the Caribbean, Africa and England, became central to how Indians abroad were seen during this early period. In a number of sites, particularly in the Caribbean and Africa, local populations directly identified Indian immigrant presence with hard labor. Through time and in more varied areas and populations, in a place like London, remembered associations have produced images of Indian workers as images of India, resulting in both distancing mechanisms, where middle- and upper-class Indians have dismissed connections to lascars or others, and solidarity, where politically active Indian-origin politicians publicly took up the cause of indenture.[27] In the United States, as we shall see, Indian workers in California and the

Pacific Northwest during the early 1900s have a confusing and suppressed relationship to the story of later migrations.

Indian migrant laborers of the middle 1800s to early 1900s should also be placed in plots of racial formation. The continuing presence of Indians within a mix of peoples—black, white, as well as East Asian—was an important effect of British colonial labor arrangements. In that racialized world of the sugar colonies in particular, Indians interacted, struggled, and had deep conflicts with former African slaves; that intercourse structured Indianness as it has taken shape both inside and outside the countries that provided the first stop in the migration process. Within the United States, Indian laborers appear within two constructed histories. First, and most locally, an important reference point for Indian laborers in the United States between 1905 and the 1920s is the broader history of Asian workers in Hawaii, California, and the Pacific Northwest that began as early as the mid-1800s, just as African slavery in the United States was headed toward abolition.[28] The racial discourse of that period generated "Asian" as a highly absorbent category for peoples from an Asia that included China, India, Japan, Korea, and the Philippines. This grouping of "Asian" bears a strong (and parallel) resemblance to that of "black" in the United States at this time, as a way to describe colorist difference for peoples who had a specific position within the United States economy. The specificity of an Asian subjectification was based on an idea of "Asians" being distinct from "blacks," having never been subjected to plantation slavery, and, indeed, as having come to the United States as free laborers in response to labor shortages. Though Indians worked in places far away from the Hawaiian sugar plantations, where many other Asian groups had initially gone, they and Chinese, Filipino, and Japanese migrants worked in similar occupations in the West, albeit in much smaller numbers.

The activities of Indians in the United States at this time might also be read within another historical framework, of British colonial subjects from India traveling to participate in agricultural and other enterprises through the world as indentured and then free labor. In that body of historical experiences, Indians, of course, played a more central role than they did in the Asian American migration story, in terms of numbers and influence; in places like Trinidad and South Africa, the racial Others were equally Indians and Africans, and those from China and other places in Asia formed smaller groups in the broader landscapes. Through this particular trajectory, Indians' racial subjectivities were formed through British colonialism. An international experience of race and labor may be counterposed to questions of "Asian exclusion" in the United States. Indians in the United States at this early point in their history lived within multiple possibilities for self- and social definition. On the one hand, they formed part of a local racial world, occupying a third, or perhaps even a fourth, racialized space, after former African slaves, native Americans, East Asians who had been in the area for a longer time and in much greater numbers, and Mexicans. On the other hand, they constituted the primary racial Other in a colonial system deeply fixated on India.[29]

How to classify Indians was a matter of much contradictory racial theorizing.[30] The broader racial categorization of humanity, as Aryan, Negro, or Oriental, omitted Indians. Within the parameters of the reigning scientific languages of race, then, "Indians" as a people comprised a variety of affiliations, among which "Aryan" was perhaps the most ambiguous. Those from northern India at various points in history have claimed that term, and the British themselves utilized racial distinctions based on the Aryan/non-Aryan dichotomy. Not surprisingly, the brown, non–East Asian, non–Native American, non-African, and purportedly Aryan immigrants posed a conceptual and political problem to racial ideologues in the United States. Indians entering the United States immediately after 1905 were not directly or indirectly addressed by the early exclusion laws, yet given their racial ambiguities vis-à-vis "whiteness," their eligibility for citizenship was a matter of some debate. On the one hand, the "barred zone" of the 1917 act was in part intended to forestall the complications presented by an avowedly "Aryan" group of working-class and brown immigrants, by prohibiting those from India from immigrating. On the other hand, Indians who had been in the United States for many years had already applied for and in many cases received permission to naturalize, and had in effect become U.S. citizens. The contradictions inherent in the period climaxed in 1923 around the now legendary case of the Indian immigrant Bhagat Singh Thind.

Having previously ruled in 1922 that Taddeo Ozawa, a Japanese man in the United States for a long time, was ineligible for citizenship because he was not white,[31] the Supreme Court was poised to determine the parameters of whiteness. By this time, Bhagat Singh Thind had lived in the United States for nine years, had fought in the army during World War I, and had applied for and received citizenship from the state of Oregon, but was in danger of being "denaturalized" by the Bureau of Immigration following recent court decisions involving Asians. In a landmark 1928 case, the Supreme Court decided against Thind, saying that though Indians were considered by academic authorities (anthropologists and sociologists) to be "Aryan," and thus thought to be synonymous with "Caucasian," they were not "white" according to popular meaning, in the understandings of the "common man."[32] The Supreme Court made race a social category, apart from social scientific renderings of the concept, and ascribed to Indians a racial representation, borne not out of origin or, necessarily, self-identification, but out of their embeddedness in local social and class formations. The judicial gesture was as much to cultural groups and labor organizations that were working to exclude Asian labor from a number of occupations and geographical areas as it was to formal tenets of the law; an ambiguous appeal to a kind of "common sense" conveyed the external pressures on the court. Broad patterns of social activism, diverse communities of immigrants, and local and national ideologies of nationalism, then, all conditioned the "race" of Indians in the United States.

Complications of nationality and citizenship during this period are further dramatized by a rather different and more unusual kind of immigration case in 1928. Cyril R. T. Moir was the son of an official of the vice-regal establishment in India who wrote to the Economic and Overseas Department of the British government asking if he should apply for inclusion in the Indian or British quota for entry into the United States. J. C. Walton, the secretary of the department, noted that were Moir to apply as an Indian, he would be admitted as part of a quota of one hundred. The logic was that because recent laws denied entry to those peoples who were ineligible for citizenship, such as Indians, there was space in the original quota. But as an "Englishman," in racial terms, Moir would be eligible for citizenship. A handwritten reply on the Economic and Overseas Department folder describing this petition reads: "Quite interesting. I was myself born in India. It seems that if I were to go to the U.S.A. then I should have to enter as an Indian."[33]

If national forces of and in the United States and Britain actively shaped Indian migrant subjectivity, so too did India, as a nation, though not yet a state, factor into these constructions. While colonialism on the most obvious level connected Indians abroad to Britain, as British subjects, it also linked them in an enduring way to India because an ambiguous nationality was a barrier to the assumption of other national affiliations, like being American or British. These peoples continued to be interpellated as Indian—colonized Indian, perhaps—but Indian nonetheless. Basic to the rhetoric for empire were places (homelands) that made sense to their inhabitants.

Developing here as well is a sense of a diaspora: a community of Indians outside of India. A 1916 article in the *Modern Review*, published in India, reveals the early investments and concerns of such a formation. Entitled "Hindu Immigration, with special reference to the U.S. of America," this piece painstakingly details the movements of Indians to England, South Africa, Australia, New Zealand, Fiji, the Caribbean, and North America, focusing on laborers and their subsequent treatment and integration into host societies. While on the surface the author of the article, Indu Parkas Bannerji, seems most respectful toward Britain and the Empire, he nonetheless subtly critiques the effects of colonialism, noting at one point:

"Some migrate to foreign lands to enjoy, permanently or for a time, political equality with free men."[34] This and other comments implicitly contrast the state of Indians abroad, as possible citizens of other nations, particularly in the United States, to their colonized status in Britain. With this migration narrative, which extends not only through the British colonies but also to North America (and, possibly, South America),[35] Bannerji establishes the reach of India itself. And in fact, the thrust of the article is devoted to a kind of admonishment to Britain to not impede such movements, which Bannerji terms "such just and natural expansion of the Indian nation within the Empire."[36] In the style of later pronouncements of anticolonial nationalists, he remarks that were England to do so, "the consequences will be more than we can see now" and "an Empire with water-tight compartments is hardly conceivable."[37] We can read in this text the presumption that India does not only exist in the subcontinent, but lives in its peoples abroad, and, therefore, in the world, however complicated and even contradictory a possibility that might seem prior to independence.[38]

Also dwelling in the midst of such contradictions and possibilities were students and other middle- to upper-class Indians in England and the United States. Beginning in the late 1800s, a number of aspiring Indian professionals arrived in London, at about the same time as the lascars and ayahs. An important discriminatory mechanism for the Indian civil service was its sole administration in London, preventing in most cases and impeding in some the integration of local peoples into the governing system. Many of those people who hailed from elite and wealthy families who had made the trip to England with the goal of becoming certified to serve in the British colonial administration stayed and established residency in London and other large cities. The Indian elite also saw the cultural value of a British education and sent their children to be educated abroad; a relationship with England was a way of signifying class status back home.[39] Indian businessmen and doctors also migrated to England, both those who had been affiliated with British companies in India and others who had skills and educational and other resources to start their professions abroad.[40]

Though the Indian population in England was extremely variegated by class, it did find common interests for affiliation.[41] The development of a kind of Indian community, with political and cultural "representatives," even elected lawmakers such as Dadabhai Naoroji and Mancherjee Bhownagree,[42] subsequently took shape without a studied or even artificial reconciling of the various elements of the Indian population that remained for the most part distinct. In these formations, middle-class Indians of course held sway. The claims of financial success and cultural equality, the mastering of a "British" lifestyle, and eventually the nationalist desire for a state all structured the rise of Indian figures in England who would influence political and social discourses preceding independence in 1947. In the United States, middle-class Indians began to hold positions of significant influence in what might be called Indian interests. Indians had gone to study in the United States, too, particularly to places on the West Coast, in California and the state of Washington. And there were also small numbers of Indian businessmen and their families in the New York area, one of whom, Sirdar Jagjit Singh, was eventually profiled in the *New Yorker*.[43]

If the classed Indian migrants of California, London, and New York had autonomous existences in different social worlds, they had some connections across space through the aspiration of a free India. Many differentiated responses to British colonialism found common ground in nationalist discourse, though, as many have argued, different ideas about the constitution of the nation have been suppressed in that production.[44] Perhaps the most explicitly revolutionary anticolonial responses were among Indian students and workers on the West Coast of the United States who formed the Ghadar Party. In 1913, student leader Har Dayal, other students, and Indian farmers established a group called the Hindi Association of the Pacific Coast in Portland, Oregon; they began a newspaper called *Ghadar* and set up a group house, Yugantar Ashram, in San Francisco.[45] While the paper was produced in the western United States, it was distributed through Indian immigrant groups allied with the cause of independence in North America, the Philippines, the Caribbean (Trinidad, Honduras), Hong Kong and China, Singapore, and elsewhere.[46] And connections with all sorts of activists in other countries were forged through an anti-imperialist consciousness.[47]

Movements for independence from India, too, radiated outward, into the diaspora. In 1885, the Indian National Congress was formed to address the emerging issues; a number of journals, including *India*, were disseminated at home and abroad for this end.[48] Many leaders of the Indian National Congress went to study in England and, subsequently, established links there with British and Indian sympathizers throughout Europe during their tenure at places like Cambridge and the University of London.[49] Eventually, with the advent of the twentieth century, more "moderate" leaders who were centered around the Indian National Congress gave way to a student movement in Britain and elsewhere directed at the goal of Indian independence in no uncertain terms. In London, groups based their work in the hostel India House; in 1905 the Indian Home Rule Society was formed. These British revolutionaries were part of a larger diasporic movement of ideas, resources, and activists; the group in London might be seen alongside Ghadarites. Such activists for

Indian independence also coordinated political work throughout Europe, via London, Paris, and cities in India.

The British and U.S. governments responded to the threat of these pro-independence activities all over the world. When Ghadarites sought aid and counsel from the German government during World War I, the United States prosecuted them.[50] The U.S. government responded to this political activity less out of pure concern for the issue at hand than because of its continued alliance with Britain. And the fact that heightened activities of the Ghadar Party coincided with the advent of a war in which the sides were clearly delineated greatly intensified the harsh light to which Indian nationalists would be exposed in the United States. The British were also keenly aware of the broad dispersion of Indians around the world and of the personal and political connections that ran through those communities. The British maintained an elaborate system of surveillance through the 1920s, 1930s, and 1940s; they kept detailed information on Indians traveling not only in the United States, but throughout the Americas. Their lists of "extremists" there in the late 1930s, during a period of stepped up activities around Indian independence at home and abroad, also provides a sense of the span of the political Indian diaspora through the Americas, including Indians in the United States, Canada, Mexico, Panama, Brazil, and Argentina.[51] In England, after the 1909 assassination of an India Office administrator, Sir William Curzon Wyllie, the British government stepped up its tactics of repression, charging many student leaders with sedition, deporting and imprisoning them, preventing various activists from being admitted to the bar, and closing down a number of important social institutions for Indian students.

Not all movements for independence were explicitly revolutionary; many were formed with multiple purposes in mind. In New York, far from California's worker and student populations, there was a constituency of Indian migrants and others who also were deeply invested in the question of British colonialism. There, in the early 1900s, a number of small groups arose, including the Pan-Aryan Association, the Indo-American National Association, the Society for the Advancement of India, and the Indo-American Club; the India Home Rule League of America, created later, in 1917, would be the longest lasting and most influential. In the early years, some Indians participated in anticolonial activities, but for the most part, Americans comprised the groups. Many scholars have observed that Indians and Irish Americans found common cause in their political organizing against British control of foreign lands; and the considerable resources in the Irish American community, of political groups, journals, and newspapers, were utilized by Indians and those sympathetic to a free India.[52]

To understand what drove some Americans to become invested in overturning British colonialism in India is, again, to be attuned to a broader international political context. Alan Raucher has suggested that the question of imperialism, regarding the Philippines, and, by extension, India, became a topic of significant debate among a range of U.S. intellectuals and public figures, including Andrew Carnegie, William Jennings Bryan, and Agnes Smedley. The ideological roots of the critiques of "empire" were heterogeneous. Carnegie opposed imperialism through a kind of pragmatism, in which he remained skeptical of commonalities between ideas of Western and other societies, and committed to the security and stability of the British and U.S. governments, which could be threatened by revolutions for independence. On the other hand, those on the left argued against imperialism from a more humanitarian standpoint, based on observations of the state of Indians under colonialism, and also through the desire for alternatives to U.S. nationalism, in full and dominating force during the world wars.[53] What might appear as primarily a debate on the fate of India should also be seen as a deliberation of what the nation of the United States was, and could become. The East-West polarity that was an important and useful component of anticolonialism, and one evidenced in the alliance of Britain and the United States against Indian revolutionaries, nevertheless reifies and makes monolithic "America" in ways that ultimately do disservice to the historical contingency and instability of that ideology. Seeing the United States as a more contested entity during this period and others allows for more nuanced understandings of a range of political developments.

In the activities of the officials of various Indian organizations and others in the United States, there seemed to be no contradictions in advocating for independence from Britain and the right to citizenship in the United States. Indeed the moves for U.S. and Indian nationality seemed to shadow one another, particularly in the late 1930s to 1940s.[54] Sirdar Jagjit Singh, the renowned president of the India League of America, wrote letters to popular news publications about the denial of naturalization rights to those of Indian origin and simultaneously campaigned for a Gandhian transition to home rule and for support to those Indians adversely affected by British colonialism.[55]

Indian independence refracted internationalist issues for a range of peoples. One interesting example is that of the writer Kumar Goshal. Having immigrated to the United States from India in 1920, Goshal exerted himself very specifically for the overthrow of British colonialism, but also worked for many other causes; as a leftist, he enunciated a politics that was broadly global.[56] Goshal wrote articles for the *National Guardian*, the *Nation*, and other periodicals on matters largely concerned with Asia and Africa and opposed to various forms of imperialism. From 1942 until

1947, just after Indian independence, Goshal had a regular column in an African American newspaper, the *Pittsburgh Courier*. A closer look at his writings there reveals Goshal's expansive sensibilities, in critiques of foreign influence in the Philippines, Burma, and Indonesia, as well as in discussions about lynching and racial representation.[57] In a 1942 article, Goshal issued a series of challenges to "progressive" movie directors such as Frank Capra and Lewis Milestone:

> Let these directors show us that the Chinese are not all Fu Manchus, nor are they Charlie Chans. . . . Let them present the Negro people as they truly are, stripped of the tradition of plantation mammies, smiling mint julep servers, corn pones and magnolia blossoms. Let us see the Negro people carrying on a heroic struggle against terrific odds. . . . Let us see the people of India, not as Gunga Dins and elephant boys, bejeweled maharajahs and snake charmers, naked fakirs and nautch girls—but as a people who, given the opportunity, would repeat the glorious story of the Chinese. . . . Let us see the real Indian people who have made incredible sacrifices in their fight for national freedom.[58]

Goshal's solidarities with what would shortly be called "third world" peoples are mirrored in the decision of a black newspaper to include this column, as well as one by other international citizens, such as a Chinese columnist. Developing at this time, clearly, is a complex network of affiliations based on divisions between north and south, east and west, and more and less industrially developed nations, and their peoples. In a description of the lack of segregation between Indian and white British pilots preparing for an offensive against the Japanese, black intellectual George Padmore refers to the Indians as "colored."[59] What is important to understand about this period is both the internationalism of Indians and also the cosmopolitanism of African American political communities.[60]

By the 1940s, the sociopolitical landscape in England was changing, too. Punjabi Sikhs came to London and northern England, and subsisted by working in factories and by selling textiles in the neighborhoods in which they lived. These immigrants formed the Indian Workers' Association in 1938 to represent their interests as workers in Britain, to provide institutional space for a developing "community," and also, to advocate anticolonial causes in England and in India.[61] Student organizations at the universities in London, as well as at Oxford and Cambridge, multiplied, with both political and more broadly cultural aims. A great majority of Indian groups in the period preceding independence addressed the problems and aspirations of immigrants in England while remaining committed to the broader goal of independence from British colonial rule; they were therefore carefully watched by the India Office and other arms of the state. Given the increased presence of Indians in Britain, the British state was also fixated on the possibilities of large-scale migrations from India to the West, without the natural inhibition and control that the imperial relationship had once provided. During these years, the British government kept detailed files on the movement for naturalized citizenship in the United States.[62] And Britain continued to monitor closely the number of Indians who actually went to the United States.[63]

The radiating effects of Indian nationalism took shape through other national formations of politics and culture: American and British, to name just two examples. And, furthermore, this occurred within various social landscapes, inflected in important ways by class and race. The efforts of Indians for naturalization, and therefore full citizenship in the United States, ultimately bore fruit in the 1946 Luce-Celler bill, just one year before Indian independence. Here the relationship between two forms of nationality, American and Indian, seems to be best expressed not through mere coincidence of chronology, but by a complementarity between the developing epistemologies of national identity. This was a way of thinking and living nationality that, even in its tamest forms, demanded some sort of critique of international-geopolitical power arrangements, and effectively took issue with the nations of the United States and Britain. Cultural diversity or worlds of many cultures in the 1940s emerged in both places as national ideals. This is why even Sirdar Jagjit Singh, a less radical, more middle-class proponent of Indian nationalism, could be just as concerned as Kumar Goshal or Ghadar Party members with questions of racial-national representation, and assert solidarities across emerging non-Western states.[64] Pro-independence Indian students in England developed their own alliances, with working-class and leftist causes, to influence visions of British nationality, which would be under increased scrutiny after the Second World War.

By the time of Indian independence, small populations of Indian migrants remained in the United States, in California and New York especially, but altogether not more than 4,000.[65] Many who had in the 1920s and 1930s been deprived of citizenship rights were also subject to the greater implementation of alien land laws; denaturalized and immigrant Indians who owned land in California were thus stripped of an important investment not only in the region itself, but also in a broader vision of life in the United States.[66] Disgruntled with discrimination and exclusion from basic individual liberties, Indians had begun to leave and the immigrant population dwindled.[67] Indian communities in England, while larger than those in the United States, were limited, too, in their reach and diversity; prior to independence there were largely those who had worked in some capacity in the apparatus of empire, such as lascars or ayahs, more upper-class students who settled in large cities and small but growing groups of recent migrants. Though the structure of this social geography would to some extent endure, the numbers and variations of peoples after 1947 would dramatically transform the British landscape.

1947—A New India and a New Indian

In the last section of the 1991 Cultural Festival of India exhibit entitled "Message of India," the binding element for subcontinental peoples around the world is the transhistorical nation, made vivid through the discourse of culture. The introductory text read: "India has always implied to the world, the luminous light of wisdom which is more needed today. . . . Her lofty ideals of non-violence, peace and purity are not superficial but filter through. . . . Indian culture is an eternal stream of human values that continues to inspire the youths, the men and women of the world." But of course, particular Indias, indexed to specific historical renditions, have had their hold on peoples through the diaspora. As a discursive formation that organized the imaginative and social worlds of migrants, the drive for independence had broad and multiple forms: anticolonialism, anti-imperialism, regionalism and communalism, pan-Asian and pan-African—what would come to be known as "third world"—solidarities, racial identification, and, finally, statehood. And herein lay the complexity of being Indian, in all places in the world. If immigrant cultures before 1947 were being created through the as yet unfulfilled fantasy of the overthrow of British colonial rule, their continued development would be forever marked by the actual fact of new nationality.

Indian independence in 1947 hugely affected diaspora consciousness and sewed together a wide range of political and social interests. For those abroad, for those who stayed home and for would-be migrants, the construction of the nation-state of India established a form of citizenship that would bestow a new form of subjectivity in a world determined by hierarchies of value based on national economic power in a capitalist market, and, by extension, military prowess to maintain those positions. The border between the fantasy and materiality of the nation can never be unporous and the citizenship of a state with geographical borders and a government produced different kinds of nationalisms both inside and outside India, and new social, economic, and cultural networks to support those ideologies. National liberation, the memory of colonial subjugation, antagonism toward the colonizer, and an exploited position with regard to the West, through a knowledge of England, all became important elements in a transformed and structuring nationalist narrative that Indians carried with them through the diaspora. What was "national" and what was "foreign" could be reimagined, on some level, with an independent nation-state. But the memories and affiliations hardly made for the "eternal stream" that the festival ideology asserts; indeed, they were variegated, interrupted, and contested.

The development of the Indian state had been a profoundly conflictual endeavor; among other things, the partition of the subcontinent into "Hindu" and "Muslim" states of India and Pakistan wreaked a kind of havoc that would continue to reverberate through immigrant communities that had in large part been held together by the glue of anticolonialism in the period before 1947. An increasingly complex field of affiliations began to distinguish the histories of "Indians" from those of "Pakistanis," and later "Bangladeshis," and other South Asians.[68] And, likewise, the state of India began to have distinct meanings in the world at large, and more specifically for its migrants; Pakistan, Bangladesh, and "Islam" became with this shift important influences on subgroups of the colonial category of Indian peoples. While previously many (though not all) kinds of diasporic difference had been rigidly grafted onto the desired object of nation, now the state itself opened up wider spaces in which to translate differences from home into contemporary lived realities. Thus identities in the diaspora became more particularized after independence because of the many issues at stake in state, regional, religious, and linguistic conflicts. The perceived falling to the background of the external enemy of the British colonial state disrupted real and abstract forms of solidarity among diasporic Indians in the pre-1947 period.

So India seemed to take its rightful place in a world of nations. But that world, too, was in flux. Indian independence coincided with the end of World War II in 1945 and with the broader onset of the postwar period. The end of the war, as well as the accelerating demise of British colonialism, had created not only the formal assignation of sections of the globe as "first" and "third" worlds, but a significant shift in the relationships between those places, based on economic, political, and, not least important, cultural hierarchies.[69] With the United States taking responsibility for vanquishing Nazism and Britain claiming that they "gave up" India, both nations devised new public languages for racial justice that took shape both domestically and internationally. These two nations were as much in the midst of processes of construction as recently independent India.

As Britain entered the postwar period, it initially defined its new role in the world through the tradition of colonial empire, and ideologies of largesse and paternalism in relation to former and present colonies. In 1948, the British government passed the Nationality Act to permit easy movement among countries of the colonial empire and British Commonwealth, with the assumption that the major direction of the flows would be, as in the past, from England outward.[70] The state's touting of free movement and inclusion, twinned with its self-image of benevolence, continued to have a significant impact in a number of quarters both inside and outside England, for proponents of a postwar liberalism and for those about to migrate.

Somewhat differently, the United States inaugurated the "American Century" with the rise of intellectuals and policymakers like Henry Luce and others in the 1940s, who espoused an aggressive nationalism to combat disruptive political trends around the world, including socialism, anti-imperialism, and anticolonialism.[71] The close of World War II intensified domestic aspirations for guaranteed U.S. political domination of the world, and thus affected relationships between the United States and the emerging "third world." Though both the United States and British cases are important on their own terms, what also stands out at this critical historical juncture is the contrast between those nationalisms, and the perception of that difference through the 1940s and 1950s by other developing nation-states such as India, and especially by future migrants. The British state publicly committed itself to accepting the movement of peoples from former and present colonies and the U.S. government, despite granting the rights of naturalization to Indian immigrants in 1946, installed a quota of only one hundred immigrants from India per year. This quota effectively worked against the possibility of the building of active new migrant communities and also deferred the development of lived connections with the emerging independent India that would be so important in a later era. In the entire period between 1946 and 1964, only 6,319 Indians immigrated to the United States.[72]

Britain and the United States also offered different postwar possibilities for the script of the nation—for the migrant subject and for the emerging Indian state. England was saddled with the legacy of colonialism, while America could recast its imperial involvements and its history of exclusion into triumphant stories of combating Nazism and other forms of intolerance and, by the early 1950s, ensuring citizenship rights for all. Small wonder, then, that when Indian immigrant and U.S. congressman Dalip Singh Saund described his passage to the United States by boat through Britain, he remarked: "I was not interested in empire builders. Abraham Lincoln's statue, however, evoked in me quite a different response."[73] As a congressman in the late 1950s to early 1960s, Saund was extremely concerned, as was the U.S. government, with what road independent India would take, whether toward socialism or toward "American democracy."[74] What kind of nation India was had a relationship to what kind of migrant subject, in another nation, an Indian could be.

India's independence was an initial sign of broader decolonization efforts and ideas about autonomy all over Asia and Africa. Jawaharlal Nehru, India's first president, had been meeting with Asian, African, and North and South American nationalist leaders since 1927, and by the time of his own country's independence he was already part of a broad network of political formations that were militating for independence and against the forces of imperialism. Nehru, with Gamal Abdel Nasser, Josip Broz Tito, and Achmad Soekarno, was central to the 1955 Bandung meeting in Indonesia that served as a statement of collective pan-Asian, African, and Arab solidarities in the face of postwar U.S.-European political domination, and was an important precursor to the Non-Aligned Movement formally instituted in 1961.[75] The principles of nonalignment remained deliberately broad and open-ended, and the many nations that participated in the summits and conferences from 1961 on were by no means consistent in their adherence to constitutive issues like economic independence and political autonomy; how to support liberation movements and how to negotiate relationships with "superpowers" were sorted out in various ways by member countries. Yet questions of territorial integrity and social justice continued to shape the development of the nationalisms of third-world states, most especially India because of its prominent role in the nonaligned movement, and, necessarily, ideologically influenced national-Indian subjects all over the world.

Postcolony in the World

A central exhibition in the Cultural Festival of India in Edison was entitled "Beautiful Borderless World" (see fig. 4). Upon entrance, the attention of participants was directed to an overhead sign with the message:

> Our World was born with borders.
> Today it is caged and confined,
> torn and tortured by a thousand divisions.
> Let us not further disunite and disfigure it.
> As children of mother earth,
> We ought to heal her wounds, promise to be
> nice to her, to each other and help
> rebuild a BEAUTIFUL BORDERLESS WORLD

The festival elaborated the borders of the particular nation, of India, and the Indianness that is a result, in the framework of a world without borders. But that paradoxical construction could only be sustained by giving India (and the world) a stability—temporal and spatial—that was thoroughly undone by transnational migration, among other things. To those

Figure 4. Beautiful Borderless World (courtesy BAPS).

who moved, the borders were very real indeed, and thickly layered by complex histories. While the festival glibly and spiritually asserted collective ownership of the earth, being a citizen of the real world was fraught with tensions. Subjective living in a new world was the setting for alternative diasporic constructions of India and other nations. And that world was built of systems based in the continual erection of borders.

As the world realigned, Indians were becoming reinscribed as "workers" in postwar England. The economies of many western countries, including those of the United States and Britain, enjoyed significant expansion and prosperity after the war. Britain required new sources of labor for burgeoning industrial enterprises in areas of London and northern England, and this development coincided with both the 1948 Nationality Act and Indian independence, though not without some consternation. Pushed by social and cultural conflicts unleashed by the withdrawal of British forces and pulled by the prospect of steady employment in British industry, Indians began to go abroad as labor in the early 1950s, much as they had traveled to various parts of the British empire, including England itself, but with different expectations. As new nationals, Indian migrants now had access to narratives of immigration, particularly those that stressed individual betterment, group legitimacy, and settlement abroad.

Beginning in the 1950s, Indians abroad would become consolidated as "immigrant populations" in an unprecedented fashion. Turning first to the society they knew best, Indians migrated en masse to England, and only later to the United States. Indians' experiences as British colonial subjects were easily, if resentfully, transmogrified into identities of racial otherness. And numbers begin to tell a story of both magnitude and classification. Most scholars agree that the peak period for Indian migration to England was between 1955 and 1965. Beginning with numbers near six thousand for the years 1955 through 1960, the number of migrants jumped to 23,750 in 1961 and continued in that fashion through the 1960s. Until the 1962 Commonwealth Immigrants Act, most of the migrants were assumed to be new immigrants; after the middle of 1962 (when the act was implemented), a good number of the migrants were relatives of those already here and/or meeting qualifications of entry by way of professional status.[76] The numbers of Indian migrants before 1962 were much smaller than those for West Indians and, after that, consistently exceeded the West Indian figures.[77]

Most of these Indians, especially prior to the middle 1960s, exhibited a distinct downward mobility. A variety of factories engaged in heavy industrial production recruited or served as magnets for Indians in both developing cities in northern England as well as in what was beginning to be known as greater London. Performing a wide variety of types of unskilled and then skilled labor, these workers established themselves as visible and significant parts of the British working class. India's place in the world had changed, from a British colony to a "third world" country, and so too had the nature of the British Indian immigrant population in shape and form. The image of the "immigrant" was no longer an ayah, lascar, or prince, to borrow the title of Visram's book on the pre-1947 period,[78] but now a factory worker.

Going mostly to cities, Indians also became a metropolitan diaspora in England. Very much embedded in urban formations of work and culture, Indian communities themselves embodied many of the highly popularized contradictions and tensions of a "changing London" or a "transformed Birmingham." The timing of the larger-scale migration of Indians to England coincided with a period of massive industrial growth in British cities, and these phenomena were ultimately linked in the British popular imagination as well as in the daily life of Indian immigrants themselves. Indian migrants carried the symbolic weight of economic expansion, geographical growth, and racialized cultures as much as they themselves constructed those developments. Their location in cities also laid the groundwork for the later emergence of a more international urban Indian community; the experiences of Indians in London in the 1970s and 1980s would be claimed as those of the diaspora of Indians in New York, Bombay, and London. Still, the seemingly wide dispersal of immigrants all over England should be qualified by the concentration of Indians in specific areas, in communities or enclaves.[79] Such geographical characteristics of this population were influenced by work patterns (where the jobs were), the quick building of areas of concentration from the original immigrant presence, and the persistence of housing discrimination that restricted Indian immigrants to particular locales.

The spatial aspects of the Indian immigrant presence in England testify to the discursive and material tensions within the term "diaspora," of concentration and diffusion, of the international and national. While England was a constitutive force and a developing national identity for Indian immigrants, so too were Southall, Birmingham, Blackburn, and Leicester local signifiers for Indian community.[80] There have been volatile political debates on the very nature and alternating desirability and disagreeability of dispersal and concentration in England, but there is a certain universality to the experience of minority enclaves and a particularity to its incarnation in Britain.

The largest number of immigrants in this early period came from Punjab and Gujarat, due to the centrality of these states within the British colonial establishment (and hence the familiarity of Britain as an imagined site) and also the high levels of unemployment in the rural and business sectors of these state economies. The relative regional specificity of the early Indian populations in the England of the 1950s and 1960s facilitated the development of tightly knit and communally oriented groups in various British cities. In western London, Punjabi, mostly Sikh immigrants gravitated to areas where other family and kin from home had already settled and associations and networks of employment and housing counsel had developed. In Bradford, Gujaratis congregated in particular areas of the city to participate in cultural and religious activities and provide shelter and jobs to recent immigrants.

Despite the numerous examples of active community construction, there were also pockets of migrants who were more isolated, such as students and businessmen, and who required "ethnic" services from Indians living elsewhere. Rashmi Desai, one of the early historians of the Indian immigrant community, wrote in 1963 of Gujarati grocers who traveled to different places on the weekends (Friday evening through Sunday), provided Indian foods from vans, and maintained social and economic relationships with a wide variety of Indians through this commerce.[81] This kind of activity evokes the earlier examples of other Asian immigrants in countries with new Asian populations, the image of the Chinese grocer in the American West during the late 1800s among them.[82]

Increasing numbers of Indians, the changing political landscape of the nation, as well as economic shifts in urban centers like London stimulated the more formal organization of these Indian populations; cultural and political associations served a number of different ends in the construction of more self-conscious forms of community. In Bradford, Gujarati Indians started a group in 1959 called Bharatiya Mandala (Indian association) to organize the celebration of festivals and holidays like Diwali; the group also built a physical structure to house a library and residential facilities. During the same period the Indian Society of Great Britain formed in Birmingham and mediated factional divisions in the Indian community in the interest of unity. Structured as they were around a type of cultural trade, of practices and goods, these groups gave life to an Indian cultural identity; and the recent birth of the independent Indian state further nationalized that identity.

Various Indian communities in England also organized themselves into specifically political organizations. While mostly Sikh immigrants formed the Indian Workers Association in the 1930s to argue for the cause of Indian independence and coordinate cultural activities among Indian immigrants, the 1958 formal centralization of the group emerged from the formulation of political objectives that were based on the interests of those cast as Indian laborers, in relation to the British labor movement, and constructed around a consciousness of the particular forms of racism that Indian immigrants encountered. The late 1950s and early 1960s witnessed the rise of an "Indian" population within the British national space and the growth of connections between local immigrant communities, in places like Bradford, Southall, and Wembley, and a broader "Indian" ethnic formation.

By the early 1960s, many developments had combined to change profoundly the broader popular interest in Indian immigration, the responses of English citizens to Indian immigrants, and subsequently the very character of the population itself. The significant rise in total numbers of Indians in Britain by the early 1960s indicated that the phenomenon was not temporary; Indians had become more economically and socially established in Britain, both as individuals and as a group. As their tenure extended, the population diversified; if not advancing to skilled jobs in the manufacturing sectors in which they had worked, Indians branched out into other occupations. Many, for example, saved money and purchased small shops, while others tried to pursue careers that had been interrupted by migration, such as teaching or engineering. Indian ownership of shops in white (and minority) areas became a symbol of the presence of a population and its power in a community. It also illustrated shifts in class status, however minuscule, at a time when the economy was no longer expanding at the same postwar rate as it had in the 1950s. Finally, Indians were located in broader racial contexts, in particular one in which large numbers of Afro-Caribbean peoples were also beginning to be noticed by British society. A series of 1958 riots in the Notting Hill section of London, where white youths had attacked blacks, was only one manifestation of the increasing hostility of whites toward immigrants of color, both Afro-Caribbean and Asian.

Race, as a collection of categories, as a process of subjectification, and as a field of power, structures one telling of a story of Indians in England. The rise of the hostility of white residents toward nonwhite peoples and the construction of immigration as an issue in British political discourses led to the development of new collective social identities in the Indian population. Seen as one group by the British population, Indians, Pakistanis, and later Bangladeshis began to assume the category of "Asian" in a number of different contexts. The dominance of the term "black," again both in British colonial languages and within politically constructed groups of immigrants, began at times to be applied not only to Afro-Caribbean immigrants but also to a wide variety of Asian immigrants, so that nonwhite immigrants as a whole began to constitute a "black" population, in largely political terms.[83] Given the complex debates on Indian racial identity and particularly the desire among immigrants to be identified as "Aryan," the application of blackness to Indians in England was a contested move indeed.

As the Indian population grew into larger and more organized communities all over England, anti-immigrant fervor reached a high pitch, with national and local manifestations. Riots in Nottingham and Notting Hill persuaded national policymakers that violence against minorities was on the rise and that political solutions were necessary to address these issues. Initially, the responses from the Labour Party and the Conservative Party were very distinct, with the Labour Party interpreting the racial violence to necessitate antidiscrimination measures and a firm commitment to a multiracial society, without legislation controlling immigration.[84] The Tories, on the other hand, responded with an express sympathy for those unhappy with changes in the British population, not always articulated in bald racism, but often taking a more problem-solving form: British society could simply not adapt so quickly to recent demographic shifts, and thus needed regulation. For that set of interests, numbers of migrants and population percentages were mobilized in the service of dramatizing change and classifying otherness.

The divergent philosophies of multiracialism and immigration restriction are less important for their association with a particular political party (because that would shift) than for their simultaneity. While the government led by the Conservative Party passed the Commonwealth Immigrants Act in 1962 to limit and regulate the entry of immigrants, it was a Labour-dominated government that in 1964 renewed the legislation to control immigration and produced in 1965 a White Paper recommending the further reduction of the number of allowable vouchers for immigrant entry. In 1965, the Labour government, with the support of the Conservative Party, passed a mostly symbolic antidiscriminatory bill that would become the Race Relations Act. The national goal, then, through the 1960s, was to limit the entry of New Commonwealth (colored) immigrants and to manage the changed racial dynamics of British society through a series of proactive antidiscriminatory measures.

On a local level, the experiences of the period reflected general ideologies of multiracialism and racism and also contained specific manifestations. Intense hostility against immigrants resulted in racial attacks on Indians (as well as other immigrants) in areas of high residential concentration, in London especially as well as in cities to the north like Birmingham. In the workplace, employers and then unions actively discriminated against Indian workers.[85] As much as Indians had become a community in Britain, they had also become a minority group, and one that was in many ways despised.

The manifold responses of Indian communities to these local and national crises illustrated the growing stratification and diversification of that group. Just as late-nineteenth-century and early-twentieth-century Indians in Britain had been divided over how to best approach issues of India's sovereignty, so too did mid-twentieth-century Indians experience political differences over their minority status, with perhaps many more issues to process, including generation, gender, and class. Newly middle-class groups eschewed direct conflict in order to secure the broader and long-term goal of assimilation. Younger populations adopted more confrontational tactics, like protesting everyday forms of racism. The affiliations of Indians with other minority groups also reflected a measure of diversity; calling oneself "Indian," "Asian," or "black" would come to suggest a political orientation even more powerfully in the 1970s. Still another reaction within the wider circuit of migrant Indians, who had in some cases not yet come to Britain and in others had only recently migrated, was to turn to the United States as a destination with its own racial conflicts but still free of the weighty legacy of strained relations between the colonizer and the colonized.

New Indians in a New America

The Cultural Festival of India's exhibit "India—A Cultural Millionaire" opened to a room filled with banners of quotations from writers, politicians, and imperial apologists (such as Lord Macaulay). The first quota-

Figure 5. What do we mean by an Indian face? (courtesy BAPS)

tion, from Arnold Toynbee, glibly delineated the undergirding premises of the festival: "It is already becoming clear that a chapter which had a Western beginning will have to have an Indian ending, if it is not to end in the self-destruction of the human race. At this supremely dangerous moment in human history, the only way of salvation for mankind is the Indian way." In a mirror image of Hegel, here India was the solution for the future because it was at once stunningly exotic, wildly diverse, and very old. Accordingly, the first section of the exhibition documented the natural wonders of India with huge photographs and lengthy descriptions of the coastline, the mountains, the rains, rivers and forests, the animals, the flowers, the arts, and finally the faces of people. A descriptive panel asked the question that may have already been in the minds of curious fellow travelers: "What do we mean by an Indian face?" (see fig. 5). And, a Benetton-like photograph was accompanied by these words: "All these faces belong to India. Covering the entire scale of skin tones, from fair to dark, from sharp and squarish features to the roundish mongoloid features of the Gurkhas, India comprises a surprising diversity, matched by no other Nation. Yet a common lustre of hospitality and friendliness binds them to the soul of India that remains eternally One." This construction of a Nation assumed diversity and difference—indeed, even racial difference—while at the same time asserting that spirituality, or "soul," held it all together.

The Cultural Festival of India rehearsed a mythology of Indianness fundamental to the formation of a simultaneously political and cultural nation. Well before independence, the father of modern India, Jawaharlal Nehru, expounded on antecedence, diversity, and essence in similar language:

> The diversity of India is tremendous; it is obvious; it lies on the surface and anybody can see it. . . . It is fascinating to find how the Bengalese, the Marathas, the Gujratis, the Tamils, the Andhras, the Oriyas, the Assamese, the Canarese [et al.] have retained their peculiar characteristics for hundreds of

years, have still more or less the same virtues and failings of which old tradition or record tells us, and yet have been throughout these ages distinctively Indian, with the same national heritage and the same set of moral and mental qualities. . . . Ancient India . . . was a world in itself, a culture and a civilisation which gave shape to all things. . . . Some kind of a dream of unity has occupied the mind of India since the dawn of civilisation.[86]

But it is impossible to singularly associate this idea of unity in diversity with Nehru, or his time and place. British colonialism employed such mythologies in its exercise of cultural-political power. And none other than Mark Twain was seduced by India's antiquity and multiplicity, that he presumably did not find or perhaps could not see in his own America. Those who emigrated from India to the United States in another period, however, could carry diversity with them and give it another grammar in a place that was developing its own language for inclusion.

Diverse unities had always, in some way or another, been a stated public ideal of America, though with a working model of novelty rather than antiquity. And especially in 1960s America, newness was being rearticulated on a number of fronts that impacted the flow of Indians and that created the social worlds of multiplicity in which they would be able to claim a place. In 1965, when President Lyndon Johnson signed the momentous Immigration and Naturalization Act in the United States, he ensured that the contours of the worldwide Indian diaspora and the relationship between India and its citizens would change in spectacular fashion, just as it would for other migrant populations. In the context of the civil rights movement and at a time of increasing national attention to discriminatory legislation and applications, quota systems for people of non-European origins seemed yet another symbol of the injustices protested by large segments of black, Latino, Native American, and Asian students and activists. By abolishing the old quota system, the government opened the doors to some 170,000 immigrants from the eastern hemisphere, 20,000 per country annually; the act also allowed entry for relatives of U.S. citizens.[87] The numerical effects of the act were variously forecasted, amounting to only small changes or constituting a racial transformation.[88]

The symbolism of the Immigration Act itself in 1965 was even farther-reaching than its immediately perceptible policy or demographic changes. During this year, the United States was deeply involved in Vietnam, had only recently emerged from two other wars in Asia, and was at the same time crafting an image of itself as the leader of the "free" world. Paternalism—being the nation with "open arms"—virulent anti-communism, and foreign intervention all occurred together. The national and international reverberations of the civil rights movement had contributed to a rearticulation of American mythologies of racial democracy in the early 1960s and also created backlashes. Confronted by protesters demanding inclusion and equal rights before the law and in the practice of the law, policymakers and scholars both produced a renaissance of new writings on America's pluralistic society and also tried to contain the radical possibilities of civil rights and then black power. African, Asian, Caribbean, and Arab countries, meanwhile, were producing discourses of opposition to U.S. political hegemony all over the world in the nonaligned movement.

The United States readvanced the idea that the nation could comprise many races and ethnicities.[89] Though such formulations resonated with older renderings of diversity, such as the concept of the "melting pot,"[90] they also had certain meanings and contradictions in the immediate context of violent social division and were part of a different vocabulary used in public forums to address a range of cultural transformations. Certainly, the new languages of pluralism contained an anxiety and tentativeness for minority populations already contending with racial injustices at home. But this vision of America, in the form of state rhetoric at home and abroad, and alongside the very act of loosening immigration regulations, held tremendous promise for new immigrants from the third world, most particularly in contrast to the more familiar reality of British efforts to tighten her borders to impede the entry of peoples from the former empire. Here in the United States was an ideal model of diversity that Indians could comprehend and see themselves within, as it seemed to be free from the trauma of British colonialism and disconnected from an earlier history of exclusion. The slate of the past could be washed clean and a set of histories with 1965 as foundational moment could begin, for the United States and for the Indian diaspora.

In the 1960s, members of the first large-scale Indian migration to the United States were greeted by an economy in a period of expansion. The occupational experiences of mostly middle-class and credentialed Indians during this period seemed to match the ideals and actualities of growth and opportunity. Technological transformations meant new jobs in medicine, the sciences (natural and applied), business, and education, for which this group of Indians was exceptionally qualified. As in the early 1900s, Indians came also to a social world deeply stratified by race, and a biracial formation—"black" and "white"—in which there was no clear place for the racial identity of non–African Americans who were not white; this was especially true in the northeast, where most Indians initially immigrated after 1965. The public image of Indians was not a matter of great importance to policymakers or social critics, especially with regard, in relative numbers, to other minority groups, and this ultimately enabled a kind of mobility (both in terms of ethnicity and class) that was denied to Indian immigrants elsewhere, particularly those in urban areas of England.

It was not that India did not exist in U.S. popular culture, but that Indians were yet to be recognized within the complex of an awareness of Indian things. During the 1960s, in segments of middle- and upper-middle-class society, Americans were greatly fascinated with Indian music and Hindu religious spirituality.[91] The Beatles' widely publicized forays into psychedelic visions of Hinduism and sitarist Ravi Shankar's extraordinary popularity in the United States echoed the Boston Brahmins of the early twentieth century, but now found wider audiences and became articulated to a new kind of cultural politics, of openness, of multiculturalism, and of a less rigid personal lifestyle. It is on this level that anthropologist Margaret Mead understood such developments: "Ten years ago it was the thing to be Existentialist. . . . This interest in India is a similar psychological rejection of the United States, only it's more important, I think, and more serious. India, after all, has so much to offer on every level. It's phenomenally rich."[92] Throughout the 1960s, there was a palpable public silence about the relationship between this somewhat exoticized perception of national Indian culture and actual developing Indian communities; and little work has been done on this period, or succeeding ones, to explain whether or not we might consider the two phenomena side by side. I would suggest that it is useful to broadly paint the cultural landscape, as one in which many ideas about America, as well as the rest of the world, were being newly formed, and also where different peoples were newly visible in U.S. cities especially. In this more abstract sense, then, immigrants cannot be far removed from the perception of India. Even more important, migrants themselves have always been deeply invested in how their country of origin is represented. Though Indians in the 1960s were not numerous or organized enough to exert influence over this process, in later years they would certainly create highly politicized programs around the issue of representation.

In the years following the 1946 Luce-Celler bill, which permitted naturalization and thus also small immigration quotas, most Indian students and professionals who qualified settled all over the United States, and owing to their small numbers and their dispersal, they did not form visible communities.[93] The dramatic shift in numbers after 1965 is vital to understanding the more subjective aspects of community transformation. The Immigration and Naturalization Service reported that while 582 immigrants had come from India in 1965 and 2,458 in 1966, in each year following, that number increased by thousands and in 1974 reached 12,795.[94] The striking increase in the numbers of immigrant Indians, and the distinctive character of that shift in class and cultural terms, have led a number of scholars to begin Indian American immigration history in 1965.

Indeed, the thousands of Indians who came to the United States in the decade following 1965—largely concentrated in New York and then other urban centers, highly educated and professionalized, who began upon their arrival to develop what would become strong ethnic and cultural ties to each other and to Indians all over the world—embodied radically different subjectivities from those immigrants of earlier years. Maxine Fisher was one of the first scholars to lay out the activities of this immigrant formation in New York City in detail, and in that project she noted both the heterogeneity of Indians during this period as well as the inception of local efforts to produce more general "Indian" articulations of immigrant identity.[95] Fisher's detailed and careful study of the activities and ideas producing the early stages of Indian American consciousness, for 1960s and 1970s immigrants, might be creatively juxtaposed to Rashmi Desai's study of early British Indians for comparative purposes. The decade and a half between Indian immigrant flows into Britain and the United States accounts for the groups' relationships with very different worldwide economic and cultural phenomena: in the earlier period, 1947–65, with expanding industrial economies and decolonization, and in the later, post-1965 period, with the imminent rise of post-Fordist economic arrangements and struggles for racial justice at home and abroad. The class characters of the two communities shape how Desai and Fisher describe ethnic association and consciousness; Desai cites workers' organizations, while Fisher underscores the importance of professional identifications. Notwithstanding these differences, through both studies, Indians' urban identity and continued relationships to the homeland form an important subtext for unraveling the "immigrant experience," even in its early stages.

The high representation of doctors, engineers, and professional scientists in the first decade of the post-1965 Indian immigrant group produced an anxiety back home about the constitution of a national population without the necessary technicians essential to economic growth. Using the term "brain drain" that had previously been used to describe the flows of people from Britain to North America, the Indian government began to decry the tendency of educated and upwardly mobile Indians to move to the United States.[96] The widespread usage of the term accentuates the broader representation of Indians going to the United States, both for those who had already immigrated as well as for countries and populations around the world, in India and in places like Britain and East Africa, where Indians had not achieved quite as pronounced a level of professional success and with such apparent consistency. Indians in America, then, as a public category and actual population, began in the early 1970s to have a particularly eminent role in the diaspora.

The 1970s were marked by a kind of ambivalence through Indian society and government about migration and particularly about how to treat those who had emigrated. A 1973 article in the *Illustrated Weekly of India* on Indian Americans begins with the observation: "There are 50,000 Indians and Pakistanis in New York. Unlike their compatriots in Europe who do menial jobs and live in congested lodging houses, those in the States are educated, affluent and believe in gracious living. They are to be found in all professions as well as in industry and government service."[97] These authors hold Indians in the United States in high regard because of their class position, in contrast to more working-class Indian populations of Britain, as the reference to "Europe" seems to suggest. Being the beneficiaries of less discrimination also accrues to Indian Americans' value in the authors' eyes: "They are, by and large, valued by their employers, suffer from a minimum of discrimination and are affluent."[98] Special attention is paid to the immigrants' efforts to reconnect to India, by engaging in Indian cultural activities, and in their plans to help those back home; various sections of the piece also document the bevy of representations of India in art, film, and music. For the readers of this article in India, immigrants in the United States appear less as wayward sons than as part of a formation related to the nation and in the interests of the nation.

The project to interpellate the migrant as an extension of the nation was most clearly manifested in the financial initiatives of the Indian government to develop the category of the nonresident Indian, or NRI. In the early 1970s, the Indian state, like many in the third world, faced the increasing concentration of growth in narrow segments of its economy and the approach of stagnation in its broader industrial sectors, all in the context of a balance-of-payments crisis. Indian state officials' convictions in the importance of outside investors existed alongside persisting fears about economic autonomy that had energized and still informed the powerful languages of nationalism. Turning the traditional family remittance from currently petit bourgeois (and in the past, peasant) investment into large-scale capital formation was seen as one solution. The increasing economic success and community coherence of Indian immigrants in the United States, as well as in England and places like Hong Kong and Singapore, came to be seen by India as a less threatening source of funds for expanding economic enterprises, and so the state began actively seeking financial remittances from abroad. In 1973, the Indian Foreign Exchange Regulation Act discussed for the first time in official governmental documentation the "person not resident in India,"[99] and by 1975 members of the Indian Investment Center had begun to approach and hold seminars for immigrant associations in the United States, with the purpose of soliciting monies for new Indian industries.[100]

The term NRI did a great deal of signifying work: it symbolized financial prosperity and the successful Indian community abroad. From this period on, NRI became a common way in India and elsewhere to describe the Indian migrant; its usage was generalized. Understanding the NRI as a mode of subjectivity, however, requires attention to its origins in an economic program of the Indian nation-state, and the simultaneous glorification of Indian immigrant communities, in a sense as something reflected in the different kinds of 1973 representations, of the Indian Foreign Exchange Regulation Act and the *Illustrated Weekly of India* article. The nation had begun to aggressively claim its peoples, just as immigrants were expressing complex desires for India.

The process of translating difference and similarity from back home into lived (and represented) experiences in the United States operated through the multiple vectors of regional and religious affiliation, national identity, and spatial distribution. Cultural and political associations all over the United States, but certainly concentrated in California and New York, began to form in the 1970s with various constituencies, such as the Sikh Cultural Society, the Indian Association of Long Island, and the Indo-American Cultural Association of Westchester.[101] The emergence of the Association of Indians in America (AIA) in 1971 signaled the development of a broader formation through an *Indian* identity that serviced some kind of representation within the United States. Not surprisingly, part of the work of the AIA entailed a struggle for the inclusion of a category in the U.S. census for "Indian."[102]

The 1970s were a time of great diversification and significant growth of Indian American as well as Indian British populations. Public discussion of Indian presence was very different in the two nations, though, as American ideology seemed to embrace new immigrants while the state of "Britishness" established more rigid and hostile boundaries to greater influxes of peoples. And this had everything to do with the historical production of these groups in the United States and Britain in racial, class, and national terms. To Americans, Indians brought exotic heritage to bear on the existing diversity of U.S. cultures, and their insertion into middle-class society confirmed notions of immigrant ascent. In the early to middle 1970s in New York, Indian immigrants were in some way representative of transformations of the urban space: the incorporation of "peripheral" areas like Queens and Westchester into the cultural life of the city and the development of ethnic areas throughout a designated *metropolitan* site. Concentrations of Indian shops and services, "Little Indias," developed first in Manhattan, in the East 26th–28th Street and Lexington Avenue area, and a bit later in the Jackson Heights and Flushing areas of Queens. Associations in New Jersey, Westchester, and Long Island grew as credentialed Indian immigrants dispersed into the suburbs, not unlike their white ethnic predecessors. Newspaper and magazine articles celebrated these new and richly diverse urban cultures.[103] Indianness, in contained form, had become part of the U.S. urban and national landscape.

Borders between Peoples, Borders of the State

In a series of exhibits on social pathologies, Cultural Festival participants were asked to approach the limits of national culture. Though the Cultural Festival persistently strove to capture a broadly sweeping (and consuming) vision of India, it did compulsively return to the question of borders. In language resonant, again, of Nehru, the introduction to the exhibits read: "A world without borders seems a wishful dream yet it is possible. . . . First we must understand and eliminate the root reasons that split our world, the real elements that create borders." If most of the festival had to this point been structured around the comforting presence of the Indian nation in a (beautiful) world of multiplicity, these exhibits, however briefly and tentatively, suggested that the construction of Indianness, and its manifestations in community and identity, was by no means a fluid process. For those in England and the U.S. engaged in their own personal and group negotiations around what it might mean to be Indian abroad, the acknowledgment of "borders" came as a welcome reality check.[104]

Of course in the festival, the borders were first turned inward, to the family. Exhibits focused on marital difficulties and the other issues that divide the idealized family unit like "anger," "doubt," and "suspicion." Partly this had to do with the social conservatism of the religious sect that sponsored the festival, and with the notion of Indian culture being advocated. And in fact the family romance was the structure for the nation. But given that the nation here was projected into diaspora, into a context of other social conditions, the festival could not completely occlude the dilemmas that face racialized migrants, though it located that reality secondarily, almost on the margins. One panel description read: "What a distortion we create when we cage ourselves in compartments, saying: I'M BROWN, I'M BLACK, I'M WHITE, I'M YELLOW. Racism is rooted in Prejudice which reflects a grotesque image of humanity. Even a small PREJUDICE is like a Brick that slowly builds up into barriers between Cultures and Races."

Here racism was articulated in terms of individual perceptions and images; an almost pre-1960s consciousness was evident in the use of the dated term "prejudice." Vast divisions of economics and history were leveled in the return to the formulation of racism as a problem of attitude. A universalism, in the title of "humanity," made intelligible the apparent contradiction between, at first, derision toward colorist classification, and then acceptance of separate Cultures and Races. Perhaps in the midst of the stress of racialized experience, this was a desirable formulation for middle-class diasporic Indians who were working hard to make a place for themselves within multicultural nations. And yet the ordeals of racialization were embedded in diasporic memory, as stories of the past and present illuminate.

Indians in 1970s Britain faced more dramatic and material barriers to the creative production of a national identity. Questions of migrant-racial difference had become particularly acute and race had also destabilized again questions of nationality, as English society understood race through colonialism and its effects. That history of India intervened in the developing story of the Indian diaspora in Britain. By the early 1970s, anti-immigrant feeling in resident white English populations and within the Conservative Party had succeeded in producing tighter regulations on the flow of family members and dependents. Yet developments in the world continued to conspire against the efforts of the British state to determine who could come in and who could not. As Kenya began increasingly to favor those who were Kenyan citizens in labor and property ownership in 1967, many Asians, particularly middle-class Indians who had held onto their U.K. passports, began to be assailed as disloyal and greedy and fled to England.

Not included in the categories of the immigration controls prescribed by the 1962 act, this wave of Asian entry reintensified debates on how to control the shape of the national population. Consequently, a 1968 Commonwealth Immigrants bill included a provision that would allow only those who had one U.K. citizen-parent or grandparent to apply for entry outside strict immigration controls; this effectively pushed back within the controls most African Asians who had only attained British citizenship in the first generation. The bill also increased regulations on children under the age of sixteen immigrating to join a single parent, a status that had previously been unrestricted but that was now limited to cases in which children were joining their only surviving parents; the intention behind this was to prevent employable male children coming to Britain to join their male parent workers in the search for jobs.[105]

Tensions in British society among those older residents antagonized by changes in the English social fabric, new immigrants, and the state erupted in 1972, as Britain struggled to deal with Asians who were being expelled from postcolonial Uganda. Recent legal history in the response to Kenyan Asians had on some level prepared for this moment while the international (and relational) legacies of colonialism complicated matters considerably. The 1948 Nationality Act specified only two forms of citizenship, for Commonwealth countries and for Britain and her colonies; the 1962 act reworked and restricted Commonwealth and formerly colonial citizenship by way of immigration control, and the 1968 bill introduced generational connections to England into the requirements, with allusion to East Africans. Ugandan Asians had been entering Britain en masse since

1968; they had arrived both before the implementation of new regulations and later when they were subject to immigration controls as the consequences of Idi Amin's coup d'état started to play out.[106]

Amin's brand of anticolonial, anti-Western, Africanist nationalism interrogated first, Asians' cooperative role during British colonialism and second, their unintegrated commercial and social presence in postcolonial Uganda. In a sense, he brought the past to bear on the present, refusing the historical ruptures that were celebrated in a variety of quarters. The framing of the "Asian problem" by Amin in relation to the history of British colonialism in Uganda posed a different kind of problematic for Britain from the quieter, smaller, and less politically expressed issues surrounding the Kenyan Asian case. The hysterical fear of the destruction (and defilement) of cultural integrity within Asian communities in Uganda and all over formerly British colonial Africa raised the issue of the British state's obligation to its former colonial subjects. When in August 1972, Amin prepared to expel summarily all Asians from Uganda and declared Britain responsible for their resettlement, a political crisis broke out in England over the prospects of admitting thousands of Asians at a time when citizen outrage over immigrant presence was at a high pitch.

The ensuing controversies in both political parties and in newspapers and other cultural institutions engaged, perhaps for the first time, broader conceptual issues of the determination of who was and was not a citizen, and more practically how the postwar British state would come to terms with the legacy of colonialism.[107] Twenty-five years after India's independence, the United Kingdom was finally forced to reckon with the demographic consequences of imperial and racial divisions of labor. The subsequent decision to admit the Ugandan Asians, however, largely evaded these contentious and in some sense unanswerable queries, in part because to declare publicly the porousness and continuity of these histories would be to question the discretion of the British state and its voters to determine the profile of its own population.

In total, some 30,000 Ugandan Asians came to Britain in 1972, in addition to about 13,000 in earlier years,[108] with a much smaller number, about 2,000, going to the United States.[109] While a good number of the British group settled in the city of Leicester,[110] these Ugandans, with different experiences of class and community cohesion, also greatly diversified the population of Indians in general. As solidly middle-class subjects, these people came into Indian spaces and communities with a strong sense of entitlement and skills to develop enterprises in England, and without the possibilities of entering into industrial labor as early Indian immigrants of the 1950s and 1960s had been forced to.

Operating in ways that diverged from other already-settled Indian groups, these Ugandan exiles nonetheless shared many experiences with other Indians, not only in terms of class as they carved out their own spaces in the service industry, but also in their retreat to India for the construction of an identity. As stateless peoples, many Ugandan Indians began to see the cultural and psychic usefulness of "becoming Indian" and submitting to the sense of a past rooted in a more abstract "homeland." Ugandan and Kenyan Indians brought to existing Indian immigrant communities a set of experiences that both complicated and buttressed pan-ethnic nationalism. The memories of multiple migrations, the histories of indentured labor, the triangulation of colonial sympathies and anticolonial resistance all broadened the discourses of Indian identity. Likewise, during this period, the presence of Indians from the Caribbean—from Trinidad, Jamaica, and Guyana—challenged the linear narratives of class ascendancy being created by an earlier generation of now middle-class Indians in Britain.

Affiliations varied greatly; in some cases, Indians from a variety of different countries saw themselves as primarily "Indian"; in other cases, members of East African and Caribbean communities asserted the specificity of their process of migration, calling themselves Ugandan Indians or Trinidadian Indians, for example. Formations of class and race influenced all identities. While the lines between "newer" and "older" immigrants were on one level formed by socioeconomic position, the influx of "new" middle-class Kenyan and Ugandan Indians altogether complicated the mapping of those divisions by accentuating different experiences of migration, based in African racial landscapes and more attenuated relations with India.

Despite and through the rapid diversification of immigrant communities, the late 1970s and early 1980s brought into being new formations and articulations of identity. Indian youth, particularly in areas of high Indian concentration like Southall, developed forms of resistance that took shape through new forms of racial consciousness that had international reference points, through black power movements of the United States, and national meanings, in connections with West Indians.[111] Many Indians also participated in leftist and antiracist organizations like the Institute of Race Relations and theorized the relationship between race and leftist politics.[112] Working with issues of race foregrounded the need for coalitional activities with other groups for activist Indians and also kept alive issues of class that many increasingly middle-class Indian groups eschewed. These developments in England might be seen as helping to construct complex identity maps for Indian migrants. Ethnicity, race, and nationality, and the overlapping spaces therein, provided important though shifting coordinates for subjects to locate themselves in new and old places.

In developing a sense of group identity, or peoplehood, there has to be a reckoning with the past, an articulation to the present, and an imagination of the future; the choices Indian migrants made in that process had a great deal to do with lands of settlement.[113] In the United States, the process of identity formation for post-1965 Indian migrants entailed a functional silence around a prior history of Sikh workers. Given the small numbers of the early group of Indians, relative to other immigrant and minority groups during the period, it seems at first glance somewhat curious that they should not have revived the knowledge of Punjabi Indians migrating for work to California in the early 1900s in order to claim a kind of historical continuity of "Indians in the United States." But early Punjabi immigrants had not left behind large visible communities, even in California, that could participate in the process of establishing connective power with newer groups, and had not forged public proclamations of ethnic solidarity or even identity in the ways that other immigrant groups had. Even when Indianness was important, it remained within the relationship of Indians to the emerging nation-state of India, not through a referencing of a local experience in or an articulation to the United States.

The differences between the post-1965 and early 1900s Indians were also too profound to allow for the conflation of the groups. Most significant, the class background of Punjabi workers who came to the United States to engage in agricultural work and other manual labor sharply distinguished this group from the more professional and middle-class Indians in a North American imaginary, much as it had and would back home in India. Divisions in India between those who worked with their hands and those who had the credentials to avoid that kind of work were scrupulously maintained in the form of educational access, government representation, and caste and other cultural institutions. Indeed, it is hardly likely that those Indians who had moved to the United States for financial betterment and with the promise of class ascendancy would seek out connections to a group of laborers that had suffered racial and economic discrimination. Finally, the East Coast location of the larger group of post-1965 immigrants was, literally, a long way from the Pacific Northwest and California history.

Indians in the United States in large part eschewed a racial category of Asian American that might have drawn meaning from the elaboration of homologous histories of a pre-1965 period. Numbers illustrate important aspects of this dilemma; while by 1978, the number of immigrants from India had reached 19,100, much higher than the number for Chinese (14,500) and Japanese (4,500) immigrants for that year, the total number of those of Indian origin since 1820 was still 163,000, much less than the corresponding numbers for Chinese (523,000), Japanese (406,000), and Filipinos (390,000).[114] Indians' relatively small numbers with regard to large and already established Asian groups obviously played some role in the absence of identifications with Asianness.

But identificatory strategies were very much in flux. While those in the Association of Indians in America (AIA) pushed for the recognition of "Indianness" in the U.S. census, others clung to descriptive models of whiteness that were seen to bestow a kind of cultural power, in a manner reminiscent of Bhagat Singh Thind's citizenship case. These various positions were staked out in the context of the 1970s, when what it meant to be a "minority" following vigorous civil rights movements, implementation of affirmative action policies, legacies of discrimination, and profound changes in urban populations was yet to be fully worked out. Debates within the Indian American community bore the marks of these complex historical developments. A 1976 exchange of letters to the editor in the *New York Times* illustrates these points. Under the headline "Denying Racial Heritage," Ranjan Borra decried the AIA's protest of the decision of the Federal Interagency Commission to categorize Indians as Caucasian: "While Indians continue to be racially discriminated against in many other parts of the world, it must be considered no small honor to have been given this rightful recognition of their national distinction in a country other than that of their birth and ancestry. . . . It is time Indians abroad, especially in the United States, merged with the mainstream on grounds of racial affinity and not walk with the motley crowd of the minorities."[115] In this scheme, being recognized as a national-racial group, as Indian-Aryan, allows entree into another nation, of the United States. The desire for whiteness is apparent, as is a kind of disdain for being a minority. But it also seems important to read in these 1976 comments the presence of another historical experience of the diaspora, namely, contemporary events in East Africa, wherein Indians had been expelled from countries in which they occupied the category of racial Other and had not joined the "mainstream." The trauma of that rupture, from elsewhere, might in fact influence this writer's concern with an Indian diaspora in the United States.

Manoranjan Dutta, in another letter, takes a different and more presentist tack. As president of the AIA, Dutta's charge is a more direct orientation toward inclusion in the United States polity, and various forms of representation for Indians. Dutta distances himself from the racial chauvinism of Borra: "The suggestion . . . that to be in the mainstream of the American life one has to belong to the Caucasian race is an insult to all sensible persons"[116]; the multiracial America is the ground in which claims for Indian Americans must be made. Dutta expresses the need for a proper counting of Indians in the United States, under their own category in the census, and as well a more pan-Indian sensibility, "so that Caucasian and non-Caucasian Indian immigrants can continue to share their common heritage." Yet the head of this national association of Indians is also careful to instantiate Indians within the existing political possibilities of the time, which means the periodic affiliation with the category of "Asian American," particularly as affirmative action programs recognize Asian Americans. For these purposes, Dutta writes, "America's multiracial, pluralistic society has drawn on immigrants. . . . The Asian-American population, a small fraction of the total population, remains a minority for all administrative purposes . . . and the Indian immigrants shall be honored to join this class, to which they naturally belong." Both 1976 letters anticipate discrimination against Indians and minoritization in the United States, though with divergent solutions. Not far from the minds of these writers were the experiences of Indians in other countries, like Kenya, Uganda, and Britain.

Within the trappings of the former British empire, Indians were always and already racialized; unlike their U.S. counterparts, they could not have even imagined existing in the national-racial space of English whiteness. But 1970s Britain, too, was undergoing changes into a more pluralistic sense of itself. Racial uprisings, other forms of community rebellion, and popular and scholarly writings had prompted government studies and commissions that translated the need to respond to social change into a more generalized "multicultural," antiracist program, implemented in educational curricula, the Greater London Council, and measures to prohibit or at least discourage discrimination in employment and housing. Among the many important and complex effects of these developments was the rise of ethnicity as a concept, and as an identity for British minority groups. An emphasis on origin and cultural specificity—the building blocks of ethnicity—was appealing to those newly middle-class Indian groups who were invested in stressing their assimilative achievements and for whom the more insurgent racialization model threatened to propel them into prescribed alliances with Afro-Caribbeans, and support of labor struggles as well as relationships with working-class elements of their own population.

In light of these deeply fractured histories, how could a "unity in diversity" that the Cultural Festival proposed, that Mark Twain's romantic India conjured forth, or even that multiculturalism idealized, contain the Indian diaspora? Unity in diversity presumes, on the one hand, continuity, and on the other, stability. Post-1965 Indian migrants in the United States did not wish, in their production of a history of themselves, to include early 1900s Indians in California; what has been Indian in America, then, becomes discontinuous. Multiculturalism cannot fully account for that complexity, just as the emanation of an Indian past from the festival makes for a disjunctural relationship with these histories, precisely because of the rather different senses of narrative time and affiliation. And as much as Indians from Uganda or Kenya might have attempted to claim membership in the story of Indianness in diaspora, their traumatic date of entry, 1972, is not only a boundary crossing for their own group, but also a source of disruption for the broader historical narrative. India and Indianness are in flux in the diaspora, while stability is the feel of the nation that the Cultural Festivals seek to create. And yet both models held their distinct appeal for migrants creating identities in the United States and England.

New and Old Identities

Current debates on issues of different peoples within state boundaries may often unwittingly accept the newness of the phenomenon of diversity. British colonial strategies in India give diversity a historical depth, and in fact allow us to see the Cultural Festivals within a broader trajectory of political and cultural practices. In the 1860s and 1870s, the British colonial government undertook a massive ethnographic enterprise to document the varied forms of Indian culture and Indian peoples.[117] This "People of India" project, instead of pointing to the difficulties of national cohesion, provided justification and information for colonial rule. The careful attention to historical and cultural detail of the different peoples of India in no way asserted national similarity but instead proposed that these British subjects were highly diverse. Surprisingly, also absent in this text was any effort to make the peoples or their characteristics analogous.

Similarly, the British colonial administration's 1877 Imperial Assemblage to institute Queen Victoria as the royal head of India heralded diversity rather than submerging it. Lord Lytton, the viceroy of India at that time, remarked at the Assemblage that one could see the splendid results of royal rule in the very empire, "multitudinous in its traditions, as well as in its inhabitants, almost infinite in the variety of races which populate it, and of the creeds which have shaped their character."[118] These examples concretized and propagated the construction of India for the British empire, for the Indian aristocracy, and for the outside world as well. The British colonial administration shrewdly understood that nation formation and a concrete though broad proposition of what was Indian would establish the terms of the debate and ultimately make an extremely diverse entity conquerable.

Bernard Cohn suggests that British colonial authority was exercised as much through an idiom as through sheer physical suppression and that this specifically British idiom served to codify what was Indian for western eyes.[119] This became a more general discourse on India for those inside and outside India; governing a diverse group of peoples while respecting the plethora of (discrete) cultural traditions has been the lexical means for the Indian state to maintain a relative degree of legitimacy, and for it to contain dissent. When the 1985 and 1991 Cultural Festivals spectacularize the same Indianness that the British themselves formulated, the lines between "colonial" and "postcolonial" textuality are not at all clear. Establishing authority over the traditional and the modern, by instantiating Indianness in the present with new technologies and references to diasporic contexts, the festivals, too, enacted a number of conflations that spoke to the contradictions of migrant culture.

The situation of Indians in England by the 1980s had shifted in many important ways. They had achieved the highest per capita incomes of all ethnic groups in England, had almost fully moved into nonmanual labor, and had produced professionals at double the rate of white British citizens.[120] Indians were increasingly associated with economic success and counterposed to less successful Pakistani and Bangladeshi immigrants, as well as Afro-Caribbean and African peoples. The effective extraction of an identity from broader groupings, like Asian or black, constitutes the formation of non-Muslim Indian ethnicity at this historical moment.

In the United States, the Indian population was also changing. Beginning in the late 1970s and extending through the 1980s, Indians became more visible, more organized, and more diverse. Departing considerably from the celebratory coverage of years past, a 1977 *New York Times* article, entitled "Immigrants from India Find Problems in America,"[121] documented the hostility faced by new immigrants as well as the dilemmas surrounding assimilation and the preservation of Indian culture. Less credentialed migrants entering an economy in recession began to appear in a wider variety of professions, and even clustered in businesses like news stands, motels, and gas stations.[122] The status of the prototypical Indian immigrant was no longer so undeniably middle or upper class; it depended on a range of factors that included time of migration, area of residence, and occupation.

The concentration and growth of this population also began to be felt regionally, both for the group itself and also for other possibly referential populations. Indians were most numerous in New York, California, and Illinois, with large concentrations in New York City, Los Angeles, San Fransisco, and Chicago,[123] but their status as Asians fluctuated within those figures. In New York, they were the second most numerous group of Asian Americans (surpassed only by Chinese Americans), while in California they were outnumbered by Filipinos, Chinese, Japanese, Koreans, and Vietnamese, and in Illinois by Filipinos. In New Jersey, which had the fourth largest Indian population in the United States, the number of Indi-

ans was larger than any other Asian American group. Many college organizations, political interest groups, and social formations began to name
themselves Indian American.[124] The consolidation of an Asian American
politics, and the resulting process of identification, occurred in the late
1960s through the movement of mostly second- and third-generation East
Asian groups, well before the arrival en masse and community cohesion
of Indian immigrants.[125] Ethnicity as a concept and identity rooted in na-
tional/regional categories began to assume dominance, most especially in
the face of racial categories; even "blackness" became reconstructed into
the quasi-ethnic grouping of "African American."

The late 1980s, however, interrogated and complicated the choice of
ethnicity over race as Indian Americans became visible targets of racial
violence. A group called the "Dotbusters" emerged in Jersey City and
other New Jersey suburbs to declare their hatred of Indian presence in
what had previously been majority white and Latino spaces; a number of
physical attacks against less wealthy Indians elicited greater consciousness
of American hostility to local Indian communities. Students and political
groups composed largely of second-generation Indian Americans responded to the situation more quickly than first-generation groups who
felt that they had a good deal to lose in being identified as victimized
minorities.[126] Arrangements of race and class, at times overlapping and at
others widely divergent, provided a complex framework for Indians to
negotiate the influence of factors like relative success, education, racialization, and political solidarity in the production of self and group identities.

In both the United States and British Indian communities, class formation has been an important axis of difference. Representations of elite
British Indians and lower middle-class shop owners, though constructed
along independent trajectories, resonate with an earlier period in which
it was difficult to capture the world of lascars and at the same time sons
and daughters of the Indian upper class. In the United States newspaper
vendors and motel owners of the 1970s and 1980s could still be embraced
and incorporated into the American dream, but poorly paid service workers who entered a bit later were more difficult to write into triumphalist
narratives of the nation. And the new Indian millionaires in California's
Silicon Valley are yet another kind of population diversification and tell
an altogether different story of immigrant ascent.[127]

Indian immigrants functioned within broader possibilities of what is
American or British, among other national mythologies, and this has profoundly impacted what is received as the coherence or content of identity.
The comparative arrangements of multiculturalism, in which spaces exist
for imagining oneself in many different worlds, allow for a great deal
of flexibility in the contemporary moment. And race and ethnicity, as
intrinsically ambivalent and contingent processes, are open to continual

negotiation, particularly as the question of who and what a migrant is changes over time. In a 1996 piece on the op-ed page of the *New York Times* entitled "Under My Skin," Sunil Garg seems to reiterate the concerns that Ranjan Borra had thirty years earlier: "I am a person of color— or at least that is how people often categorize me. . . . Certainly I am brown. My parents emigrated from India. . . . But I have never seriously thought of myself as a brown man or as a person of color."[128] By 1996, the taxonomic ground for Indian identity had shifted considerably, and while Garg seeks a script outside that of "racialized victim," he is much more inclined than Borra was in 1976 to be an ethnic minority; the arrangements of a fully formed multicultural society required a different kind of address, and Garg responds in the requisite language: "As the ethnic and racial composition of our nation changes substantially, we need to understand and relate to one another, regardless of the color of our skin."[129] The ideal here of a postracial future is echoed by Indian conservative and public intellectual Dinesh D'Souza, who habitually employs his own immigrant background to authorize his critiques of the development of multicultural education.[130] While these renderings of immigrant identity discomfort progressive political groups and intellectuals, they symptomatize an enlarged public sphere in which Indian American and perhaps all ethnic identities are being invented. This "new" ethnicity is also a claim on a developing discourse on race that, to be sure, is far more complex than in times past, and has in some ways to contend with racialized and internationalized migrants as part of the mix.

Divergent interpretations of British Indian experience were expressed in the multiple terms *Indian*, *Asian*, and *black British*. Most of all, these identity categories were a way to evaluate racialization historically and in more contemporary terms. Describing all peoples from the Indian subcontinent, "Asian" had links to the languages of British colonialism, particularly as it did not recognize distinctions between post-1947 nations; its racial effect came, most obviously, from the sense of all South Asian peoples being phenotypically similar, as well as the similarity of this term to that in the project of dividing the world's populations into three major racial groups. Indian, Bangladeshi, and Pakistani people in Britain also described themselves as Asian, not only because they had been explicitly named as such in Britain, but also to represent a collective racial interest— mitigating national divisions from back home, and distinguishing from Afro-Caribbean and African populations. But many, including some in a younger generation, sought out connections with other former colonial subjects and those who were similarly excluded from the category of whiteness and, in effect, Britishness. The effort to launch a critique of British society through the desire for inclusion alongside racial difference was crystallized in the assumption of the term "black British." This was particularly true in the sphere of cultural production; many British Indian filmmakers, artists, and musicians saw themselves as part of this black British constituency. The rise of second and third generations of Indians, the various points of origin—in the subcontinent, in the Caribbean, and in East Africa—and the broad stratification of class position all gave rise to the growing sense of diversity in the Indian community, of multiple answers to the question of what it means to be Indian. Writers and intellectuals began to speak of Indian and migrant subjectivity as hybrid, as composed of discrete and complex parts.

Caste, region, language, and religion have also attenuated pan-Indian identifications in a population that is experiencing tremendous growth. In the 1980s and 1990s especially, global integration gave way as much to increasing diversification as to tighter circuits of influence. Changes in the geopolitical context laid bare the longings of many regional and ethnic groups, like Sikhs and Muslims in India, to create social space in the form of real and imagined international communities for independence and/or enhanced civil and economic rights. If immigrants of an earlier period moved with relative ease from a regional affiliation to an identification with India, it was because this shift was specified by the processes of nationalism that created the nation-state, with which colonized peoples were well acquainted through insurgent movements for independence. Today, for many migrants, regionalism may be alternatively counterposed to or function in the service of the nation. At any rate, national fissures are pronounced in daily life, and the choice of how to articulate a response to that reality remains a contested one.

India in Its Diaspora

The unpaid workforce for the 1991 Cultural Festival in Edison was composed of 2,600 men, women, and youths who spanned a range of middle-class occupations; professionals and college students had taken between three and twelve months off to work on the festival, in some cases performing mundane tasks like selling food. Various Indian American organizations had solicited volunteers, with some people coming from India, Britain, and East Africa and others from off the street. The mechanisms for inclusion, then, were both flexible and thorough.[131] This figure of 2,600 volunteers was constantly rehearsed, in festival literature, on the website, and in conversation. To be sure, it was an impressive number, but coupled with a notion of local voluntarism, it conferred legitimacy to the festival as a diasporic formation with broad forms of membership. And Bochasanwasi Shree Akshar Purushottam Swaminarayan Sanstha

(BAPS) has also been very keen to stress that youths volunteered, to suggest that there is an appeal of Indian culture across generations.[132]

Given the wide diversity of people working on the festival, there was a striking degree of content similarity in comments about the festival.[133] At times, it seemed that only regional accents distinguished the men, women, Indians, Indian Americans, Indian British, teenagers, businessmen, English majors, and CEOs from one another. When these people were asked a wide variety of questions regarding the size of the festival, the makeup of the workforce, and the projected audience of the festival, they answered directly and specifically; but any questions about the hierarchical structure of the organization or the sentiments in the ranks were shunted to evocations of the greatness of Indian culture and the prominence of Pramukh Swami Maharaj, the spiritual saint of BAPS. The presentation of India at the Cultural Festival was meticulous and studied. Volunteers scrupulously policed the exhibitions.[134] The sadhus, or priests, maintained ultimate financial, administrative, and ideological control over the event. The functionaries had no knowledge of financial details, yet the festival had an extremely organized process for collecting money; tickets for food and crafts were sold in only a few booths at a central location at the beginning of the festival.

The control of BAPS and the omnipresence of Hinduism suggest agendas both inside and outside the West. The Swaminarayan Temple represents a Hindu religious sect that has been growing in India and among Indian immigrants since the 1950s. But as Raymond Brady Williams has noted: "A tension exists between the oft expressed view that the message of the Swaminarayan religion is universal truth for persons of all cultures and religions and the fact that the religion is restricted in membership primarily to Hindus from Gujarat and functions to maintain cultural, linguistic, and ethnic identity."[135] Unlike other Hindu religious sects, like the Hare Krishnas, the Swaminarayan does not conduct itself in the manner of attracting non-Indians, nor necessarily non-Gujaratis, suggests Williams. Its address to the diaspora, then, is highly specified regionally and culturally, despite the group's seeming investment in a broader Indianness. In the United States, the majority of Indian festivalgoers were northern and western Indian. In light of turbulent conflicts in India, the submergence of regionalism in the material presentation of the festival was astonishing. The only physical indication that the state of Gujarat might be of special interest to the architects of the festival was in the larger space accorded to that state's pavilion in "India—a Cultural Millionaire." The whole and integrated India was of primary concern to the festival ideology in a context where nations matter. The link between that national articulation and religious absolutism was suppressed by the text of the festival (and by the ever-persistent myth of Hindu tolerance), but also by the festival organizers themselves. When BAPS met in January 1990 to discuss the development of the following year's festival, they suggested five aims to promote Indianness and universality, none of which even mentioned Hinduism.[136] BAPS, in this festival, reproduced the Indian nation's consumption, occlusions, and repressions of regional/religious/linguistic difference and provided a blueprint for the kinds of exclusions that might occur in diaspora, too.

The concluding paragraphs of the promotional material for the British festival indicated a specific kind of transnational agenda: "This Festival will contribute immensely toward eliminating race and religious differences in today's society. We are confident that the citizens of the United Kingdom will welcome this event."[137] In the context of 1980s debates about the extent to which British Indians should claim a racialized ethnicity, the festival seemed to take a particular stand, "to eliminate difference." Nowhere in this text were there familiar markers of racial identity, like the terms "Asian" or "black," nor was there any reference to specific episodes of British Indian history. The foregrounding of a timeless Indianness was the festival's choice for ethnic identity, as it may have been the choice for many middle-class British Indians at the time. And in Edison the presence of Indian immigrants had generated hostility from racist gangs, with posters affixed to buildings surrounding the festival area that read: "Bindi go home. Who are you going to call? Dotbuster."[138] In the midst of lavish celebrations of Indianness and a collective desire to render this event an unqualified success, the president of the Indo-American Cultural Society for Middlesex County (in which Edison is located) explained the racializing posters as a response to parking problems created by the festival.[139] Clearly, the Indianness projected in this production could not easily accommodate race.

Both the British and U.S. Cultural Festivals of India were unambiguously directed at diasporic Indians, and mainstream publications recorded this fact.[140] But the diaspora receiving this cultural production was hardly a passive receptacle; its members generated their own challenges from different conceptual and representational sites. Articles in Indian migrant newspapers noted that neither the Taj Mahal nor the Golden Temple of Amritsar, architectural representations of alternative regional-religious (Muslim and Punjabi-Sikh) traditions, were among replica structures of the festivals,[141] effectively questioning the inclusiveness of the representation of a historical "India." And a major axis of contestation to this nation, as to all nations, was gender. Women objected to the Swaminarayan practice of seating men and women separately at religious events; as a female delegate to one of the conferences put it, "I think they have already built concrete borders between men and women. . . . Women are not being treated at par with men, and as a woman I am very much offended."[142]

Whether associated with the political state of the homeland or the cultures of the diaspora, nation necessarily is exclusive in its very structure. Repressive mechanisms, be they the policing of popular protest, the surveillance of dissent, or the control over cultural representation, are not just a distortion of an ideal, but a necessary means to maintaining the unity that always threatens to disintegrate. Given that the festivals were embedded in the project of building a nation, it cannot be a surprise that they enacted the exclusions—of gender, regionalism, religion—that might open up counternarratives to the story being told. This, however, is not to diminish the fact that nation is an incredibly powerful force, to which many submit with full knowledge of its inherent limitations. In a way this is the very contradiction of diaspora, too, that it constructs itself through an identification with the homeland, even when the homeland is an acknowledged fiction.

The Cultural Festivals' story was on some level successful because it was able to seize upon extant longings and the political-cultural force of nationalism within migrant communities. That desire for the nation comes not only from a "homeland" but also from the local conditions, in which to have a nationalized identity is to have a place in a cultural or social order and to be able to participate in interest group politics, as "ethnics." Visiting the Cultural Festival in Edison was a range of world political leaders: the governor of New Jersey, U.S. congressional representatives, a British Minister of Parliament, a cabinet minister from Kenya, and others who spoke simultaneously about India and Indianness in the world. Keith Vaz, the British (Asian) Minister of Parliament, depicted the festival as "India created in the world . . . the greatest event by the Indian community in America."[143] What is clear is that in the conceptual-political world in which migrants live, Indianness has a cross-temporal legibility—it can be read and understood in terms of the past, present, and future—that other forms of subjectivity may not.

The Past, Present, and Future of India Abroad

The Cultural Festivals of India very materially manifested what is by now a theoretical truism: that nation is far too expansive a concept to remain within state-geographical boundaries. And the experience of these events also shows how as various colonial empires developed and eroded, and as the world has become realigned very much continuously with those imperial relationships, the concept of nation has provided a helpful and necessary salve for migrants all over the world. As Homi Bhabha has so aptly put it: "The scraps, patches, and rags of daily life must be repeatedly turned into the signs of a national culture."[144] What the festivals brilliantly achieved was a delicate balance between the pedagogical (the intimations that "this is India") and the performative, that dynamic process by which both viewers and actors could elaborate their cultural longings in a distinctively public space. As cultural identity must be located in a place and time, advertisers must provide a story for that place. Narration became an ideological process for the purpose of providing a functional and national history of India. Articulation through other nations (the United States and Britain) was the subtext of identity, or Indianness. And a text like the Cultural Festival operated through a special compression of time and space. It portrayed the dynamics of culture by breaking apart the easy separation between strategies of the colonizer and colonized. The story being told was colonial, postcolonial, and migrant at one and the same time. The festival took the mythology of "unity in diversity" and grafted it onto contemporary locations, rehearsing the historical coincidences and simultaneities of U.S., British, and Indian nationalities. Even popular articles in the *Times* of London were able to see the profound disjunctures between those efforts and the lived experiences of Indians in the diaspora. Multiculturalism may need nation, but diaspora is more complex than a singular nation.

It is against and alongside the tightly conceived occasions of the Cultural Festivals that various other stories, created histories, of the Indian diaspora may be posed. Though the festival was able to speak to a desire for unity central to the diaspora, the histories of movement capture a subjective experience that escaped its elaborate productions. Most profoundly, the transformative psychic power that nationalism has exercised for Indians before and after 1947 is one that may be repeated and recalled at the moment of migration. In this way and others, histories are drawn on to create complex notions of memory that support the formation of migrant identity. The reason for providing such detailed stories of movement is, then, to suggest that they function as more than background. Those stories have created understandings of self and group that function in moments of cultural transformation and translation; they are a conceptual site in which to become Indian. The dates on the one hand describe actual occurrences, and on the other metaphorically structure the beginning and the end of a narrative of displacement, and become a powerful means for many people to imagine how a community is formed. The stories of movement, through time, are also a way for Indian migrants to understand themselves and create new forms of subjectivity. As Michel de Certeau put it: "History is probably our myth. It combines what can be thought, the 'thinkable,' and the origin, in conformity with the way in which a society can understand its own working."[145]

The festival's history is of one nation, of India, projected into the diaspora. Yet as that story has taken shape within a diasporic circuitry that is our concern here, it becomes clear that three nations are in formation: India, the United States, and Britain, just as migrant communities themselves have been forming. Rendering all those nations as contingent and flexible may challenge dichotomized understandings of nationalism as subversive or reactionary, though exclusions remain stubbornly exposed. In a global framework, Indian independence has shadowed American nationality; citizenship in India has enabled Indians to imagine becoming American. This has led to a transformed sense of what it means to become a citizen. In the postwar period, and as multiculturalism has become the cultural apparatus of globalization, in both the United States and Britain, nationality becomes a language of inclusion, in more than one nation. Desires for unity meet up with experiences of multiplicity, and in that encounter nationality can also become deeply conflicted.

The global space exists here not simply as a set of locales from which and to which peoples move, but instead as a constant force for migrants: this is *lived* diasporic history. While much of this book focuses on the post-1947 period, the lines between historical periods are not unporous: stories that draw upon the past refuse to be bound by dates. These points about history are essential to understanding what makes Indians not only groups of migrants but a complex set of diasporas. Members of Indian diasporas went to a festival about a historical India not only because it had been directed at them, but also because it elaborated some of the stories that they needed to bridge the distance between their past and present. When New Jersey governor James Florio said at the closing ceremony of the Edison festival that it gave him his "shortest visit to India without jetlag,"[146] he articulated the compressions of time and place that histories of India and Indianness have enacted in the diaspora. In spite of, or perhaps because of, that fact, citizens of the diaspora still look for India in the places where they stand.

TWO

LITTLE INDIAS, PLACES FOR INDIAN DIASPORAS

WHEN AAMIR KHAN, producer and star of *Lagaan*, the first major Bollywood film to be nominated for an Academy Award, was looking for India in the United States in 2001, he went straight to Jackson Heights, New York.[1] There he found over a thousand admiring fans who spilled out onto the street from a music store to create a notable traffic jam in an area known for its congestion. To promote an Indian project for which he had actively solicited funds and viewers from abroad,[2] Khan quite logically sought to make an appearance within the symbolic space of diasporic Indianness that a place like Jackson Heights could offer. Part of what made this moment spectacular was the odd (and engineered) feeling of India coming home to the diaspora. But borders, of nations, of cultures, and of the practices of cultural membership, were not altogether transparent. The financial success of a movie founded on a fable of a small Indian village overcoming the unfair taxes of the British empire (self-consciously likened to the French comic *Asterix*), Khan admonished, would depend on stemming the widespread practice within Indian migrant commerce of distributing pirated copies of Hindi films and music. One could hardly miss the ironies of this Bollywood star articulating such warnings in Jackson Heights, a U.S. community space built on free, almost unregulated traffic in Indianness, where it is always easy to find cheap videotapes of current movies.

On this occasion, it seems that all the conceptually diffuse and physically dispersed productions of diaspora have come to settle on a place. And yet the meanings for culture, community, nation, and space, and the relationships therein, continue to emanate outside the geographical coordinates of the several block radius of that which has come to be associated with the "Little India" of Jackson Heights. In other words, this place is an urban locality, with translocal significations. Beginning to comprehend that set of structural paradoxes, this chapter suggests, is essential to a deeper inquiry into the nature of Indian diaspora.

Indian diasporas, and diasporas more generally, have come to exist with particular force and energy in postwar cities like New York and London. A backdrop of the discussion that will appear here is the postwar transformation of a variety of urban economies by intensified processes of globalization. As sociologist Saskia Sassen has made manifest, there is a distinct character to the capital flows and accumulation patterns that have remade and newly centralized cities as part of a service-based and free-trade-dependent world economy. Points of concentration, such as London, New York, Paris, and Tokyo, are marked as "global cities" in this scheme.[3] Sassen orients her very important discussion of global cities to changes that began in the 1960s, including the decline of older forms of economic arrangements and the rise of the informational industries that are central to the broader trajectory of globalization. It is those processes, and the different interrelationships they have engendered, that form one aspect of the categorical difference between "world cities" (of an older form of empire, presumably) and "global cities." Of course, as a space caught within the always incomplete transition from colonial to postcolonial arrangements (economic, political, and cultural), particularly as it exists for a population like Indians who are similarly enmeshed, a city like London might be seen as a site of mediation: of the colonial-imperial and postcolonial, of the industrial and deindustrializing, of the modern and postmodern, and of the world city and global city. More squarely within the model that Sassen elaborates is the city of New York that is inhabited by Indians.

The term "global city" has a particularly wide reach for the imagination. In its evocation of the porousness of boundaries, the fluidity of capital, peoples, and goods, and the situatedness of each point in a broader circuitry of influence, the global city may approximate the cosmopolitanism that is basic to the contemporary experience of urban life. Aamir Khan's address from Bombay to New York, which evidences his own subjectivity as a citizen of the world, does not seem so unusual when viewed alongside other everyday occurrences in so many cities. Just as important to the conception of the city is what changes in world economies have enabled, if not compelled: the massive migrations of peoples from Asia, Africa, and Latin America and the consequent constructions of diasporic cultures. The efflorescence of restaurants where international foods are served, the growth of neighborhoods where there are few advertisements in English, and the proliferation of business partnerships between U.S. or British citizens with those in other countries all indicate a new urban cosmopolitanism. The "first world" cities of New York and London have been changed by formerly "third-world" peoples, and consequently the conception of a singularly national space has been troubled. When being black and from Brooklyn is seen, for example, to connote having recent origins in the Caribbean, we might say that a quintessential "American" urban site has been transformed. And when the Little Indias of Jackson Heights and Southall are claimed by Indians all over the diasporas as "theirs," conceptual boundaries of the state have become exceptionally porous.

And so the meanings for New York and London have become increasingly multiple and heterogeneous.[4] This has meant a breaking up of representational totalities that were formally if not tenuously held together as central cities of the nation-state. Cities like New York and London became divided, or differentiated, with component parts sustaining discrete social and cultural lives.[5] And that process has had a mutually generative relationship with diaspora formation. While the formation in and through diaspora of the postwar enclaves that I will discuss here have become particular kinds of spaces for the nation-state, ethnic enclaves and racial ghettoes themselves are hardly new. They have existed as differentiated spaces within the modern city for as long as there has been international trade and the movement of peoples around the world. Black or Jewish ghettoes, Chinatowns, Little Saigons, or Koreatowns and the like have contained migrant or minority populations and have also been spaces for tourism and consumption of otherness.[6]

There has long been an imperative to create, in Michel Laguerre's terminology, "minoritized space."[7] Central to the conceptual architecture of that kind of space, suggest Laguerre and others, is a built association between race and place. All of the many responses to either a racialized minority, like African Americans in the United States, or an immigrant group, like Chinese or Koreans, that constitute an epistemology of otherness, correspond to the specific territory, simultaneously physical and symbolic, of those peoples, like a Harlem, Chinatown, or Koreatown. This relationship becomes central to the apprehensions of those outside and, to some extent inside, the groupings. In a wonderful study of Vancouver's Chinatown, Kay Anderson discusses how the relationship between the category of Chineseness, and the site of Chinatown, has been produced in a racializing imaginary of whiteness and that which is "other" to it.[8] Anderson notes that in this process there is "an object for a subject."[9] And similarly, Laguerre writes: "The production of the minoritized subject is concomitant with the production of minoritized space."[10] The way in which a notion of minoritized space establishes a connection here between the place and the individual-group subjectivity, of blackness or Chineseness, is essential to understanding how any of these places conjure forth Orientalist or racialized images for popular consumption and also dynamic sets of social and symbolic relationships within a particular population, and between those populations and a wider society, both inside and outside the nation.[11]

That complex web of relationships is what this chapter seeks to unravel for two "Little Indias," Southall, London, and Jackson Heights, Queens—spaces in which, through which, and for which Indianness is being made. Southall and Jackson Heights thus make vivid the *production* of social space that Henri Lefebvre has theorized.[12] The territory that these places cover is always and already representational as their status as "Little Indias" might imply: connected to the symbolics of diasporic Indi-

anness, bearing the weight of transformations in first-world urban landscapes and their economies, and mapping the enclosure of lived
experiences of migrant inhabitants. The cosmopolitanism of Southall and
Jackson Heights is at once the cosmopolitanism of the cities of London
and New York and the cosmopolitanism of a set of diasporas. And yet,
there is a specificity of locality, of what might be provisionally termed as
place.[13] What becomes a problematic of place might be cast in this question: What does it mean to be Indian in New York, and what does it
mean to be Indian in London? The problematic quickly becomes a deeper
dilemma when we consider how to describe such a difference, without
reducing the difference to place. Locality can be seen in the languages of
indentity, race, ethnicity, and nation, and may not always be fully synonymous with place. In some respects the temporal unevenness of the development of Jackson Heights and Southall permits a sidestepping of the
trap of place as ultimate difference.

Jackson Heights and Southall have held together diverse elements, and
each in its own way has become a site of community formation for Indian
migrants. Beginning in the late 1950s, mostly working-class Indian migrants lived and worked in Southall to build a veritable ethnic enclave,
with political organizations, shopping establishments, and the use of public resources. It was not until the early 1970s in the United States that
Jackson Heights developed as a sign of Indianness, through the rapid
emergence of Indian-owned stores and restaurants on a few blocks in
Queens, but with the noticeable absence of large Indian residential populations. What is important to foreground here as a similarity between
Southall and Jackson Heights is the association between place and a conception of Indianness, for the migrant subjects themselves and others. But
the very dissimilarities, of class, nation, and nature of relationship to the
place (residential, wage work, entrepreneurial), may help distinguish how
community is lived in the two examples. Group identities are constructed
and performed through events specific to each place just as they might
appear to be resolutely "Indian."

As nodal points in the Indian diaspora, New York and London are
quintessential urban sites to contain the communities of Jackson Heights
and Southall. For many years, Indian migrants have made New York and
London their homes, places of work, and centers of cultural reproduction. These cities have figured centrally in both the social experiences of
Indians and the imaginary of the Indian diaspora, as stories about Indian
migrant life circulate around the world. Significant concentrations of Indian migrants in both places have also impacted the public discourses of
these cities, as it has become impossible to speak of New York or London
urban cultures without in some way acknowledging either the popula-

tions themselves or the foods, art, or musics of India as being integral to the social mix.

But though New York and London each have significant and perhaps even competing importance in formations of migrant culture, they do not exist on the same plane: these cities are differentially located in terms of the time and space of the Indian diaspora. As the seat of the British empire, London was most real to potential migrants, while New York, symbol of the American dream, appeared later in the field of possibilities for those Indians who would not or could not go to England. Looking at these places side by side gives the temporality and spatiality of the "Indian diaspora" a kind of depth that would be missing were we to look only at one period, or at one country; doing so serves the important function of guarding against any temptation to conceive of diaspora too literally, as one large Indian community that would ultimately flatten out the particular and contingent ways Indian migrant culture is lived.

It should be evident by this point in the development of the disciplines of history and sociology, as well as anthropology, that the very term "community" is a deeply contested formation. In the past it has been a unit of analysis for social group formation, and also acquired the connotations of geographic territory, of bounded place. Locales were perceived to create groups of people, just as those groups molded the place. But many have rightly asserted that indeed groups spill over the boundaries of their locales, and the meaning of the locales cannot be solely derived from the internal logics of peoples defined as a group. Nor do overt expressions of commonality mean that groups within a formation necessarily see themselves as linked. Community, then, is a provisional and flexible term at best, and often uttered with some degree of irony. And to be sure, globalization has conferred a special contingency to notions of community.

Perhaps if we can conceive in the stories of the making of community the production of a representational space, then something more dynamic, and transformative, can be found. As Lefebvre has noted: "Representations of space are shot through with a knowledge (*savoir*)—i.e. a mixture of understanding (*connasisance*) and ideology—which is always relative and in the process of change."[14] For unraveling that knowledge, I think that we can read Lefebvre as offering a method of historical reading: "Representational spaces, on the other hand, need obey no rules of consistency or cohesiveness. Redolent with imaginary and symbolic elements, they have their source in history—in the history of a people as well as in the history of each individual belonging to that people."[15] For Southall and Jackson Heights, the production of social space that is a notion of community may be read through the processes by which ethnic, racial, national, and other identities are formulated. Again, the subjectivity of "Indianness" is essential to understanding the place. The argument is not, of course, that we can extract full meaning from a place, nor that such a place will have any precise correlation with "community," but simply that the question of what happens when place becomes a conceptual site for Indianness, even when it is spilling over, will enable a sharper view of diasporas. In many ways, the limits of multiplicity are elaborated, because the meaning is always in excess of the stories told and the politics enacted. Most of all, this process of reading the *production* of Jackson Heights and Southall will pluralize community, place, and diaspora.

Communities, places, diasporas, and nations, too, become conflated when Southall and Jackson Heights are represented, in shorthand, as "Little Indias." The term "Little India" suggests at once the reproduction of a national (Indian) formation elsewhere, as well as the building of an ethnic enclave within the United States or Britain. "The notion of an India" within first-world countries may assume the aura of the exotic, and, at the very least, the foreign. But in England, a land in which India is thought to be known and in which there is the memory of possession, a "Little India" testifies to the inclusions of empire, though here, of course, the structure is inverted: India is part of the whole, inside rather than outside Britain. In the United States, the discursive production of an Indian immigrant community in the 1970s as a "little India" more closely resonates with that of other ethnic Asian communities, especially Chinatowns. New York and San Francisco Chinatowns always functioned metaphorically for local populations as the other within, and were attended with imaginings of a necessarily exotic origin, in the Far East. Yet they also referred to significant immigrant populations that grew to have a stake in extant understandings of the United States as a multicultural unity. Ambivalences surrounding this idea of the exotic other as both a part of America and from another place outside the nation structured local perceptions of Chinese enclaves, just as they did Irish, Italian, German, and other immigrant ghettoes. In the dominant political language of the United States, the inclusions are not of British empire, but of America. Of course America has always been an empire of a different sort at various critical junctures of racial formation, too. Though open discourses of nation-building, of the "land of immigrants," may obscure histories of exclusions, within and without, postwar U.S. hegemony constructed for itself an imperial role in the world that has had an impact on all its peoples.

Both Southall and Jackson Heights present profound complexities for the question of political and cultural citizenship. Discursively, is being part of a "little India" to be part of Britain, the United States, or India? The equivalence between territory and collective experience that is the basis for the social architecture of Southall and Jackson Heights has different renditions in each case. Largely this difference has to do with the specificities of place. A transnational subjectivity has been generated from Southall and its particular arrangements of race and class, while that Indian subjectivity itself has created Jackson Heights. Being part of the nation-state of India and feeling affiliated to the United States or America or Britain are propositions influenced by a relationship to the community space, which certainly changes over time. Images of Southall and Jackson Heights transmitted home to India, and the participation of the Indian state in discussions about its migrants in specific places around the world that amount to a kind of claiming, further muddle not only the citizenship of Indian subjects but also the nationality of specific Indian communities.

Southall and Jackson Heights also exist as places with goods to offer residents and visitors. These veritable marketplaces, replete with Indian restaurants, food stores, sari stores, beauty salons, record stores, and the like, evoke images of an exotic bazaar, or of a self-sufficient ethnic community, and perhaps both, through which India as fantasy is made real. The presence of new migrants in areas of London and New York where others have dwelled and continue to live further corporealizes these Indian spaces and produces the negotiations and conflicts that inevitably arise when neighborhoods change. Jackson Heights to a large extent and Southall only a bit less so are spaces of consumption. Indians meet there, eat there, and buy and sell there, and essentially perform an Indianness that functions to consolidate their migrant subjectivities. Through these multiple acts of consumption, migrants become citizens of the local space, of Southall or Jackson Heights (and London and New York), of England and the United States, of the diaspora, as their experiences have a life outside immediate boundaries and perhaps too of India, and as this sense of becoming culturally Indian is translated into maintaining Indian political activity. If in the postwar and perhaps postmodern age consumption qualifies as participatory citizenship, then Southall and Jackson Heights become ideal sites in which to comprehend how nations function, and function differently, for distinctly diasporic actors. When these sites become spaces for ethnics' own tourism, the picture becomes even more complicated.

The production of identities in Southall and Jackson Heights works first in the various constellations of race, ethnicity, and peoplehood in which Indian migrants appear and to which subjectivity is articulated, and second in a diaspora that is a collection of images and a circuitry of movements. In a very basic way, Indianness here in these two communities is indexed, as always, to what is possible in England and the United States, to who else is a minority and why, and how color, class, and citizenship have been historically manufactured through specific contexts. As Southall and Jackson Heights become part of the lore and lived realities of the Indian diaspora, be it in a film like *Wild West* in which local second-generation Indians caught in a web of social expectations in Southall as-pire to country music success in Nashville,[16] or in the plans that travelers from India make to stop off at Jackson Heights to pick up inexpensive goods en route from Kennedy Airport, there are broad diasporic fields that create a sense of what it means to inhabit these two communities.

Jackson Heights and Southall are very much Indian places that signify something for Indians migrants, a range of British and American residents and Indians all over the diaspora, including in the homeland. Multiple and often contradictory meanings have created community spaces that are tenuously held together and in a state of continual formation. Even as Jackson Heights and Southall, for Indians, may connote Indianness, the names of these spaces may circulate in other diasporic imaginaries as locations for, respectively, Colombian-American cultural formations or Somali refugee settlement. Rather separate worlds compose any commu-nity and perhaps even more so these two postwar, multi-ethnic, and highly globalized sites. These places may enable us to think about difference, multiply represented, as a defining feature of urban life, just as we compre-hend the local as always being constituted by citizens of the world. While places of Indian diasporas may at first glance seem geographically fixed, interpreting their spatiality creates a sense of boundaries and symbolic meanings as always in the process of being crossed. Those crossings, along with their necessary limits, are at the heart of this chapter.

Urban-Suburban Enclaves Both

The origins of the bustling urban-ethnic areas of Southall and Jackson Heights in sleepy rural and white enclaves might give contemporary ob-servers and inhabitants alike a great deal of pause. Early histories of these two areas just outside London and New York seem wholly disconnected from the realities that are experienced in the postwar period. But if we commit to considering the formation of Indian communities in these spaces as historically contingent, the *development* of Southall and Jack-son Heights, in which Indian migrant presence comes to have a special role, becomes of great significance. In the case of Southall, the shift from one kind of place to another, in terms of the organization of physical and social space of the area, is one that is submerged in both official local accounts and insurgent and politicized histories of Southall. So, too, do stories of early Jackson Heights, and later more multicultural Jackson Heights, read as narratives of entirely different entities. How and why those divergences exist tells us something about a variety of experiences of place.

Developments of Southall symptomatized transformations of the industrial city. In the beginning of the nineteenth century, developers built a new canal to link the village of Paddington to the main body of London and to stimulate new economic activities in a vast and integrating city.[17] With this canal, manufactured goods from recently developed industries could now be distributed a long way from their production site, and previously self-sufficient villages and towns could now be economically (and socially) linked to central London in efficient ways. Even more important for the formation of the town of Southall, to the west of Paddington, was the construction of a railroad line between Paddington and western England in 1838; the Southall station opened in May 1839.[18]

Prior to these developments, Southall was little more than an isolated hamlet with an intensely local social and economic life. Its integration with larger commercial networks accelerated the shift to a more modern and self-sufficient town. The late Victorian period in Southall was characterized as much by rapid economic and social consolidation as it was by the formation of an intrinsically local, genteel middle class. And through a great number of local histories that constructed Southall as the prototypically bucolic "community,"[19] we can see a palpable anxiety about the area changing and being "corrupted" by influences of the city. As early as 1907, in the book *Middlesex*, local historian A. R. Hope Moncrieff wrote: "There was a Southolt once, which, corrupted by the evil communications of the high-road, has changed its name as well as its nature. I can remember Southall when it could still be called a pleasant country nook, half village, half distant suburb; but in one generation it has waxed to what it is now, a somewhat commonplace outgrowth of London, which for a time was the train terminus."[20] The competing impulses of the romanticization of the local space and the voicing of alarm at its established course defined Southall like they did many other towns and cities that were experiencing rapid cultural and economic change during this period. Over the next few decades, Southall's distinction as a center for progress seemed to flow almost organically from its beneficial location—close to London but not within London city limits—and a tacit acceptance of the role of this area in the economic development of the larger county of Middlesex soon followed.[21]

By the early 1900s, Southall had become a highly industrialized town with a variety of large enterprises, including chemical and foodstuff production. One of the largest Southall industries was a margarine factory.[22] Accompanying these economic developments in Southall were other physical and social changes characteristic of urban centers; people from outside the isle of England began to slowly head to this part of Middlesex County with its increasing job opportunities and perceptible economic progress. In the midst of a depressed economy in the 1930s, Welsh people and others from western England came to the area in search of employ-ment and diversified a still predominantly white population; later, post–World War II labor shortages attracted some Irish, Polish, and West In-dian workers. Changing fortunes after the war as well as the return of area servicemen contributed to a problem of overcrowding. Though a county council proposal to send people and industries to different towns outside of Southall was at first mildly effective, heterogeneity of workers and residents had already become a defining characteristic of the area, even before the massive immigrant waves of the late 1950s and early 1960s.

On the opposite side of the Atlantic, Jackson Heights was part of an-other kind of urban trajectory. In 1898, the five boroughs of Queens, Brooklyn, Manhattan, the Bronx, and Richmond were consolidated to become the City of New York. The expanding and sprawling metropolis of New York became a site for new forms of industrial production, major population increases through the movement of people from more rural areas toward New York, and the subsequent rise of land speculation for the area. New York became a symbol of progress, as well as of corruption and iniquity.

At the time of consolidation, many of the areas outside Manhattan were still mostly rural enclaves of the landed gentry. Six or seven wealthy families owned land in the area of the borough of northern Queens and in the Trains Meadow section of Newtown that would become Jackson Heights. But rapidly developing industry in Long Island City and the pros-pects of new transport links between Queens and Manhattan recom-mended this part of Newtown for commercial and real estate ventures. The planned Queensboro Bridge between midtown Manhattan and in-dustrializing areas of Queens and anticipated extensions of the Long Is-land Railroad and IRT through East River tunnels produced a frenzy of land speculation and farmer buyouts in northern sections of Queens dur-ing the early 1900s.[23]

While Southall's development of residential arrangements had a more organic relationship to changing industrial fortunes, Jackson Heights's so-cial space was deliberately planned. In 1909, Edward A. MacDougall and a number of other prominent New York investors formed the Queensboro Corporation and purchased six farms that totaled 325 acres. They gave their new holding a name: Jackson Heights.[24] Over the next several years, the Queensboro Corporation directed itself primarily and aggressively to the task of making a place out of these newly associated lands. The planned community of the Queensboro Corporation and Edward MacDougall ex-pounded on a specific class vision by serving as an alternative to high rent areas in Manhattan, but catering to those who worked for high salaries in the city and wanted a comfortable and safe residence for their families. The community envisioned, then, was a highly exclusive one.

But in contrast to suburbs that had begun to be built through swank single-family detached housing, Jackson Heights was developed into a site for the "garden apartment." Built around a large interior garden, the first apartment complex in 1917 was intended to maximize area and yet provide a community space. Indeed, as housing shortages in the second decade of the twentieth century arose, the Queensboro Corporation promoted its apartments as "homes" that could and should be owned; though at first they named it the "Collective Ownership Plan," they later changed it to "Cooperative Ownership." Local historian Daniel Karatzas notes that this name switch was probably made to avoid the socialist implications of the original term.[25]

MacDougall developed and expanded his goal of the planned community in Jackson Heights by shrewdly navigating the social and economic changes of the 1920s. After World War I, the United States economy began to expand, and in the 1920s local Queens industries as well as residential housing grew to unprecedented levels. Changes in Jackson Heights during this period reflected and responded to regional and national developments; Queensboro Corporation efforts succeeded in transforming this area into a vital residential and commercial space. The interests and activities of the corporation had also been fused together with those of the "community." Early issues of the *Jackson Heights News*, a local paper, read like promotional material from the Queensboro Corporation; for example, Edward MacDougall's private business ventures were frequently described as being in the interest of Jackson Heights. An article on the first page of the *Jackson Heights News* in 1929, entitled "Brief History of Jackson Heights from the Investment Point of View," recounts the early history of the area and then concludes: "With such a history and such prospects, it seems safe to predict that real estate investments made at Jackson Heights are both safe and sound and that the immediate future holds out great prospects of continuing the rapid increase in values which has been so marked in the immediate past."[26] The Queensboro Corporation stimulated a variety of economic changes in Jackson Heights in an effort to diversify and develop a "town"; the commercial area around the 82nd Street subway stop, for example, greatly benefited from the corporation's work. The corporation also helped to form a community board to oversee the development of institutions such as churches, theater groups, and civic organizations.[27]

In 1929, the Queensboro Corporation opened new executive offices and celebrated its twentieth anniversary. On the occasion, Edward Mac-Dougall, by now acknowledged to be the founder of Jackson Heights, commented on the area's progress to date: "Jackson Heights is the result of both a sound financial plan and a housing ideal. It is one of the few examples of these two elements being yoked together successfully."[28] He also laid bare the intentions and effects of the by now twenty-year-old venture: "The Queensboro Corporation is closely related to every resident. Our interests are inter-dependent. Those things which are beneficial or harmful to one are beneficial or harmful to the other. . . . The purpose in the development of Jackson Heights was to provide a restricted home section in New York City where discriminating families could secure homes."[29]

Interdependent interests had purposely created an exclusive and exclusionary upper-middle-class community; the discourse, interestingly enough, was silent on the matter of occupations and work life. In a Queensboro Corporation list of the "Reasons Why Jackson Heights is the Most Attractive and Important Housing Development in New York City," the compilers cited, in addition to "Location," "Transportation," and "Appearance," "Values Protected": "The Queensboro Corporation has followed a policy of reasonable restriction in accepting tenants thus bringing together tenants having ideals and living standards in common."[30] This "restriction" was a euphemism for outright racial discrimination aimed at African Americans, Jews, and probably other white ethnics such as Italians and Greeks. In 1925, MacDougall was known to have told visiting urban planners from abroad that because of the well-planned system of "cooperative" development, "undesirables" could be kept out.[31] But when the Depression slowed down the housing industry, MacDougall could no longer exercise such strategies of exclusion.

When the Depression hit Jackson Heights, the Queensboro Corporation responded with various tactics to stay afloat. They formed the Jackson Heights Merchants Association to organize and consolidate business interests and to shift responsibility for neighborhood maintenance to private businesses. Even more important, huge and luxurious apartments that had held exclusive interest for the moneyed upper and upper middle classes were now marketed for other groups. Apartments were broken up into less extravagant living units and rooms were rented.[32] Though the area eventually recovered financially, the intersection of economic difficulty and general social changes in New York at this early point in the 1930s made Jackson Heights, like most sections of the city, a place of changing demographics and self-descriptions. It is this aspect of the early history that seems to fade in contemporary expressions of nostalgia for another Jackson Heights.

While economic pressures made Jackson Heights more accessible following the Depression, the general vision of a "suburb in the city" remained undisturbed. MacDougall died in 1944, and his son took over as president of the Queensboro Corporation.[33] Despite the change in leadership, the corporation's articulation of community interests persisted in similar form. In 1947, the New York City Housing Authority's efforts to develop public housing in Jackson Heights were roundly defeated by citizens' protests. Residents claimed that such a proposal would have caused the original MacDougall to "turn in his grave."[34] Through the 1950s, with the expansion of an already established commercialism of the area and with generational shifts, many older residents moved out to newer suburban areas in Long Island and Westchester and younger families moved in to replace them.[35] Jackson Heights, like many urban-suburban areas, entered into a new phase of transformation.

It bears repeating that nations and their cities are never fully complete; they are always in a process of formation. The idea of a historical shift is useful less for its proposition that change has occurred than for a description of how and why a particular change enables a new way of seeing. So it is with the "postwar period" of world history that does the work of signifying development on a national level in terms of economic and political transformations, and of suggesting how such changes are articulated to the aftermath of a war that took place in the global arena. And the postwar world is also a postcolonial world, most especially for those in and from India.

As Indians began to newly experience nationality after 1947, the economies of Britain and the United States underwent significant changes. Despite the quasi-isolationist efforts of many United States policymakers and the desire to retrench in British political circles, economic expansion and fissures in national ideology all helped to put cities like New York and London on the road to becoming even more complex, international, cities than before. New York and London already figured prominently in the imagination of the world as cosmopolitan points of destination for peoples, cultures, and capital. The social architecture of these spaces had been anything but static; as cities constantly in formation, London and New York inspired movements of peoples and development in residential and work space that became distinguishing features of what was urban in both countries.

But in the 1950s, London and New York expanded to accommodate industry and residential populations differently. What happened in Jackson Heights's planned community much earlier, which was at that time so distinctive, became in both New York and London a more generalized strategy for containing and controlling the organization of space. Models of cities as composed of cores and peripheries were reworked to support the development of suburbs, residential (often called "bedroom") communities for those who worked in the industrial and financial centers but wanted to live outside them. Increasing populations of nonwhite peoples in the city proper accelerated the appeal of cultivating outlying areas, particularly for the middle classes. Into the 1960s and 1970s, this would become a more pronounced phenomenon, referred to as "white flight."

We might situate Southall and Jackson Heights at the meeting point of a range of these urban transformations. In areas outside the "centers" of London and New York, these two communities, and their formations, enliven changing notions of the relationship between the core and the periphery, precisely because they contained some of the elements thought to be essential to the city, like multiclass residential life, industry, self-sufficient economic enclaves, and, perhaps most of all, immigrant and minority groups. Beginning in the early 1950s in Southall, and in the middle to late 1960s in Jackson Heights, massive migrations of third-world peoples would further emblematize just how urban these areas were.

Southall—A New Indian Community

British Bobby
Before I came to this country
I heard about this person
This 'British Bobby the Best'
And admired him from a distance

But then I saw him here
In his smart uniform so dear
Killing Blair Peach, my colleague in Southall
Prowling with SUS in hand on blacks innocent
His image still such serene, so versatile
Embodied on his community role;
What happened to that adorable image?
How was it tarnished? I wonder at all.

In my eyes he's still that majestic
Though wounded physically, strong yet in
heart
He knows his difficult job well;
Don't despair, dear Bobby, you're still the
envy of the world.[36]

This poem by Balwant Naik, a Gujarati-Ugandan immigrant to Britain, expresses the ambivalences of migrant life: effects of the transmission abroad of romantic visions of English icons like the "bobby," the contradictions of British policing of the world as well as the domestic space, and the specific connotations of the police in communities like Southall. And in Naik's mention of Southall a broad set of images are meant to spring to mind—images of immigrant presence, nativist backlash, and community organization—those that starkly contrast with textual productions of a sleepy rural enclave. But making Southall over as a new kind of social space is very precisely a story that belongs to Indian migrants.

Migrants from India began to arrive in the area around 1957 and permanently changed the face of greater London. Many major industries in the city, and those of Southall in particular, had found themselves with a shortage of workers for their prospering production plants. Woolf's rubber factory in Southall ingeniously began to procure workers from Punjab and presumably the news that work was generally available in Southall was then quickly disseminated outside those initial networks.[37] Heathrow Airport, a short bus ride from Southall, also provided jobs for new residents, as it continues to do to this day. And it was not long before a wide range of Southall area factories that produced plastic, foodstuffs, and textiles began to hire only Asians for particular tasks, and specifically for low-wage, unskilled jobs.

Most Indians of this first stage of migration were Punjabi Sikh, and from the two areas of Jullundhur and Hoshiarpur. Ethnically, then, there was a homogeneity to the arriving population that faciliated both consolidation and continuance. Punjabis who arrived in London during this early period sought to settle at first with other Punjabis; family connections or affiliations of region, language, dress, and culture proved to be a comfort in a still deeply stratified and discriminatory London. Though many might have chosen to go to the United States instead, those Indians in particular who had participated in political activities like student movements faced obstacles above and beyond already strict U.S. immigration regulations, where very strict quotas were still in effect. Activists and others found it much easier to migrate to England in the late 1950s and early 1960s and the flow to Southall continued. As Piara Khabra, later a Member of Parliament, described it: "It was hard to get a visa [to the United States], especially for the ones who had participated in student movements. There was a network of spies who knew. . . . Some people said go to the U.K., from there apply to go to the U.S. . . . Friends picked me up in the airport and brought me to Southall. I became a victim of circumstances and stayed in the U.K."[38] By the early 1960s, then, Southall had become a popular destination for Indians who had been agricultural laborers as well as for middle-class professionals, like Khabra, previously a schoolteacher in Punjab. Most, however, discovered that factory work was the easiest to find and maintain at a time when Indian institutional credentials were thought to be substandard; and so a moderately diverse group of Punjabis became more occupationally concentrated upon arrival in London.

Until 1962, when the Commonwealth Immigrants Act severely curtailed immigration, the Indian population in Southall greatly increased. In figures from the 1961 census that tell a story of dramatic, almost sudden change, 1,678 Southall residents were Indian-born and an additional 2,500 to 4,500 were British-born Indian children out of a total population of 53,000.[39] The 1962 act theoretically prohibited new immigration, but a massive rush just before institutionalization of the policies and subsequent immigration by dependents, relatives, and brides and grooms of pre-1962 migrants contributed to the development of majority Indian populations in two voting districts of Southall by 1977.[40] That specter of a new majority, with prospects for representation, was certainly one motivating feature of the explosion of responses to make competing claims on the territory of Southall and the narrative production of the space. Groups emerged as new participants in this expanding social arena: the Southall Residents' Association, in association with the British National Party, was founded in 1963 to object to the rapidly increasing Indian population in the area and also to the large numbers of Indian children in Southall schools.[41] More complicated if not more subtle responses can be gleaned from the personal recollections of R. J. Meads, a longtime Southall resident who wrote a number of highly nostalgic and romantic local histories of the borough. In the introduction to his last (1983) book, *Southall 830–1982*, Meads wrote: "The whole of Southall has become badly run down. Our new citizens seem to love bright colours which shows when they decorate their houses—some very good, but not all— and add to this, the rubbish left on the front gardens has a very bad effect on our terrace type streets."[42] Meads focused on garbage left on the curb, and more generally on dirtiness, to denigrate the immigrants. An ethnocentric address utilized the language, and lament, of change, of the main thoroughfare, of the face of the streets, and of other effects of growth. Transformations of the physical and social spaces were linked in this local historian's diagnosis of the times.

What would come to be understood as the cultural dominant of Southall emerged not through studied negotiations between the new and the old, but instead through huge increases of the Asian population and, subsequently, from the ways that these new residents defined Southall life on their own terms. While the Indian and white populations employed a number of strategies to define themselves and react to change, "integration" was curiously absent from that repertoire of means for substantial community transformation.

Despite the difficulties and complications of migrating, by the late 1960s Indians (and South Asians in general) had established a large and formidable presence throughout the whole of England. Labor opportunities in areas like London as well as constraints on economic advancement in a depressed Indian economy had made the process of migration appealing and the pattern of settlement predictable. In a little over ten years, Indians had developed majorities or at least significant minorities in a number of neighborhoods not only in London but also in other places with large manufacturing sectors, like towns and cities in northern England.[43]

Such rapid changes in the physical appearance of the British population should also be seen in the context of world historical developments, in which the demise of British colonialism had left behind huge populations around the world with a complicated history of national and cultural identity formation. Indeed, one of the many effects of colonialism was the categorization of "brown" and "black" peoples as British subjects, and in effect *as connected* to the British state. The possibilities of "postcolonialism" gave those third-world peoples not only a sense of mobility, but also the occasion to exist in the West while retaining their own national subjectivities. This rich but contradictory historical moment gave rise to manifold complications, including a deep and unprecedented uncertainty on the part of the British state about denying former British subjects entry to the erstwhile center of the empire. Compounding these ambivalences were the actual Commonwealth passports that many of these diasporic migrants still held (in places like Kenya and Uganda), and more broadly the extant claims to Britishness that black populations expressed through a range of activities.

A number of national social and political agendas emerged in the middle to late 1960s to respond to the population changes and new patterns of race relations. They might be broadly categorized under the headings of "race relations management" and "immigration restriction." During this period, ensuring that the rate of growth in the black, or immigrant, proportion of the British population did not increase coincided with and corresponded to the elaborate efforts to assimilate into the English polity those immigrants who could not practically be sent back. Complicated and often contradictory sets of strategies were employed against the backdrop of periodic race riots and insurgent political organization.

National tensions manifested themselves locally in the sphere of education, where the political ideologies necessitated a new praxis. The espousal of a vision of multiculturalism, and of its possibility that many cultures and races could constitute the nation, was new for this era of British history but had its roots in the very colonial empire itself. While in the late 1800s inclusion referred to a country's position as a colony, in the 1960s it served the general objective of the immigrants' assimilation into British culture. And so Southall schools, like those of many districts, introduced new materials on immigrant cultures into the educational curriculum for the general aims of reformulating the nation and facilitating the process whereby immigrants could become "British" (residentially), if not "English" (ethnically).

In purported support of this general goal and in response to other pressures, the local authorities of the Borough of Ealing (into which Southall had been incorporated in 1965) developed a system of "dispersal" to distribute immigrant students such that no particular schools would have large concentrations of those populations and in any case would have no larger a proportion than 40 percent.[44] Ealing authorities had clearly aimed this measure at the populations of Southall; commonplace wisdom held that busing Indian students out of Southall would prevent the possibility of majority Indian Southall schools and consequently the consolidation of certain areas as "Indian areas."

The ideologies behind the dispersal plan were far more complicated than a cursory glance at the policy would suggest, in ways that come alive in stories about this school experience. By the late 1960s, the British state found itself in the position of having to address vastly different interests. The state's approach to the immigrants came out of tried and true traditions of the colonial empire that employed both the purported protection of culture and more generalized paternalism. Responding political strategies effectively converged around two specific aims: the prevention of segregated schools and the assimilation of the non-natives by instructing them in English ways through the mastery of the English language. The effects of these programs are perhaps even more ambiguous as Sukh Sandher, a local resident who came of age during this period, describes it. He notes that in this 1960s policy of distributing Asians, "there was ESL [English as a Second Language] at first and so the Asian kids ended up in the same classes and afterwards hung out together."[45] Sandher's point highlights the problematic nature of integration in general, as well as the high degree of cohesion in the Indian community in Southall.

Given concurrent struggles across the Atlantic by "liberal" forces against the evils of segregation and "conservatives" allied against the plan to bus children, the British case is interestingly divergent. The government authorities in London that argued for mixture rather than separation occupied a "conservative" and "racist" position in the perspectives of Indian minority communities. In the United States, both black and white students were bused out of their communities to make all the schools in a town or city more integrated.[46] In England, however, the Borough of Ealing bused only Indian students out of Southall to prevent more than 40 percent in those schools. Effectively, the authorities did not require any white children to attend school outside of their communities; the problem was perceived to solely accompany the presence of Indian children. Many said that this policy of dispersal stigmatized Indians and was ultimately racist in its methods and objectives. In 1973, after several years of dispersal, the Ealing Community Relations Council, comprising teachers, social workers, neighborhood activists, and scholars, produced a report that recommended the termination of the dispersal program. One of the reasons cited for restoring the neighborhood-based schools was that: "fear of almost all-immigrant schools is less now among teachers. . . . Educationally, a

Figure 6. A new Southall? (photograph by author)

school consisting only of immigrant children can be as good a school as
one containing only "white" children. Most of the immigrant representatives on our committee feel that the attitudes of many of those who insist
on dispersal undervalue the immigrant cultures. As one member put it
simply: " 'to preserve one's culture is an honourable aim.' "[47] That the coun-
cil-supported commission described opposition to the program of dispersal in terms of "cultural preservation" in some ways mirrors the overall
ideological objectives of the state at this time, in the interests of a multicultural England. Teachers and the authorities no longer feared the clustering
of these communities. Another reason cited for abandoning the "dispersal" policy was that, to make it fair, white students would also have
to be bused (as in the United States) and English parents would certainly
protest such a plan.[48] Keeping things separate, it seemed, would maintain
the most peace with the native white and immigrant communities.

This moment is also a key to another kind of shift: from the goal of
assimilation to the acceptance of strict divisions between residential racial
communities in the city. The exaltation of the city as a space with shared
meanings across a range of social groups had effectively been worn down,
and what emerged in its place was a sense of multiple, even contestatory
meanings for what was urban: differentiation (see fig. 6). The transformation, indeed the destruction, of conceptions of the city as a collectivity
was activated by new racialized minorities from former colonies. In this

way, third-world and postcolonial peoples were beginning to have a real role, not simply in occupying places of a city in the seat of the former empire, but in giving those very important spaces meaning.[49] The correspondence between race and place, in that notion of a "minoritized space" like Southall, in its locatable Indianness, was now a fact of life that a range of interests coped with.

The significance of the dispersal issue itself extended far beyond the actual process of busing, or not busing, children out of the area; it was a window onto the struggles over the representation and constitution of a community of local concentrations of migrant peoples. Many leaders from a variety of community organizations described the beginnings of their political development through the consciousness of the enormity of political stakes attending the issue of dispersal.[50] Though a number of obstacles were cited, including the long commute to another school and the stigmatization of bused children in the schools themselves, much more important was the manner in which this formalized scattering was employed to dilute the strength of the growing and rapidly consolidating Punjabi Indian community in Southall. Members of that community built arguments centered on both the preservation of immigrant culture and also the power of immigrants to determine the place of their children's schooling.[51]

Given the publicity of matters having to do with education and immigration, the issue of dispersal gave Southall national media attention. The new problems and issues of the urban space—immigration, race, racism, and community incorporation—all came to bear on Southall as part and parcel of London and stimulated an intense focus on the area. In metonymic systems of the popular imagination, Southall became "the city," much as other black areas in London, like Notting Hill, had once been.[52] This marks an important shift in the history of London as well, because Southall had previously been considered to be technically outside the city of London. What was, in many respects, a physically liminal space now became symbolically central. Changes in the kinds of languages used to describe the urban entity and in its actual existence as a geographical space, from more strictly defined cities to large sprawling metropolitan areas, took place around the world; similar changes occurred later in the United States, as the example of Jackson Heights demonstrates. In Southall, however, it is noteworthy that Indians were central to the process whereby new notions of what was urban were being created.

Connections between the "local" space of Southall and the urban space of the nation were continually being made. On November 5, 1971, Member of Parliament Enoch Powell, who was associated with virulent anti-immigrant racism because of his "Rivers of Blood" speech, came to Southall to speak to the Chamber of Commerce. Both the Chamber's decision to invite Powell and Powell's use of that podium to make a number of general programmatic and controversial points further reflected the centrality of Southall to debates surrounding issues of race and immigration at the time. Powell began his talk with a quote from a *Daily Telegraph* article from 1966: "The best I dare to hope is that by the end of the century we shall be left not with a growing and more menacing phenomenon but with fixed and almost traditional 'foreign' areas in certain towns and cities."[53] Powell then proceeded to compare the British racial situation with problems in contemporary U.S. race relations; he raised the specter of events in Detroit and cited "Black Power" as a real possibility for England. As Powell was suggesting that the name of the British analogue to Detroit "could be Bradford, or Birmingham, or London," a person in the audience shouted "or Southall," to which Powell replied, "Somebody in the audience has said 'or Southall,' and of course you know it's true."[54] Powell's comments continuously moved between local "racial" circumstances and international reference points. For him and others, immigration reworked notions of what was foreign in its collapsing of the spatial divisions of "inside" and "outside"—divisions studiously maintained during the British empire but those that were no longer possible, as Indians and others now occupied places in London.

And social and political developments around the world did affect the shape of the Indian population of Southall in the late 1960s and early 1970s. The particular contours of nationalism in African countries that had recently liberated themselves from colonialism excluded Indians; in 1967 a number of Kenyan Indians left to come to London and eventually settled in Southall. In 1972, Ugandan leader Idi Amin expelled Asian Ugandans following several years of class and racial conflicts between them and black Africans. Because of its role in the settlement of Indians in Uganda and the particularities of Commonwealth citizenship, the British government was forced to accept into England thousands of Asians who held British passports, but this time not without a great deal of public debate.

Like the city of Leicester that already had large Indian populations, the Ealing authorities tried to prevent expelled Ugandan Indians from settling in their borough. In this and in many other racial conflicts during this time, the political lines between "progressive" and "conservative" forces proved hard to draw: overwhelming opposition to additional immigration constructed a set of voter interests to which both the Conservative and Labour Parties were compelled to respond. The main local paper for Ealing that served a largely British white constituency, the *Middlesex County Times and West Middlesex Gazette*, on August 11, 1972, reported on the Ealing-Southall Conservative Association's "call to the Government to halt all further immigration, from all parts of the world, except for the immediate family of people already here. . . ."[55] Another article in the same local paper that day noted that Sidney Bidwell, a much renowned Member of Parliament from the Labour Party who had been touted as being sympathetic to the interests of Indians, was "concerned at the possible effects of increasing numbers coming into areas such as Southall."[56] Later in his 1976 autobiography, Bidwell made explicit the political exigencies of his position, noting that "natives . . . have a fear that further immigration will result in more overcrowding. . . .They fear the social effects. Naturally this has been reflected in the views of many Labour councillors . . . who take the brunt of any problems that arise."[57] The Southall Tenants Association actively tried to stem growing tides of Indians; in August 1972, they warned: "You can't squeeze an extra sock into a full suitcase."[58] But despite the consensus against increased immigration, the East African political situation and its special complexities vis-á-vis the British state could not be resolved in the contemporary public sphere; it had to be administered on another level. Ultimately, the British government was forced to admit thousands of Ugandan Asians; some went to Leicester and others eventually made their way to Southall.[59] And by 1973, the borough of Ealing, which had tried so hard to keep Asians out, would have the highest percentage of the Indian-born population in Greater London.[60]

Discourses of Race, New Formations of Southall

A number of important phenomena converged in middle to late 1970s England to produce a historically specific politics of race: a rise in xenophobia fueled by the growing numbers and prominence of Indian residents in the area, a virulent and explicit racism that manifested itself in physical attacks on Indian youth in particular, and a growing degree of organization of Indians through both cultural and political associations and the daily life of a geographically concentrated and economically interdependent community. What emerged from these many and complicated developments was a city space starkly divided by race and political interest.

During this period, Southall had become, for many, Indian. Not only had Indians achieved sizable populations in a number of Southall districts, but they had also developed a cluster of business activities in a number of the main streets like King Road and the Broadway. Restaurants, sari shops, and news stands, owned by Punjabi Sikhs as well as middle-class Gujaratis from Kenya and Uganda, serviced the growing Indian population and replaced white-owned enterprises in the central areas of town. Consumption was an important shared practice, but it did not fully define the space. Southall had a social life, with theaters, religious institutions, and recreational clubs; it also had work and residential lives. Sikh, Hindu, and Muslim inhabitants maintained discrete cultural spaces so that by no means was Southall homogeneous. But increasingly, a broader, if not more simplistic production of "Indianness" became correlated to this physical space by worlds outside, including the city of London, the British state and national media, and the Indian diaspora. In the languages for identity that were available within British society at the time, community was territorially defined, and Southall could comfortably exist within such a framework as a majority "minoritized space."

An Indian public, in India, too, gazed upon Southall as an Indian place. In a July 1976 article in the *Illustrated Weekly of India*, Manohar Singh Gill discusses the differences between his first visit in 1967 and another eight years later. He charts, with considerable admiration, the ways that Indians have come to occupy the space. Of 1967, Gill remarks:

> As one came to Southall Broadway, one was confronted by a remarkable scene. While the backdrop was indubitably English—the shops, the chimneyed houses, the grey asphalt footpaths, even the lowered sky and constant drizzle—the actors who moved against this canvas were from another clime. The sidewalks in front of the shops were peopled by every hue and colour of turbans. . . . Most of the shops were English owned, but already the odd board could be seen proclaiming Banarsi saris, Indian home provisions or jewellers. Many signboards preferred Urdu and Punjabi to English.[61]

Here, Englishness is the "backdrop" and Indianness interrupts the homogeneity of the image, popping up as periodic points of color. But by 1976, Gill encounters a rather different spatial organization:

> Much had changed. . . . Nearly the whole of the Southall Broadway is Indian owned. Southall has also acquired a reputation as a bit of a gourmet place. Over the years the Indians have weaned the English away from their insipid food. Today almost all of them love the sight of a curry or a tandoori chicken. There is hardly a town without an Indian restaurant. London is full of them. Peter Sellers has been known to help promote the sales of one.[62]

The importance of this place of Southall being Indian-owned seems to be that it has transformed the canvas that Gill earlier outlined. Indianness is now fully in the foreground, not only physically but also symbolically when British actor Peter Sellers acts in its service. Southall's impact, then, lies beyond its specific territory, into a broader field of signification by which the author, too, is interpellated. What is clear by the end of the piece, however, is that there is an underlying anxiety about multiplicity that remains mostly suppressed but momentarily reveals itself. Gill's closing comment is about a competing discourse:

> When all has been said, Southall remains a complex phenomenon. . . . There are many who are anxious to make Southall a truly cosmopolitan community. This may seem an odd hope in the current situation, but I will point only to

a single sign for the future. I went to see the Southall school. . . . The Head-master was English, the most popular teacher a turbaned Sikh from Amritsar. To his West Indian, English, Pakistani and Indian students, he did not seem a strange creature. . . . I asked a little Pakistani boy newly arrived from Kara-chi how he felt. He was happy as a bean. Why? I asked. "They don't beat you here as they do in Pakistan," he replied.[63]

The question of cosmopolitanism makes a good deal of sense coming from an author in India, where debates about multiplicity have always had a particular force. And yet the answer, in a glib celebration of diversity, seems deeply ironic when read in context, when a young Southall resident had been stabbed to death but a month earlier, and when tensions were in the midst of blowing open. Given the extended process of publication, presumably this article that appeared in July was already in press; and the complete absence of questions of racialization may indicate how pro-foundly dramatic the changes in the discourse about Southall were to be.

Insurgent political organizations all over London turned their attention to Southall as a site of important conflicts over immigration, race, and community, and reproduced the discursive connections that gave the place a particular kind of meaning. The Campaign Against Racism and Fascism wrote of Southall's uniqueness in the 1970s: ". . . . Nowhere else in Brit-ain does an Asian community now have what Southall provides—its own cinemas (two show only Indian films), travel agents, marriage bureaux, banks, grocers, insurance agents, cafes and clothing and jewellery stores. . . . Asians from all over Britain, and even from Europe, look to Southall for their household, social and cultural needs. Asians feel at home there; it is their town in a very real sense."[64] What this text and others highlighted was the lived experience of an "ethnic enclave"; Indi-ans now lived, worked, and consumed goods within the general bound-aries of the area and were seen to inhabit that place.[65] Southall was becom-ing known to both its own residents and outsiders as a "Little India."[66] As such, it became a haven for Indians as well as a threatening embodi-ment of the presence of outsiders for native English people, a classic dual-ism of any minoritized space.[67] The formation of Southall as "Indian" was in production and constantly in transition, because casting it thus marked out territory in what many whites thought of as a space that they owned materially, socially, and culturally. Southall bore the representa-tional weight of geopolitical transitions that were much broader than the changing consumption patterns of the Broadway; they were about na-tional boundaries and postcolonialism.

Two events in the late 1970s represent both the intensity of racial ten-sions in Southall and the ways in which the negotiations and conflicts in this area produced the insurgent political discourses of a community. The 1970s were a time of deep and violent racial confrontation; it was quite common for Asians and West Indians to be physically attacked when walking on their own streets of residence, say many. National political leaders of both parties fanned the flames by pointing to immigration as a central problem in English society and declaring their commitment to aid white residents in the struggle to retain the basic principles of "English society," in effect, policies limiting the ability of people from formerly colonized areas to enter Britain. That the climate was racist, then, should be understood as having a number of manifestations in daily political and cultural life, of which only the most obvious were outright physical assaults on minority peoples.

And at this moment a new discourse of community and race was developing, one that is illuminated in an occasion of dramatic conflict: in June 1976 when a young resident, Gurdip Singh Chaggar, was stabbed to death by a gang of white youths just outside the Dominion Cinema, a Southall theater that showed Indian films and hosted community events.[68] Chaggar's death was a flashpoint in the development of Southall and the British Indian community as well. Angry Southallians, and Indians throughout Britain, were incredulous that such a thing could happen how and where it did, outside an institution owned by a respected community organization, the Indian Workers Association. One account, from *India Weekly*, outlined the importance of this event in a charged political context: "Ours is not an immigrant journal; its range of interest is at once more specific and wider; however, the growing insolence of the racialists lobby in this country and the consequential increase in violence against members of immigrant communities, of which the murder of Gurdip Singh Chaggar in Southall last Friday night is a gruesome reminder, are matters of international, not least Indian, concern."[69] Even a relatively conservative Indian newspaper that concerned itself with political issues in India to the exclusion of problems facing immigrants in England saw it as important to comment on this seminal event.[70]

But the moment also exposed cleavages in the community itself, between younger and older Indians and, to some degree, between the different political strategies available to and desirable for those groups. Generational differences began to appear in a community that was no longer recently from India, but now a mature immigrant population with offspring that had been schooled largely if not wholly in England. The youth of this community were Indian *and* British and struggled for a number of political causes with the intention of seeing them through in rather different ways from those in which their fathers and uncles had approached political conflicts in an earlier period, both in England and in India.

An important symbol of the early political organization of the Indian community in Britain was the Indian Workers Association—Southall.[71] The IWA—Southall was formed in 1956, just as the very first Indian immigrants began arriving in Southall.[72] The group expressed its original mission in race and class terms: "The IWA was established. . . in response to the white racism facing Asian workers in post war Britain." In its early years, the IWA supported a number of major strikes by black (both Asian and Afro-Caribbean) Southall workers at Woolf's Rubber Factory, Rockware Glass Company, and Chignalls Bakery. Established white unions, including the Amalgamated Engineering Union and the Transport and General Workers Union (TGWU), turned a blind eye to those strikes and even at times expressed outright opposition to them.[73] Thus the IWA provided a space for ethnic-class politics that no other institution at the time was able to provide.

Beginning in the late 1960s, the IWA expanded their activities to deal with the more general problems that black and particularly Indian immigrants faced in British society. The IWA campaigned against various immigration bills during this period and insisted upon stronger race relations bills. The group also helped to mobilize the community against the busing of Indian children for the government's dispersal policies in the area. Indeed, by the time of the murder of Gurdip Singh Chaggar in 1976, the IWA had become the central organization of the Punjabi community in Southall; its ownership of the Dominion Cinema (beginning in 1967) symbolized IWA's cultural importance in the community. When the IWA planned demonstrations against the murder and against the increasing levels of racism, the organization was acting much as it had over the last twenty years—protesting strongly against local and national governmental institutions and building grassroots support around organized political demands.

But segments of this community had varying experiences of the same event, derived from divergent understandings of what it meant to inhabit this space. Younger Southall residents rebelled against the slow political process in which they perceived the IWA to be engaging. Having suffered the effects of racism on the streets at the hands of both marauding white English youths and the police, the youth organized themselves to act in a manner that was very different from, if not antithetical to, the tactics of older leaders of the IWA. They stoned police vehicles and shops, conducted sit-downs, and took on the responsibility of defending their own community, rather than waiting for the police to play that role.[74] They assumed the proud emblem of the lion, a Sikh signifier for bravery; and their call to struggle became "We shall fight like lions."[75]

Rather than relying on existing political organizations like the IWA, these youths started their own group, the Southall Youth Movement (SYM). Some founding members of SYM cite the initial membership as 2,500 almost at the very start.[76] Composed of informal gangs as the period of "Paki-bashing," or violence against South Asians, came to an end, the group discussed the problems that remained unaddressed by both existing community organizations and the authorities. As one of the leaders notes: "We were always aware of the patriarchal nature of the community for everybody. . . . [There was] a very real threat of being unemployed [and we were] not prepared to work in our mothers' and fathers' shops, like our elders. We were black British."[77] The subjectivity of "black Britishness" was rather different from that which had developed out of the experience of migration from Punjab to Southall; like their older counterparts, these youths saw themselves as racially marked, both with regard to other white English residents and with respect to the state, but their stance was confrontational and also articulated with struggles of other black peoples, of West Indians in the British context, and of peoples of color around the world.

A more contemporary form of racialization within urban culture was central to the process of differentiation for young British Asians, as well as for the wider public in the 1970s. Particular discursive productions of otherness were drawn on to cope with a whole set of national and local transitions. As hysteria and panic about immigration thrived in many urban areas including London, the image of the young black criminal developed to buttress claims of internal-domestic "crisis." The Asian and West Indian youths therefore walked the streets in a state of vulnerability, not only to white racist gangs but also to the authorities who, in the name of "policing," brutalized and unfairly accused them for crimes that amounted to "disturbing the public order."[78] These youths were doubly vulnerable in this respect. Being "black" at the time, for Asian men, was a response to specific events, a set of ideological apparati (of the state, particularly), and a conjunctural historical moment. It might be thought of as the development of political consciousness in this respect; it certainly has been narrated as such by those who participated in the youth movements of the time.

A number of very complicated and precariously balanced tensions climaxed in April 1979 in what came to be called the Blair Peach incident. The last several years had seen the growing strength of the National Front, a racist and anti-immigrant organization, throughout the whole of England and in London especially. Given the explosiveness of such issues and the unresolved nature of the Gurdip Singh Chaggar murder, the news that the Tory-led Ealing borough council had approved the reservation of Southall Town Hall on April 23 for the National Front catalyzed a host of violent political eruptions in the area. Though a number of organizations protested the event to the authorities in advance of the date, the council claimed that it had no legal reason to deny a rental to the fascist organization and turned a blind eye to the insensitivity and insult of the National Front holding a meeting in a building in the very center of Southall.

Armed with the knowledge that the National Front would indeed be present in Southall on April 23, the IWA held a meeting on April 11 for over one hundred representatives from a variety of political groups in the area to help develop a community strategy.[79] The meeting resulted in plans for a peaceful march on April 22, with all Southall businesses closing at 1:00 P.M. that day, and a peaceful protest at 5:00 P.M. on April 23.[80] While a number of groups disagreed with parts of the strategy, there was a general consensus on the overall objectives and the planned demonstrations.

Until the morning of April 23, all activities proceeded as planned. What followed afterward, however, became legendary for Southall activists and nonpolitical residents. The "actual" events inspired a proliferation of discourses, around community consciousness, questions of history, and desires for autonomy as well.[81] Though groups like the IWA and SYM had had extensive negotiations with the police regarding their activities and plans for peaceful action, the police responded as if such meetings had not taken place. Beginning on the morning of April 23, hundreds of policemen occupied the main arteries of Southall,[82] making any demonstration as well as any movement by residents impossible. The tension surrounding this aggressive act, that trapped people at various points in downtown Southall, the frustration of organizations that had been planning peaceful demonstrations, and the refusal of the authorities to communicate with activists who wanted to defuse the situation contributed to a siege-like atmosphere in Southall. As activists and residents reacted, the police became more aggressive, arresting and brutalizing a wide variety of people. This violence culminated in the death of Blair Peach, a member of the Anti-Nazi League. Whether Peach was knocked over or hit directly in the head by police remains unclear.

In the days following, the mainstream media and the government emphasized the fact that Blair Peach was white and a member of the Anti-Nazi League for two possible effects: to portray the agitation as produced from the "outside" and to draw attention away from the state's role in that violence. Whether the objective was a calculated one or not, it seems clear that possible divisions in the Southall community could only help subsequently to mute anger and possible protest. But the power of Peach's death in the midst of the Southall community, and in the context of an anti–National Front protest, could not be manipulated by the state; it spectacularized the tensions, fears, and disappointments that had been building up for a long time on a number of fronts. The uniting of a number of Indian organizations and the appropriation of Blair Peach as a symbol for wrongs committed against Southall signified "the community's" efforts to see itself within broader fields of race relations *and* resistance. After April 23, huge memorial services for Blair Peach were organized in

Southall and many local as well as national groups began investigations into Peach's death and all issues that related to the violence in Southall.

This event made a huge impression on the Indian diaspora. The dramatic confrontation between community residents and the police underscored the embattled position of not only Southall Indians, but of the Indian population in Britain as well. The immigrant newspaper *Asian Post* asked rhetorically: "What went wrong at Southall on April 23? Is it that the whole idea of a multi-racial society in Britain is wrong? . . . No doubt, the events in Southall have left a sour taste in the mouths of the Asians in Britain."[83] Major newspapers in India, like the *Times of India*, reported on their front pages the incidents in Southall as straightforwardly being about racism.[84] Some newspapers reproduced the language of insurgent identities in England, using the term "black" to apply to all immigrants. The Indian government made a show of trying to enter into discussions with British officials about the treatment of Indians in England, negotiating the fine line between being connected to or appearing to protect its citizens abroad, and intervening in the affairs of another nation-state with which it was seeking to maintain working relations, all of which had a broader public audience, in the geopolitics of the non-aligned movement and other international groupings.[85] Nonetheless, the Indian minister of state for external affairs did meet with the president of the IWA. While in years past, the representation of the situation of Indians in Britain had not been free of racial content, it had also comprised powerful imagery of immigrant success.[86] But by 1979, a discourse of racial crisis had settled on Indians in England. If the murder of Chaggar in 1976 could be linked to scattered killings of immigrants in East London and other parts of England and could, in a sense, be individualized, the events of 1979 suggested a community under assault; this was an image and story that greatly impacted Indians around the world. Many Indians, in fact, drew on knowledge of these 1970s occurrences to justify their decisions to migrate elsewhere, especially to the United States.[87]

Indian Worlds of Jackson Heights

The Little India of Jackson Heights came into being during the period when Southall became a symbol of Indianness abroad in the 1970s. Jackson Heights would also assume the status of an Indian place, though rather differently from Southall, and can be creatively posited as an alternative to a set of images emanating from London. The development of Indianess in Jackson Heights emerged from a particular field of U.S. race relations, immigration, and national ideology that is in its own way important for migrant cultural formation.

By the 1970s, Jackson Heights was no longer the relatively homogeneous garden apartment community that its founder, MacDougall, had tried so hard to cultivate and maintain. The political and social changes of the 1960s transformed Jackson Heights even more dramatically than the Great Depression or the 1950s, generating issues of racial and ethnic formation and debates on community membership that had previously been suppressed, particularly, and surprisingly, around relations between African Americans and whites. Conveniently enough, Junction Boulevard effectively divided African American and white ethnic populations in Corona and Jackson Heights, respectively. Of this physical manifestation of social separation, Lee Dembart wrote in 1969: "I've yet to see a black face in that playground, though there are now a few in the schoolyard of PS 149 in the Northridge co-op project. Of course Northridge is close to Junction Boulevard, the Mason-Dixon line of Queens."[88]

Demographic shifts wrought by the 1965 Immigration and Naturalization Act could not be contained in the same way. After 1965, migrants from Latin America, the Caribbean, and Asia began to arrive in large numbers to urban areas of the United States. New York City became home to many of these peoples, and the expensive rents of Manhattan recommended areas like those in Queens, in which there were also two major airports. By the early to mid-1970s, Columbian immigrants had established a strong presence in Jackson Heights and built up new sections of the local business scene. During the same time, Jackson Heights became a primary site for the more informal economy of the drug trade; many Colombian drug cartel leaders were found to be in Jackson Heights and the area was colloquially described as "Coke City, USA."[89] Structural changes in the economy made the drug trade more attractive, most especially as companies like Bulova, a large Jackson Heights employer, closed down in 1978. The simultaneity of the entry of drugs and immigrants into Jackson Heights produced deep hostilities among older white residents and created some fodder for new forms of racism, in which the figure of the (now, brown) immigrant became commensurate with crime, filth, and drugs, both for people who lived in the area and for the city as a whole. The "ethnic mix" was perceived to be no longer working, if it ever had, in places like Jackson Heights. One longtime resident used language familiar to students of urban change when he described the area in 1975: "It used to be a very refined section with a very fine class of people. It's deteriorating, that's the right word for it."[90]

A countervailing factor in this Queens racial formation was the middle-class status of many Latino migrants. The transformations that Columbians and others from Latin America became attached to in Jackson Heights also exemplified changes in the urban economy. Recent arrivals built stores and restaurants rather than factories, and they did so on a scale that surpassed the capacities of the few "Mom and Pop" shops that had been owned by local white residents in the past. One young Jackson Heights resident, Martin Gallent, put it this way: "People just assumed that they were undesirables, at the bottom of the social scale, because they spoke Spanish. But these people are middle income. Make no mistake about it—they have money."[91] Race, ethnicity, and class were arrayed in new ways for post-1965 immigrants and for the relations that resulted between older and newer residents of Jackson Heights. As former citizens of the third world, these new arrivals were racialized in ways that prevented their inclusion in narratives of "whitening" into which longtime Jewish or Greek inhabitants had already been incorporated. Yet in terms of class position, all these groups bore some resemblance to one another. Racial conflicts over space that occurred in Jackson Heights in the 1970s would bring about languages different from those developed in other historical black-white spaces, like the transformations of Harlem at the turn of the century.

New middle-class formations in the Latino population were echoed in the development of an Indian business concentration in the 74th Street area of Jackson Heights. This particular "ethnic enclave" represented a different kind of Indian community from the Southall example, precisely because it was structured around the ownership and development of commerce in the area. From the very beginning, the development of the community there came not through working-class organization but from the aspirations and imperatives of middle-class formation. Especially in the 1970s, Indians in the United States could not readily inhabit established racial categories of "Asian" or even of "minority." Formation of the place of Jackson Heights, then, resonates imperfectly with the idea of "minoritized space."

After the 1965 Immigration and Naturalization Act, people from India, too, arrived in New York City in large numbers.[92] But Jackson Heights, unlike Southall, was not the first point of destination of Indian immigrants to the country. Many of the earlier immigrants were students and professionals who settled in and around the Manhattan area. A number of Indian areas sprung up, particularly in midtown Manhattan, in the Lexington and 26th–28th Street area and lower down in the Canal Street area.[93] But the residential concentrations began to shift by the early 1970s, from Manhattan to Queens, to many different areas across the borough including Jackson Heights, Flushing, and Elmhurst.[94]

The emerging ethnic market of Queens Indians was different and distant from the Manhattan providers of Indian goods on Lexington Avenue

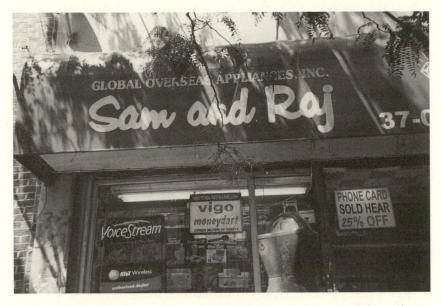

Figure 7. Sam and Raj—a legend in the diaspora (photograph by author).

and Canal Street. One story, of insertion into and a kind of production of the space of Jackson Heights, distills a number of specificities of Indian migration to New York, and to the United States more generally. In 1973, Subhas Ghai and Raj Gandhi started an electronics store, Sam and Raj, on the corner of 74th Street and Broadway in Jackson Heights (see fig. 7). This store would become legendary for Indians all over the diaspora, functioning as a kind of shorthand for easy access to Indian goods. The location and specifics of the store were hardly arbitrary; indeed, the two engineer founders deliberated over where to undertake their business venture for a long time and finally decided that Jackson Heights's convenience with regard to the subway would draw in the increasing Indian populations from all over Queens. Ghai says that the rapid move of other Indian stores like India Sari Palace and Sinha Appliances to the area was also envisioned from the very beginning: "It was our dream."[95] Interestingly, the planned nature of the Indian community on 74th Street in the 1970s was not unlike MacDougall's dreams of the early 1900s. Jackson Heights, perhaps like America itself, provided a place in which to realize fantasies of development and community, for a range of actors who had specific class resources and who therefore could tap into a tradition of entrepreneurialism. The contrast between social formations in Jackson Heights and those of Southall at this time are also striking. Just as immigrants in Southall in the 1970s were developing a racialized understanding of themselves and their space, Jackson Heights merchants were planning to make money.

Sam and Raj was wildly successful, marketing and selling highly desirable 220 volt electronic goods that could be used in India and Europe. Electronic goods had a particular appeal within a community that came of age and was consolidated during the rapid increase in communications all around the world and in particular between "third world" regions such as the Indian subcontinent and places like the United States and Britain. Many nations, such as those in South and Southeast Asia, declared their participation in a global economy in the late 1970s and early 1980s through competent and efficient production of electronic and computer goods. In addition, electronic equipment has had an important place in the history of this community with a complicated relationship to the homeland and place of residence. Electronics has allowed migrants access to visual and oral ethnic pleasures, like videos of Hindi films and tapes of Indian music, and enabled cultural commerce both to and from India. It is a kind of "symbolic good," with a range of purposes beyond its literal usage. Ghai and Gandhi in 1973 were brilliantly prescient. What is also evident is how Jackson Heights as a consumer space worked very differently from Southall. Never did electronics goods, even in the 1970s, figure so prominently in the broader patterns of visitors or inhabitants going to the Southall marketplace. Southall was better known, as the 1976 *Illustrated Weekly of India* article suggested, for restaurants. In a more contemporary moment, in the 1990s to the present, Indians continue to think of Jackson Heights as a place for reasonably priced televisions, DVD players, and the like, while that image does not have the same relevance for imaginings of Southall.

By 1980, the majority of the 74th Street block between Roosevelt Avenue and 37th Avenue housed South Asian shops. Because the goods— food, clothing, jewelry, and electronics—had relevance for the cultures more widely of people from Pakistan and Bangladesh as well as from India, non-Indian South Asian merchants also occupied stores in Jackson Heights, and almost all the businesses began to market themselves to "Indo-Pak-Bangla" constituencies. The area eventually included over a hundred stores in the area (on the block itself and a few surrounding blocks) that were South Asian–owned, and/or had almost exclusively South Asian clientele.

While some Indians lived in the immediate Jackson Heights area, they did not originally make up a residential majority or even a significant minority in the extremely diverse area, which to this day continues to have large Jewish, Greek, Italian, Colombian, Korean, and Japanese populations. The 2000 census registers 6.1 percent of the Jackson Heights population as Indian, with 1.4 percent Bangladeshi, 1.1 percent Pakistani, and an additional 0.1 percent Sri Lankan.[96] Over the years, certainly, more Indians and other South Asians have moved to Jackson Heights, perhaps partly drawn by the Indianness already in the area; more than that, however, it is clear that South Asian increases in the nearby population have to do with general demographic trends, of more South Asians on Long Island.[97] From Jackson Heights's early years and into the present, most shop owners have lived on other parts of Long Island or in more well-to-do areas of Queens, while their employees (those not related to the owners), have come from other parts of Queens. The resident and working population in the area that has frequented the shops is not necessarily consonant with the actual day-to-day running of 74th Street, most strikingly in its phase of "becoming Indian."

The more homogeneously concentrated population of Indians existed (and continues to exist) on shopping days; in that way, the "community" is both transitional and transient. The interests converged around the distribution and sale of consumer goods (like saris and appliances) and services (such as those in an Indian beauty salon). The market was an ethnic one, almost completely South Asian and in large part Indian; it was at once specific to the Queens Indian population that could most readily access the area and dispersed, extending outward to reach Indian populations throughout New York, New Jersey, and Connecticut. Indian migrants and their children in the tri-state region, particularly those from suburban areas where Indians are more dispersed, often speak of visits to the area to experience Indianness.[98] And because of its proximity to both LaGuardia and Kennedy International Airports, Indian travelers en route to India and other places in the diaspora stop off at Jackson Heights to pick up goods. Thus the local space of Jackson Heights could also become a point in the more international circuitry of mobile Indians, of the diaspora.

Just as Sam and Raj gained international name recognition and seemed to symbolize one trajectory of Indian migration—to the U.S.—and one that is entrepreneurial in nature, so too did Jackson Heights become a famously "Indian" area, a place that has substituted for broader historical and social experiences. The representation of 74th Street, even to the locals, has always had a broad, diasporic meaning. Popular renderings of such an "Indian community" occurred with reference to both the shopping area and to the shoppers that existed there every day and most especially on the weekends. Indian and American shoppers alike are surprised to hear that Indians did not make up the residential majority in the area. This space of Indianness diverges greatly from communities built by workplace or residence, and the social life that is normally an indicator of shared interests. And importantly, the power of Jackson Heights for outsiders lay in its evocations of an exotic otherness. Representative articles in the *New York Times* about the area carry titles such as "Bazaar with the Feel of Bombay, Right in Queens" and "India Casts Its Subtle Spell on Queens."[99]

The production and consumption of ethnic goods in Jackson Heights shuts off at six or seven o'clock. The community—a "virtual community," perhaps—is akin to a kind of performance, with a beginning and an end, and regulated by the customs of U.S. consumer capitalism. Ethnic production is based not in local investments, in the city blocks or the residential neighborhood, but in symbolic and material renderings of India for the most part and of Pakistan and Bangladesh secondarily. International references shape the consumer experiences in Jackson Heights and construct a set of identifications for all parties involved. The temporary, almost fleeting nature of that consumption of Indianness in Jackson Heights has made for a very different type of ethnic community from that of Southall, or even Italian or Irish neighborhoods in Brooklyn and Queens. In the ways that consumption defines this space, the place is itself commodified and turned into spectacle.

The reaction of Jackson Heights's older white community members to the rather rapid commercial development of this Indian area has been, if not always overtly hostile, then certainly never altogether welcoming. Community members have been quick to notice the increase in traffic on 74th Street and the surrounding blocks and have highlighted the resulting parking problems. Given the high volume of people going through the area and the prevalence of restaurants and more "fast food" establishments, white residents have complained most about the trash left behind by a business sector that by and large leaves at night. The language of censure, then, reserved for immigrant presence in Jackson Heights, has code words at its core that are familiar in descriptions of the "racial other": overcrowding and dirtiness. In Jackson Heights itself, Indians have met with stereotypes that Colombians encountered less than a decade earlier. And, despite the huge differences between the Indian presence in Jackson Heights and say, Southall, there are strong descriptive similarities in the responses from older white communities across national boundaries. That the older resident population may be more heterogeneous in Jackson Heights does not necessarily unmake the equation; in this case, ethnically diverse communities—Jewish, Greek, Italian—become consolidated as white, in response to forms of otherness with different racial content.

While Colombians in Jackson Heights were assumed to perpetrate crimes and engage in drug activities, the Indians there were held responsible for attracting a certain measure of crime to the area. The presence of highly valuable goods such as gold jewelry made the area vulnerable to

Figure 8. 74th Street, the Gold Corner (photograph by author).

burglary (see fig. 8).[100] In the mid-1980s, a rash of break-ins and thefts were largely ignored by city authorities and in 1988 an important set of realizations and misunderstandings arose around a particularly egregious robbery.[101] Various merchants felt that the police did not come in time, that the investigation had been far from thorough, and that this shortfall of attention was related to the area being composed mostly of South Asians. As one merchant noted: "We thought as immigrants we were not being heard."[102] Unspoken, perhaps, in this lament, is the phrase "and as nonwhite residents." Though there was an emerging critique of the relationship of this Indian area to the whole of Jackson Heights, and particularly of its racialized nature, migrants were loath to identify themselves as racial subjects, preferring the term "immigrant" to capture the complexity of their feelings of disempowerment. In conversations in the early to middle 1990s, many merchants specifically avoided the term "racism," largely because they saw themselves as different from Indians in places like London. It does seem by this time that Jackson Heights shop owners, and Indian immigrants in the United States more generally, have become more accustomed to languages of race, particularly as those languages have become more nuanced and complex in recent years. The complicated development of responses of Indians in Jackson Heights to questions of race illuminate the way that the Indian diaspora in the United States more generally has been very much caught up in the transition, if not transformation, of what the relationship between class, color, and nation would be.

While shop owners may have shunned race as a marker of identity, they were willing to participate in more collective action as a result of the 1980s robberies. They founded the Jackson Heights Merchants Association and went to the police station in a procession to protest the police inattention. The organization bears little resemblance to the one created by the Queensboro Corporation in the early 1930s, yet apparently uses the same name unknowingly. And it is different from the Indian Workers' Association in Southall, certainly in its origins. The Jackson Heights Merchants Association was founded as—and continues to be—a local "ethnic organization" composed of South Asian merchants with stores in the 74th Street district whose interests revolve around the smooth flow of commerce in the area. This investment in the workings of the market has not precluded "political" activities; the march to the local police station is just one instance of a willingness to be confrontational with established authorities. The Jackson Heights Merchants Association's ethnic interests originated in migrant subjectivity; formulations of migrants in response to questions about an agenda describe the need to develop a "voice" and "unity." These interests were further structured around economic power and interests; one merchant was quite direct about how the group had consolidated: "After all, we pay high taxes."[103] The ways in which early markers of community, through participatory and representative institutions, developed in Jackson Heights and Southall enlivens the difference between these two spaces. As migrant and merchant subjects organized around commerce in Jackson Heights, a commercial organization would come to best represent their interests. Indian migrants who built a community in 1960s Southall were *workers*, whose first institution was working-class in nature. Though each space appeared to be one for Indianness, evoked even as "Indian community," what originally held Southall and Jackson Heights together were very different modes of being: class, race, and social life on the one hand, consumption and commerce on the other. That these modes become more confused in time testifies, perhaps, to the very basic tenuousness of the notion of community itself.

The Jackson Heights Merchants Association developed a clear sense of the outlines of *its* community, hiring private security people to guard against car break-ins (which had become a barrier to encouraging people to come into Jackson Heights from wealthier and presumably safer suburbs) and also to provide area information on where to obtain certain goods or services. And the organization also spoke to the anxieties of local residents by exhorting members to keep the sidewalks outside their stores clean and have their garbage properly carted away.[104] In these ways and others, the organization laid specific claims to the territory it inhabited; it maintained and protected the streets and guided people through its own vision of what that space was for. It did so in a model of a planned and almost gated community, though the Indian area of Jackson Heights existed in the midst of tremendous diversity. The ethnic boundaries erected by residence and workplace in Southall did not appear in Jackson Heights, and therefore more deliberate means had to be employed for the project of delimitation.

The Jackson Heights Merchants Association established itself politically in a range of ways, acting as an interest group in local and city politics by developing relations with the police, administrative bureaucrats, and members of congress, and by encouraging authorities to look upon this area as highly profitable in terms of tax revenue and as highly marketable for its presentation of "Indianness" in a multicultural landscape. Members of the organization, like many Indians of middle- and upper middle-class status, now cite these positive aspects of the 74th Street enclave continuously in response to any insinuations of their having been the victims of racism. Significantly, the intersection of immigrant consciousness and business perspective produced the imperative to be seen ethnically, and yet to willfully disregard any implication of having been victimized racially. In this model social harmony is presumed to emerge spontaneously from "doing business," a rather time-worn cliché of American life.

Recent proposals to develop a more formal identity for the 74th Street area of Jackson Heights have further complicated some of these issues. For a number of years, the area's shop owners and customers have supported a plan for the city to officially name the area "Little India"; and when Mayor David Dinkins visited Jackson Heights in 1992, he declared his support for the motion.[105] The merchants and residents see the proposal as positive, in a way that speaks again to the specifics of Indian ethnic formation in the United States. Indian Americans applaud the growing public acknowledgment of their presence. This reveals as much about the current, and hegemonic, discourses of U.S. multiculturalism as it does about the particulars of this Indian place. Having a "Little India," for the merchants, is commonly seen as a step in the direction of recognizing Indian American interest groups and Indian American localities within the political and social fabric of the United States.[106] One shop owner remarked that the area becoming a "Little India" would "give [the occupants] some image and sense of belonging."[107] What this formulation suggests is that despite the fact that the term "Little India" conjures the exotic India, and the structure of another nation, the formal establishment of an enclave proffers membership in the United States. If this "Little India" is a minoritized space on the level of a Chinatown of years past,

the term "minority" seems to acquire positive rather than negative connotations in the construction of merchants.

It is clear in discussions with those who occupy, if not literally inhabit,
Jackson Heights, that models for citizenship are being actively reworked.
Here, commerce and consumption become important modes for being
part of a place, even of a nation, but construct only one field in which
desires for a place in the world are worked out. Connections with India
indeed figure centrally in the lives of those post-1965 Indian migrants
who *trade* in Indianness, who provide goods that are Indian, as well as in
the imaginative worlds of those who go to Jackson Heights to eat Indian
food or buy Indian clothing. While platitudes abound about the essentially American aspects of this correlation between capitalist commerce
and cultural identity, it is hard to overlook the fact that the fundamental
reference points exist in a place far away from the United States. In fact
the very diasporic cultural citizenship evinced by a place like Jackson
Heights results from the special characteristics of postwar and post-1965
migrations as well as through new consumerist and service economies that
define Sassen's "global cities."[108] The idea that to consume is to belong to
a place is unsettling to a whole range of popular observers and scholars
alike, particularly as what is "public" and what is "private" comes into
a sustained interdependency, through the structures of the marketplace
that create and satisfy personal and group desire.

Even though Jackson Heights seems less territorially defined, the sense
of belonging that merchants have elaborated and the claim to the space
that was activated in 1973 with the first electronics shop have led to discord, suggesting that ownership of the area still matters. During David
Dinkins's visit to 74th Street, many Indians remember longtime white
residents shouting, "Indians go back."[109] These "locals" continued to actively oppose the development of a "Little India," saying that this area
was also theirs and that to call it "Little India" would obscure that fact.
Older white residents largely constituted the Community Board, which is
the main bureaucratic apparatus responsible for approval of a neighborhood appellation; the board cited parking problems and the lack of clean-
liness in the area as reasons for stalling approval of the proposition.

In 1988, several of these local residents founded the Jackson Heights
Beautification Group. Its activities, including neighborhood cleanups and
programs to remove and prevent graffiti, converged around the general
goals of "beautification" and "preservation." More directly, members
sought to develop a community to revive, in their own words, "Edward
MacDougall's vision of an urban suburbia in Jackson Heights."[110] The
organization supported the development of a central section of Jackson
Heights (that did not include 74th Street) to be designated as a historic
district. But the group also rather emblematically opposed the naming of

74th Street as "Little India." At stake in the contest between those for and against the designation were two very different social and aesthetic visions of the city: a particularly commercial type of urbanization, on the one hand, and on the other, the nostalgic rendering of what was old, stately, and pristine. Here we might see the residue of an age-old American quandary: support for free (and even reckless) enterprise, but a desire to ban such commercialism from "private" lives. When asked why "Little India" would not be a positive development for the area, an active member of the beautification group noted that tour buses and the like would only contribute to the traffic problem.[111] The development of an Indian enclave in Jackson Heights, then, proceeded with a troubled and rather distant relationship to these nostalgic and aggressive stories of the future of the area. Indian commerce on 74th Street, like Latino and Korean markets to the north of the area, symbolized to white residents "deterioration"[112] and formations deviating from a more established and palatable history of their place.

A resident noted that these kinds of conflicts enable the media representation of an Archie Bunker racism in Queens communities like Jackson Heights.[113] To what extent the existence of divergent narratives of this space is evidence of racism might be considered from a number of different perspectives. Contemporary distaste for the influx of new immigrants and the consolidation of space for ethnic activity certainly has had a rather different content from the outright housing discrimination of the past that prevented Jews and Italians from renting in the original garden apartments. The coordinates have changed: the racial other is a group perceived to be economically advantaged; immigration has joined racial mixing as a persistent urban fear; and the subject himself is now "brown" rather than "black." Nonetheless, the language founded upon inside/outside metaphors (rather than models of assimilation), employing code words like "filth" and "overcrowding," contains a kind of fear and loathing that is at the heart of both older and newer forms of racism. Recent adaptations of racist ideologies include both a change of terminology and also a shift from assertions of biological inferiority to critiques of behavior of the group in question. While no white resident would claim that Indians or Colombians are lesser people, at least in public, they would and do criticize the cosmetic changes (trash and garish signs) that immigrant presence has brought to their places.

It is this new form of racism, more subtle perhaps, but nonetheless steeped in familiar metaphors of xenophobic distaste, that dominates contemporary urban and national politics, in the name of immigration controls and the further isolation of poor communities. And yet, simultaneously, there is an increase in racial attacks, a not altogether unfamiliar product of deep racial conflicts in society. Perhaps even more significantly, the immigrant (and African American) middle classes are the targets of this new racism, which is often but not always distinct from racisms faced by the working-class "other" (in Southall, for example) or the poor African American. In these cases, contestations over symbolic space and territory recast the black-white problem and the immigrant problem as influenced by the intense intermingling of cultures, as in Jackson Heights, rather than the attitudinal dysfunctions of modern society, as seen in the television series *All in the Family*.[114] But much as the Jackson Heights resident's efforts to distance his community's responses to the new immigration from the kind of crude racism of an earlier period ring hollow alongside an obvious anxiety about new residents, so too should the demurrals of Indian merchants to a kind of racial subjectivity be placed in a context in which identities are often conferred by broader social conflicts rather than freely chosen.

Changing Communities, Changing Nations

The space of community, nation, and diaspora was continually being made in Southall and Jackson Heights; stories about these places, like those about all places, perhaps, were thematized by change. We can see Southall and Jackson Heights as important symptoms of transforming postwar social relations. Constructions of Indianness in both Southall and Jackson Heights were temporary and open to greater flexibility and contestation, particularly because all sorts of differences were provisionally subsumed in that conceptualization of subjectification, be it Punjabi or Sikh in Southall, or, in the case of Jackson Heights, hailing from Bangladesh or Pakistan. As England, the United States, and India, too, experienced new forms of nationality based on complex models of coherence and division, Southall and Jackson Heights bore the marks of difference. Any sense of community therein, like Indianness, was always in a fragile state, threatening to come apart, just as it had come together.

Coming out of the very dramatic events and rapid developments of the 1970s and early 1980s, Southall was a web of political and social organizations that were commonly self-identified as "community groups" but that constituted an incredibly complicated and variegated field of resistance. In addition to the 1979 conflict between the police and the Southall community in the Blair Peach incident, as well as the flurry of united political action at that time, the turn of the decade brought to light a number of social and cultural changes that had been taking place in Southall. Southall had become a good deal more diverse in socioeconomic terms. It was no longer a mostly working-class community as it had been in the 1950s and 1960s; instead it was diversified, and divided, by the growth of a business class that owned shops and small industries in the area. The relative prosperity of Southall with regard to outlying areas (as well as the consciousness of "difference") produced in a number of sectors of Southall a kind of self-sufficiency and insularity. But on another level, the increase in women and the coming of age of a new generation raised in Britain had taken place in the context of social and political developments in London that included youth and feminist movements as well as the onset of a deep economic recession. New Southall populations that were constituted by interests other than the original migration, or the class position of that first group, developed identities that were assertively articulated with both the British context and also with nations and social formations outside England. Various groups in Southall developed both ethnic and diasporic understandings of themselves.[115]

The Southall Black Sisters, was formed in November 1979, seven months after the Blair Peach incident, out of concern that questions of Asian and Afro-Caribbean women's oppression were not being adequately addressed in other black political and feminist organizations.[116] As Gita Sahgal, a founding member, describes it: "The group was born in the heart of the struggle that followed the murder of Blair Peach by the police. It was a (rare) moment of community unity in the face of attack by fascists and the police. Yet, by founding a black women's group, we challenged the right of male community leaders to speak for us."[117] The Southall Black Sisters addressed a range of women's issues and, in particular, domestic violence in the community. Their actions in a number of key cases involving the physical abuse and/or death of women in violent households often placed female members in opposition to established male-dominated organizations. More broadly, these women critiqued an idealized vision of a cohesive and unified community. By interrogating the definition of "community," the Southall Black Sisters was one of a number of groups that exposed fissures and differences in Southall itself. And by consciously drawing on solidaristic notions of "blackness," and appealing to multi-ethnic and multiracial constituencies, this group participated in the broader production of new identities that departed from regionally specific (Punjabi) or nationalistic (Indian) forms of difference.

The story of the development of the Southall Black Sisters has had reverberations through a range of political communities all across England and even the Indian diaspora. In one narrative of progressive black feminism, a group that emerged from local circumstances was transformed into having national importance, able to negotiate the deeply charged political landscape of race.[118] The maintenance (to this day) of the term "black" as a signifier not necessarily for identity but for coalitional political activity explicitly distinguishes this kind of politics from a national-ethnic focus on being Indian, Punjabi, or a religious minority, that which is more familiar in a more contemporary moment. There is a surprising familiarity with the Southall Black Sisters in the Indian diaspora, especially among South Asian diasporic communities in North America invested in questions of solidarity.[119] The way in which Southall Black Sisters could move into a political-symbolic space beyond locality may be another indication of the porous boundaries of Southall itself.

In the early 1980s, two progressive groups were created to deal with the persistence of racial discrimination and the need for information on immigrant rights, the Southall Monitoring Group and the Southall Law Center. While the Southall Law Center handled more legalistic issues, the scope of the Southall Monitoring Group was broader and included all kinds of casework such as domestic violence, immigration, labor issues, racial attacks, political campaigns, and emergency service. In confronting all these issues, the Southall Monitoring Group experienced the limits of locality, too, as it discovered that basic services and support as well as a political language to address questions of racial violence were needed at a national level.[120] In changing its name to the Monitoring Group more recently, while retaining its offices in Southall, leaders and members made connections between places, like west London, Birmingham, and northern England, and spaces, such as those of the racial subjectification of middle-class Punjabi Indians and violence directed at Pakistani Muslims.

While there were many consciously activist organizations in the 1980s, the emphasis of the IWA in Southall shifted. By 1980, the IWA was widely considered to have become primarily a service organization, geared to questions of social welfare and linked to the goals of the Labour Party.[121] And certainly, recent utterances by leaders of the IWA created narratives of change that stressed "pragmatic" goals and issues centering on the day-to-day needs of immigrants with regard to local and national government regulations.[122] As Piara Khabra noted: "The IWA [could] not remain organizing marches, lobbies, etc."[123] Balraj Purewal, later an IWA board member, was more forthright: "The majority had a socialist agenda [in the past] and now it is increasingly more capitalist."[124]

For several years, Khabra has been the general secretary of the IWA, as well as a Member of Parliament from the Labour Party for the Southall area; other members of the executive board of the organization, however, include those loyal to the Conservative Party. A large percentage of current IWA members are owners of small Southall shops as well as larger area companies. The increasingly diversified constituency of the IWA signifies not only the organization's political shifts, but also changes in what were once called community interests. Attention to race and ethnicity, as the two have become increasingly conflated in that space, has been decoupled from a pro-worker agenda. Directed toward immigrant issues, the IWA still stands in opposition to many functions of the entry-regulating British state and to local authorities who continue to unfairly distribute government resources. The persistence of frank racism in such spheres of activity formulates and concretizes IWA members' identities as Indians in a country that is perceived as hostile to difference. The historical and discursive relationship between that ethnic identity and a particular class position effectively glosses over the transformations in Southall and in England as a whole that have made the easy correspondence between Indians and workers spurious.

According to Purewal, the label that empasizes the Indian *Workers* Association has been retained for national and international name recognition, but I would argue that there are other important ideologies of British class and racial formation at work in this choice. The experience of being an immigrant, and a racialized immigrant at that, often overrides what might seem to be a relatively privileged position financially in the host society. Ideas of class position for those immigrants as well as for others emerge from the contradictions inherent in what may be experienced as disempowerment rather than capital advantage. Rethinking models of class formation to encompass immigrant social experience helps us to understand the situation of Indian shop owners in Jackson Heights too, who often describe themselves as workers of some sort or another. For many immigrants from the third world, who no longer work in heavy industry and who may have access to small sources of capital to start their own businesses but whose actual wages may be lower than even minimum wages in first-world countries like the United States and Britain, traditional groupings of the working and middle classes may seem constrictive. But it may also be true that categorical spaces become better defined when recent Indian immigrants in a city like New York increasingly appear in formally working-class occupations, like construction and factories, and when they populate the low-wage service economies, such as staffing the restaurants at Kennedy Airport. In England, too, poorer Indians have arrived on the scene to diversify a high-income population. Though these demographic shifts might make it easier to identify class position, they make more difficult any attempt to establish the parameters of belonging to a particular kind of place.

Multiple ways of envisioning life in Southall came to a crisis in the late 1980s around the emergence of youth gangs.[125] At the time, older residents of Southall and local state authorities began to identify the presence of informally organized groups of youths in Southall. The description of these gangs took a variety of forms. Some local activists tried to recover these occasions of youth culture for progressive purposes, other political groups were worried about the impact of highly masculinist and sometimes violent forms of organization among disenfranchised youths, and the state embarked on a campaign to racially and culturally pathologize this emerging Southall generation.[126] The youth of Southall, as a generation, had indeed suffered in a number of ways the pressures and possibilities of the building of "community"; as an editorial essay in a publication from the Southall Monitoring Group suggested, "An entire generation of our youth has grown up in the shadow of police penetration and saturation, in addition to the pressures which their parents have experienced of racist harassment and violence on the streets and racist discrimination . . . . In addition, they have . . . emerged into life in Thatcherite Britain to experience mass unemployment, the dismantling of the welfare state, and the institutionalising of repressive trade union, immigration and civil liberties legislation."[127] The development of gangs and the reading of all insurgent (and perhaps Westernized) youth as potentially threatening set in motion another phase of stereotyping this community, as it has for other minority communities in economically depressed societies.

Indians' connections with India have grown, not only in Southall but all over Britain. While Southall Asians had always maintained a range of affiliations at home and abroad, the struggles around community empowerment in the 1960s and 1970s necessitated local forms of ethnic and racial identity, which foregrounded the importance of a specifically racialized immigrant experience in England. Various shared experiences of place within the Southall Indian community had facilitated the development of oppositional solidarities in groups like the Indian Workers Association. But greater diversification in terms of class and Indian origin opened up space for new kinds of affiliations in the 1980s, and produced a shift from race to nation as a mode of subjectivity, particularly among certain segments of the Southall Indian population.

These local developments coincided with India's increasing role in the activities of migrant communities all through the diaspora. The international activities of Indians in Southall had a broader context outside Britain. Issues of communalism and religious fundamentalism took hold in the area. In 1984, following Indian Prime Minister Indira Gandhi's storming of the Golden Temple in Amritsar, Punjab, and her subsequent assassination, movements for the creation of Khalistan, a Sikh homeland, as the political ideal was called, erupted into a global domain. Khalistani groups were very active in Southall and produced deep rifts in the local population, leading to the murder of a newspaper editor and other violent acts.[128] Many Sikhs supportive of Punjabi sovereignty articulated a more diasporic set of interests that disassociated them from broader Indian constituencies in Britain, from other Punjabis in Southall, and also from issues specific to the community that had once been so powerful, like racial and ethnic discrimination. Communalism has certainly impacted second- and third-generation Sikh, Muslim, and Hindu British citizens. Older migrants profess shock at incidents of violence, at pubs, and on the streets during religious holidays and other social events, between youths of different ethnic groupings, speaking nostalgically if forgetfully of a time when such tensions did not exist. Expressed divisions, however, have achieved a particular intensity in the last couple of decades, as youths have become isolated and alienated by continual economic downturns and have turned to religious identities as a salve (however deceptive).[129]

The continuing influx of new populations into Southall in the 1980s served to make the area much more diverse. Growing numbers of Somali refugees have settled in Southall, and the black African and largely Muslim characteristics of this population have introduced a number of complications into both internally produced spatial identities (Southall's sense of itself) and images of Southall from the outside (see figs. 9 and 10). The move from a mostly Indian to a more multicultural self-definition has not yet taken place; the Somalis are poorer and politically unorganized and many established Indian organizations have been slow to see themselves as responsible for what may be new and different interests.[130] On the first level, there is a wide gulf between the category that these newer, mostly Somali, but also some South Asian Southall residents occupy, that of "refugee" or "asylum seeker," and the term "immigrant," which was applied to Indians, even to East African Asians who had come to England to escape discrimination in black nationalist nations.[131] Embedded in the different lived experience of those categories is the fact that Somali refugees, while able to receive government benefits, are unable to work; in a community space originally built by an association between work, residence, and race, this creates a distinction around the new minority, and interrupts one possible form of membership. On another level, Somalis are black African Muslims and therefore are necessarily racialized differently from Indian and Pakistani residents. In an "Asian" space, Somali refugees are "other." Unlike other recent immigrants from India and Pakistan, Somalis can never fully assimilate into that space as it is currently defined.

Responses of older Southall residents to new populations, Somali and other South Asian, expose the limits of the discourse of tolerance and multiplicity.[132] The most common language creates a bounded spatiality, maintaining that an already overcrowded Southall cannot absorb asylum seekers.[133] Resonances of this contemporary set of reactions with earlier anxieties of white residents around the entry of Indians into Southall remain submerged, or at least unacknowledged. Many Southall Indians now fully seem to "own" their space and lament encroachment by others. New populations that also include poorer South Asian workers are seen to contribute to the cheapening of Southall; several residents pointed to the quite evident proliferation of cheaper imports from places like China, brought and facilitated by younger male Indian and Pakistani arrivals, displayed in stores along the main streets of the area. Some residents note

Figures 9 and 10. New populations, a changing "Little India"
(photographs by author).

that this development has created a form of consumption that used to be the mainstay of other less affluent areas of London. Interestingly, these comments demonstrate a contemporary identification with Southall as a middle-class rather than working-class space, despite a history of an association between this place and working-class life and politics.

Life cycles have created obvious changes in the stories told about Southall. While the youth generation always receives more discussion in scholarship about changing communities, the elderly in Southall are an important new category that also deserves attention. The British government and local authorities fund institutions for older residents, like the Southall Day Centre and the Milap Centre, where men and women meet to create their own communities, rather different from the ones outside. A women's discussion and activities group at the Milap Centre provides a primer on the heterogeneity of Southall, including a Gujarati leader, members from East Africa and Punjab, and a variety of Sikhs, Hindus, and Muslims.[134] Jostling about sustained ethnic differences, including very serious discussions about caste identity, gives way to a pronounced attachment to Southall as a shared community space, particularly when the issue of recent arrivals arises. In those moments, the most common story told is a nostalgic one about the former shared interests and ethnic harmony of Southall; moments of discord drop out of that narrativization, through a sense of racial otherness—mostly around being "Asian" or "Indian,"—and a profound alienation from British society remains embedded in understandings of how the space of Southall was built.[135]

What is changing in Southall, then, is not just the balance of populations, but also the sense of what the space means. As groups within become even more differentiated,[136] and as different categories of identity (being Hindu, or Sikh, or Punjabi, or a refugee) obtain purchase on the imaginations of residents, the cohesion implied in a "Little India" threatens to disintegrate. But moments of cohesion or the production of a community in the face of British racism or immigration policy or cultural alienation were always ephemeral and constructed for very particular conjunctures that quickly passed. Constitutively, or thematically, then, this is not really very different from the performances of community that a site like Jackson Heights might suggest. Cutting through these spaces are alternative desires for membership, one form of which is illustrated by the responses to a survey by Southall's planning board four years ago asking whether residents wanted another grocer or something else in the area. Overwhelmingly residents noted that they wanted the (prototypically) British department store Marks and Spencers. Rather than see this moment as a desire for assimilation, we might consider how respondents may be articulating a sense of the alienation of their locality from a national space, particularly in historical circumstances where certain forms of consumption are akin to membership in a broader collectivity. Similar debates have taken place around the demands among Harlem residents for chain grocery and clothing stores and movie theaters in their community. And decreasing attention to Southall is evident in the fewer urban resources that are being allocated to the area, resulting in a visibly shabbier public space, and, necessarily, a re-ghettoization.[137]

The further development of "Little India" in Jackson Heights has, like Southall, experienced greater diversification and ever more complex renderings of identity production. Most important for the case of Jackson Heights is the changing demographics of South Asian communities in the area. Originally, largely Indian-owned shops serviced mostly Indian customers; later the market was expanded to include other South Asians, as both distributors and consumers of ethnic goods. But as more middle- and upper-middle-class Indians have moved to suburban areas outside New York City and developed new residential and commercial enclaves there, the Jackson Heights market has apparently shrunk, at least in the eyes of some merchants. Over the last decade, Edison, New Jersey, has become host to its own commercial-social enclave with all the goods and services of Jackson Heights, including higher-cost items like designer clothes and more expensive restaurants, the very goods that may be particularly well suited to the middle-class Indian populations in the tri-state area.[138] A similar development can be seen in the decreasing importance of Devon Avenue, an Indian area in Chicago, for the rapidly suburbanizing population.[139]

In the mid-1990s, many predicted that the "Little India" of Jackson Heights would disappear, just as Canal Street and Lexington Avenue faded as important commercial centers for Indians. At that point in time, the proposal to name the area "Little India" could be read as a strategy of survival in the face of such demographic shifts; the designation could have helped to develop a commercial monopoly. Certainly it has helped that Jackson Heights has broadened its constituency beyond middle-class Indians who moved out to New Jersey to include more recent Pakistani and Bangladeshi Muslim immigrants, whose economic position has not changed as quickly as that of their Indian counterparts and who still by and large live in urban areas around Jackson Heights.

But surprisingly, just as the strength of Jackson Heights's commercial markets has been somewhat on the wane due to the dispersion of ethnic consumption, the representational power of the space of Jackson Heights as a "Little India" has increased, indeed has become more centered. When Sakhi for South Asian Women marched against domestic violence, it did so in Jackson Heights.[140] Protests against discrimination against South Asians, particularly after September 11, 2001, have been held in Jackson Heights; a whole range of political organizations—mainstream and progressive—spend time talking to people on 74th Street. Aamir Khan's visit is but one instance of the sense of Jackson Heights as an important symbolic space for a range of South Asians. The development of that representation, again, lies in the particularities of the place.

It is significant that Jackson Heights was never racked by the same kinds of ethnic cleavages or religious fundamentalisms that so divided Southall. The shift from an Indian consumer constituency to an explicitly "Indo-Pak-Bangla" market occurred almost soundlessly. No Muslim or Hindu merchants express unwillingness to work in the unified interests of the Jackson Heights Merchants Association. No Pakistanis or Bangladeshis have even publicly declared opposition to officially naming the business district "Little India." A 1999 article in the Indian immigrant newspaper *India Abroad* on the marking of the Hindu holiday Diwali in Jackson Heights depicts the area as specifically resembling Indian landmarks: "Seventy-fourth Street between 37th Road and 37th Avenue . . . took on the look of New Delhi's Chandni Chowk on Oct. 17 when the Jackson Heights Merchants Association (JHMA) presented its first annual Diwali Festival."[141] It is striking that the Jackson Heights Merchants Association had not celebrated Diwali until 1999, despite an obvious investment in being seen as Indian, in cultural terms, since the early 1970s. The rise of religious identities within Indian communities may be seen to have played some role in this relatively recent shift in the Jackson Heights Merchants Association's strategies, as well as having a probable social-psychic effect on individuals who constituted the group. Indian jeweler V. N. Prakash's remarks, that "although Diwali is identified as a Hindu festival, Pakistani and Bangladeshi businesses took part,"[142] may imply that there is little threat of a serious conflict in publicly celebrating a Hindu holiday.

But nonetheless, given the high pitch of religious and national conflicts in immigrant South Asian communities in the United States as well as the membership of many shop owners in nation-based ethnic organizations, like the Federation of Indian Associations, such a seamless web of common ethnic interests in Jackson Heights is astonishing. The explanation lies in the most apparent difference between this type of immigrant community and that of Southall; as Jackson Heights coheres around economic advancement, regional, cultural, and religious differences are subsumed by a kind of aggressive capitalist democracy. Unlike the confluence of residential, cultural, and political affiliations that draw out a focus on subnational identities in Southall, the singlemindedness of a group like the Jackson Heights Merchants Association keeps at bay any possible interruptions to the smooth flow of commerce.

In a twist, the easy interactions among South Asian business people in Jackson Heights may be seen to echo colonial contentions of the democratizing effect of the marketplace. None other than J. S. Furnivall wrote in 1948: "A plural society is no ordinary business partnership. In form it is also a political society and is, or should be, organized for 'the good life,' the welfare of the people. . . . its function is solely economic, to produce goods as profitably as possible. . . . As a social institution also it has an economic aspect, and is concerned with both production and consumption, supply and demand."[143] Merchants in Jackson Heights do indeed have both economic and social functions, as do those who consume goods and perform Indianness there. The wonder of this spectacle of a "Little India" lies in the blurring of boundaries: of commercial and psychic and of public and private. And, like colonial formations, Jackson Heights is constructed through a certain diasporic sensibility; the space exists between and through being Indian and American, too. Pakistani and Indian merchants may live apart and have little reason to socialize together during the Muslim holiday of Ramadan or the Hindu holiday Diwali, but they do come together to reap the rewards of the American dream, as do those consumers who wield dollars to buy all kinds of goods in an unrestricted fashion.[144] And much as local residents might evince distaste at the particular form in which these blocks of Jackson Heights appear, and the city-state apparatus might have contradictory approaches to the space, how can one deny that this bustling Indian entrepreneurial community that serves as a meeting place for some of the most affluent immigrants in the region is a ringing testament to ideologies of American ascent?

So amazingly, this "Little India" seems to hold together even as it continues to diversify within a dynamic and stratified racial context. This is not to say that Indianness in Jackson Heights does not undergo processes of transformation; in fact, it may be the very transformations that give the space a continued life. A recent article in the New York newspaper *Newsday* cites merchants' laments on the cultural decline of the sari, which has cut into sales of traditional goods, among Indian women and their children who must be cast as potential customers.[145] But more working-class South Asians who require different clothing, second-generation Americans who seek alternative goods from their parents, and a greater number of non–South Asian Americans all now visit Jackson Heights and create different meanings for this "Indian" space. Jackson Heights is still the major site for the consumption of musical and video entertainment; on any given weekend day, South Asian Americans of a variety of backgrounds, middle and working class, with roots in India, Pakistan, Bangladesh, Guyana, and Trinidad, flood the audio and video stores to purchase the latest bhangra tapes and compact discs. And the resident population of Indians in the area seems to be growing; on the one hand, immigrants are attracted to this place for the ethnic conveniences it offers, and on the other, they are simply increasing their numbers here as they are in other

Figure 11. Jackson Heights theater (photograph by author).

places in New York. The future of Jackson Heights, then, lies in the multiple and new meanings that changes in the migrant diaspora, in the United States and all over the world, will construct.

Nodes of New Diasporas

In the 1992 film *Wild West*, British Indian actor Naveen Andrews and Indian American actress Sarita Choudhary portrayed young Southallians intent on starting a country music band. The fable ends with their trip to Nashville to make an unusual dream come true. And in May 1999, I watched a World Cup qualifying match between Peru and Chile, with a fully Latino audience, at a Jackson Heights movie theater devoted to showing Bollywood films (see fig. 11). What these cultural moments represent, in rather fantastic form, is that the physical or imaginative borders of any site of the Indian diaspora are not fixed, stable, or unitary. Even the "Little Indias" of Southall and Jackson Heights cannot fully contain the "Indian communities" for which they serve as loose metaphors. Walking around the "Little Indias" of Jackson Heights or Southall today, one can perceive boundaries, of Indianness and of community, being permeated by otherness. Though on one end of Southall, on the Broadway, one still sees mostly Indian residents and shoppers, a closer look reveals clothing and other goods that seem Indian but were made in China and young male workers in those shops recently hailing from all parts of the subcontinent. Shifting to the King Road side of town, what is first apparent are several cafes filled with Somali refugees, and large groups of Muslim men spilling out of mosques. In Menka, the first Jackson Heights beauty salon to offer a variety of "Indian" services, like henna application and the threading of unwanted hair, one hears as much Spanish spoken by the clients as any South Asian language; Latina women in nearby areas have heard of these now fashionable practices and crossed streets that were previously rigid markers of "Indian" territory, entering into another cultural space. And more and more African immigrants seem to be going in and out of jewelry stores, looking for the reasonably priced twenty-two karat gold that is the fetish of many Jackson Heights third-world cultures. Both Jackson Heights and Southall are, yet again, in a moment of transformation at the beginning of the century.

These constantly shifting spaces illuminate the fact that Indianness is never a completed process, and that simultaneously ethnic, racial, and national formation is always being constructed alongside other cultural possibilities, of multiplicity. And so it is rather unsurprising that the places associated with Indianness too refuse to stand still. Though the specific sources of change are cast differently in each case—in Southall the major issue seems to be about asylum seekers, and in Jackson Heights new South Asian populations is the most obvious—the underlying problematic seems to be diversification. And in each case, diversification is simultaneously ethnic, racial, and class-based. What makes that structural and historical conjuncture so interesting is the fact that Jackson Heights and Southall were built through such divergent processes of urban development, migration, and race and class formation. It seems perhaps that globalization, which might be seen as the backdrop for transformations in each place, has created a simultaneity across differential Indian diasporic space and time.

Nonetheless, this chapter has shown how it is important to consider the ways that New York and London have offered Southall and Jackson Heights alternative forms of diasporic cultural possibilities, not only because they have been different kinds of cities, but also because they have been differently embedded in the time-space of the Indian diaspora. Those distinctions have enlivened not only specific histories of movement but different processes of becoming Indian. Agency is a complicated question here, as Punjabi Indians first claimed Southall as theirs, and Sam and Raj made good on their dreams in Jackson Heights, while all migrants were caught up in the trends of the postwar, postcolonial world. Functioning as "Little Indias," Southall and Jackson Heights have served as important if hastily assembled representations of the nation abroad, for non-Indians and Indians alike. These places are invested with a range of meanings that converge on this terminology and that may seem flattening or reductive of complexity. For those people looking for a place for Indianness, I have suggested in this chapter, here are the localities of Jackson Heights and Southall. But nothing is solely produced at the local level: such sites always have translocal significance and meaning.

I would propose that these Little Indias affirm *and* challenge other nations. An intense attachment to locality in Southall militated against a particular conception of Englishness, precisely because it actually remade the practice of inhabiting a British urban place in race and class terms. Jackson Heights affirmed America through its self-inclusion in stories of entrepreneurial success and the community of marketplace, while at the very same time it reinstated Indianness as a primary source of identification. In this way, it produced a transnational sensibility of what it might mean to be American, a sensibility that has become increasingly common among post-1965 migrant-minority populations within cosmopolitan cities like New York. Both "Little Indias" might be multiply mobilized, to explain the question of what role postcolonial migration may play in the more general and complicated representation of race and ethnicity in postwar histories of the United States and Britain, to ponder the limits of any space of community, and to realize a fantasy of urban cosmopolitanism. In other words, the places of Jackson Heights and Southall do some of the cultural and theoretical work of the space of diaspora itself.

THREE

AFFILIATIONS AND ASCENDANCY

OF DIASPORIC LITERATURE

I N THE LAST several years in the United States and Britain, there has been an explosion of interest in the Indian diaspora and in things Indian. While we may observe this trend in cinema, fashion, and music, Indianness is particularly apparent in the field of literature. Many Indian authors who have lived in Britain and the United States have become household names since at least the early 1980s. Novels by Indians, both immigrants in the first world and those in the subcontinent, have won a range of international literary prizes, not the least of which is the 2001 Nobel Prize for Literature to Indo-Trinidadian V. S. Naipaul. And recognition of a different kind can be seen in the appearance of Indian Canadian Rohinton Mistry's novel *A Fine Balance* in Oprah's Book Club.[1] Certainly the growing visibility of Indian literary work has particular emphasis and energy in the individual contexts of the United States, Britain, Canada, or the Caribbean, but the simultaneity of the national developments, the gestures to elsewhere (India and other places) in the writings themselves, and the intertextuality among the authorship signals a diasporic type of production.

In this chapter we turn to literatures that provide comparative narrative possibilities for diasporic Indianness. The readership, which receives, claims, and is claimed by literature, offers a number of complexities to the framing of this kind of cultural production. A lead editorial in a 2000 issue of *India Currents*, a magazine from San Jose, California, discussed the plethora of recent fiction by both Indians abroad and back home and explored in particular the disjuncture between different community members' expectations of texts and what those texts can deliver. With the echoes of a classic generational split, editor Arvind Kumar remarked: "I can't but feel for my father who valiantly waded through the grinding poverty and the bleak outlook in Rohinton Mistry's *A Fine Balance*. . . . None of it was new to him. . . . Still, he could not see the India he knows and loves in that book, no matter its considerable merits."[2] Embedded in these comments, and in their placement in an immigrant publication, were important questions about knowledge, nation, and community. When Kumar "feels" for his father, he also asks his own readers to sympathize with a generational and possibly national location that may be different from their own. In the space between recognition ("none of it was new") and subjective desire ("the India he knows and loves") is an Indianness that may not be fully revealed in the current popularity that Indian diasporic writers have been recently enjoying.

A rather different production of India can be found in the formulations of much celebrated author Salman Rushdie in an introduction to a 1997 special issue of the *New Yorker* devoted to what then seemed a special efflorescence of Indian writing: "Indians—and following the partition of the subcontinent almost fifty years ago, one should also say Pakistanis—have long been migrants, seeking their fortunes in Africa, Australia, Britain, the Caribbean, and America, and this diaspora has produced many writers who lay claim to an excess of roots."[3] Even as he was writing an introductory essay to a collection of nationally derived Indian fiction, Rushdie implicitly celebrated a range of affiliations among Indian migrants all over the world. His own signature interests in hybridity informed a view of diaspora writers as multiply shaped, laying "claim to an excess of roots."

At first glance, Kumar's discussion in the more immigrant-centered, middlebrow *India Currents* may seem to explore the notion of a nation standing still, while in Rushdie's comments for the highbrow audience of the *New Yorker* we see a familiar evocation of Indian nationals on the move.[4] Such an opposition has a structural analogy, perhaps, in the polarized possibilities of diaspora, of rest and movement. But a closer look at the two enunciatory moments could reveal less familiar associations: of the older (and alienated) father with a represented India as a relatively unstable signifier (between that which is familiar and that which is known and loved); and of the cosmopolitan Rushdie with a quite specified nation or set of nations (India and also Pakistan) from which migrants have scattered. Ironically, there may be more meanings, more of a sense of constructedness for India, in the discomfort of Kumar's father than in Rushdie's celebration of multiplicity. Desire for a nation might be a realm of active identity-production, a mode of living in the world of transition, while hybridity may leave its component (and national) parts intact.

Both extended quotes usher us, then, into a vexed field of questioning: what does it mean to belong, to a nation, to a community, to a canon, and what languages are available to express that? How and where do Indians abroad see themselves, and what relationship to the world is embedded therein? In attempting to answer these questions, this chapter returns to a basic preoccupation of *India Abroad*: the construction and production of Indianness in diaspora, with a more sustained focus perhaps on the technologies of the imagination. Employing the concept of the imagination here is not to suggest that something unreal is being created in Indian diasporic writings, but serves to highlight the process of working out questions of recognition, self-construction, identification, and desires for collectivity. Literature translates the self and group for a wider public, for that which may be cast as other.[5] The navigation, I suggest, is of two psychic structures for the construction of subjectivity, of the individual and the group.[6]

If a diasporic imagination effectively breaks down the separateness of the spheres of individual and collective consciousness, then it may also fail to respect the boundaries between prototypical fictions of the self and the group: the autobiography and the novel. For Indians who live abroad, the self created in an autobiography is inextricably linked to the possibilities and difficulties of the national *collectivity* of India. And the communities and relationships of the novels of diasporic Indianness illuminate, necessarily, deeply felt ideas about *individual* belonging in nations. The genres may create different kinds of formational narratives, wherein the novel presents temporary closure to conflict, while the autobiography writes the self as primary symbol, but the focus of this chapter is how diasporic time and space may allow us to see some blurring of those lines, particularly as they have been traditionally cast. And the chapter ends with letters, perhaps the most obvious example of individuals actively connecting to one another as individuals, yet evidencing here some of the most profound longings for grouphood, or community, that are at the heart of diaspora.

The Indianness constructed in the space of the diasporic imagination creates a repertoire of images and narrative negotiations that cannot be easily categorized as part of the familiar camps of "immigrant" or "postcolonial" literature. To a large extent, postcolonial critics have structured their work around British writers' contemplations of colonial India and Indian writers' relationships with and imagination of the homeland. They have elaborated the more superstructural aspects of the colonial project and colonialism's effects more generally by examining how notions of India have influenced the literary works of writers like E. M. Forster, Rudyard Kipling, Joseph Conrad, V. S. Naipaul, and Salman Rushdie.[7] Though postcolonial scholars have theorized the trope of displacement, the actual experiences of migration have largely been left to another set of critics, particularly those in fields like Asian American literature that consider "immigrant writing,"[8] and that have focused on more recent writers like Bharati Mukherjee.[9] Postcolonial literature and Asian American studies have become marked by some polarities organized by "the international" and "the national," including cosmopolitan versus immigrant, diaspora versus national community, and homeland affinity versus state citizenship. An emphasis on international cultural formations has occluded questions of new nationalities (American and British), while the focus on immigration and national integration downplays the persistently global character of Indian migrant communities.

To read the diasporic literature of this chapter, marked by movements and pauses, is to map diasporic subject-formation (individual and collective). And therefore these writings constitute an alternative space to that of "immigrant" and "postcolonial" production. Indianness is created in the texts surveyed here through the shared territory of postcolonial and migrant experience, and is engaged with the building of complex and varied forms of nationalisms. Writing and reading across nations is what might be understood as the transnational strategies of these works. The orthographic similarities of "transnational" to "translational" can only further emphasize that there are agents and audiences for all this textual and cultural production. Desires to represent an individual or group and create the possibility of identification are central to the logic of diasporic literature, as perhaps these elements are to all forms of literature.

In this mode of diaspora, as in that of history or place, there is a dialectic between, on the one hand, how Indianness is experienced and created by those subjects constituted as Indian across time and space, and, on the other, how such an Indianness is received by a world perceived to be outside that. Indianness and India itself lie as much in this basic dialectic as much as in any nation-state. And this fact seems to be recognized in a variety of quarters. Even when their meanings are contested, as was the case with *The Satanic Verses* by Salman Rushdie, novels and autobiographies and their authors have been claimed as part of a community and as sharing an ethnicity. Sometimes, I would suggest, even the content of the books is less important than the simple fact that they have been written by Indians; they can be appropriated without being read. There has been an increasing attention to the role of Indian American and Indian British texts in migrant cultures, as the growing and mature referent populations strive for greater representation within the social rubrics of the lands of settlement. Immigrant newspapers like *India Abroad* now feature regular sections—both broadly inclusive and quite current—on books by migrants, and the *India Currents* discussion that opened this chapter is another indication of the perceived importance of the work of Indian writers.

This chapter offers kaleidoscopic moments of an imagination taking shape in diasporic literature, wherein nations are being crossed and lived within, and through which a complex and contradictory Indianness is broken down and built up again. In the constructions of selves and groups in various fictions—novels, autobiographies, and letters—the working out of the complexities of migration occurs in diasporic time and space, where the local is always and already transcended and where the past must be invoked to support the present. Again, it must be reiterated that all the texts undermine simple dichotomies of the symbolic and the real, precisely because they do their work in the space of diaspora. Most of the texts discussed here, with the possible exception of Amitav Ghosh's *Shadow Lines*, are those that have not received high literary praise, nor have they garnered much attention in the literary criticism of Asian American or postcolonial studies. They are not in this sense *canonical*, in the way Salman Rushdie's or V. S. Naipaul's works have become. Because these texts allow us to turn the lens slightly, to work outside of familiarly received scripts of the postcolonial or migrant, they can give us another story of diaspora, to revisit questions of periodization for postcolonial migrancy, and to look anew at Indian national independence, or post-1965 U.S. immigration law for different concerns. The possibilities for India infuse the realities of India, America, and England. The material of this chapter, constructed as a group of readings, can hopefully illuminate diasporic collectivities that begin to break down singular notions of nation, community, and identity.

And yet, this alternative space, like any other, is nonetheless marked by polarities of similarity and otherness. Thus many of the texts examined in this chapter, and their themes of affiliation, ascent, dislocation, and exile, compulsively return to colonial writer Rudyard Kipling and that notorious line: "Oh, East is East, and West is West, and never the twain shall meet."[10] I will argue, though, that this sense of incommensurability, that what is Indian and Western (British and American) cannot be compared, is successfully challenged in diasporic literature, through its very fixation on bringing imaginative national maps into a kind of dialogue, even into conflict. This remains true despite the fact that contact with and imaging of otherness seem fundamental to any enunciation, of identity, of self, or of a collectivity.[11] Perhaps the constitutive pressures of Kipling, which initiate the possibility of the borders of East and West being crossed by its very denial, is the constitutive tension of diaspora itself. And the simultaneously impossible and possible articulation of what it means to be equal subjects in a globalized, multinational set of arrangements serves also as a statement of the dilemmas of postwar and postcolonial citizenship that are ignited by the process of migration.

Loving India, Loving America

Though the preceding chapters have opened with the mapping of postcolonialism through British space, we begin here with travel to America to contemplate the possibilities of what it could mean to be Indian vis-à-vis other languages for identity and belonging. And becoming a national was indeed a complex process for those Indians who had gone to the United

States. The absence of a colonial relationship between America and India has meant that the United States did not invite the forms of vilification that colonial England had in India. This was true despite consciousness of the mistreatment of immigrants and political activists and the harshness of immigration laws. Indians could project a whole set of desires onto the nation of the United States that they simply would not and could not do with colonizing Britain, though, as we will see, they did not have the same ability to imagine the map of America. Ideologies of America, including democracy, individual rights, and freedom and the accompanying stories (and realities) of a society less hierarchical and thus more permitting of class mobility, gave new ideas of nationality, of Americanness *and* Indianness, a flexibility unmatched by British national discourses.

Krishnalal Shridharani's *My India, My America* is a text that relies on travel through America as a strategy to work out the tensions of being from another, and emergent, nation. Written in 1941, six years before Indian independence, it serves as a harbinger of multiple national investments of a later generation of Indian immigrants to America. Arriving from Gujarat in 1934, Shridharani was a playwright and writer of children's books who was also heavily involved in the independence movement, at one point joining Mohandas Gandhi on his famous 1930 March to the Sea and being imprisoned for the protest.[12] Shridharani's nationalist sentiments influenced his perceptions of life in the United States, where he came for further study at Columbia University's School of Journalism. But arriving at the moment he did, aboard a ship to Ellis Island where his first sight of the United States was the Statue of Liberty, Shridharani inclined toward acceptance and absorption of U.S. national sentiments. A keen and at times ironic observer of American life, Shridharani documented the various intersections of Indian and U.S. experiences.

The textuality of *My India, My America* achieves a set of crossings itself. Part travel account, part political tract, and part autobiography, the book cannot be easily categorized. If a single agenda of the book can be named, however heuristically, it might be the construction of a new diasporic Indian self. Given that self-construction occurs in America, it is most fitting that Shridharani should write some kind of autobiography. The discovery of the autobiographical genre has certainly been associated with the building of the United States, and the narrative itself in the United States with betterment, ascent, and conversion.[13] *My India, My America* plainly employs those tropes, concerned as it is with America as ideal. But it does more than that, too. Shridharani's writing, structured by travel and by two nations, stimulates us to think beyond the familiar plots and conceive of an Indian national self and Indian nationality through diasporic space and time that take "America" as caught in a moment of transition, just as other nations are. It therefore becomes possible to formulate what relations between and among nations could be.

Most immediately striking in *My India, My America* is Shridharani's ability to hold in a tense balance strong Indian nationalist sentiments, the current language of internationalism, and a persisting admiration and even awe for the United States. In a representative and imaginary dialogue between an Indian and an American on the subject of Indian independence from Britain, Shridharani demonstrates this remarkable disposition:

AMERICAN: But can't you see that the trend is toward a larger and larger international order? By proposing a splitting up of the British Empire, aren't you also upholding the old and ruinous idea of nationalism as opposed to internationalism?

INDIAN: Our nationalism is only a stepping stone to internationalism. The very term *inter*nationalism presupposes nationalism. Nationalism is something like the measles; the sooner we get over it, the better.[14]

This exchange illustrates the perceived inability of the average American to understand the depth of India's desire for national independence and also the complexity of existing nationalisms; deeply embedded in this Indian's (presumably Shridharani's) ideology is a long-term plan for a version of regionalism and ultimately a sense that the new nation-state of India should exist in a broader world order. In this, Shridharani sounds very much like other political critics who at times of transition have contemplated the role of their nation in global frameworks. The geopolitical program echoes American intellectual Randolph Bourne's arguments in the midst of the First World War, those that have become canonical for transnational American studies. Bourne wrote that "the contribution of America will be an intellectual internationalism which goes far beyond the mere exchange of scientific ideas and discoveries."[15] Shridharani turns Bourne's arguments inside out, making India's political and cultural developments occupy center-stage in the ideal of internationalism articulated during the Second World War.

In searching for conceptual models for that new *international* nation-state, Shridharani finds himself in the United States not by complete coincidence. Indeed, he compares Britain most unfavorably with the ideal of America; describing the apparent contempt toward American education among British colonial officials in India as one of a fear for "dangerous ideas," Shridharani explains his own move to the United States as an example of extraordinary foresight: "My speculations were based on the idea that the United States was gradually but surely becoming the center of western civilization. . . . Not only will the United States emerge from the present conflict as the strongest nation in the world, but it will . . . stand out as the bulwark of western culture, the 'arsenal of democracy.' New York has now become in the field of international education what Paris, Rome, London and Berlin have been" (71). America is appealing to Shridharani precisely because it has transnational possibilities and importance. Shridharani sees ethnic diversity as further cause to celebrate America; in this he even finds important comparative possibilities: "India, like the United States, has always been a melting pot of creeds, colors, races and religions. So Indian sociologists can learn more in America than anywhere else in the world" (72–73). Interpreting the United States in this fashion, through a similarly multicultural national lens of India, becomes the means to critique the English nation, cast as more homogeneous.

Shridharani views the United States as having a less class-divided society than Britain and the absence of birth-derived hierarchies as a real source of progress and promise for the nation. Both caste-conscious England and India serve as negative points of contrast to the perceived social freedom that exists in the United States: "If the Hindu goes to Oxford or Cambridge, his notions of a caste system are apt to be bolstered up by the more sinewy, and sinister, British caste system. Snubbed by British society, such a student is almost sure to seek a strange psychological compensation in constantly behaving like even more of a snob among his own people back home. Thus he is made unfit for the great tasks of building a new nation" (74). Populism informs Shridharani's nation-building project, and he finds a convenient set of practices and ideologies in the United States to aid such work. He praises at length the practice of "working one's way through college" (73), and slips into American mythologies of success through hard work when he claims that: "the practice of supporting oneself . . . teaches the Hindu the dignity of labor, a concept which has helped make America great" (74). In an autobiographical convention, Shridharani sees the construction of the autonomous and independent self as linked to the creation of a nation.

Yet even in discussions about the greater degree of class mobility in the United States compared to Britain, and the explicit and implicit portrayals of the differences between Indians' experiences in Britain and the United States, Shridharani is gently critical of the United States. In enumerating the reasons for the greater migration of Indian students to Britain than the United States, he cites the United States's higher standard of living, costliness, and distance from India but ends ironically: "In the third place, there are those severe and even unfriendly immigration laws" (69). During his travels across the country, Shridharani discovers and reports laughable ignorance about India and Indian people and undertakes in his book to educate an uninformed public about the humanity and complexity of other parts of the world. If Britain is seen as an unmalleable entity, the

United States is taken to be a nation with which one can engage and presumably change. In other words, America can be situated on the same plane as a new India.

The extent to which Shridharani considers American national ideologies to be flexible is evidenced in the title of chapter 4: "Becoming Americanized." American political and social analysts had been quite concerned with the ways in which new arrivals, particularly immigrants from eastern and southern Europe, became integrated into the national formation, and acquired values deemed to be "American."[16] The process of "Americanization" for these critics had assumed cultural, political, and economic trappings, and immigrants' success in one sphere or the other contributed to buttress notions of the melting pot.

In the time when Shridharani was writing, Americanization was largely a white ethnic affair. The appropriation of the term "Americanization" and allusion to the process and possibility of national integration by an Indian in the United States is interesting here. Shridharani's "doing the country," as he subtitles the first section of the chapter, presumes an ability to traverse the national landscape with an ease untempered by racialization. Race does not impede the author's agency to become Americanized, either here or at any moment in the text, very much in contrast to the assertive disarticulation between race and nation in the texts that we will consider about Indian experiences in England. For Shridharani, two forms of knowledge—of the United States and of India—pave the road to a form of nationalization. He engages and dispels the persistent stereotypes of Indians; he explains the practice of betel nut chewing, why cows are sacred in Hinduism, and the tendency of some castes to maintain long hair. And in this way, Shridharani broaches the subject of ethnicity, which actually emerged as a concept in the 1940s; he describes the origins, customs, and ways of life of a people, for purposes of inclusion into, or at least comparison with, the national whole.[17]

Shridharani goes on to cover a wide range of topics in *My India, My America* that include the form and substance of Indian life, the need for national independence, and profiles of Indian leaders like Gandhi, Jawaharlal Nehru, Abdul Gaffar Khan, and Rabindranath Tagore. It is hard to ignore the gender composition of Shridharani's list of movers and shakers, and the masculinized nature of his mobility in the service of grand nations. The construction of multinations, indeed, is linked to a powerful new subject, the author himself, as an Indian in the world. Shridharani's juxtaposition of India and America, evidenced in the title of the book as well as through the substance of the text, leads almost inevitably to the moment where the two nations, one not yet formed and the other soon to emerge unquestionably as the world's most powerful country, become for Shridharani counterparts in the construction of his own self, in the struggle for Indian national independence, and in the path of world history; as he says on the last page of the epilogue: "The twain have met" (607). Directly referring to the quintessentially colonial Kipling, as well as to a whole tradition of British perceptions of India, Shridharani concludes with an assertion of partnership and affinity between India and the United States, just as his personal journey has revealed a place and people willing to accept otherness in their midst: "The United States is the apex of western civilization. India and China are still the two pillars of the East. Thus any story of India and America has to be a fable of East and West. There is so much in common between the two—there is a real union which springs from the same spirit. What differences there are complement each other" (602).

Because England would not and did not acknowledge India to be an equal independent partner at this historical moment, Shridharani proposes the United States as a model for the new Indian nation. He reworks Kipling's impossibility within a new, and freer, landscape of America, in which one can write a different kind of international history. Largely because of the lack of a historical relation colored by British colonialism, a new set of national connections between India and the United States can develop. In the promise of America, Shridharani can see the hopes of India: "I came to the United States in the summer of 1934. Since then almost eight years have gone by. . . . I have tried to understand America's central drives and to dream the American dream. Gradually I have come to admire the texture of the American character . . . thoroughly enough to believe that the hope of the world really lies in this country. . . . And yet my American experience has underlined my strong belief that much of the hope of the future also lies in the renascent India" (602).

These experiences allow Shridharani to live even his own identities and affiliations in less singular ways; both the title of the book and his final comment—"But I am twice-born now!" (607)—are an interesting contrast, in 1941, to the inability of much later Indian immigrants to Britain to see themselves as part of England. Amazingly, Shridharani can construct the Indian self as American, too. Shridharani's dual nationalisms set the scene for the interpretation of Indian experiences in the United States, for the perceived contrast between American cultural expansiveness and British racial exclusivity and ultimately for the complex forms of nationality that Indians would develop abroad in many places.

Man from India, Citizen of America

Dalip Singh Saund's 1961 text *Congressman from India* provides a representational link between the small migrations of Indians to the United States in the early twentieth century for agricultural labor and schooling and the later, huge influx of Indians after 1965. Saund's book, like Shridharani's, occupies no one genre space fully: it is simultaneously an auto-biography and a political tract. As a congressional representative up for reelection every two years, he is keenly aware of the need to disseminate a constructed self to his constituencies. That self, though, in the context of the late 1950s, cannot be built entirely separately from the nation with which it is always associated; Indian American Saund, in the public eye, is never *not* Indian, in spite of the fact that he can be American. To address this complex social reality, Saund creates an Americanized fiction of India in the guise of his own autobiography. Through the course of the text, and through the trajectory of his life, Saund learns to become American by becoming an Indian citizen-subject, and becomes Indian by becoming an American politician. Any apparent contradictions in this flow are man-aged by powerful ideologies of multinationalism that attend assimilation and immigration. For this imaginative moment, the postcolonial can be articulated through diasporic sentiment, and India is no longer only about homeland, but always and already abroad.

Immigrating to the United States in 1920 from the Punjab region in India, Saund had already attended university and intended to study new methods of canning food on the graduate level. Like earlier Indian mi-grants of the 1900s, Saund was agriculturally oriented; yet both his prior education in India as well as the time of his migration, 1920, placed him outside that class of laborers.[18] Saund's educational achievements, his pro-fessional success, and finally his stunning public achievement of being the first Asian American congressman in the United States install him in a historical trajectory of Indian Americans in ways that are yet to be for-mally realized.[19] While certainly not necessarily representative of Indian community life, Saund's life and reflections, in their own way, illuminate the evolving complexity of the experiences of Indians in the United States.

At the beginning of *Congressman from India*, Saund sets out his frames of reference, in the two nations of India and the United States: "My guide-posts were two of the most beloved men in history, Abraham Lincoln and Mahatma Gandhi."[20] Locating himself within a broad set of political traditions, Saund creates a narrative that moves from his childhood in India through his increasing achievements in the United States to, finally, a trip back to India as a U.S. congressman. In several important ways, *Congressman from India* tells a story of ascent and, to some degree, assim-ilation, but the terms in which the climb takes place, American as they might seem, are also framed by origin from and continued affiliation to India. Even the very title of the book reminds us of this orientation.

The first chapter of the book, entitled "Beginnings in India," describes in painstaking detail the kind of circumstances in which Saund lived be-fore coming to the United States and forms an anchor of the subjectivity he builds through the text. Born and brought up in a village, Saund presents himself as a young man deeply invested in education, yet loyal to family and culture. He explains to unfamiliar American readers the folkways of his people, such as religious ceremonies, foods, and community rituals, and suggests how formative of his own aspirations this world was. Saund's portrayal of India also contains a critique of British colonialism. Much like Shridharani did in *My India, My America*, Saund finds it necessary to rehearse the historical background of Indian resistance to the British, their efforts for national independence, and the injustices of the colonial administration. Saund too relates Gandhi's 1930 Salt March as a formative event for Indian anticolonialism. Not only is the Salt March an archetypal moment of simple resistance to injustice, this event compares well to American anti-British actions such as the Boston Tea Party. Saund makes such anticolonial analogues explicit when he comments, "The British rulers of my country had thought it highly important that English history be thoroughly taught the youth of India, but they did not think it important to pay any great attention to the American Revolution—a revolution which, in my opinion, has done more to bring joy and dignity into the lives of men than anything that has happened before or since in recorded history" (29). Struggles against British colonialism in this construction can make one Indian and American. Such is the underlying sentiment in Saund's resentment at having received a biased education from the British and the rational contrast he intimates with an assertion of the United States as a model of democracy. Somewhat prototypically, Saund's prospects for membership in America are authorized by having origins, and in this chapter he utilizes the ideals of Indian village society to prepare him for a full life as a citizen of the United States.

Interestingly, even Saund's depiction of his voyage to the United States in 1920 includes a reference to a stopover in England that then becomes an occasion to further reflect on a comparison between western countries. At the time of publication of Saund's book, this was of course an ensuing preoccupation for future Indian migrants, who in the early 1960s were facing the tightening of British immigration regulations and the prospect of liberalization of United States laws on entry. Saund's choice of America over England as a place for education and settlement, and as an ideological model, was echoed by many who would come to the United States. He recalls seeing historical sites in London: "I noticed how reverently the British people passed by the tombs of Lord Nelson in Saint Paul's Cathedral and the Duke of Wellington in Westminster Abbey, those two great builders of the British Empire. While I could respect these men for themselves, their achievements in building the Empire did not have much appeal for me. I was not interested in empire builders. Abraham Lincoln's statue, however, evoked in me quite a different response" (34). For Saund, Britain and the United States evoke different histories of colonialism on the one hand and more proletarian and antislavery sentiments on the other. They also embody different models for a political state. Britain represented empire in the past and in the present, while the United States promised a different form of nationality, which Saund had assumed in the United States and could also graft onto India. Saund's act of passing through the story of empire on his way to myths of America compressed time and space, so that Lincoln could be processed for his own, present, and new subjectivity.

Once in the United States, Saund goes to California, like many Indian farmers and students before him. Indeed, Saund finds a number of Indians in the Bay Area, a Sikh temple, and a set of institutions including the Hindustan Association of America. Promptly enrolling in the University of California at Berkeley, Saund becomes a speaker for various events associated with the struggle for India's national independence. As he notes: "All of us were ardent Nationalists and we never passed up an opportunity to expound on India's rights to self-government" (38).

Saund's specifically Indian identifications did not prevent him from expressing at various points an understanding of himself as an Asian.[21] While he does not describe immigration restrictions in detail, nor his ability to get around them, he does invoke a broader history of discrimination against Asians on the West Coast and includes his experiences under that rubric. Contemplating a speech he made that advocated greater friendship and communication between Americans and Indians, Saund observes in retrospect: "But such acceptance was very difficult to obtain in the atmosphere of California in those days, particularly for students from Asia. Prejudice against Asiatic people in California was very intense in the early twenties and I felt keen discrimination in many ways. Outside of the university atmosphere it was made quite evident that people from Asia— Japanese, Chinese, and Hindus—were not wanted" (40–41).

Saund's position as an Indian student, and the class status that it implied, did not therefore overcome the longer history of anti-Asian nativist sentiments, particularly in California and the Pacific Northwest. He goes on to describe the Alien Land Act, in which those not eligible for United States citizenship were unable to legally hold land in California. But Saund is also eager to recover America. After these more critical points, he ever so quickly retorts, "Despite the prejudice and discrimination that I saw, there were many other American practices that made a more favorable impression on me" (41).

Though entering Berkeley's Department of Agriculture with the intention to go back to India and work in food preservation, Saund switched to the field of mathematics and eventually earned a doctorate. It was in this period that Saund made the decision to stay in the United States, not because of professional opportunities, but out of admiration for American political philosophies. Unlike other immigrant narratives in which economic possibility is cast as the major impetus for settlement and where patriotism is a by-product,[22] here a distinctive Americanism is a prior logic for Saund's represented desires. This political sympathy came despite the fact that in 1924 he was still denied citizenship: "America exemplified for me the highest form of democracy. . . . Even though life for me did not seem very easy, it had become impossible to think of a life separated from the United States. I was aware of the considerable prejudice against the people of Asia in California and knew that few opportunities existed for me or people of my nationality in the state at that time. I was not a citizen and could not become one. The only way Indians in California could make a living at that time was to join with others who had settled in various parts of the state as farmers" (44–45). Presumably the experience of eventually becoming a citizen and later a public figure contributed to his tolerance of past injustice. And Saund's strategy, to become a farmer with the aid of other established Indian farmers in Imperial Valley, is a familiar one in the annals of Asian American history.[23]

Becoming American for Saund was a process at once political, intellectual, and personal. It was also a psychic identification, for his life possibilities were fused together with the United States ("it had become impossible to think of a life separated"). Yet never does Saund fully assume the conventional language of assimilation marked by the loss of a country upon the assumption of a new one. In some very important ways he remains the congressman *from India*. His thirty-eight-year marriage to an American woman is still described in terms of two cultures coming together, rather than as two melting into one. Saund's contemplation of this partnership is in fact not unlike his belief in the comparative possibilities between India and the United States. Saund's wife, Marian (Kosa), is everywhere present in the text, as is her racial-national otherness. And, in fact, in the preface to *Congressman from India*, Saund says of his marriage: "Kipling said 'East is East and West is West and never the twain shall meet.' Clearly he was wrong, for a Saund from the East met a Kosa from the West" (v).

Turning to and explicitly contradicting Kipling, Indians in the United States like Saund and Shridharani evinced a forthright and also masculinized disbelief in the British colonial assertion of the incommensurability of cultures. In these occasions of an Indian diasporic imaginary, then, America functioned as a very different kind of symbol of the West; it could for migrants represent the possibility of cultures and nations meeting even as it exerted tremendous national-ideological power over its citizens and residents. Much as America was revered, however, these Indians never lost their own sense of Indian national-cultural subjectivity. And it is precisely because they were no longer colonial subjects, neither infantilized nor emasculated, that these Indians could now be interpellated by myths of new nations. Indeed, there was something useful about being national in an emergent multinational multiculture.

Part of Saund's described sense of difference took the form of class position. As a farmer, Saund addressed a particular constituency even when he became a county judge and later a U.S. congressman. Relating stories of difficulty among small farmers allowed Saund to engage his differences in ways that follow well in the traditions of U.S. politics, most notably like those of his hero Abraham Lincoln. In the 1956 congressional election, Saund faced an opponent for the Democratic nomination who contested his candidacy on the grounds that the election fell before he would complete the requisite seven years of citizenship, though that milestone would pass before he would take office. This opponent and later the Republican candidate also quoted passages from Saund's earlier book, *My Mother, India*. Of these strategies, Saund writes: "Every effort was made to make it appear that I was an Indian, not an American. In newspaper ads I was not called D. S. Saund, but Dalip Singh in big letters and Saund in small letters. This sort of practice was widespread, but apparently it did not hurt my candidacy either in the primary or general election" (101–2). But he spends much more time describing the fame and fortune of his opponent in the general election, Jacqueline Cochram Odlum, a celebrated aviator, wife of a multimillionaire, and friend of President Dwight Eisenhower. By emphasizing these aspects of his opponent's résumé, Saund seems to be both questioning Odlum's political legitimacy and dramatizing the uphill struggle of running against her extraordinary financial resources. He countered by rallying friends and family from throughout the district to help him campaign. He also strongly advocated for farm subsidies, an issue of considerable importance in the rural counties. Overall he attempted to project a folksy image, portraying himself as a local and as a symbol of the American dream; at one campaign stop he pointed out, "You have been listening to the insidious propaganda of the Communists that there is prejudice and discrimination in the United States against your people. Look, here I am. I am a living example of American democracy in action" (108). Saund's victory must have seemed an extraordinary testament to the idea that anyone can make it in America, even those who are from other nations. And this victory also illustrated a more complicated development: that Saund could be seen as more American precisely because he was Indian.

Saund's self-symbolization of the American dream only intensified at a time when the United States faced increased criticism for intense segregation and discrimination, as well as for aggressive foreign policies. Though Saund periodically asserts his commitment to civil rights and racial equality in *Congressman from India*, he does so quite briefly; the turbulent atmosphere of the period does not shape the narrative itself. And the fact that his commentary on the world outside the United States occurs often through a reaffirmation of anti-Communism shows that his political sensibilities are much less shaped by India's nonalignment than they are by the United States' Cold War ideologies. It is therefore not surprising that the House Foreign Affairs Committee supported his trip to India and other Asian countries to report on the "mutual-security program." Saund approached this trip with a variety of interests in mind. One intention was as he says, to "present [himself] as a living example of American democracy in practice" (152). But he also sought to rewrite popular perceptions of Asians, into a (highly Americanized) discourse to which he was attached: "In preparing for my trip I was convinced that in the minds of the people of India and the Far East, the Middle East and Africa there was no doubt that, given the choice, they would inevitably choose democracy and freedom. . . . The blaze started in 1776 in the United States of America. . . . There is no need for the people of the United States . . . to instruct Asians in the meaning and value of democracy. . . . But there is one burning question uppermost in their minds: *Are the American people ready and willing to accept them as their equals in every respect?*" (154; italics added).

While Saund here invokes comparisons between core beliefs of Asians and Americans, he also intimates that behind the West's distrust of the East is a sort of political paternalism, and so he is led to ask provocatively about American prejudices. His positive perceptions of Japan, Taiwan, Vietnam, Indonesia, Singapore, and the Philippines function as replies to the questions he has posed before departure. Saund's own professional identity very much exists on these terms, and both his travel to other Asian countries and his guarded replies and dispassionate response to questions about forced integration at Little Rock's Central High School[24] suggest a choice of Indianness and to some extent Asianness over other coalitional possibilities. Though he may be racialized in national-regional terms, he maintains a studied emotional distance from the turbulent issues of the time concerning the civil rights of African Americans. Saund's identifications are elsewhere. It is possible that to become American for Saund is, on at least some level, also to become symbolically white, most especially given the polarized options that would have been presented to a brown-skinned, non–East Asian, middle-class, upwardly ascendant male at this time.

That Saund's international physical journey (and narrative) leads back to India is illustrative of the structuring premises of the life of this Indian American, deeply committed to U.S. capitalism and its democratic institutions, yet always marked by the experience of migration and the development of the young nation-state of India. Such sustained and framing attention to India makes class ascendancy and becoming a new American a less linear process, despite the easy consumption of what reporters and a camera crew from CBS television record when Saund returns to his village home. Saund had certainly become a representative of the United States; he was self-consciously American: "The people of India and the Asiatic world knew the story of my election to the United States Congress in 1956 and were proud of the fact that a man born in India had been elected to that high office" (183). Yet his desire to go back to India and his confidence that he could properly portray the guiding philosophies of Indian political society, and more generally Asian peoples as well, signified much deeper connections to India than any simple model of contemporary Americanization can reveal. Though Saund's identity as a congressman is deeply defining, so too does his origin "from India" play a fundamental role in both how he seems to have been consumed at that historical moment and how he constructs himself for posterity in this narrative.

In 1960, Saund is as interested in defining America's role in the world as in laying out a life story; the links between the two are enlivened by his trip to India and the rest of Asia, and through the guiding principle of internationalism. To some extent, Saund reestablishes the terms on which the United States would have a role in the world; like Shridharani in 1941, Saund speaks in his own period to a set of historical circumstances that are articulated through concepts of ethnic and racial diversity. His experiences as an Indian immigrant who becomes a U.S. citizen and then a member of Congress advance the United States as flexible and absorbent in a postwar period in which there was much restructuring of the domestic and international policies of nations all over the world. Turning again to one advocate of transnationalism, Randolph Bourne wrote earlier that such a political program "will be an intellectual sympathy which is not satisfied until it has got at the heart of the different cultural expressions, and felt as they felt."[25] In some sense, the combined geopolitical and cultural power of American transnationalism emerged through anticolonial and inclusionary ideologies. This was also the special achievement of U.S. nationalism.

With the demise of Indian colonialism, the United States was well poised to assume a new role in the region, and this did not escape Saund: "The era of colonialism has come to an end. Its death knell was sounded on the fifteenth day of August 1947. . . . Since that time more than six hundred million people on the continent of Asia alone have achieved political freedom. These people are now struggling to build their new societies. The leaders of these revolutions were inspired by the same ideals that burned so fiercely in the hearts of the fathers of our own great republic" (184–85). Saund links the future of Asia (and particularly India) with the past and present ideals of the United States; he cites the Declaration of Independence and the Bill of Rights as integral to the construction of United States foreign policy in Asia, and to the development of these countries. Steeped in the language of anti-Communism, Saund makes arguments here for the political dominance of the United States: "In some instances in keeping with our own program of national security, we may be obliged to give military aid to countries ruled by dictators. But in such cases we should never permit the image of America as the champion of a democratic way of life to become in the least bit blurred" (188).

Certainly, Saund's words forecast more intense and developed discourses on the paternalistic and interventionist policies of the United States in Asia and elsewhere. Yet Saund's interests, as an Indian, cast a slightly different light on such formulations. America is very important to both his conception of himself as an Indian, and ultimately, as he asserts, to his conception of India as a nation. Saund becomes part of one nation, India, as he becomes part of another, America.

Saund concludes his autobiographical fiction by reiterating what he sees as principles essential to the future of the United States as both a nation and an international power. Reasserting his loyalty to the United States takes shape in a glorification of the United States Information Agency, support of a strong national defense, and a continued belief in free enterprise. But he gives equal treatment to issues of social importance, like collective bargaining, senior citizen and veteran pensions, and water resources. Finally, Saund suggests his own investment in America as a space for becoming a full subject: "There is no room in the United States of America for second-class citizenship. In Uncle Sam's family there are no foster children. . . . Discrimination . . . is repugnant to the ideals which all Americans cherish" (192). Despite or perhaps because of his Indian origin, Saund can have a place in this constructed nation, not as an adopted child, but as a full adult citizen.

That he can be "from India" and still be American suggests that the process of nationalization need not require "melting in," but political and social absorption. India remains present in a diasporic imagination, to the extent that Saund returns there after becoming a congressman, and yet its presence (much more than a trace) does not forestall the possibility of becoming American. By the end of *Congressman from India*, a certain transnationalism underlies the new Americanism that Saund proposes. If Saund advances a sense of American identity for himself, it is also one deeply influenced by an international referent, of India; here again it is possible to extract a marker that can be seen as "ethnic" inasmuch as it contains difference that has a racial aspect. In this scenario, becoming two kinds of nationals, in fact, is not completely at odds with an immigration narrative.

Fictions of Nations, of India in Britain

Amitav Ghosh's 1988 novel *The Shadow Lines* brings the question of Indianness in diaspora to Britain, and then back to India.[26] It explores the period in which Saund was writing himself as an American, and arrives at very different possibilities for postcolonial subjectivity and nationality.

The novel's structure is itself very self-consciously diasporic, moving throughout a number of sites at home and abroad, and its content comes to terms with contemporary theoretical questions having to do with nationalism and post-nationalism.[27] *The Shadow Lines* is concerned with groups, communities, and relationships among them, but like the autobiographies discussed above, this novel is at least as illuminating about individual subjectivity. Characters in a small (and local) story continually ask what a variety of forms of "Indianness" might look like in a vast postcolonial world, when India is a new nation-state. And *The Shadow Lines* also engages questions having to do with the postwar period more generally, beginning in a pre-independence migration, detailing life in India and Britain through the 1950s and 1960s, and ending with characters in England sometime in the 1970s. It is a novel about the status of history and how history impinges on its subjects.

As a text illuminating the diasporic imaginings of this chapter, *The Shadow Lines* sits within multiple literary fields. On some level, this novel about Indian characters in the subcontinent and beyond articulates the central concerns of "Indian" and "postcolonial" literatures. The musings of a nameless narrator, first a young boy and later a young man, showcase the effects of an Indian upbringing in the post-independence period. But the book also offers, centrally, a contemplation of the meaning of migration at this historical moment, if the first line of the text serves as any indication: "In 1939, thirteen years before I was born, my father's aunt, Mayadebi, went to England with her husband and her son, Tridib" (3). Divided into two sections, "Going Away" and "Coming Home," the novel is peopled by characters who travel between the worlds of England and India, in actual and symbolic terms. Though it is a novel about the subjective experience of nation, it is not geographically defined in a nation: its field of identifications, experiences, and possibilities is constituted by diasporic space and time.

Charting the narrator's odyssey through a range of cultural and political experiences in Calcutta, *The Shadow Lines* critiques the idea and reality of modern nationhood, and thus the meaning of Indianness. The "shadow line" marks boundaries, separating the narrator's Hindu Bengali family from their relatives in Dhaka, Bangladesh, between the experiences of the narrator and his cosmopolitan-migrant cousin Ila who lives in England, and among histories of England and India. Partition of the subcontinent, and all the divisions that resulted, haunt the novel at every turn. Seeming chasms are filled as the narrator crosses those limits assigned by nation-state formation. And toward the end of the book, Ghosh has the first-person narrator come to terms with the compulsion to divide peoples in world history: "It seemed to me then that . . . there were only states and citizens; there were no people at all. . . . I was struck with wonder that there had really been a time, not so long ago, when people, sensible people, of good intention, had thought that all maps were the same, that there was a special enchantment in lines; I had to remind myself that they were not to be blamed for believing that there was something admirable in moving violence to the borders and dealing with it through science and factories, for that was the pattern of the world" (233). Nations may pose no obvious impediments to the narrator's literal movements through the boundaries of geographical spaces, chronological narratives, or social formations, but the heavy symbolic weight of nationalist histories exacts psychic costs of all the characters, including the narrator's cousin Tridib, who dies in a communalist riot. And so both the absurdity and terror of boundaries are continually present in all the spaces that the narrator occupies.

England presents another set of "shadow lines" to be understood, crossed, and lived within. As in many contemplations of diasporic Indianness, here the postcolonial nation is the postwar nation. The international shape of India has been formed by interactions with and incursions by other nations. And putting India and England into a continuum, the novel asks us to consider whether, in fact, nations can be compared when they are inextricable. From the very beginning of the novel, the world outside is symbolized by the narrator's cousins' lives in England. The character of Ila, the female cousin of and object of desire for the narrator, illustrates the compromises and contradictions of a woman constituted as "Indian" and marked by narratives of Indian national history that have particular operations in the British postwar context. Diasporic and cosmopolitan, Ila is also displaced and lonely. The narrator's grandmother, Tha'mma, a figure of complex nationalist sentiments says, "Ila shouldn't *be* there. . . . She doesn't belong there. What's she doing in that country?" (77) The question of why Ila is *there* can be answered in literal terms: education and social freedom; but at the same time the broader question of desire for another place—for England and its people in particular— remains more elusive than anything the characters can say or do, much as the act of migration itself.

As an effect of the colonial project, however, knowledge of the other, and in this case of England, is far more easy to gain and express. Interestingly, the narrator's fascination with and knowledge of London, its streets, and its people (and the white characters in the book, the Prices) is fostered not along the Thames but back in Calcutta during the 1950s through stories told by Tridib. Tridib traveled to England with his wealthy parents when he was younger, but makes his adult life in India, as part of both the narrator's extended family network and also local urban culture, on street corners and in tea shops. Mapping London and Calcutta simultaneously is a way for this postcolonial national character to compress space and time. An enigmatic figure for family members and street acquaintances alike, Tridib imparts amazingly rich and lucid understandings of history as he tells of his and others' lives, particularly as they exist beyond the nation-state of India.

As Tridib informs the narrator about life in England, he transmits an unobstructed geography of London that enables him to become a conduit for a set of interlocking histories. When the narrator is in London later, as a young man, and is about to meet the Prices for the first time, he notes: "I've known the streets around here for a long time" (55). He proceeds to lead his cousins and Nick Price from the tube station to the Price house: "Since this is West End Lane, I said, that must be Sumatro road over there. So that corner must be where the air raid shelter was, the same one that Robi's mother and your mother and your uncle Alan ducked into on their way back from Mill Lane, when one of those huge high-calibre bombs exploded on Solent Road, around the corner, blowing up most of the houses there. And that house, that one, just down the road, over there . . . an incendiary bomb fell on it, and burned down two floors. That was on the 1st of October 1940, two days before your uncle died" (56). This particular realization of known physical space accentuates the extent to which Indians carry with them geographies of London as a symbol of Britain, but also, and perhaps more independently, as a site of diasporic circuitry. Here the inclusion of this metropole is into a popular understanding of what it means to be Indian, as well as American and British. This urban identity, like most, is forged through a diasporic experience, and yet it is very different from what Dalip Singh Saund experienced when he stopped over in England on his way to the United States. What is worth contemplating here are the very different ways that particular nations might be narrated for experiences of migration. For Saund's representative story of becoming American, Britain is a site of misrecognition ("I was not interested in empire builders. Abraham Lincoln's statue, however, evoked in me quite a different response" [34]); in Ghosh's imaginary, imparted to his characters, England is always and already part of Indian consciousness.

Though the London underground, the A to Z street atlas, and houses on street corners provide the structure of the narrator's knowledge about the city, and in some ways about himself, the broad sweep of historical events with no physical manifestation fills out a deeper understanding of the national-social formations that his grandmother alluded to in her defense of nationalism. But ironically, here it is the narrator, Indian born and bred, who can tell the British citizen about his family and national history and in effect contest traditional assumptions about national authority in the postwar period. The construction of a British place as already his own allows the narrator to permit a new conception of belonging to take shape, one very different from his grandmother's. In this way, the process of colonization is temporarily reversed through the acts of knowledge and recognition.

But the narrator, moving as he does from India to England and back again, cannot in those acts fully extricate himself from markings of attachment, to his family, to his life in India, and to a historical perspective that has nationalism at its center. The continuous intervention of the grandmother into the translocal narrative, her unfailing belief in the nation-building project, but also her roots in Dhaka shape the powerful sense that even contradictions and boundary crossings can be absorbed into national locations and national longings for Indians at home and abroad. Indian identity is not the sole national aspiration in the story; constant migrations produce multiple sites for affiliation. Ila's yearnings for England mirror Tha'mma's desires for India in a way that escapes the two characters in the text. As Ila invents stories about her popularity in school, cloaks the reality of her racial victimization, and eventually becomes unhappily married to the cowardly Nick Price, she is shown to seek escape from India and its social world by participating in the fantasy that the colonizers promoted: that England is a superior nation with a superior national culture. Though the narrator, too, holds a much glorified vision of Britain, his represented Indianness contrasts with Ila's desire to become British; but her racialization and loneliness become important variables in the broader impossibility of her integration. Through the characters of the narrator and Ila, Ghosh reveals at once the ease of travel, the difficulties of settlement, and the content of otherness.

Making a powerful commentary not only on postcolonial histories but also the problematic of migrant identity, exile, and nationhood during this period, Ghosh gives us different possibilities for diasporic subjectivity from what either Saund or Shridharani, mired as they were in multinational state projects of their time, could do. *The Shadow Lines* imagines a future utopia, embodied in the character of Tridib and his stories; the narrator observes: "I knew that the sights Tridib saw in his imagination were infinitely more detailed, more precise than anything I would ever see. He said to me once that one could never know anything except through desire, real desire, which was not the same thing as greed or lust; a pure, painful and primitive desire, a longing for everything that was not in oneself, a torment of the flesh that carried one beyond the limits of one's mind to other times and other places, and even, if one was lucky, to a place where there was no border between oneself and one's image in the mirror" (29).

It is hard to miss the resonances here with Jacques Lacan's discussion of the Imaginary and the Symbolic; Tridib's stories, which operate in the realm of the symbolic, are the means of becoming a subject.[28] In some respects, too, this discussion of the possibilities of yearning—in Ghosh's terms, desire—in a postcolonial world of social contradiction reflect the very negotiation between individual and collective subjectivity that is the hallmark of the diasporic imagination. The possibility of Indianness is in this sense already fissured, but it is constantly on the verge of reconstruction while the nation of India exerts its force around the world.

As the story of Tridib's death at the hands of an angry nationalist mob is unearthed, so too does the dream of life and love beyond nationality seem unforeseeable in the near future, for Indians at home and abroad alike. This anticolonial and diasporic novel cuts both ways for readers, to constrain and enable, to define the parameters in which one must live but also to proffer multiplicity and ethnic diversity that can be utilized for experience or a perspective when in a state of "going away" or "coming home." In this way, I would suggest, Ghosh has successfully worked in and through critiques of the liberatory and regressive aspects of nation-building without having to return to Kipling, precisely because the imaginary worlds (of East and West, or India and Britain) are no longer counterposed, but instead deeply connected.

New Indian Lives in London

The alternate distance and closeness of the worlds of India and Britain certainly came to crisis in 1970s London. Indian migrants had developed significant populations there and in other cities, and were contemplating new forms of citizenship amid the construction of highly defined community spaces, like that of Southall, and an atmosphere of racialization, including physical harassment on the streets and public stereotyping in media and state discourses.[29] This is the background to Anita Desai's 1985 novel *Bye-Bye Blackbird*.[30] In this book, when the narrative tension is framed as the difficulties of life in England and the dream of a return to India, the polarities between East and West are resurrected, producing a very different kind of story of diaspora than the one Ghosh tells in *The Shadow Lines*. Ostensibly centered on the relationship between two Indian cousins in London, one of whom has been living in England many years and is married to an Englishwoman, with the other a recent visitor from India, the novel's themes are not unlike those of *The Shadow Lines*, about the contrast between immigrants and travelers to England, the lure of Indian nationalism in the face of asserted British superiority, and the enduring and somewhat fantastical desires that both England and India inspire. But it is largely in the way that the books manage the question of nations—in Desai's text as fixed in structure and content, and in Ghosh's, flexible and with porous boundaries—that they produce very different kinds of Indian subjectivity.

Desai presents a continuous dialogue between the cousins Adit and Dev as a running commentary on the motivations, process, and effects of making the choice to live in England or India after independence. Informed by varying degrees of nationalism and idealization, the act of immigration comes under direct scrutiny here, albeit in highly ironized fashion. A conversation between Adit, longtime British resident, and Dev, recent arrival, distills the possibilities and difficulties of life and possibility in diaspora:

> "At home you would just take carrot *halwa* for granted but here you go ga-ga over it. You get your proportions all wrong, you emigrants."
>
> "Immigrants I think we are, and it's values you mean. . . . I wouldn't live in a country where I was insulted and unwanted."
>
> "No? Why have you come then?"
>
> "To study. You know that. I will go back to India an 'England-returned' teacher." (16)

As Adit and Dev begin to discuss a recent incident of racial hostility, their feelings about migration spin out of different approaches to otherness, belonging, and home:

> "Laugh. Go on. That's all you people do—you lazy immigrants. . . . You should go mad—*mad*, when even schoolboys can call you names on the streets, when you find the London docks have three kinds of lavatories. . . ."
>
> "Stop it, *yar*. You've come abroad to study and see a new country. Stop making . . . storms inside teapots.". . .
>
> "Adit, aren't you coming back at all? Do you mean to stay on?"
>
> "I do. I love it here. I'm so happy here, I hardly notice the few drawbacks. . . . I like going into the local for a pint on my way home to Sarah. I like wearing good tweed on a foggy November day. I like the Covent Garden opera house. . . . I like thatched cottages and British history and reading the letters in *The Times*."
>
> "Like being called a wog . . ." "I like the freedom a man has here: Economic freedom! Social freedom!" (17–18)

While Dev at this moment sees Britain as a racially exclusionary national space, Adit experiences the nation through a culture that he can easily consume, and also through his own personal economic success. The significance of this exchange at an early point in the text is to set up competing images of migration and settlement; Adit represents a naive or at least repressive migrant who is unconcerned with broader patterns of racial discrimination, while Dev exemplifies not only the more nationalist visitor, but also the Indians at home who caricature those abroad as greedy and accepting of daily forms of humiliation.

In *Bye-Bye Blackbird*, just as in *Congressman from India*, marriage is a symbol of national unions. Adit's marriage to Sarah becomes a sign for desired assimilation and ultimately a springboard for the deeper exploration of questions of psychic displacement and enduring attachment to location. While in Saund's masculine narrative of ascent his white wife appears only as a facile testament to opposed cultures meeting, Desai's story gives a great deal of space to Sarah's inner life. Rather unconventionally, readers begin to comprehend Sarah first before Adit, as they formulate the effects of immigrants living in British society. In this move, Desai pries open the closed or at least very specific nature of diaspora experience to disclose that the legacy of British colonialism affects not only the social worlds of Indian immigrants but also the consciousness of British citizens more generally. Sarah is in fact racked by an anguish that results from an understanding of the racism that she and her husband face daily as an interracial couple as well as from a subsequent alienation from her own cultural context; as Desai writes of Sarah:

> In the centre she sat, feeling the waves rock her, and then the fear and the questioning began. Who was she—Mrs. Sen who had been married in a red and gold Benares brocade sari one burning, bronzed day in September, or Mrs. Sen, the Head's secretary, who sent out the bills and took in the cheques, kept order in the school and was known for her efficiency? . . . They were roles . . . and then she wondered, with great sadness, if she would ever be allowed to step off the stage, leave the theatre and enter the real world—whether English or Indian, she did not care, she wanted only its sincerity, its truth. (34–35).

Initially Sarah's disaffection stands in contrast to her husband Adit's apparent contentment with life in England. But as the novel progresses, Adit is afflicted by an intense nostalgia for India and ultimately a desire to return to the home he has conceived of there. What is striking is that despite Desai's obvious attempt to deal with white British women, and gender more generally, the discourse of nationalism in a sense overtakes that intention, for it is Adit and Dev who assume primary roles in national formation while Sarah's subjectivity drops out of the last third of the novel.

Adit's deepening dissatisfaction with British society, while catalyzed by the presence of his cousin Dev, emerges from a formulation of the two spaces, of India and England, as very distinct though contiguous. Unlike in *The Shadow Lines*, here Desai's histories of those nations intersect only in a distant past; migration in the present produces stark choices, to stay in England and become part of British society, however imperfectly, or to go back to India. Desai's narrative predictably ends with the realized fantasy of a return to India functioning as a reply to the failures of Indian settlement in Britain. As Adit becomes irretrievably depressed about life in England, and also conscious of anti-Indian racism, he has no other choice but to ask Sarah to go back to India with him, which she does.

While political trouble between India and Pakistan serves as a pretext for making such a dramatic choice, the narrative thrust is toward a resolution of the quarrels between Dev and Adit about the possibility of Indians ever really being at home in England.

And yet, in *Bye-Bye Blackbird*, Desai, much as Ghosh did in *The Shadow Lines*, maps the urban space of London through its streets, monuments, and cultural institutions. Peppered with references to the city, this novel, too, decenters geographical knowledge by suggesting that it may be gained not only by the fact of migration, but also back home in India. Upon being introduced to Hyde Park, and Rotten Row, Dev replies: "Of course. I know. . . . You don't have to tell me. And here is the Serpentine." In response to Sarah's surprise, he returns: "I have always known them. . . . Always. Ever since I could read" (64). This moment almost perfectly reproduces the scene in *The Shadow Lines* when the narrator show the Prices different physical locations of their past. But for Desai, the matter of deeper cultural knowledge is rendered more elusive than the act of reading (in Dev's case) or even experience (in Adit's) can address: "Another thing to which Dev cannot grow accustomed, in all his walks and bus rides through the city, is the silence and emptiness of it. . . . All, to his eyes and ears, dead, unalive, revealing so little of the lives that go on, surely must go on inside them. The English habit of keeping all doors and windows tightly shut . . . of guarding their privacy . . . cannot quite be explained to him by the facts of the cold and the rain. It remains incomprehensible to him" (63). Though Dev knows the streets, Desai seems to suggest, he cannot understand what broader experiences they represent. In a way that recalls colonial ideologies in reversal, the Indian cannot really know the Englishman or his world. A fundamental dichotomy between India and England produces alienation for a group of diasporic citizens of one place or the other in this new version of the Western world. On the back of the paperback edition of the book, a quote from *The Statesman* sums up quite nicely the informing philosophy: "Anita Desai touches on a very real problem, a facet of 'east is east and west is west' which has been hitherto little explored in novel form." Cultures here, very much as in colonization narratives, function to a large extent without historical reference points, and therefore cannot representationally contest such simplicity attending to "east" and "west." The late reference in the text to trouble between India and Pakistan, alluding to the war in Bangladesh, marks the narrative as taking place in 1970s London, but the absence of other clear historical markers, especially for a period that might have offered Desai a bevy of possibilities, gives migrant communities in the text a particularly flat and dehistoricized feel.

In fact, the representation preserves a studied distance between the characters and more particularized Indianness in Britain by bringing colonial images to bear on what could certainly have been rendered in more complex fashion. When Sarah and Adit take Dev to Petticoat Lane, an area of Bengali immigrants, Dev first remarks: "This could be one of our bazaars" (60). But that asserted authenticity is quickly cast as highly commercialized for British tastes, and thus artificial; Sarah suggests that "the East India Company has come to take over England now," and Dev indulges in wild fantasies about camels, elephants, and gurus having come to the London cityscape to avenge colonialism through new forms of cultural imperialism. Later in the book, when they go to a popular Indian restaurant called Veeraswamy's, Dev notes: "Here you have the real thing—the very essence of the Raj, or the role of the sahib log—in its fullest bloom" (195). The three main characters in the book view all things Indian in England as inauthentic and through the lens of the history of colonialism. The very real nation-state of India makes appearances only through sporadic fantasies of Adit's childhood and can thus become an object of desire in a fairly static process. Though nationalist desires propel a kind of return, they do not allow for deeper understandings of the space of India. In the way that Desai produces a strict separation between England and India she also rehearses colonial stereotypes that become embedded in Indian nationalism itself. In contrast, India, for Amitav Ghosh's novel is more dynamically constructed as a site of diaspora and involved in the making of diaspora.

Ultimately, Desai seems to have a clear agenda: to challenge the myths of immigration that influence the Indian population in England and are carried back home, in particular the idea that Indians could ever become part of British society. Adit's return to India at the close of the novel illustrates such an impossibility. Incommensurability guides the choices that face immigrants, intimates Desai, and the angst that the characters in the novel endure is a result of that. Indian cultural nationalism functions as a salve for the experience of exile; while in this novel it propels a return, it might also be understood to be part of the fantasies mobilized in response to experiences of racial discrimination and displacement.

In two very different novels, Desai and Ghosh elaborate the diasporic imagination of Indians that construct the nation and create the complex forms of affiliation and alienation wrought by the act of migration. For the characters of each text, Britain functions historically and culturally as a site of a variety of forms of displacement; and India exists within and through all travelers' and migrants' subjectivity, as a fantasy projection, negatively and positively. The narrator, Ila, and Tha'mma of *The Shadow Lines* are all caught in the postcolonial historical moment in which boundaries between nations are increasingly thick yet patently artificial; Dev, Adit, and Sarah of *Bye-Bye Blackbird* exist in much less historicized cir-

cumstances and predictably evidence a much easier separation between
national-cultural spaces. Ultimately, however, in both texts, Indian nationality in some form or other provides the interpretive framework for British
Indian settlement; Tha'mma's disapproval, Ila's failing marriage to an Englishman, and Adit's return construct limits for the fictive ability of Indians in Britain to achieve psychic integrity or even real happiness. Identity
formation in these works takes place in the ground worked over by British
colonial presence, consciousness of racism against India and her peoples,
and opposition to the status-quo, all in some imagined space of India.

These two books employ the metaphor of travel to create a set of relationships between England and India and between English and Indian
identities, and in fact the diaspora itself, though with vastly different results. In *The Shadow Lines*, the travel is imaginative; the educational en-
deavors of colonialism unwittingly pave the road for the postcolonial subjects' decisions to go abroad and in the process gain thorough knowledge
of the metropole that they will later come to literally inhabit. Before the
narrator of *The Shadow Lines* personally visits London, he has traveled
the streets of London via Tridib and Ila, and Ila too has traveled at the
same time as she emblematized "the immigrant." Adit and Dev's travels
in *Bye-Bye Blackbird* likewise enable new forms of subjectivity, in a place
that may appear to be physically outside India, but can be understood to
be another space for the nation. But while travel produces a knowledge
of London that functions to signify migrancy, it also limits the scope of a
set of experiences that constitute the process of migration. Ghosh and
Desai articulate a traveled but sustained distance between Indians and
Britain largely shaped by the impossibility of settlement. In fact, a certain
incommensurability, while differently performed, conditions all the migrant characters' travel and becomes fundamental to the relationship between "colored" immigrants and the British nation. This occurs even at
the same time as knowledge about the other can seem intimate, as in
Ghosh's narrator's ability to sympathize with the white character Nick
Price and Adit's companionship with Sarah.

In both novels, as well as in the more autobiographical pieces by Shridharani and Saund, there are continual shifts between "home" and
"abroad." Importantly, routes and dwellings are the central terms of diasporic fictions. Saund goes from India, to England, to the United States,
and then back to India; Ghosh's characters make many moves back and
forth between India and England, as do Desai's protagonists. We might
read this representation of movement alongside a long tradition of English
men and women visiting India and other places and writing about their
experiences.[31] In distilling questions of affiliation and being marked as
other in "foreign" space, travel articulates the very possibility of a na-

tional community. Much as white women like Harriet Tytler and Fanny Parks were never more reassured of their Englishness than when in India,[32] so too might the subjects of the Indian nation-state *feel* Indian upon contact with the cultures and peoples of England, resulting from, on the one hand, independent feelings of alienation and, on the other, imposed patterns of racialization. And yet, as represented moments of recognition in England or a view of Abraham Lincoln's statue might reveal, these subjects might also feel British and American. While memoirs more specifically about the experience of travel assume temporary aspects to the move abroad, Ghosh's and Desai's texts most clearly address the problematic of settlement. It is a troubled experience, and one shaped by the ever-present incommensurability of cultures and subjectivities that the nations of Britain and India have inscribed. Migration, indeed, can have a hopeless quality, rather than the liberatory potential often accorded to travel.[33] The question of what it means to leave India and yet *be* Indian remains one of great anxiety in large part because of its lack of resolution. Finally, *Bye-Bye Blackbird* and *The Shadow Lines* may suggest that Britain's exclusive and exclusionary processes of nationalization, most especially in contrast to America's inclusion, are keys to unlocking that distress.

Newly Gendered Stories of Americanization

Throughout the autobiographical texts of Dalip Singh Saund and Krishnalal Shridharani, mostly isolated individuals in the two national landscapes of India and the United States assumed representative roles for the process of Americanization. And, indeed, Saund and Shridharani exerted tremendous power on the shape of their own lives, evidenced in a number of ways, including the very fact that they wrote and published personal memoirs. I would suggest that a form of masculine privilege informed the sentiments expressed in both *My India, My America* and *Congressman from India*, and also influenced the ability of Shridharani and Saund to cross certain kinds of borders. While both authors were obsessed with the first line of Kipling's "Ballad of East and West," they also embodied the third and fourth lines:

> But there is neither East nor West, Border, nor
> Breed, nor Birth,
> When two strong men stand face to face, though
> they come from the ends of the earth![34]

If we think carefully about this framework, of the ability of strong men from different places to stand face to face and write themselves into narratives of multiple nations, it is hard to imagine a female subject within. And unsurprisingly, there is no equivalent first-person piece about migration to *My India, My America* or *Congressman from India* written by an Indian woman in the United States before 1965, due in large part to the fewer female immigrants prior to the legislation that enabled families from a range of Asian, Caribbean, and Latin American countries to resettle in the United States, and also the differing access that male and female immigrants have had to literature as a mechanism to survive, to make sense of the world, and to express themselves publicly. In fact, it is only recently that memoirs of female immigrant experience have appeared and gained popularity, particularly in the United States.[35]

Nonetheless, the first Indian authors to have U.S. literary celebrity have been female.[36] Perhaps the first of these is Bharati Mukherjee, originally an Indian immigrant to Canada who subsequently moved to the United States. Mukherjee sees herself very much as an American, and her writing centers on the experiences of Indian women who have migrated to the United States. An early work, *Wife*, published in 1975, was one of the first novels about the post-1965 immigrant experience. It serves as an interesting window onto the times of a just-developing Indian community in the New York area in the 1970s, and also of the particularly gendered experiences of migration and exile.[37] She constructs a sense of Indianness with clear gestures toward the possibility of becoming American.

Wife centers on more psychic experiences of displacement than the autobiographical *Congressman from India* or *My India, My America* could. The main character, Dimple, comes to the United States with her engineer husband and undergoes a process of alienation from her past, her community, and her partner that symptomatize broader forces at work in this historical moment of migration. As a female figure isolated from the homeland that imparted her sense of self and an accessible identity, Dimple serves as a device for Mukherjee to trace the ways that conditions in migrant New York have affected Indian women.

Even before Dimple's departure for the United States, Mukherjee suggests a closer look at the terms in which migration is being understood and experienced at this historical moment. The late 1960s were a heady time for those people in countries like India who had wanted to go to the United States for a long time but were unable to because of restrictive immigration rules. And the development of a Fordist mass culture between the 1920s and 1960s, and its export around the world, meant that many post-1965 "new" immigrants had already assimilated much of the United States before arriving in the country. During the late 1960s and afterward, those mostly middle-class people who could afford the fare could actually experience what had been so much the substance of unmediated fantasies. America constructed itself and was constructed by others as a place of unbridled economic and political success. Some Indians who came to the United States undoubtedly lived those inventions, by greeting an expanding economy and being among a group so small as yet unable to rouse racial discrimination. But by the early 1970s, enough Indians had immigrated so that more sober understandings of life in the United States began to take hold. Difficulties in obtaining jobs and advancing in well-established industries and fields as well as tightening immigration rules in response to the unexpected influx of people under the 1965 Immigration and Naturalization Act shaped new understandings of the Indian migrant, for those abroad as well as for those back home.

Mukherjee's protagonist experiences the act of migration and settlement in the United States in ways that mirror the complicated and contradictory perceptions of life abroad. To set the scene, Dimple is made to face a skeptical view of immigration just before leaving India; she goes to a party of one of her close friends, Pixie, who remarks: "You're so lucky! . . . I wish *I* were leaving tomorrow" (45). As Pixie then excitedly relays to another woman, Ratna Das, that Dimple is going to the United States, Das says: "It might be fun to go for a vacation. . . . But I wouldn't want to settle there." Pixie replies: "Me too, I wouldn't want to feel a foreigner all my life." As Dimple struggles to understand this interrogation of her fairly simple dreams of a life in the United States, she asks: "But why would you feel like a foreigner if you went as an immigrant?" And Das quickly retorts with: "*You* may think of it as immigration, my dear, but what you are is a *resident alien*" (46). Mukherjee counterposes immigration to foreign status, and her delineation of the "resident alien," as distinct from "the immigrant" or presumably "a U.S. citizen," is interesting here in 1975, particularly in light of her later formulations.[38] While the character Das imbues the category of "resident alien" with racial undertones that distinguish Indians from other immigrants and Americans, Dimple's own dreams of a new life, and in general a more romantic vision of migration, economic success, social freedom, and independence from extended family responsibilities, are tempered by this thorny question of status in the United States.

To paint the realities of Indian immigrant life in the United States, Mukherjee chooses New York as a site for a set of conflicts and resolutions. New York, particularly Queens, where Dimple first goes to live, contains the post-1965 Indian migration that produced quickly concentrating communities, a growing professional class, and in general far more Indians relative to the total population of Asians than in places like California or even Illinois or Texas, other popular destinations. The place of New York also distinguishes this group of Indians from the earlier history of Indians who had gone to California as laborers. Prototypical migrants of this period, Dimple and her engineer husband, Amit, armed with good college educations, arrive in the United States with few economic resources, but they do have friends there who had emigrated earlier (but are not yet family members).

And when Dimple and Amit go to stay with their friends, the Sens, in Queens, there are interesting portrayals of an Indian community taking shape. Describing their social strategies in the United States, the resident Jyoti explains: "Only one way to keep a *saheb* from complaining . . . and that's the way we do it: never invite one over"—which his wife elaborates on: "What he means is that they eat nothing but beef. . . . Anyway, who needs *sahebs*? There must be a thousand Indians in just this neighborhood!" (54). Indian communities in places like Queens were growing rapidly at this time, and Mukherjee's descriptions of Indian families socializing together, Hindi films being shown in public school auditoriums, and the formation of immigrant organizations echo sociological accounts of this period.[39] As the characters of *Wife* travel between Queens and Manhattan, frequenting delicatessens and pizza parlors, Mukherjee maps a migrant experience within the urban space of New York. Much like London had for Ghosh's and Desai's British Indians, New York becomes an important space for Indians in the United States in Mukherjee's novel. The absence of a colonial history in the relationship between Indian and American cultures, however, also means that Indians migrate with less detailed imaginative maps to the United States than they possessed when they went to England. Nonetheless, as more and more Indians in the diaspora chose the United States for settlement, New York assumed a symbolic role in Indian diasporic literature, and this 1975 text forecasts such narrative trends.

The subject of *Wife* is the intersection of gender and migration and is embodied in the figure of Dimple. Dimple's unhappiness extends over the course of the narrative and intensifies upon her arrival in the United States. In large part her subjectivity is defined, controlled, and ultimately limited by her husband Amit, though in ways that Mukherjee does not satisfactorily explain.[40] As a migrant woman, Dimple exists between two ill-defined, largely stereotypical models: Meena Sen, at whose house she initially stays, and Ina Mullick, who is a friend of the Sens. Meena has a small child and is pregnant with a second, stays at home, wears Indian dress, and socializes only with other Indians; as a mother and devoted wife, she adheres to most traditional conceptions of Indian femininity. In direct contrast, Ina Mullick is childless, wears pants—a symbol of westernization—flirts with white American men, and expresses dissatisfaction with traditional roles. Dimple becomes exasperated with both women and has difficulty not only seeing herself through them but also through the communities from which they emerge; she exists very much as an isolated and alienated individual through the entire text. Driven to a kind of murderous hysteria, Dimple can be seen to represent the inaccessibility of psychic, social, and cultural choices, for migrants far displaced from their homeland. Though Mukherjee does not succeed in giving life to a complex character, she does, through a number of absences and frustrations, imply that female Indian migrant experience is more complex than any of the standard narratives can allow.

Indeed, the writerly aspects of the novel may be less significant than the sociological lessons that Mukherjee's text imparts at this historical moment. Ultimately, Mukherjee succeeds in critiquing both gendered and glorified notions of immigration. Post-1965 experiences, while especially economically lucrative in the early part of that period before 1975, nonetheless endowed the concept of "America" with a realism previously unrealized as smaller numbers of Indians were allowed to enter the United States and actually cope with life abroad. Unlike the autobiographical selves constructed by the more politically minded Saund and Shridharani, Mukherjee's characters experience displacement and ultimately Americanization in more critical ways. They live within Indian communities, and that creates difficulties of a different sort than the struggle for citizenship created for the more exceptional Saund. The question of economic survival and success figures more centrally in this and other post-1965 narratives of migrant life because that forms an important vector of expectations and desires for America. Political liberation lies further on the horizon for this group of travelers; cultural orientations, in some ways, replace earlier forms of anticolonial identity.

Mukherjee may be seen to critique here facile conceptions of America and belonging in ways that are curious, especially in light of her recent reputation as an outspoken proponent of Americanization. A 1996 *New York Times* op-ed piece by Mukherjee has been the focus of much negative attention from those who have been critics of immigration mythologies. In the article, Mukherjee juxtaposes her own and her sister's different trajectories of immigration and affiliation: "I am an American citizen and she is not. I am moved that thousands of long-term residents are finally taking the oath of citizenship. She is not."[41] Mukherjee describes various factors in her and her sister's lives, including their marriages, her sister's to an Indian graduate student and her own to a white North American. But strangely, she cites only her own marriage as a means to liberation: "By choosing a husband who was not my father's selection, I was opting for fluidity, self-invention, blue jeans and T-shirts,"[42] in essence equating freedom and westernization. Again, the marriage, in fact the *mixed* marriage, bears the symbolic weight of nations, nationalization, and the subjectivities that might result. That mixed marriage served different ends for Desai's sense of what might happen in the diaspora in *Bye-Bye Blackbird*, but for both Mukherjee and Saund, it is a means to becoming a different kind of Indian, and American.

Mukherjee also examines her sister's resistance to becoming an American citizen in the face of new legislation denying government benefits to immigrants alongside her own deep satisfaction in citizenship: "In one family, from two sisters alike as peas in a pod, there could not be a wider divergence of immigrant experience. America spoke to me—I married it— I embraced the demotion from expatriate aristocrat to immigrant nobody, surrendering those thousands of years of 'pure culture,' the saris, the delightfully accented English. She retained them all. Which of us is the freak?" For Mukherjee, becoming American entails giving up Indianness, and thus the two national-cultural identities remain altogether distinct, not unlike the conceptual reasoning behind the "east is east, west is west" model. Yet here the west is not the exclusionary Britain, but an expansive idea of America, one that Mukherjee can and does choose to be absorbed within; as a result, she herself changes in ways that were not constructed as really possible for the character of Dimple in *Wife*. As she describes the difference between her sister's choice and her own, she sets up the dichotomy: "She is happier to live in America as expatriate Indian than as an immigrant American. . . . The price that the immigrant willingly pays, and that the exile avoids, is the trauma of self-transformation."[43] It is difficult to read this formulation even against Mukherjee's earlier work in *Wife*, where Dimple's distress was about the difficulties of making clear-cut choices, of nations or cultures, and where the "resident alien," or immigrant, was held in some disdain.

In this respect, Mukherjee has recently subscribed to a more linear narrative of migration and nationalization. Her sense that she as an Indian can move to the United States and become American and in effect give up the affiliations of the homeland distinguish her from other writers like Ghosh, Desai, Shridharani, and even Saund, though there are some continuities as well with those earlier experiences of the United States. Citizenship is ultimately the mode in which Mukherjee experiences America; in response to literary critic Aijaz Ahmad's accusation that she is right-wing,[44] she notes: "If 'right-wing,' for Ahmad, applies to anyone who agrees with the spirit behind the American Constitution and the idea of democracy, then I suppose I am."[45] Like Saund, Mukherjee is attracted to political ideals that underlie American public discourse. But quite differently from Saund, she abdicates a primarily Indian subjectivity. While Saund remained the "congressman from India," her preferred self-description is "an American writer of Bengali-Indian origin."[46]

Mukherjee, however, unlike the other authors, has achieved an iconic importance within the United States; she has in some sense become representative of Indianness to Americans, even though Indian critics may not like her. Her books are widely consumed through high school and college literature curricula. Partly this has to do with issues of scarcity; until more recently there have not been many Indian American authors to include in multicultural canons, despite the fast-growing populations of Indians in the United States. But also, her writing fits well within paradigms of ethnicity that stress origins of writers who now see themselves as American, much as Mukherjee puts it herself. Hyphenated identity, of being Indian American, is a product of the 1970s, well after Dalip Singh Saund's *Congressman from India*. While Saund can become both Indian and American through his own text, it is Mukherjee who finally makes the transition from the multinational possibilities to become American and fully realize the possibilities of assimilation.

Ultimately the formulation of America that emerges from the work and figure of Mukherjee is at odds with both broader and complex conceptions of diaspora that have been elaborated here as well as with the discipline of postcolonial studies. Mukherjee in fact advances such distinctions: "Postcolonial studies seems an inappropriate category in which to place my works. I don't think of myself as a postcolonial person stranded on the outer shores of the collapsed British empire. . . . If I had chosen to return to India after writing that book in 1977, or if, like Salman Rushdie, I'd spent my entire adult life in Britain instead of in North America, I might have evolved as a postcolonial whose creative imagination is fueled primarily by a desire to create a new mythology of Indian nationhood after the Raj's brutalization of Indian culture."[47]

Simplifications of postcolonial literature aside, what is interesting here is Mukherjee's sense that her investments in immigrant status both preclude the incorporation of anticolonial issues into her work and also emerge distinctively from choosing to live in North America rather than Britain. And rather consistently, she does cite as guiding philosophies quite stock elements of American mythologies: "The mission of postcolonial studies as a discipline is to level all of us to our skin color and ethnic origin, whereas as a writer, my job is to open up, to discover and say 'we are all individuals.' "[48] The theme of individualism in her comments here resonate with the life story of Dalip Singh Saund, but with different cultural reference points.

Mukherjee's brand of assimilation emerges from a deep belief in singular forms of nationality, whereby you can give up one national affiliation for another and subsequently invest in a whole new set of political, cultural, and psychic concerns. Though the stirrings of "ethnics" are her literary subject, the possibility of diaspora, a mode of life for many new ethnics, and abiding connections to the homeland, which are almost always present in some form or another for first- and even second-generation Indian Americans, are pointedly absent from her texts. While she does not disavow her earlier work, her recent public discourse in some way undermines the complexity and contradictions of migration that the

character Dimple in *Wife* embodied. Mukherjee is committed to seeing
immigration and postcolonialism on opposite ends of the spectrum, and
she therefore effectively dismisses what Shridharani and Saund saw as
constitutive of their own identities, connections to the past and present
of India that are the substance of diaspora. She explains: "Those who
decide, 'all right, I'm going to go on with my life, the past is going to color
my present and the present is going to color my future, but here and now,
I'm a different person,' these people reflect the spirit of immigrant writing
by keeping themselves open to new experiences. . . . This energy is completely opposed to the postcolonial who, if he or she is not within the
immediate postcolonial context, is simply talking about the past and ig-
noring or obliterating the present."[49] It is hard to imagine writers from
Britain, perhaps "within the immediate postcolonial context," formulat-
ing the immigrant present without contemplating how contemporary race
relations might be influenced by, or at least resonate with, historical colonial arrangements. The lack of a colonial past and the accessibility of
national languages of inclusion in the United States construct Mukherjee's
and other Indian Americans' migrant subjectivities in ways that are distinct from their British counterparts.

By the 1980s, Mukherjee successfully negotiated a self-identificatory
move from "Indian" to "immigrant" to finally "ethnic American." These
were simply unavailable choices for Saund and Shridharani and they are
fully impossible renderings of British Indian experiences. Though Mukherjee self-consciously places her work within the canon of "ethnic literature," which extends from white ethnic traditions, she can be seen as part
of a continuum of works about the Indian migrant experience that have
in some way or another negotiated diaspora, the affiliation with a multiplicity of nations and states, and the anchoring of those identities to complex historical understandings of Indianness in a postwar global system.
Her texts occasion diaspora, even when she herself chooses resolutely to
stand outside that kind of definition. And, Mukherjee's insistence on "ethnicity" and "immigration" indeed fit very well within other bodies of literature, of Asian American literature, of multicultural literature, a fact that
continues to make her work both very popular and representative.

New Countries for Indian Americans

Quite another future of Indian diasporic writing is suggested by the 1994
work *My Own Country: A Doctor's Story*, by Abraham Verghese.[50] Verghese's book, while autobiographical, is intertwined with accounts of the
AIDS epidemic in a small town, Johnson City, Tennessee. Both Verghese's
location there and his interpretations of how his individual experiences

interact with broader phenomena serve as meditations on new Indian diasporic arrangements. Verghese arrived in the United States as a doctor
in 1980, and this fact makes his an always self-conscious life story of
conditions for the second wave of the post-1965 immigration. His circumstances of entry were not clearly linear; he moved to the United States
from Ethiopia for a short time early in the 1970s and then returned to
India to complete medical school before resettling in the United States.
Though his parents were brought up as Christians in Kerala, they moved
to Ethiopia and raised their family there. Verghese's status as a diasporic
Indian, with roots in India but experiences in an Indian community in
Africa, distinguishes him and many other new Indian migrants from the
earliest wave, who had for the most part come directly from India. Verghese expands the imaginatory reach of the diaspora and thus of his own
identity: "When my parents tell me the story of their arrival in Ethiopia—
the tough times in India, the struggle to get a college education, the word
of mouth from friends about jobs overseas . . . I understand the migration
of Indians to South Africa, Uganda, Kenya, Tanzania, Mozambique,
Mauritius, Aden, Ethiopia. And the next wave on to Birmingham, Bradford, Bristol, London and Toronto. And to Flushing, Jersey City, Chicago,
San Jose, Houston and even Johnson City, Tennessee" (16).

In 1994, Verghese is deeply conscious not only of the changes in the
nature of Indian migration, but also the impact of new immigrants on the
broader racial landscape of the United States. Part of this shift had to do
with the steady proliferation of Indian doctors into city hospitals as well
as in more rural areas of the country. While in the 1960s and 1970s, the
prototypical locale of the Indian migrant was in the world Mukherjee
described in *Wife*, places like Queens, Manhattan, or perhaps near Chicago or Los Angeles, by the 1980s and 1990s Indians had begun to move
to other places in the country, "even Johnson City, Tennessee." As the
Indian American diaspora diversified, it also expanded its reach. When
Verghese decides to go to the unlikely site of Johnson City to be the area
hospital's infectious diseases specialist, he is but part of a broader immigrant phenomenon that he discusses later in the book. He and his wife go
to Indian parties held in local school gyms, much like the groups Mukherjee described in Flushing, but with a distinctively suburban and
southern identity here. As he describes it: "The Indian community in
Johnson City was growing logarithmically. The new complement of in-
terns and residents always included three or more Indians, most of them
married. . . . They were the friends, relatives or classmates of those who
had gone through the ETSU [East Tennessee State University] residency
program, people who now put them up, lent them the rule book to study
for the Tennessee driving license exam." While the developing community
Verghese describes is diverse, it is nonetheless held together by various

conceptions of Indianness that Verghese is both part of and outside of, particularly as he battles the medical epidemic of AIDS. And given the essential cosmopolitanism of AIDS, it is not surprising that Verghese's medical experience gets counterposed to this Indian community, as well as to his wife, who is allied with that more parochial space. Verghese's marriage to an Indian woman, in fact, cannot enable absorption into the new space, of America, as Saund's and Mukherjee's mixed marriages could. In the end, as Verghese's involvement in his work and in this community increases, his wife is pushed to the background of the narrative; eventually, when he leaves Johnson City to embark on new travels across America, he leaves his wife behind.

Through his work with AIDS patients, Verghese surveys rural America, and this alternative landscape allows in turn different readings of migrant experience and identity. In his narrative interactions with the locals, Verghese, though to some degree ethnicized, is very much the cosmopolitan. He describes the space in terms that are highly ethnographic. Descriptions of life and people in Tennessee stand in contrast to what he frequently calls urban war zones and his experiences of anxiety in Boston. The second chapter, in which Verghese recounts his decision to go to Johnson City, is rife with references to his inability to feel safe in the urban space. His approach to Johnson City, on the other hand, is marked by this observation: "Going from India to Johnson City, Tennessee, had been a bit of a culture shock. . . . Not even reruns of *The Beverly Hillbillies* that we had watched in India prepared us for this" (31). Verghese at once glorifies and reduces the local residents by asserting their essential goodness: "To describe them, I found myself borrowing a term they frequently used themselves: 'good ole boys' " (41), and by frequently referring to their earthiness and simplicity, echoing, among others, James Agee.[51]

As Verghese portrays the local residents of the area in highly romantic ways, he also, remarkably, excuses their racism. In describing a man he befriended early on, he writes: "Even if he could not read well or if the word 'nigger' was much more natural to him than 'black,' he was well aware of the world" (42). Later he uncritically notes: "Essie's directions involved taking a left turn at a house with a lawn jockey (an 'artificial nigger,' as Essie termed it)" (87), The "country" that Verghese refers to in the title of his book is one that is unapologetically white. In a classic ethnographic strategy, the extraordinary absence of blacks in the book and his silence on racism and race relations effectively mark him as the only outsider to this folk white Appalachian culture, which can then be easily categorized. Verghese's brand of diasporic identification seems not to mark him racially, or implicate him in broader racial landscapes.

What is important here is how Verghese's story of an Indian diasporic experience is very much about an Indian abroad and an accepting and absorbing site; Johnson City becomes for Verghese symptomatic of a new stage in migrant life, of settlement, acceptance, and ultimately of new forms of nationality. For writers like Saund, Shridharani, and Mukherjee, "America" played the broader conceptual role that here the local space does. Verghese's autobiography illustrates both the increasing diversity of the Indian diaspora in the United States that now includes those who have not only migrated from India, but also from Europe, the Caribbean, and Africa, and its proliferation of sites, in New York City, California, and now Johnson City, Tennessee.

Despite the fact that "community" is an increasingly, or perhaps continuously, vexed issue, Verghese can winningly find various kinds of homes in the United States. Though he eventually chooses to leave Johnson City to go to Iowa for another position, Verghese expresses real attachment to the people and places of this small Tennessee town; they become his "own country," as in the title of the book, which is taken from Malcolm Cowley's poem "The Long Voyage." The first and last stanza of the poem read:

> Not that the pines were darker there,
> nor mid-May dogwood brighter there,
> nor swifts more swift in summer air;
> it was my own country,
> . . . .
> Now the dark waters at the bow
> fold back, like earth against the plow;
> foam brightens like the dogwood now
> at home, in my own country.[52]

Verghese, like Saund, who contemplated his paradigmatic American experiences, but unlike Mukherjee, who aimed for single-nationality, eventually finds a home in both the United States and a border-crossing, diasporic space. Yet all four of the U.S.-based authors—Shridharani, Saund, Mukherjee, and Verghese—write of various forms of freedom that become formulated in and through the national space of America. It is for this very reason that Shridharani and Saund can elaborate on the twinned destinies of India and the United States and Mukherjee and Verghese can experience more personal forms of liberation in this national space. The three male writers all become "Americanized" without losing India or Indianness, while Mukherjee's Americanism is constituted by some chosen loss. One might presume that gender shapes the difference between Mukherjee and the others; as she describes her westernization as a woman, she also objects to arrangements of family and sexuality that are left largely intact by the male writers, including Verghese.

Writing across Diasporas

Though this book has widely constructed diasporic time and space *through* England, the United States, and India, much of the action may seem to occur *within* specific nation-states, as the project of becoming specifically American or British overlays productions of Indian subjectivity. Any notion of Indian homeland may be thoroughly deconstructed by these processes, but the exchanges seen in the texts discussed here maintain some structure of duality: India–United States, India–Britain. Urmila Mohapatra's *With Love, from Britain*[53] (1999), a small and relatively undistinguished collection of letters from an Indian American mother to her children about her trip to England, creates a different comparative network, between England and the United States. When Saund and Shridharani made related comparisons before the 1960s, it was largely the dominant nations and their political discourses that loomed large, and that created a slate for identificatory possibilities. But Mohapatra, an American, reads England through its Indianness, and in that move quite profoundly displaces a range of national formations. Interestingly, the text that results ends up being produced in India.

England is the site for a four-month sabbatical that Mohapatra and her husband take before continuing to India for a five-week trip. The circuit of travel, from the United States to England to India, certainly contrasts with those made by migrants on their way to constructing new diasporic spaces. Mohapatra's less familiar and inverted diasporic journey is marked by an obsessive concern with locational coordinates; letters are full of references, in particular, to the differences between British, U.S., and Indian zones: "It must be around 1 A.M. in America, while we landed in England at 7 A.M. As we gathered our carry-on baggage to leave the aircraft, most Indian passengers stayed on board. They were going to fly to Delhi or Bombay. Again I felt a little sad. These passengers will be in India soon" (2–3). The author's regret is generalized by a desire to see India, after twenty-four years of not having visited, but it is also a statement of a certain melancholy of disidentification. Having flown Air India for the first time, Mohapatra encounters people who ask her about the United States and sense her own distance from India; her response is an extreme desire to *be* in India immediately and to not have to spend time in England. In this way, Mohapatra's stopover initially seems to echo Dalip Singh Saund's unsatisfying pause there many years earlier.

Yet what Mohapatra discovers in England, and creates in epistolary forms of development, is not the alienation represented in Anita Desai's novel, nor the unwelcome reminders of British empire that Saund had expressed disdain for, but instead India. Beginning with her arrival in

Leicester, Mohapatra's letters to her children are filled with a sense of wonderment and satisfaction in seeing Indian people everywhere, and discovering spaces for the consumption of Indian food, clothing, and films. All sorts of recognition occur in the diaspora, when Mohapatra affirms her own Indianness and that of others: "Once while waiting at a bus stop, an Indian girl from Africa named Nita, who now lives in Leicester, conversed with us. She has never been to India in her life. She wanted to know why we came for sabbatical to Leicester instead of another British city. She asked, 'Do you have any relatives in Leicester? Is that why you chose Leicester?' Your dad replied, 'Yes. You all are like our Indian relatives. We wanted to come to Leicester because it has a large Indian population.' Nita smiled and agreed with us" (16). Mohapatra here conceives of family as diaspora, and as that which is deeply wanted. In fact, the actual homeland nation-state recedes, as it does not seem to matter if a subject of Indianness, in this case Nita, has ever been there. Affiliation now occurs in places outside an India that Mohapatra had once so envied as a site of travel for her fellow passengers on Air India. And even political connections can result from diasporic affinity; when the author discusses the couple's trip to Ireland, one of her first points is that "many people of Indian origin know about the long struggle of the Irish people for their independence from the British rule" (16).

And finally, in leaving England, Mohapatra expresses, again, a loss of India. Never is the experience of India in Britain posed as inauthentic or treated even with the mildest form of questioning; an almost seamless reordering of place has occurred, when Indianness can really be present elsewhere:

> As we wind down our brief sojourn in Leicester, we both are becoming more and more attached to this city. When in America, we will miss our short bus ride to Belgrave Road where we have soaked up the Indian sub-culture. Your dad will miss the little Indian fast food places where he could buy a motichoor or magaz laddu for 20 pence. . . . We will miss the many youthful faces of Asian students in Kimberly Library. . . . We will miss the Saturday afternoon shoppers . . . who bought sarees, gold jewelry, and sweets. We will miss the huge posters of Bollywood Cinema displaying the latest Indian Cinema shows. (76–77)

In elaborating the connections that she is able to make between nodes of Indian diasporas, Mohapatra makes an even more powerful commentary, on the ability to recognize India in the diaspora. Her own Indianness is articulated not in America, even now as Saund's once was, but in a construction of Indian community *abroad*. In this sense, the journey implicit in Mohapatra's letters, a journey for self and group, reaches a satisfying endpoint.

Diasporic Imagining and Claiming

If this chapter has covered a long historical trajectory and broad geographical parameters, it is because Indian diasporic literature has evidenced a tremendous ability of its purveyors to cross boundaries of time and space. Given the impossibility of representativeness, of any one text or set of texts fully expressing the many and complex imaginings of Indianness, this chapter has instead presented flashpoints of the negotiations of Indianness abroad, and the contemplation of what it means to be a multinational citizen in a postwar world. Neither the writings of Dalip Singh Saund or Bharati Mukherjee should be seen as central to the experience of migration, or to the broad reading practices of a widely dispersed set of populations. It is difficult to imagine any text or set of texts having this kind of role for the Indian diaspora; the constituent populations are too dispersed and diverse for a real collectivity to emerge around coherent forms of representation. But what I have read in the texts of this chapter are stories of diaspora that are drawn on by those making and remaking an Indian subjectivity.

What we see here is that India continues to be created in and through America and Britain. And the location for Indian subject formation is very much in the diaspora, not in the homeland, though ideas about homeland circulate across time and space. This is not to say that the meetings of nations are always friendly. If Shridharani and Saund were committed to seeing the possibilities for the Indian nation-state in the American nation, Mukherjee's protagonist was unable to live that multinational encounter without deep alienation. And though the character of Tridib created imaginary maps that transcended facile borders of the nation that colonialism had drawn, the narrator of *The Shadow Lines* was all too conscious that knowledge of another country did not equal psychic comfort there.

While the Indian American Urmila Mohapatra has created an epistolary representation of finding India in England, and reversed the trajectory of Indian migration moving from Britain to the United States, renowned Indian writer Salman Rushdie has paved an imaginative path that is more conventional in terms of diasporic histories, writing of India in *Midnight's Children*, of England in *The Satanic Verses*, and making the move finally to America in his two latest books, *The Ground Beneath Her Feet* and *Fury*.[54] But more than any sort of authoritative rendering of migration in a broader structure of diaspora, these and other literary representations do suggest complicated and nonlinear directions of development and, ultimately, another configuration of the Kipling East-West divide that had once been an obsession in the diasporic imagination.

The diversity of recognition can be seen as well in two recent, very public moments of celebrating the Indian diasporic imagination. In 1999, Indian American author Jhumpa Lahiri won the Pulitzer Prize in the United States for a work of short stories, *Interpreter of Maladies*, and in 2001, Indo-Trinidadian V. S. Naipaul was awarded the Nobel Prize for Literature. Lahiri's text is saturated with India, even as it crosses all sorts of conceptual boundaries of nation. In the last line of the book's final story, "The Third and Final Continent," the narrator remarks on his experiences of thirty years outside India: "As ordinary as it all appears, there are times when it is beyond my imagination."[55] The expression here is largely of a sense of wonderment at the tremendous travels the narrator has made, with a particular attention to the past. Naipaul's feelings about the past seem rather different, when he was reported to ask at a conference entitled "Shared Histories: Issues of Colonialism and Relationship with the Past": "Why do you keep drumming up the issue of colonialism?"[56] Indianness in the public eye is both associated with and detached from the past, and relates to a wide variety of histories: colonialism, postcolonialism, migration to America, indentured labor to the Caribbean, and, in the case of Naipaul, an Anglophilia that defies all of the above.

Yet Indian migrant newspapers cover both Lahiri and Naipaul, celebrate the public affirmation of Indian writing in the West, and, in effect, claim the heterogeneity of expression as part of an Indian diaspora to which everyone belongs. Identifications with and receptions of Indianness can even accept contradiction. While narratives of "Indians in America" have often begun with the post-1965 migration of middle-class and credentialed Indians from India, more recent celebrations of Indian diasporic ethnicity make reference to Dalip Singh Saund too, who signals, if not represents, a different phase of movement (of agricultural laborers, to the U.S. West).[57] In suggesting that Saund's narrative of ascent may be an important story to recover for newer constructions of ascendant Indian ethnicity, celebrants may also see the reflection of contemporary constructions of diasporic subjectivity, as this U.S. congressman from India holds India in formation alongside a changing America.

FOUR

INDIA IN PRINT, INDIA ABROAD

I N 1970, just five years after the passage of the Immigration and Naturalization Act in the United States, an immigrant from southern India
living in New York, Gopal Raju, started a newspaper called *India
Abroad*, which would become the preeminent publication for South
Asians in the United States. The name of the paper wonderfully captured
a principal theme of diaspora: that the nation exists and continues to be
created abroad. The title and object reference of "India Abroad" also
evidence what is now an almost commonplace dictum, from the seminal
work of Benedict Anderson, that of a newspaper as another technology
for imagining nation.[1] Newspapers of the diaspora like *India Abroad* construct the nation of India and the nationality of Indianness, too, but also
mediate various and contradictory effects of the development of new social formations that are located alongside India in the global field.

For groups formed by complicated and divergent histories of movement, in which there might seem to be nothing shared, newspapers indeed
impart a sense of community. This occurs not only through the practices
of reading, but even through the fact of the publications themselves. As
a self-described organ of the migrant community, *India Abroad*, in its
very existence, signals a coherent referent population with interests and
needs. Successful development of the project of building a newspaper inspires a closer consideration of the strength of the desire for representation in the public sphere. How that public sphere is constituted, what it
includes and excludes, are questions that have been the source of much
debate in the work of Jürgen Habermas and others, and that parallel the
problematics of nationalism.[2]

This chapter establishes immigrant publications, mostly newspapers but
magazines, too, as sites for developing Indian diasporic nationalism and
multinationalism, for constructing new Indias, and for mapping out what
it might mean to become British or American. In this way, print is both a
medium for nationalism and a means of nationalization, as product and
process. Indian print media do not transparently give us the news, but
instead buttress circulating narratives of affiliation that are the building
blocks of community in the diaspora. Here India as a powerful entity in
the lives of its citizens is created by stories about politics, culture, and
economy that originate not necessarily in Bombay or New Delhi, but instead in London and New York. For immigrants, news from "home" may

appear authentically Indian, even though it is produced on their own door-steps, and in this way the question of origin—where these forms of imagining community are *from*, and where the nation of India lives—is reworked.

Newspapers also track the social formation of migrancy, that which encompasses broad experiences of race, ethnicity, and class. Papers in both Britain and the United States, but perhaps especially *India Abroad* in New York, have concerned themselves with what it means to be a citizen-subject of a country of domicile, a "new land." In 1922, sociologist Robert Ezra Park designed an outline for the ideological work that migrant newspapers do. His comments in *The Immigrant Press and Its Control*, a volume of the Carnegie Corporation–funded "Americanization Studies" series, although in the language and presumptions of its own period, find surprising complementarity with Anderson's work, particularly regarding questions of national belonging. Park considered foreign-language papers of European immigrants of the late 1800s and early 1900s, but his points about the role of the genre remain deeply evocative: "Editors . . . have claimed that their press is not merely a medium for the communication of news, thus initiating the immigrant into American environment, but is likewise a means of translating and transmitting to him American ways and American ideals."[3] It is interesting that Park should use both the constructionist, almost textualist notion of "translation" and the more literal term "transmission" in a discussion of what the press does.

Park suggests the ideological function of information undoes the seeming transparency of "the news" in ways not unlike Anderson. In a footnote in *Imagined Communities*, Anderson very precisely writes: "Reading a newspaper is like reading a novel whose author has abandoned any thought of a coherent plot."[4] Though productions of "the news" impart a sense of urgency and currency, that what is happening *now* is what is being *transmitted* in what Anderson calls "homogeneous, empty time,"[5] they look backward and forward, in historical understandings of any developments, with agendas for the future. While there is a chaos to the narrativization, there are, nonetheless, historical "plots." Those plots, in the case of diasporic print culture, have to do not only with the individual nations of America, Britain, or India, but of the relations among those three nations, and within the processes of nationalization that occur.

The work of these publications, which this chapter maps, is the bridging of geographical-conceptual distance between experiences of and desires for nations in multiple sites of diaspora. The print culture also takes the sutured nation and national community that exists "abroad" and creates a greater sense of flow as the news of India becomes almost indistinguishable from news from other places. It creates a continuum, a "horizontal comradeship" of diaspora that Anderson has written about, for the imagined communities of nations. Both implicitly and explicitly, this print culture invokes diaspora as a form of belonging that allows producers and readers to simultaneously process the local and the global; the local articulation makes sense only with global reference points and the global comes to exist locally. Immigrant newspapers like *India Abroad* in the United States or *Asian Times* in England provide at once texts for a representative performance of identities and exemplary translations of the hopes and dreams of Indian migrants in their lands of settlement. Specific stories in these papers may depict the day-to-day narrative of what it means to be an Indian in Britain or the United States just as the producers—publishers, editors, and writers—are developing a keen sense of how to construct ideologies basic to new ethnic formation. The publishers of these papers do not loftily sit above their own productions; they participate in the activities that are covered and they share in the constitution of the groups that emerge from the newspapers' audience. In this sense they are both "ethnicity entrepreneurs" and "organic intellectuals."[6] The publishers of immigrant newspapers, predominantly men, have a role in immigrant culture not unlike the merchants of Jackson Heights or Southall, the novelists in New York or London, or the leaders of political groups for independence or U.S. citizenship: they simultaneously *represent* and *construct* Indianness by establishing a public.

By closely considering a number of Indian diasporic publications and their development, this chapter attempts a rethinking of some basic questions raised by seeing print as a form of "imagining community" (Anderson), of creating a "public sphere" (Habermas), and of creating space for "translation and transmission" (Park). Some of those questions might be rephrased as follows: How, if at all, might communities be built through this medium, and what kinds of communities are they? What is the role of a literate set of actors in creating a sphere in which it is possible to articulate longings for membership? And how does the diasporic space of and in print culture allow for different possibilities that move beyond the focus on nationalism that is the primary purview of Anderson, Habermas, and Park? Preliminary answers to these questions lie in the very fact of a diasporic set of arrangements working to create an extraordinary heterogeneity, with autonomous productions that ultimately challenge any singularity associated with identity or nation. The translation of the nation of India through diasporic space can never be a perfect reproduction; it is a process of recreation. And here we return to a basic idea of this book, about the subjectivity of nation and nationality, in which India and Indianness are deeply fissured, heterogeneous, and yet tremendously powerful. Some forms of print culture, just like symbolic communities, novels, or histories, make their readers-consumers part of multiple nations and create India through that move. In utilizing strategies of transnationalism, these cultural forms have had to move between the local and global. Though most of the publications emanated from (were located in) New York and London, they also more broadly addressed Indian populations of the United States and Britain, respectively. The daunting task of determining coordinates—spatial and psychic—of a reading public in many places at once was part of the agenda faced by those who presented one kind of news at each stage of the formation of Indian diasporic cultures.

The specificity of this site, of this kind of "public," may be a key to important shifts in diasporic culture and the whole notion of belonging. The publications considered here are in English, and the products of a literate, male (petit-) bourgeoisie, much as Habermas envisioned for his public sphere. Yet the making of citizenship is of a rather different kind in our case, where the building blocks include diverse racial and ethnic identities, differential relationships to the ascendant nation-state of India, as well as economic and political success in multiple nations; participation in such an unruly set of possibilities may be more expansive than the class background of the cultural producers would prescribe. As the heterogeneous formation of diasporic print culture expands the meaning of citizenship beyond voting, identities based in acts of consumption become increasingly important, most especially as ethnicity becomes annexed to the development of new markets within the United States and Britain. More broadly, the parameters for belonging to a nation have been transformed by the most recent phases of globalization, and necessarily the notion of a public has changed too.

Indians as new citizens and as new consumers in the United States and United Kingdom, reflect such trends. Creating another historical map of Indianness, this chapter outlines the many and fractured publics of Indian diasporic print culture. While on the one hand there is a stronger argument here for the ways that Indians in the United States or Britain have at times been primarily, even solely, identified with India, the transnational strategies of identification, in their multiplicity and diversity, can also break apart the imagined communities of Anderson and the public that Habermas spoke of. Truly autonomous productions, they may organize under the sign of some ethnic-national identity (Indian, Asian), but need not always create a totality. In these publications, as in much other cultural work that is "diasporic," India and Indianness are so multiply constituted as to be at times mutually unintelligible to the actors concerned. Yet some sort of mediation does occur. In these texts, then, we see the possibilities and the limits of translation.

Hopes and Dreams for a Free India

Before 1947, Indians in the United States and Britain largely defined their relationship to a variety of states and to the very fact of being abroad through perspectives on the issue of Indian independence from British colonial rule. In 1920s New York, an organization named the Friends of Freedom for India in New York published a short, single-paged issue of news accounts from India, with a distinctly pro-labor and anti-British stance.[7] Articles described independence activist Taraknath Das's address to the American Labor Party convention,[8] strikes in India, and international relations more broadly. One article in 1920, "Boycotting the Briton," recounts a meeting at a restaurant in Manhattan involving Indians who put together a resolution to critique the Allied Treaty with Turkey, on anti-imperialist grounds, including the words, "Whereas, such an enslavement to European imperialism is a menace to all other Asiatic countries. . . ."[9] The image produced, of Indians at this time gathering in New York to denounce Western imperialism, is a particularly memorable one, especially given their small numbers.

On the West Coast, where Indians were more numerous and there was a great deal of political organization, the Hindustan Gadar Party in September 1920 began disseminating the *Independent Hindustan*, subtitled "A Monthly Review of Political, Economic, Social and Intellectual Independence of India." The ideology and rationale were noted in an article entitled "Our Aims": "Actuated by a definite, determined and deliberate purpose, we are before you to interpret and inform concerning revolutionary and progressive spirit which is guiding the destiny of India. It is our sincere desire that no pains should be spared to acquaint you with the Indian affairs in a manner that will enable you to formulate your own opinion for the guidance of your own action"[10] Other articles in the *Independent Hindustan* included profiles of important revolutionary leaders, depictions of Ireland and Persia, and discussions of the role of women in a "new India." Yet the Gadarites were also interested in the situation of immigrants in the diaspora and, not unlike more recent publications, detailed incidents of unfair treatment at the hands of American and British administrators and business officials. "Plight of Indian Labor in Fiji"[11] examined a 1920 post-indentured labor strike, and "Doing England's Dirty Work" questioned the ideals of American justice when thirty-nine Indian workers at the Bethlehem Steel factory in Bethlehem, Pennsylvania were arrested and deported by United States immigration officials, according to British wishes.[12] The producers of the paper were keenly concerned with the state of the Indian diaspora, at this time working-class in nature and widely dispersed. The more upper-class Indians, in London and some in New York, did not appear in the *Independent Hindustan's* field of vision. The paper articulated the radical possibilities of Indian independence and built an audience around that. But despite the variations in address, both the *Independent Hindustan* and the publication of the Friends of Freedom for India located their goals for India in a broader, global, framework of imperialism in which many nations, including the

United States, were perpetrators and many countries of the third world were victims. The texts of these papers developed anticolonial nationalisms and built alliances and solidarities that their authors in the independence movement would eventually build as well.

Publications in Britain during the period before independence were rather different, largely due to the special role that upper-class Indians played not only in the popular cultural understanding of what India was and could be, but also in the independence movements themselves. The contradictions of living in British society were manifested in these texts, and constituted by simultaneous attachments to English culture and feelings of victimization by British society and politics. Much as abolitionists had done in the past, groups critical of the British government's role in India mobilized Indian and English reformers to bring injustices to light and influence popular opinion. And so in the 1930s, a group called the Friends of India published the *India Bulletin*, to provide news about India and advocate independence.[13] The group was quite clear about its propagandistic intent in the very first issue: "Our object is to awaken England and to attack the century old prejudices and ignorance which prevail among Englishmen in regard to India. . . . India wants her freedom. She wants to be rid of the exploitation which has continually impoverished her during the past 150 years, and which is leading to a revolt of the starving masses. . . . Can any Briton deny these legitimate rights?[14]" Educated Indians in England and liberal anticolonial English men and women could join forces to express their common interests in home rule and incidentally raise the specter of revolution in India. Whether this was a strategy or a genuine anxiety is hard to determine for sure, but that gesture functioned at any rate as a keen reflection of the ways that British popular opinion would come to be shaped in the years preceding Indian independence. When the Friends of India commented in the pages of their newspaper, "We would convince the best minds in this country that the only way of avoiding a disaster in India is to let India choose her own path"[15] and proceeded to cover instances of violence and unrest in India,[16] they presaged the rationale that would be employed in public discussions about the inevitability of independence and the need to "leave India." The elite Indians who made their home in Britain and retained particular kinds of attachments to the homeland were as invested in a peaceful transition as their English counterparts, for their class identity was inextricably linked to images of India in England. The issue of how India would be perceived abroad would become even more important, not only to Indians in Britain, but also to those in the United States and all over the world, because it came to be centrally related to their experiences as immigrants from a new nation.

Productions in the Seat of Empire, from a New Nation

This intense focus on India and Indian politics, and the concern with the image of India abroad, lasted well after independence had been achieved. For small numbers of upper-class Indians in London, whose national identity was at best tenuous and who wished to have some distance from communities of manual laborers like lascars and ayahs, India as a place of cultural interest was integral to their self-formation. Few venues for such perspectives existed in these early years; one such publication, *India News*, was first published in 1949 by the Public Relations Department of the High Commissioner for India.[17] Its likely audience was Indians in London as well as "friends of India," those English people who had valued Indian culture and supported Indian independence. In addition to general news about India, *India News* featured notices of Indian films, dance performances, and other cultural events in London. The section entitled "Indians Abroad" covered less the activities of ordinary immigrants than it did those of diplomats and other government officials who traveled to England on business.

The familiar tropes of immigration—assimilation and national integration—were absent from this version of India-centric postcolonial reportage. Given that *India News* was for a long time the only publication of its kind, it can be seen as reflecting the ways in which Indianness was both constructed by and dictated to a class of people that claimed an Indian British subjectivity. Diasporic affiliation, to India as a particular kind of place, constructed the logic of the paper. Both the recent nature of Indian independence and the urgency of the state-building process functioned to create the only available language of identity, in Indianness, for a British Indian population small in number and faced with a society and culture that, on the whole, was deeply hostile to the former racialized subjects of the empire. This production anchored class status to a glorification of India, internally and externally. By looking outward, toward India, elite British Indians could avoid looking downward, toward their working-class brethren. In this way, then, material and social resources structured the very representational possibilities of the diaspora among Indians in Britain in the late 1940s and 1950s.

Beginning in the late 1950s, large numbers of Indians began to come to England, and new and diverse interests began to take shape in resident populations. Places like Southall began to house concentrations of Indians. The rise of an Indian British community took place under the rubric of entirely different class, racial, and national subjectivities from an earlier period in which elite Indians maintained control over *India News*. Immigration as a term and concept began to have meaning for Indians abroad;

so too did an immigrant press newly address the needs and desires of a constituency encompassing (at least) two countries and cultures.[18] While all papers dealt with the contingencies of Indians' lives in Britain, they also maintained important links with India and saw as part of their central mission the reporting of news from the subcontinent.

The first among these papers was *India Weekly*.[19] First published in 1964, with the subtitle "News of India and Indians Abroad," it described a dual set of interests, in the nation of India and its peoples who have gone abroad. The first issue described the lack of cohesion among Indian immigrants: "There are over 150,000 Indians scattered throughout Britain who have no regular link as between themselves, or with their homeland, or the British people in whose midst they live,"[20] and thus disclosed the paper's deliberate efforts to create an interest group. The paper treated a range of activities within the Indian community, including academic honors gained by schoolchildren as well as meetings of the Indian Workers Association in Southall, and also held forth on the general goal of unifying the community. In a 1965 article entitled "Unity in Diversity," the editorial staff wrote: "There is a large number of Indian organizations in Great Britain, much larger than justified. Many of these are fully representative and rendering useful service. . . . But their activities are often hampered and their energies dissipated through duplication of effort, which creates an impression of Diversity without Unity. . . . The remedy certainly lies in the application of the time-honoured Indian principle of Unity in Diversity."[21] What was becoming a varied set of communities, whose differences of class and racial experience could quite distinguish the many elements from one another, was one that *India Weekly* sought to address in an appeal to and construction of a more nation-based identity, in Indianness. Not surprisingly, it imported a language for multiplicity, "unity in diversity," from India, to construct a more cohesive sense of nationality for those abroad, and to representatively iron out any difference that could level a real challenge to the whole of Indianness.

A good deal of space in *India Weekly* was accorded to news from India, in a format very similar to the High Commission's *India News*. A common title for celebrating the paper's work, and for elaborating the activities of immigrants was, in fact, "India Abroad," which implied obvious attachments to the symbolic and material world of "India." The founders, T. P. Basu, Iqbal Singh, and K. S. Shalvankar, specifically assigned to *India Weekly* the role of promoting nonalignment and India's "point of view"[22] as a counternarrative to British-influenced material on India, as well as to the Cold War and Commonwealth ideology. Indian nationhood was the main concern of this publication from its very outset.

For a long time, *India Weekly* served the community as the primary English-language paper for Indian immigrants. Smaller papers appeared and quickly disappeared from the scene throughout the 1960s and early 1970s as the immigrant populations underwent a series of transformations.[23] In part, the relationship of immigrants to both their homeland and their place of residence had changed. While the early years of post-independence immigration had seen small numbers of Indians scattered around England, slowly building centers of social, political, and cultural activity, by the 1970s established communities had formulated new kinds of consciousness as well as a stated commitment to the representation and, to some extent, reproduction of Indian interests within British society. While Indians' investments in a vision of the India back home (in terms of politics and culture) endured, immigrants now also felt the need to develop languages to describe their experiences in British terms. Just as the new and proud Indian citizenship of the immediate postwar period ignited the imaginations of the earliest immigrants, citizenship within the British nation now began to emerge as also important in the words and deeds of Indians who had been in the country for some time. Dual imperatives of citizenship, in more than one country, engendered complex, multiple, and even performative identities that would be worked out in politics, culture, and also in print.

One primary sphere of identification was race. As formerly colonized peoples of the empire, Indians had always been racialized by the British state, by British society, and more generally by its national cultures. Yet in the pre-independence period, the propagation of a racial approach to India and its peoples existed largely in international terms, as a way to organize and understand the place of countries in the world, and particularly as justification for British political control of the more inferior India. As Indians began to settle in England, racism changed in form and content and turned inward, such that what developed were almost distinct formulations of colonialism and postcolonialism, depending on the moment of construction, as well as on the referent population. Early immigrants of the 1950s and 1960s battled a racism that they understood through being formerly and very recently colonized; national and nationalist attachments to India provided useful foils to the exoticization of, condescension toward, and degrading of the country from which they had moved yet toward which they continued to retain ties. To portray India as a serious geopolitical (and nonaligned) power contradicted and challenged the prevailing assumption that Indians were racially inferior. The print culture of the earlier period, then, was not free of "racial" content even as it framed its address in "national" terms; for this and other examples, the assertion of Indianness was at once a national, transnational, and racial strategy.

But the different forms of racial victimization of Indians in Britain during the 1970s produced new kinds of identities and a surprising critical consensus around the perceived role of the British state in abdicating its responsibilities to its English and non-English citizens. As Indian workers and professionals saw doors of employment closed to them, regardless of their qualifications, as they witnessed the hostilities of white residents to their continued presence in the cities of England, most especially London, and as their children began to be attacked by white racist youths, Indians developed a racial consciousness with a number of designations, the most popular of which were "Asian" and "Indian."[24]

Gurdip Singh Chaggar's murder in 1976 and the Blair Peach incident in 1979, both in Southall,[25] were acute representations of the blatant forms of racism that existed in British society, directed both at Indian peoples and at the idea of an immigrant presence in London. These local events had effects on national representations, as they forced Indian journalists to develop a discourse that could clearly address the problems of immigrants and their settlement in England and thereby define constituencies of opposition. More mainstream venues like *India Weekly* only reluctantly confronted the issue: "Ours is not an immigrant journal; its range of interest is at once more specific and wider. [H]owever, the growing insolence of the racialists lobby in this country and the consequential increase in violence against members of immigrant communities, of which the murder of Gurdip Singh Chaggar in Southall last Friday night is a gruesome reminder, are matters of international, not least Indian, concern."[26] In the very next issue, *India Weekly* had both an article citing the Indian Workers Association's efforts to maintain calm in Southall and also an interview with Margaret Thatcher, then opposition leader in Parliament, who stressed the work of the Conservative Party in trying to end discrimination against Asians from Uganda.[27] In this gesture, the publication effectively institutionalized a more "middle ground" vis-à-vis racial insurgency and racism.

Thus *India Weekly*, a mainstream Indian newspaper in London, shifted its sense of itself at this politically critical moment; though it had originally eschewed the label of "immigrant journal," it did indeed cover what became an "immigrant issue." Developing a public argument about how the newspaper was compelled to deal with the Chaggar incident because of its "Indian" and "international" importance, the editors then went on to decry *racial* violence against Indian *immigrants*. Arguably, this was a formative moment for the ways in which *India Weekly* addressed and formulated publics, and also acted to reflect political shifts in its referent population. Given that class-diverse British Indians at this moment could not extricate themselves from the racial and national worlds in which they resided, and to which they had to respond as immigrants, their organs for expression, too, mirrored those changes.

But in this representational crisis we might also see the clearing and expanding of the field for other kinds of narratives, in print culture and elsewhere. An entirely different set of ideologies from those of *India Weekly* was portrayed in *Asian Post*,[28] subtitled "The voice of Asians in Britain." In December 1979, a photograph of Indians at a protest accompanied the lead article "What we want is Asian Power," with the subtitle "We have come here to stay." The pseudonymous Anand Naidoo discussed the merits of subcontinental unity, and treated Indians, Pakistanis, and Bangladeshis as collectively Asian, requiring both solidarity and power in the face of the historical efforts of the British state to deny their human rights. He questioned the tactic of nonviolence: "The image of the Indian as a peaceful non-violent chap has sometimes done him a great deal of harm. Instead of regarding it as a highly civilized virtue that there are human beings who are genuinely against violence, the people among whom the Asians have settled have often interpreted this as weakness and cowardice."[29] Significantly, the article ended with an implicit plea not only to non-national identifications, but also to crossracial solidarities through a critique of Indians' lack of support for black nationalist regimes in Africa. As a category for identity, "Asian," then, afforded entree into the more progressive, transnational, and racially articulated politics of the period. Yet its functional importance also lay in a gesture toward a quasi-racial grouping that could be anchored to an immigrant experience. In addition to the inclusive nature of the identity, "Asian interests" also suggested international reference points, not only India, but Pakistan, Bangladesh, Uganda, Kenya, Zanzibar, and other points of settlement for the diaspora. In this way, *Asian Post* reflected the more militant aspects of Indians' political struggles in the late 1970s and early 1980s: racially identificatory as well as aligned with critiques of global power arrangements. Its decline a couple of years after its initial publication indicates less the disappearance of those ideologies, and more their suppression and absorption by liberal institutions created out of struggles during the 1970s.

Efforts to create a counternarrative to the more militant ones being espoused by a publication like *Asian Post* were evident in the revival of *India News* in 1978 by the High Commission,[30] at a critical moment when responses to racism in British society were taking shape. In the first reissue of the paper, no less than N. G. Goray, High Commissioner for India, wrote: "We are resuming publication of *India News* after a pretty long time. A lot of water has flown down the Thames during this period of self-imposed silence. Back home in India, the people have reaffirmed their commitment not merely to the form of a parliamentary Government but a democratic way of life. . . . The foreign news media cannot be expected to convey in an adequate measure our country's significant achievements in many fields."[31] Subsequent issues were filled with highly glorified descriptions of the achievements of India and Indians in Britain. Two institutions in particular received a great deal of press: Bharatiya Vidya Bhavan and the Commonwealth Institute, the first of which deserves attention here.

The Bharatiya Vidya Bhavan, or the Institute of Indian Culture, stands as a perfect manifestation of the efforts of middle-class Indians to promote a glorified vision of India in the West. It is in this sense very much a diasporic organization, with links to Indian communities all around the world; as such, immigrant newspapers, particularly those with predilections toward a more middle-class, specifically Indian identity, have often devoted a good deal of space to its activities.[32] Supported by Mahatma Gandhi, Dr. K. M. Munshi founded the Bharatiya Vidya Bhavan in India in 1938, and its British branch was started in June 1973 in London.[33] The Bhavan's activities in London have always included both religious and nonreligious high cultural events, like dance performances, literary readings, and musical concerts, all with the express participation from and support of British government officials and Indian commissioners. The opening of more elaborate premises in 1978 was attended by the British prime minister,[34] and established the organization as a special and chosen representative of respectable Indian community. The rise of Bharatiya Vidya Bhavan coincided, then, with more general attempts to construct distinct international stories about the Indian immigrant that focused on India as a site for the production of identities, in the face of developments like progressive activism and attraction to black power within Indian communities. Covering the events of the Bhavan was more than a service by *India News*; it was a demonstration of the ideological contours of its own choices, however unconscious, to advocate and sustain the organization's nonradical vision of India, Indian society, and immigrant presence in London. A counterpoint to this formation could be seen in the short-lived *Asian Post*, and its announcement of crossracial political meetings. The ways in which immigrant newspapers covered the activities of one organization or another more generally reflected their location in a political spectrum. The public that was constructed through certain forms of print culture may overlap here with those created in and by associational cultures.

Yet at the same time, even *India News* could not completely ignore the racial violence that beset Indian immigrants during the late 1970s and early 1980s. Indians were simply unable to disavow a specifically racial experience and had on some level to acknowledge their victimization by English society in a way that set them apart from Indian American migrants at the time, as we will see. The glories of India and the potential successes of her immigrants were cold comforts in the face of the National Front meeting in Southall's Town Hall. The May 3, 1979, issue of *India*

News published an article on the hostilities in Southall, but framed it, like *India Weekly* had, as an international and/or Indian issue, citing the statement of concern made by Samarendra Kundu, the Minister of State in the Ministry of External Affairs in India, in the Lok Sabha (Indian parliament).[35] Ventriloquizing their protest through the Indian Foreign Office circumvented an analysis of racism in British society; the paper effectively cast a racial attack as the product of a poorly managed "racial environment,"[36] and thus exceptional.

The events of this period in Southall and elsewhere produced a range of political, social, and cultural strategies for coping with the changing realities of being an Indian immigrant in England. After the continued opposition of an impressive coalition of political forces, involving students, the working class, and Asian and Afro-Caribbean peoples, British society and politics experienced dramatic transformations. The Labour Party returned to power in 1974 and began to respond to issues of inequality more forcefully than they had in the past. The Race Relations Act of 1976 instituted the Commission for Racial Equality (CRE), which came to have an important role in politically progressive responses of the state to social stratification. In the early 1980s the Greater London Council (GLC) developed strategies for working on antiracist measures at the local level with much success. Yet the National Front and other anti-immigrant groups and sentiments also grew during this period and succeeded in pressuring the state to limit the effects of progressive policies, if not to adopt its racist perspective during a time of high inflation and unemployment. Multiculturalism, as a pedagogic strategy to incorporate racial minorities into British society, became prevalent in educational institutions (as well as in political appeals) while at the same time stimulating questions about the real meaning of equal opportunity for immigrants and other racial minorities.[37]

Indian Print in North America

It was not until 1970, five years after the 1965 Immigration Act, that a weekly newspaper emerged in New York to address a broader immigrant Indian community. South Indian migrant Gopal Raju began to see in the late 1960s the development of significant populations of Indian immigrants in the United States and other places and, concomitantly, the need for a publication to provide news to these diverse peoples. He started *India Abroad* first as a monthly, then as a fortnightly, and finally as a weekly paper. His original intention was to "cover all Indians outside India, including the United States, Canada and Britain,"[38] and his choice of a name for the paper reflected this broadly diasporic address. Yet the rise of *India Abroad* also perfectly coincided with the inception of a coherent and self-conscious Indian American immigrant community, a national immigrant community that, like others in the past, could be identified through community institutions like temples and political organizations, as well as its own newspaper.

India Abroad operated as the only weekly newspaper for Indians in the United States through the 1970s. Both its status as the first Indian immigrant newspaper and its central location in New York, the emerging center of Indian immigrant life, ensured its extraordinary role in reflecting and constituting political and social formations of the community. The cultural project that was *India Abroad*, though, was extensive and in-depth, and news stories beginning in the 1970s did a wonderful job of explaining the many contradictions of life in the United States, and the texture of becoming a multinational: a citizen of India, the United States, and the diaspora.

Articles in *India Abroad*, like those in London's *India Weekly*, centered on the Indian nation-state, and often just briefly mentioned Indian events in New York.[39] India's political position in the world was of special interest, particularly as that was understood to impact the received images of its far-flung citizens. In the 1970s, nonalignment was still an important geopolitical arrangement and axis of alliances for India. And nonalignment profoundly shaped how Indians experienced social division and nationality. Not surprisingly, it was a major theme in *India Abroad*'s news of the period. One article heaping praise on India's great ally Mexico, for example, evokes the third-worldist sentiments of a generation. The first paragraph of the 1974 piece entitled "Mexico, Another Indian Counterpart" reads: "For Indians, Mexico is the only country which provides all that is missing in the Western hemisphere. People are warm and friendly. They eat the same sort of food with lots of spices and, above all, they have a sense of respect concerning anything related to India. Here there is no color bar. Mexicans look so much like Indians that there is no possibility of racial discrimination."[40] Despite the careful maintenance in most other contemporaneous articles of the absence of racial discrimination in the United States, this author's fondness for Mexico has both racial and national dimensions that become somewhat conflated in the context of nonalignment. Exalted here is the sense that not only is there "no color bar" in Mexico, but also respect and admiration for India. The author comments later in the article that there is even a statue of Mahatma Gandhi in Mexico. In the desire for Mexico we might read the disappointments and melancholy of the migrant experience in the United States, an experience that provides an unstated and comparative point of reference.

Clearly migrants' locations in the United States posed a particular set of problems to any seamless support for a nonaligned India. And so, in

India Abroad's pages, there are stated ambivalences about India's relationship to the rest of the world. In a 1974 opinion piece, Rita Fawaz writes of the need for India to be less aggressive in its articulation of nonalignment, in order to cultivate the United States: "India certainly needs economic aid at this stage, and it will be in India's national interest if she expresses restraint in areas of disagreement."[41] And in 1979 in particular, Cuba proved a particularly vexing issue for Indian immigrants who were also invested in their position in a United States that was in the midst of Cold War tensions.[42] Yet at the same time, the paper did report a historic twenty-five-year commemoration of the Bandung Conference in Kuala Lumpur by India and other countries.[43] Multiple affiliations produced a dense, overlapping, and sometimes conflictive field of nationalisms. What these and other articles suggest is that while it was possible to be Indian and American, such an endeavor was marked by the profound strain intrinsic to postwar geopolitical arrangements.

Though *India Abroad* through the 1970s focused on the politics and economy of the Indian nation-state, a concern with what living in a new country meant was also present. Unsurprisingly, anxieties about a new nationality, about "becoming American," were manifested in discourses of assimilation, particularly as the decade drew to a close. Perhaps the most evocative of this inclination was a piece by Jane Chandra entitled "Up the Corporate Ladder," which appeared in May 1979. Beginning with the rhetorical questions: "Is it possible for an Indian in the United States to achieve a top position in his company or profession? Or is there a form of discrimination which allows him to climb only so far?" the article goes on to suggest that there may be "social reasons" for the disappointments of professional limits in the United States. Chandra then constructs a survey to investigate that possibility, with questions about bathing and dental habits, clean clothing, command of English, and table manners. She ends by asking: "How well do *you* fit in? . . . Have you become part of the American scene?"[44] Chandra's understanding of what it took to succeed in U.S. society was not unusual among Indian immigrants, in fact, especially in the 1970s among earlier and more credentialed immigrants, it was a widespread view.

The economic successes of many produced special investments in individualistic and entrepreneurial philosophies, often at the expense of structural or, for that matter, racialized understandings of the host society. And so in June 1979, when Mayor Ed Koch called on Indian community members to help revitalize less prosperous neighborhoods in New York, he said: "People admire hard working, middle class, ethnic-oriented people. They pay taxes and the City needs them desperately. They create jobs. We need more Indians in the City."[45] Almost a perfect encapsulation of model-minority mythology, this view of immigration was no doubt rather compelling to readers and, to be sure, it was not completely untrue, either, as a large majority of Indians in the United States at this time had achieved significant levels of financial success. The strength of the appeal of Koch's language was reflected in the editorial decision of *India Abroad* to report this event on its first page, though that coveted space was normally reserved for news from India.

But these expressions in support of assimilation were hardly left uncontested. Even in the 1970s, fissures in the productions of a desire for becoming American could be found within the paper, most especially in the "Letters to the Editor" column. In general, the letters sections of newspapers are useful sites in which to see commentary on the constructions that editors, publishers, and writers together make. Even though the space is patrolled by publishers, the genre itself demands a reasonable degree of dissent with what has been written in the past, and therefore produces a rendition of "experience" that is akin to ethnographic information. And of *India Abroad*, I would also suggest that the mechanisms of inclusion were relatively loose in the 1970s when the readership of the newspaper was small, and Gopal Raju, the publisher, was more actively involved and invested in the broad expression of Indian American communities. Two months after Jane Chandra's article on social assimilation, a reader responded in a letter subtitled "A Poor Sermon": "Her suggestions are a superficial and simplistic solution to an extremely complex problem."[46] In the use of the term "sermon," even the newspaper seemed to recognize, perhaps unconsciously, the patronizing didacticism inherent in Chandra's piece.

It is also in the letters section that one can appreciate the difficulties of Gopal Raju's project. In seeking to create a notion of India abroad, the paper had to not only provide information about the nation-state, but generate an audience with common, shared interests. While in later years the prospect of sublimating regional, religious, or linguistic differences in the interest of Indianness would become more tenuous, in the 1970s, this possibility was still being actively pursued in a variety of arenas, most vividly demonstrated in the ultimately successful push for an "Asian Indian" category in the 1980 census. But by the late 1970s, as the effects began to be felt of another wave of post-1965 migration, of family members and some less credentialed peoples, regional and class diversity proved more difficult to manage, even for the "ethnicity entrepreneurs" like Raju. It was somehow fitting that in 1979, the year before the turn of the decade, and the institutionalization of Indian ethnicity within a major U.S. governmental agency, as well as just before more politically conservative approaches to immigration grabbed the spotlight, a major controversy about regional and class prejudices should break out in the pages of *India Abroad*.

Initiating a vitriolic debate was a letter responding to an article about the increase in the number of motels owned in the United States by Gujarati Patels. S. N. Rao of New York wrote: "I dislike discussing the drawbacks of Indians but after reading . . . about the influx of Indians, particularly those from Gujarat into the motel business, I would like to add something. . . . This community's business ethics are notorious and not acceptable in any country but India, where it has to compete with another community more adept in the same business ethics. . . . What worries me is that problems might be created similar to those in Burma, Uganda and Singapore, where the whole Indian community was victimized."[47]

Rao betrayed anxieties over the representation of Indians and their national integration, those that many Indian migrants of his generation harbored, especially after the recent expulsions from Uganda and Kenya in the early 1970s.[48] But the articulation of these fears through a set of thinly veiled class and regional prejudices inflamed Gujarati Indian immigrants, who were becoming as devoted to their regional identity as to their Indianness. There was a flurry of responses, including one from the president of the Gujarati Samaj of New York that decried the "degrading of the Gujarati business community,"[49] and another that remarked that "Rao's reaction was indeed disappointing in that a man thousands of miles from India continues to stereotype his fellow countrymen on the basis of where they hail from."[50] Raju himself then intervened with a "Letter from the Publisher" on June 29, 1979: "It is unfortunate that a letter . . . has created misunderstanding, hurt, and even hostility among some of our readers in the Gujarati Patel community. . . . The last thing we would like is to hurt anyone's feelings or be accused of parochialism. We try our utmost to be the source of impartial information on India and the Indian community in North America."[51] Raju continued to stress his own nonpartisanship, citing the fact that he wrote nothing about Indian electoral politics or anything else on the editorial page. But partisanship in 1979 was not only political in nature; it was also inflected by region and class. The Indian migrant consciousness that the pages of *India Abroad* were able to capture in eight pages in 1970, had grown and diversified by 1979 far beyond even its recently allotted twenty pages.

In many ways the newspaper functioned best, and most uncontroversially, around the broader identity of the nonresident Indian: a migrant culturally and socially connected to his Indian homeland and intent on fostering a deeper, economic relationship with the nation-state. The growth of *India Abroad* converged with India's stated interests in garnering increased investments from its citizens abroad, particularly from its wealthy offspring in the United States. And the producers of the paper provided a space in which to actualize those goals of India and its migrants. Articles like "Indian Scientist in US Discusses Ways to Help India

Meet her Needs," or an Indian Embassy–sponsored seminar series, "India Gives Foreign Investors High Returns," or "How to Invest Funds in India,"[52] each testified to not only the active role that India played in producing transnational financial networks, but also to the participation of *India Abroad* in these negotiations; indeed, prominent businessmen and government officials from India often first visited the offices of the newspaper before continuing their travels in the United States. Yet the newspaper also reported fluctuations and uncertainty amid the boosterism for continued flows of capital to India, just as actual migrant investment in the homeland waxed and waned.

Often, connections with India themselves were the subject of questioning within the pages of *India Abroad*. In a piece entitled "Reorientation Program Urged for Indians," Jagannath J. Desai remarked: "It is time [for] some reorientation program about Indian culture and Indian conditions . . . for Indians visiting their motherland after a lapse of five or more years, so as to save them from the intellectual snobbery and condescending airs they often show toward everything Indian."[53] Many readers also wrote letters protesting the enormous attention paid by the newspaper and Indian associations more generally to events back home, to the detriment of political and social matters in the United States, particularly those involving some form of discrimination.[54]

What is striking is the relative noncoverage in this venue of important incidents in Southall throughout the 1970s. Often news about these events came not from England, but through Reuters in India, or via the comments of an Indian government official.[55] At this crucial period in the development of Indian migrant populations in the United States and Britain, cultural producers across the ocean seemed not to be in much contact. If and when *India Abroad* did depict England, it was with regard to experiences of racialization. In fact, race was first discussed in this Indian American immigrant paper with regard to those Indians who had gone to Britain, instead of to the United States. Clearly anxieties about the racialization of Indians in the United States could be assuaged through a distancing (it was worse over there), or simply repressed, particularly at a time when migrants were coming to terms with a choice to immigrate to America instead of to England. Print affirmed all those decisions.

British Indians of the 1980s:
New Identifications and Old Allegiances

Though British Indians were an older community and a greater percentage of the overall population, their publications did not approach the breadth and reach of *India Abroad*. Still kicking around was *India Weekly*, but its narrow concerns simply could not capture the transformed imaginings of a set of varied and growing immigrant communities in the 1980s. The decade was a period of new dissatisfactions, desires, and oppositional co-alitions to the state as well as to interest groups working with established power structures. Emerging from these complex experiences among Indians were new discourses for individual and group subjectivity and, con-comitantly, new ways of experiencing immigrant status in British society.

Though numerous and complex, the discourses fall into two general categories, corresponding to two emblematic responses of the first genera-tion to the experience of migration. The first response was more racially articulated. It stressed an ethnic identity that centered on the immediate realities of racial life in Britain, on the ever-present memory of having once been colonial subjects, and on the felt need for political connections among racial minorities in England—particularly Indian, Pakistani, Bangladeshi, and Afro-Caribbean peoples, despite the acrimonious wars of the early 1970s involving Pakistan, Bangladesh, and India. This group of interests tended to adopt with more frequency the identity of "Asian," and functioned at some remove from subcontinental antagonisms. The second type of political discourse, more nationally defined, foregrounded Indian origin and maintained an interest in national politics in India; like-wise its cultural focus was on things Indian. Though this strand of identity formation did not completely eschew the term "Asian," an oft-used cate-gory within mainstream English society, it nonetheless mostly employed "Indian" as a descriptive tool.

Two migrant newspapers of the 1980s illustrate these diverging trends of Indian debate in London and also, more important, the subsequent trajectories of political development and identification. The first, *Asian Times*, explicitly defined itself as "a campaigning weekly." Formally begun in 1983,[56] *Asian Times* directed itself to covering issues of immigrants who were Asian, which encompassed Indians, Pakistanis, Bangladeshis, and Sri Lankans but also Indians (mostly) and other Asians who had come to England via the West Indies, from places like Trinidad, Jamaica, and Guy-ana. The paper explicitly defined a constituency in non-national terms and implicitly through racial terminology. In the first issue, editors were unreserved about their political agenda: "The first thing to remember about the *Asian Times* is that it is a campaigning newspaper. It is not being published for profit nor will it be a tame spokesman for the very tame conservative Asian establishment. While we welcome Asian enterprise and success in small business . . . it will be highly misleading to suggest that Asians in trade comprise the majority of the population."[57] Reacting against a trend among Indians and other Asians in England to newly define themselves as a successful class of business people, this paper spoke to another reality, of the perspective of many Asian peoples in working-class occupations. While being careful not to dismiss the petit-bourgeois strategies of capitalism out of hand (as the first *Asian Post* had), the paper did argue for a more class-diverse representation of the community.

This particular deployment of the term "Asian" in the 1980s reshaped the ways in which readers were invited to consume the news and imagine themselves as subjects in British society. On the one hand, *Asian Times* buttressed a left-of-center politics in the face of a rightward turn in British mainstream politics. In its first issue it critiqued the (new) *Asian Post*: "The *Asian Post*, one of whose founders is the Liberal Lord Avebury, has come out strongly in defence of apartheid [it had protested the exclusion of South Africa from international athletic competitions] while taking a swipe at General Zia's regime in Pakistan."[58] Later in the same article, it implied that the Asian editor was being disregarded by more conservative elements. Within the ideology of *Asian Times* there was an apparent correspondence between an Asian racial identity and a liberal political position, all through a more internationalist framework. Hospitality toward the apartheid state and hostility toward a Pakistani military regime aligned with a white British perspective, and were deemed contrary to an Asian point of view. This strategic positionality intervened in the mainstream British public sphere as an oppositional force, both for its articulation with racial communities within England and its third-worldist orientation.

Asian Times defined its own concern with immigrant activities within such a political framework by expressing support for the Commission for Racial Equality (CRE) and discussing cases of racial discrimination within immigrant communities. The paper's coverage of more "cultural activities" included both the Indian high cultural forms, like Bharatnatyam dance and classical music, and also Bollywood stars and the more hybrid activities of British Asian filmmakers and artists. Though the cultural producers who appeared in the pages of the *Asian Times* were most often Indian, the specific labeling of this work as "Asian" was a direct product of antinational and coalitional political interests.[59] A shift also resulted partly from the growing economic divergences among segments of the "Asian" community, those differences that were to some extent nationally specific. In large part, Indians were becoming more solidly upper- and upper-middle-class as larger segments of Pakistani and Bangladeshi populations remained poor and working class.[60] More affluent Indians tried to maintain control over the use of the term "Indian," if not explicitly then certainly implicitly with the constant marshaling of their cultural superiority and high per capita income levels. Pakistani and Bangladeshi groups, though involved in their own processes of self-representation, were nonetheless more economically diverse groups with accordingly less cultural power in England.

That more exclusive rendering of the identity of "Indian" simply could not accommodate the complicated subjectivity of Arif Ali, the owner of the *Asian Times*. Ali, an Indian Muslim immigrant from Guyana, had been in the business of publishing material about British racial minorities since 1970. His company, Hansib Publishing Ltd., published not only newspapers such as *Asian Times*, *African Times*, and *Caribbean Times*, but also monthly journals and many books about immigrants and the third world.[61] Ali himself was self-conscious about his role in the production of coalitional, cross-racial political cultures and in this way was very much a contemporary "organic intellectual."[62] The concerns of *Asian Times* and its construction of itself as "a little radically minded," in Ali's words, centered around implicit and explicit critiques of British racism, advocacy of third worldist politics, and a celebration of cultures related in some way to or originating from the Indian subcontinent.

A rather different interest in the Indian subcontinent was reflected in the rise of *India Mail* in 1989.[63] The entry into the market of this new major weekly signified another trend in the articulation of "Indian" interests from those previously addressed by publications that had invoked India. A group in India started the paper and divided its production staff between Bombay and London; its content and editorial perspectives revolved around business interests and unsubtly encouraged larger and deeper investments in the Indian business sector. But with the editorial control for the paper based in London, *India Mail* covered issues pertaining to the Indian immigrant community, including cultural achievements of the first and second generations, race relations, and medicine; as editor Shiv Sharma noted, the paper has been "mostly aimed at professional people."[64] Sharma also suggested that the newspaper's role in the immigrant community was to provide a counterpoint to mainstream media's negative constructions of Indian communities, that there was in fact a great deal of "positive" images of immigrant achievements in England, what he called "good news stories."

Shiv Sharma, like Arif Ali of *Asian Times* or, for that matter, Gopal Raju of *India Abroad*, was an organic intellectual in his own right. Not only did Sharma see for himself and his work a role in a community of British Indians, he also wrote fiction and in 1990 published a novel entitled *Dimly Before Dawn* about a photographer in Bombay and the alienation that urban life has produced.[65] Born in India, Sharma came to Britain in 1960 and worked on various British newspapers including the *Manchester Daily Telegraph*, the *Daily Mail*, the *Guardian*, and the *Daily Mirror*. His personal experience of being marked as an Asian journalist and his knowledge of general stereotypes about Asians within the mainstream media seemed to influence his social goals for *India Mail* that existed quite separately from the other aims of the paper.

India Mail seemed to contain two different papers: the news section, over which Sharma retained editorial control, and the "Business Mail" section, dominated by business news from India and presided over by a chief executive with specifically financial objectives. This latter section was a quasi-distinct publication, save for its numbered pages that fell into sequence with the other parts of the newspaper. It consisted almost entirely of accounts of economic trends in India and the health of Indian commercial enterprises; periodically, though very seldom, the section also contained a photograph or short piece on the Indian government's activities outside the business realm. The chief executive, Anil Tandon, had a vision for *India Mail* that more vigorously elaborated the economic interests of the thoroughly middle-class Indian immigrant community, noting with obvious pleasure that Indians were "extremely successful in comparison with other groups of immigrants, certainly in comparison with other groups of Asian immigrants but also in comparison with other groups of immigrants generally."[66] Tandon intimated that the readership the staff sought to address was composed, for the most part, of Indian professionals who were well regarded within British society. It is that professional class that the India-produced "Business Mail" section of the paper seemed most interested in tapping for future investment, via coverage of issues more immediately relevant to their British-centered lives. Tandon remarked that there were a "lot more Indians aware of opportunities in India, an astonishing amount of progress in India, a very upbeat feeling there that the country is developing economically in contrast to [a] very downbeat feeling in Europe . . . [that] things are getting worse."[67] The comment was striking not only for its straightforward nationalist pride, but also for its counterposing of progress in India to depressed circumstances at home in England (or Europe).

While *India Mail* presupposed that social experience in Britain was important, its primary economic interest lay in the promise of investment in India, and in this way the publication constructed Indian economic success as a kind of commodity, an object of desire, and ultimately a salve for immigrant life. By containing a business section that could be easily removed but was not, the paper implied that it was not sufficient to live the day-to-day of social and educational achievement in Britain. The conception and production of this paper in India (and an Indian company's full control over the "Business Mail" section) suggested important business interests that strove for greater investment in India and also a British Indian–generated surplus to be invested. The participation in and shaping of that goal by journalists with first-hand knowledge of the experiences and desires of the immigrant community itself made such ambitions possible through the obvious divisions in the text as a whole.

Though the paper drew on transnational connections, it did so within geographical limits. The links here were to the nation-state of India, and not necessarily to the United States or other sites of the Indian diaspora. While periodically there were references to Indian communities elsewhere in the world, there was never any aggressive effort to recover Indianness in the ways that other nationally oriented (Indian) productions did. *India Mail*'s angle on India remained in the domain of economic activities of the Indian state and as such prevented a dabbling in other ideological spheres, particularly that of nostalgia. The India that *India Mail* accessed and had a role in creating was steadfastly a new, postcolonial, and ascendantly capitalist state. Its address to an Indian migrant public created that India abroad.

Maintaining British social life and Indian economic investments separately for Indian immigrants, as *India Mail* did, enabled a frank discussion of racism and a stated commitment to diversity, precisely because those subjects could exist in a realm that did not seem to affect the healthy economic future much farther away, and might even lead Indian immigrants back to India, if not to a place of residence, then perhaps to a place of investment. Both Sharma and Tandon acknowledged the continued prevalence of racial incidents in England and the need for a migrant paper to deal honestly with the discrimination that Indians faced in the present, not just relate it as a problem of the past.[68] A 1994 issue of *India Mail*, for example, featured five major stories on racism.[69] Targeted as the paper was to an audience that saw itself as specifically Indian, *India Mail* nonetheless remained committed to diversity in the Indian population, and worked to smooth over quite intense rifts between different religious groups by including stories about Muslims (like having a special Eid issue in 1994), as well as Hindus and Sikhs, a not altogether common practice within India-specific cultural work.

Strikingly for the time, and despite the title of the paper, *India Mail* did not eschew the use of other terminology for Indian immigrants, though it did advance "Indian" as the more accurate of the terms.[70] The paper employed "Asian" to refer to ethnic minorities, particularly when discussing issues of governmental regulation or public forms of discrimination. Thus the development of a national "Indian" constituency did not necessitate the denial of the political reality of Indians being racial minorities within England. The producers noted simply that using the term "Asian" deployed common usage. While that singular fact was not extraordinary, its coupling with the specific intentions of the business-oriented group in India was notable for the suggestion of increasingly direct strategies of transnational capitalist interests.

That very functional nationalism and frankness about migrant life were in notable contrast to the earlier coverage of *India News*, and the activities of *India Weekly*. Ideologically, *India Weekly* remained true to its original intentions by constructing its constituency as specifically Indian, covering political news from India with a bent toward Congress Party affiliations, and detailing the cultural activities of Indians in London. Its position on "immigrant issues" has persisted in remarkably similar form in the early 1990s to its original promise to refrain from dwelling on such Indian British experiences. Peter Pendsay, the editor at the time, remarked that they are "not involved in racism," and that discrimination is "exaggerated by ethnic minorities themselves."[71] Pendsay observed further, with some disdain, that there were sections of community workers that have "allied themselves with West Indians"[72] and that there was not much in that possibility. These comments expressed how the editorial construction of "Indianness" could exist very much in an imaginary terrain untouched by the racial experiences of Indian immigrants in London. National origin here (being from and concerned with India) in this text functioned differently from that espoused by *India Mail*, precisely because it obscured a whole set of experiences crucial to a full understanding of the immigrant community. Pendsay, like Sharma and Tandon of *India Mail*, drew on ethnicity, but not race as did Ali of *Asian Times*; *India Weekly*'s focus on Indianness was intended to eclipse the racial experiences that *India Mail* granted.

All three papers, *Asian Times*, *India Mail*, and *India Weekly*, through the 1990s, cultivated constituencies and constructed identities by selectively drawing on the varied experiences of Indian immigrants in London. For the most part, the address was to the first generation of immigrants whose memories of another place outside of England were fresh and very much related to needs and desires of the present. The papers created a set of diasporic subjectivities and cultures by processing a range of affiliations. Third worldist and racialized experiences of the world that were defiantly positioned with relation to Western (and particularly British colonial) domination of Asia and the Caribbean marked the ways that *Asian Times* appealed to readers in the lower middle-class immigrant community. Editor Ali's very Caribbean Indian subjectivity and left-of-center, racially articulated perspective interrogated the linear migration that the term "Indians" seemed to presume.[73] In contrast, *India Mail* was specifically intended to promote the Indian state as a place for financial investment. The paper's producers made use of transnational connections purely on economic terms, and left to the British context the development of migrant sensibilities; Sharma and Tandon were conscious of but not consumed by racial experiences in England. Finally, *India Weekly* depicted the world outside Britain for immigrants in the form of an Indian political state and a glorious Indian culture.

These three papers, *Asian Times*, *India Mail* and *India Weekly*, all created different publics with national and international reference points.

Ultimately, these papers of the diaspora did the work of translating diverse affiliations into equally varied and complex migrant subjectivities or ethnic identities. The terms "Asian" and "Indian," while helpful for several descriptive purposes, do not, however, fully convey the various possibilities engendered even by these three presentations. *Asian Times* did indeed manufacture "Asianness," but of a very particular kind: one that was both racially informed and politically oppositional to mainstream British culture. In this sphere, "Asian" was an ethnic identity distinct from "black" (and the identificatory effects of coalitions between Afro-Caribbean and Indian, Pakistani and Bangladeshi peoples), yet was not without racial connotations in the British context. This ethnicity, then, was racialized, particularly in contrast to other articulations of ethnicity. *India Mail* developed extant Indian ethnic identities, as they processed both racial experience and originary affiliation into transnational economic practices. The identity of "Indian" has been important, but the nationalist aspect of such ethnic formation, through the news and editorial expression of *India Mail*, also proved rather fluid and flexible enough to accommodate issues of discrimination often relegated to the sphere of racial experience. The Indianness basic to the subjectivity presumed by *India Weekly* was not nearly as pliant; it repudiated in all but the most egregious instances (like the Chaggar incident in Southall) the predication of an ethnic identity on racial experiences. In its employment of the international referent of India, *India Weekly* made a diasporic subject position supplant a racially inflected ethnic identity in the British context. Its readers were to look to India for their satisfactions, consolations, and investments. Ethnicity here existed purely through origin and not by dint of experience or association. Through various languages of diaspora, ethnicity, and race, and the silences and articulations therein, the print media of these British Indians offered multiple interpretations of what it meant to be Indian and British for a generation.

Diversity, American Style

By the 1980s, the Indian American population began to have the kind of diversity of British Indian populations and the critical mass that British Indian populations had attained much earlier. New and different publics emerged, and a more diverse print culture addressed their interests. *India Abroad* was still the major migrant newspaper, but contestations began to appear from not only within the pages of the publication but from outside as well. And the needs and desires of migrants, while continuous with the past, also assumed new shapes that could not be easily molded into what was previously known.

Gopal Raju, a consummate organic intellectual-entrepreneur, was intensely aware of the process of change. Over the years, Raju himself noted two important shifts in the content of the newspaper, toward a focus on financial affairs between the United States and India and toward the second generation. Like other middle-class cultural producers, he favorably cited the rise of India and the expansion of its economy into one that could compete with some success in a global market. His paper's focus on that development through the 1980s seemed to a large extent market-driven, and though Raju noted *"India Abroad* is clearly for Indians,"[74] the publication was in fact much less determined by an Indian cultural nationalism that guided other kinds of India-centric work. In fact, Raju tried to start a more broadly Asian newspaper and launched *Asian Monitor* in the early 1980s. He employed Pakistanis and Bangladeshis and used this forum to address a broader audience of South Asians. In describing its ultimate failure, Raju notes that it was difficult to get advertisers, especially Hindu Indians; others have speculated that non-Indians were unwilling to read or otherwise support the paper because of Raju's Hindu name on the masthead.[75] Whatever the combination of reasons for the demise of *Asian Monitor,* many in the immigrant Indian newspaper sector continued to look back on this incident as deeply indicative of the impossibility of a broader South Asian audience for any one publication, and ultimately as justification for the specifically national interests of an Indian American newspaper for the first generation of immigrants. The political/racial space that *Asian Times* occupied in London did not seem to exist in 1970s and 1980s New York City.

For the most part in the United States at this time, an intense focus on India militated against a consideration of Indian migrants in racial terms; that was often true among Indian ethnic enterprises in New York and was likewise demonstrated within the cultural production of *India Abroad.* In this, as in other cases, the reluctance to racialize the experience of Indians took place on a terrain marked not only by Indian nationalism, but also by migrants' class position and American national ideologies of inclusion. The entry of Indians into the United States in the late 1970s and 1980s with many fewer economic and educational resources than their earlier counterparts posed new issues of diversity for middle-class agents of Indian community formation like Raju. And new migrants' far less exalted existence within working-class areas of the city as well as their vulnerability to class-articulated forms of racism served to narrow the projected audience of a paper like *India Abroad.*

Raju, like others of his profession, was quite frank about the increasing diversification of the Indian migrant community, yet in no way did he suggest that his paper's readership changed or needed to change: "In the late '60s and '70s, we had the cream of the community; now they have

brought relatives, people coming now are not of the same quality."
Through the 1980s and 1990s, *India Abroad* remained deeply committed
to a base of first-generation, middle-class Indian immigrants who had
succeeded in America. This paper evinced little sympathy for victims of
contemporary forms of racism, either because its constituency refused to
define itself in racial terms, or because it did not wish to acknowledge its
own experience with the barriers of race in the United States. Raju himself
commented, quite tellingly: "Racial things are increasing just in the
ghetto. . . . Only working class living in worse neighborhoods is affected
by racial issues," and as if to explain, "America is one country where the
individual is rewarded if you can prove your mettle."[76]

The role of presenting news to the Indian community and the lure of
possibilities of the American dream compelled John Perry, the editor-
owner of *News-India*, to produce his own publication. Perry, a journalist
from India who spent fourteen years as a reporter for the Indian newspaper *Indian Express*, came to the United States in 1979 and worked in
various positions before deciding to purchase *News-India* in 1984 and
transform it into a news weekly. From its inception in 1975 in New Delhi,
the paper had been mostly concerned with Indian movie stars and film
gossip. Very much in Perry's mind was the space for a competitor to *India
Abroad*, and his mission to have *News-India* perform that role was at
first almost a one-man operation: "I worked hard and that included not
only editorial and advertising, but also cleaning carpets in the evening
and even cleaning toilets."[77] This particular kind of construction, of doing
both the white-collar and "dirty" work, is rampant in stories of immigrant ascent; in fact, almost all middle-class Indians that I spoke to utilized this script. And the facts of the story, of course, may be real too:
the subsequent rise of *News-India* to become one of two major Indian
American weeklies, with all the financial achievements that that implies,
confers an authenticity to Perry's own tales, as it does to the success of
Indian (and other) immigrants more generally.

While the narrative employed by this Indian migrant in the United
States has many stock qualities, Perry's identity as a Jewish Indian wove
a number of complexities into the texture of this "representative" life
story. His background was of multi-national affiliations. Prior to coming
to the United States, Perry had spent ten years as a correspondent in Tel
Aviv, and a connection to Israel formed an important part of his identity.
Indeed, being of a small non-Hindu minority in India shaped Perry's feelings about the country: "So much has been said about India, the largest
democracy, but what is understated is the sense of tolerance and sharing. . . . We were not the only ones to be treated as such. . . . In Hinduism
even strangers were treated like honored guests. [When Jews settled in the
country] there was a straight caste system in India; still, my people were

treated well, and we prospered. Even the mayor of Bombay at one time was Jewish."[78] His experience of the tolerance of the Indian state and Indian culture stood in marked contrast to the claims of India's largest minority, the Muslims. Perry commented, tellingly: "Being . . . from a minority community, we never had trouble with our Hindu neighbors . . . because of our willingness to adopt some of the local customs."[79] It is hard to miss how this construction, of adapting to established social norms in India, resonates with the *India Abroad* article by Jane Chandra suggesting that Indian professionals could overcome limitations by becoming more socially "American." But what Perry did not wish to consider is the possibility that tolerance of Jews in India was another way of discomforting Muslims. In fact, Perry's perspective on the Indian Jews' ability to integrate into Indian society and their subsequent financial and social success implicitly took to task the well-documented history of discrimination and impoverishment faced by Indian Muslims during the post-independence period.[80] This narrative also echoed the ways in which immigrant experiences in the United States operated to uphold tales of the American dream vis-à-vis the realities of other racial minorities, which surely contradicted the legend of widespread access to a range of resources.

Imported ethnic and class distinctions were mapped onto the American structure of opportunity when Perry sought to explain Indian immigrant life in the United States. With the use of a classic succession model, he reached back to the exemplar of Jewish American educational and commercial achievements to provide a reference point for Indian Americans. Perry compared in detail the ways that Yiddish-speaking Jewish immigrants and Indians who spoke very little English went into the news stand business; he also suggested that the values placed on education are very similar in Jewish and Indian cultures. Perry imagined a trajectory of class mobility for Indian Americans along the path of successive generations of Jewish Americans. "The good thing," he concludes, "is that Jews worked hard, sold their newsstands, and their children are now bankers or journalists. I hope the same will happen to the children of these [Indian] newsstand owners."[81] Here the models of ascent and assimilation fueled the correspondences among Jews in India, Jews in the United States, and Indians in the United States.

Yet Indian nationalism was in a very fundamental way the *raison d'être* for *News-India* and for Perry's work in the United States. The paper made quite clear its support of the Indian state and of the Indian nation's integrity in the face of all territorial disputes, including those in Punjab and Kashmir. Perry and others from the paper, as well as those from various publications, had relations with both the Overseas Friends of the Bharatiya Janata Party (BJP), the fundamentalist Hindu party in India as well as the Indian National Congress of America, the U.S. organ in support of the

Congress Party in India. Affinities with the former, of course, strained relationships with the latter, and *News-India* was widely known in the Indian community as being supportive of the BJP. A stated admiration of the tolerance of the Indian state seemed not to be contradicted by the extreme intolerance of a political party bent on making a formally Hindu nation.

While *India Abroad* buttressed the Indian nation, too, it also tended to be more critical of the state's methods for suppressing dissent; and though it did not have a formal editorial stance, it regularly published articles and letters decrying anti-Muslim actions in India and questioning the terms of the 1947 partition. Part of this difference, apart from the personal beliefs of its editors, lay in the readerships of *India Abroad* and *News-India*. As an older migrant weekly, *India Abroad* carefully guarded its base among a wide variety of Indians, from the north and south, and of Hindu, Muslim, and Christian religious backgrounds. Its appearance, during the 1970s, occurred at a time when regional and religious conflicts originating in India had not yet taken such strong hold in the community of Indians in the United States. Pan-Indian ethnicity had a broader set of reference points in the early years of the paper's development, than certainly it has had more recently.

The readership of the more recently developed *News-India* tended to be more north Indian and largely Gujarati. In courting advertisers and readers from this region, *News-India* either already had an advantage in its more conservative stance vis-à-vis the Indian political sphere or constructed itself in relation to that; the frank political and entrepreneurial views of its editor suggested both. A mostly anti-Muslim, pro-India position, however, was hardly remarkable or uncommon. The editor of a third New York–based weekly, *India Monitor*, larger than any other of the numerous immigrant papers that emerged in the early 1990s, but posing no real competition to the dominance of *India Abroad* and *News-India*, noted about the India-Pakistan conflicts of recent years: "Pakistan is always wrong."[82]

Through variations in regional readership and support of political trends, both *India Abroad* and *News-India* located their mode of address in a diasporic field, of imagined and material connections to the homeland. The prioritized dissemination of news from India seemed to subordinate the local, domestic roles of the papers to a more transnational agenda. But editors and publishers disavowed racial consciousness in an entirely different ideological context from their counterparts in England. It is not accidental that Gopal Raju and John Perry advocated a vision of Indian migrant life tinted by dreams of middle-class ascent and lit by aspirations of eventual integration into U.S. society, contradictory as that might be to their transnational articulations; their own experiences as immigrants and the populations they imagined speaking to seemed to confirm such hopes. As newspapers that took philosophical shape in the 1970s and 1980s, *India Abroad* and *News-India* were produced by and for post-1965 migrants who had the resources to be successful and developed a set of communities that defined themselves around those very accomplishments. The omnipresent idea of the American dream deeply informed prior and subsequent understandings of the experiences of those immigrants.

But herein lie the ironies of connections across national boundaries that make the very concept of nation central to lived experience. In fact, "news from home" was composed of stories *of* India told *from* New York. Migrants' profound and enduring connections to India could only be made visible through America, and as a result not one but two nations were in the midst of construction as a reading public and public address were themselves being fabricated. A certain seamlessness was produced most especially in the context of the United States, where in this period of the 1970s and 1980s the imagined community built through Indianness could map onto the ascendant nationality, of becoming American. The allure of a "new land"—in ideology, spirit, and grammar—had a powerful edge for the Indias and Americas produced in New York, much more than it could for their counterparts in London, given both the embedded histories of colonialism and the experiences of postcolonialism that precluded any easy identification with England.

In the late 1980s structuring premises of the inclusions of America were beginning to be shaken. When white racist groups in Jersey City called themselves "Dotbusters" and attacked Indian immigrants, middle-class Indian groups and their cultural producers, like the publishers of *News-India* and *India Abroad*, found themselves scrambling to develop responses to forms of racialization that less successful Indian migrants faced daily in a changed racial landscape in which South Asians were now being targeted along with other newer immigrants. To a large extent, immigrant newspapers initially neglected to deal with these more contemporary realities, and began to be taken to task by a range of interest groups, including youth and other progressive organizations. This period, of the late 1980s, in some ways marked the end of an era of first-generation Indian American control over the means and content of representation, and cleared the ground for the emergence of ever more diverse cultural forms.

Diversifying Audiences, into the Present

For some fairly obvious reasons, Gopal Raju and John Perry in the 1990s discounted connections between Indians in Britain and the United States, noting that the ideological influences as well as community pressures seemed divergent. And British Indian newsmakers expressed wonderment (and to be sure, curiosity) in response to questions about Indian American communities. What was striking is how little the self-appointed cultural representatives of each of the national communities knew about one another, and how differently they saw themselves. While the Indian American newspapers' role had indeed been explicitly transnational, in its promotion of the Indian nation (state, culture and economy), a broader diasporic address to Indian communities around the world, like that of the *Independent Hindustan* in the 1920s, seemed largely a phenomenon of the past. And even the direction of *India Mail* from India, the cultural-nationalism of *India Weekly*, and the third worldist concerns of *Asian Times* in London made little or no effort to envelop Indian American communities through the 1990s.

This throws into some question the presumed diasporic connections among Indians around the world. An affiliation to and investment in the Indian homeland by one or another migrant community, in other words, does not necessarily imply transitive correspondences between those individual communities, especially in the first generation of Indian migrant cultural formation. And, as this detailed exploration of Indian American and Indian British papers was meant to demonstrate, even the diasporic sensibility that I have argued is central to the way each and every Indian migrant newspaper conceptualized itself and its community is *located* in the ideologies and racial formations of their specific contexts.

One magazine, *India Link International*, emerged in 1990s London, independent of the interests of established immigrant newspapers, and courted an international audience of Indians in that more broadly "diasporic" form that other publications of the first generation could not achieve. Its first issue intoned:

> The Indian Republic has a longer tradition of democracy than other nations of the sub-continent. But Nepal, Sri Lanka, Bangla Desh, and Pakistan are not far behind. . . . "India Link" will strive to be a link among people originating from this subcontinent and settled all over the world. . . . Problems facing people originating from the Indian sub-continent are numerous; but so are the privileges and opportunities enjoyed by them in their adopted homes. . . . Not that they have wiped off the memory of the land of their origin. Rather the opposite. Love of the country of origin is more acute.[83]

It is through the category of nonresidency and eventual return, which other first-generation papers understood to be unlikely, that this new magazine has sought its base. And in the last eight years, *India-Link* has developed named contacts in other areas of the world, in India, Los Angeles, and New Jersey, but the magazine is not usually available in U.S. Indian spaces, like Jackson Heights or Edison, New Jersey.[84] The content of recent issues ranges widely, veering from coverage of a fund-raising event for the Conservative Party candidate for Parliament for Ealing-Southall, to an in-depth story on Satpal Ram, an incarcerated "Asian man" (as the newspaper itself notes) who defended himself against a racist attack, which resulted in the death of his attacker.[85]

In 1994 Anil Tandon of *India Mail* noted that there was a "new generation of Indians, born and brought up here in Britain with a very different relation to India. . . . Maybe they will need a very different kind of newspaper."[86] By the middle to late 1990s, Tandon's vague sense of change would be manifested in shifts in the face of British Indian print culture. While these transformations would partly be about audience, about new interests of different generations of Indian (and more broadly Asian) communities, they would also be about the increasing commercialization of news and print that took place throughout British society. In the case of diasporic print media, "ethnicity" became a commodity within new strategies of address and the development of new reading publics.

The futures of print culture for increasingly numerous and diverse Indian populations in England, as it turned out, lay not in formulaic productions of the NRI, but in the reformulation of a racialized ethnicity. The development of the publication *Eastern Eye* narrativizes these trends. Begun in 1989, *Eastern Eye* was specifically directed toward events in Britain concerning a diverse group of Asian immigrants at a time when the purview of other newspapers was reporting news from abroad alongside material on immigrants. Other papers focused primarily on India as a site for primary identification, but even a paper like *Asian Times*, which sought a broader audience, nonetheless constructed internationalism as a major axis of affiliation, as a point of entry into British affairs. Not so *Eastern Eye*, which consciously chose England for the direction of its gaze, and whose investment was in an identity that was cross-national—Indian, Pakistani, and Bangladeshi mostly—and cross-class, to encompass interests and predilections that an older group of affluent Indian migrants might not authorize. Unlike, say, the very serious *India Weekly*, *Eastern Eye* contained material on music stars, dating, and matrimonials, as well as forthright discussion of cases of discrimination. And, importantly, most of its editorial staff was initially and continues to be Muslim Asian, signaling, perhaps, a rather different set of possibilities.

The differences of ethnicity and class could partly be felt through the mode of generation, which here in *Eastern Eye* was a set of populations newly defined by the time and place in which they lived. But even more than that is the alternative form that this newspaper chose: tabloid instead of broadsheet. While *Asian Times*, *India Weekly*, and *India Mail* were presenting the news as news, and using industry-established standards of presenting themselves as "objective," *Eastern Eye* opened up a different kind of space with its more sensationalist writing and color graphics to appeal to a broader audience and to produce a different kind of reading practice. While consuming *India Weekly* might require a significant investment in time, reading *Eastern Eye*, its producers conceived, would be easier. The public that *Eastern Eye* constructed was more in the realm of the popular: literate but not necessarily highly educated, and self-sufficient but not affluent. The mainstream British equivalents for the broadsheet were the *Guardian* or the *Times*, while *Eastern Eye* saw itself more akin to the *Sun*. As the managing editor of *Eastern Eye* noted recently: "Any Asian that reads *Eastern Eye* reads it for entertainment, for the features, for other information, not just news."[87]

While in the early years, *Eastern Eye* was run by a smaller company, in more recent years it has become affiliated with other ethnic newspapers, under the rubric of a group called Southnews; the group was acquired in late 2000 by the Trinity Mirror Group, which also owns the *Daily* and *Sunday Mirror*, a leading British tabloid.[88] Though editors and writers say *Eastern Eye* has remained independent in terms of content and production, they acknowledge a significant infusion of resources because of the new relationship. Southnews, which is the immediate holding group of *Eastern Eye*, had also bought *Asian Times*, *Caribbean Times*, and *New Nation*, to make component parts of a concern called the Ethnic Media Group, a group that receives and distributes advertising among its publications. By 2001, all the "Asian" newspapers available in London, including *India Weekly*, which had changed hands, had a similar appearance, with sensational headlines and color. The content of the individual papers became less distinct, with the greatest focus on British Asian affairs, a broad address to those of various Asian backgrounds, and some international news from the Indian subcontinent seen in each paper.[89] Institutional arrangements in which all the papers now seem to be embedded suggest broader financial interests, that of advertising especially, linking profit to ethnicity. In part this was an acknowledgment of the growing sources of capital within Indian and other South Asian communities, as most advertising in the papers came from those ethnic businesses.

Increased consciousness of new ethnic consumer constituencies can be seen most dramatically in the recent development of Asian fashion magazines in London. One magazine in particular, *Asian Woman*, first published in 2000 by a holding group called Smart Asian Media Limited, directs itself to women in their twenties and thirties who are interested in Asian beauty, fashions, and entertainment, but as the editor-at-large notes, it "stays actively away from politics and religion."[90] In fact, the magazine almost seamlessly moves between various national-ethnic interests in the name of "girl power," with much space devoted to Asian clothing distributors and designers, and advertising for traditional wedding clothing and jewelry, more westernized versions of salwaar khameez, dresses made out of South Asian fabrics, and makeup appropriate for darker skinned women. Interestingly, *Asian Woman* in its first couple of years has been able to generate interest among women in the Indian and other South Asian diasporas more generally, despite little organized distribution as yet. Like many "ethnic" beauty and fashion magazines, *Asian Woman* has faced criticism from readers for featuring largely light-skinned models.[91] But it has succeeded in creating a gendered consumer subject that crosses lines of origin and nations of domicile but is not cast in political terms as feminist.

Commercial interests define the most recent developments of the still-largest Indian weekly in the United States, *India Abroad*, but the transnationalism of the address has intensified, even changed direction. In April 2001, *India Abroad*, once a paper associated throughout Indian diasporic communities with the name of Gopal Raju, was acquired and relaunched by an Indian media company, Rediff.com India Limited. Increasingly, as more Indians emigrated to and settled in the United States, and became more self-conscious about themselves as Indians in the diaspora, *India Abroad* expanded in the years leading up to the transfer of control to cover issues in the United States with greater frequency. But an attention to local context for this publication did not necessarily mean an expansion of the categories for identification, and *Indianness* still remained powerful as an organizing rubric for news from abroad and news at home, muddled as those possibilities were. In 1999, *India Abroad* had already created a website hookup to an Indian company that provided financial information, particularly on Indian markets.[92] The actual purchase of an Indian American newspaper by an Indian company formally reversed the flow of the diasporic address, often thought of as migrants recalling and making connections to a homeland, or point of origin; the nation-state of the subcontinent now reached out to other spaces to recreate itself abroad.

For Rediff, an important audience for the consumption of Indianness itself, in terms of all sorts of products that the company organizes in India and throughout the diaspora, was seen to be in the United States.[93] And yet, the content of the paper has not changed much; there is still an insert on local communities in the tri-state area and close attention to events important to Indians in the United States. From the perspective of profit, then, there has been a surprising complementarity between the national spaces, so that diasporic citizenship can be found in the possibilities of consumption. Importantly, more conventional forms of reading that take place with the printed copy of the newspaper are now linked to new technologies, where "readers" can access spheres of information on the Internet, and, in a sense, connect even to those who might never know of *India Abroad* but have some shared interests nonetheless.

India Abroad has so far navigated important challenges to the centrality of newspapers to a culture, to migrants, and to others in a new technological world, by annexing itself to those changes. Partly because the publication is now owned by an Indian communications company, but also as a result of the diversification that had been occurring earlier, the newspaper is not in any way opposed to but working in concert with other sources for information. And the newspaper has established political interests that are not displaced by even its most recent and most transparent commercial orientations. The *India Abroad* Center for Political Awareness, started in the 1970s, has now mushroomed to sponsor internships for second-generation Indian American students and to lobby the U.S. Congress on matters relating to Indian immigrants. *India Abroad* also has a news service to distribute source materials to other organizations. And, evidencing the flexibility of this publication, and not unlike the adaptations made by first-generation immigrants more generally, *India Abroad* too has opened itself to interventions and all sorts of challenges; the "Opinion/Letters" section of the paper is now filled with second-generation and other Indians' writings on how to newly construct that "Indian" identity which previously seemed to be in the hands of far fewer agents. The paper may have departed most dramatically from older ideas of positive-popular ethnic visibility in its recent celebration of two adult models of Indian origin, Nicole Narain, January 2002 *Playboy* Playmate of the Month, and Sunny Leone, *Penthouse* Pet of the Month in March 2001.[94]

In its more than thirty years of existence, *India Abroad* has become a significant institution in the Indian diaspora, especially in New York, but in other places too, as its website, news services, and various editions are accessed throughout the world. Its duration and its tremendous reach across populations constituted in some way by "India" give this cultural production a representational role unlike the more locally based papers in England. *India Abroad* produces news and relationships that have an impact on the shape and content of nationality. There are a set of publics constituted by their consumption of and participation in the information of *India Abroad*. Though the newspaper has a multilingual wire service, its primary form appears in English, which necessarily marks the limits of the social that is created through *India Abroad*. Of course this is not solely about language, as there are channels in Hindi, Kannada, Malayalam, Tamil, Telugu, and Gujarati on its news service, but more about class formation. Originally begun in 1970 as a small newspaper to serve the immigrant community, *India Abroad*'s English text addressed literate, financially secure, diasporic Indians; today as a conglomerate of internet and print communications, in a variety of languages and from a number of places in India and the United States, *India Abroad* still largely addresses literate, financially secure, diasporic Indians. And the basic issues that construct the publics of the different addresses of *India Abroad* have not changed all that much: cultural ties to the "homeland" of India, financial relationships with developing (inter-)national economies, strategies of life in local social worlds, and the expression of multiple experiences of life abroad. These issues—the content of Indianness and the very parameters of border-crossing diasporic citizenship—have a certain pull on many different groups that see themselves as Indian, though their specific rendering may be authorized by more exclusive social formations.

The diversification of forms of information, or "news," that *India Abroad* now provides may expand the field for membership. Now Indians in India, Saudi Arabia, and other places can access this formation of diaspora, though, as always, the resources—to have a computer, to watch television, or to read—significantly constrain distribution. But simultaneously, the growing presence of Indians in U.S. social landscapes, in urban centers like New York and Chicago especially but also throughout the country, means that Indianness itself is more accessible, to non-Indians and to a wide variety of Indian migrants. News stands in New York subways now often carry *India Abroad*; and Indian restaurants and shops, increasingly common in all parts of the city, not just in Jackson Heights, also sell the publication. Even for those recent immigrants, who may have little in common with the producers and business interests of the newspaper, *India Abroad* now has a representative role and can be read for information on local activities, or "news from home," without necessarily being identified with.

India Abroad began with a broad appeal to those from all over the subcontinent, and sought to occupy a multinational, South Asian territory in the midst of many divisive issues. Although it claims to continue in those efforts, the newspaper's title and its increased links with business concerns in India make for a more restricted audience. With few other South Asian publications as widely available, Pakistanis and Bangladeshis might certainly read but feel alienated from a paper called *India Abroad*. Even recent working-class Indian immigrants who perhaps come from the Caribbean and have a more attenuated relationship to the nation-state of India might have very different interests and less at stake in the public that *India Abroad* has had a historic role in creating. They do not yet, however, have an organ for representation on the scale of this endeavor, now more than thirty years old.

Discourses of Diaspora

The development of Indian print cultures in the United States and England provides one space for understanding the multiple national discourses of imagining communities and imagining publics of diaspora. Incredibly diverse productions of print represent the heterogeneity of responses to the question of what it might mean to be Indian, and British, and American. While both the process of imagining community or creating a public sphere may have implied, for many scholars, certain forms of coherence of nation or citizenship, the print cultures outlined in this chapter, I would suggest, combine to create a picture of striking incoherence. The stereotype of media as homogenizing might be unraveled by these complex and rather dynamic performances of identity. The most widely read Asian ethnic publication in England today, *Eastern Eye,* speaks to a class and culturally diverse (and racially conscious) South Asian audience in the language of sensationalism, while the most prominent instance in the United States, *India Abroad*, has sustained stronger and stronger links to the nation-state of India through a broadsheet and diversified informational format. If these moments evidence the varying arrangements of capital formation of migrant communities in the United States and England, of who has the resources to produce a newspaper, they also nicely distill varied histories of migration, and the differential pull of various publics created out of migration on the processes of representation. Yet the representativeness of these representations themselves must be called into question when we consider how the market has, ultimately, shaped the rise and fall of various constructions of Indianness in print, and shifted the notion of participatory citizenship from traditionally political concerns like voting to commercial acts like consumption. Indeed, the explanation for the duration of both *India Abroad* and *Eastern Eye* lies not so much in their popularity, but their deliberated construction of ethnic markets, of a broad Indian diaspora in the case of *India Abroad*, and of the Asian British population for *Eastern Eye.*

Nationality, being a member of broad constructions of India, Britain, or America, has been central to the projects of most of the publications considered here. At times the nationalities were exclusive, when *India Weekly* in the 1970s, for example, saw its purview to be in conveying information from India, and not engaging too deeply with racial problems in England. But more often than not, being constituted in and through multiple spaces of the nation has been an experience that was carefully managed in the texts of the publications and embodied in many of the cultural producers themselves, who were able to articulate their role in rearranging coordinates of "home" and "abroad" by bringing India to, indeed constructing India in, other places. And in the glossy fashion magazine *Asian Woman*, we might see the post-national, gendered consumer subject whose desires, in the sphere of style, are still created by some deeply felt identification with the Indian subcontinent.

As it turns out, there is no single public of nationals, even in the Indian nation–created diaspora, or in the British or U.S. multicultural worlds of immigrants, and the diversity that is inherent in print culture's address to nationals buttresses that point. Robert Park, champion of Americanization, in 1922 may have presaged such a possibility when he wrote, "No newspaper is a free agent. . . . If we know what these influences are . . . we shall know how . . . to give America at least an equal chance with foreign interests."[95] In more recent years, the competition of nations has become submerged, and the singular community that might be periodically imagined through some production of India seems ever more impossible.

FIVE

GENERATIONS OF INDIAN DIASPORA

WITH THEIR increased presence in countries like the United States and Britain, Indian diasporic cultures of the postwar world have created conceptual problematics to shape anew how we look at both migrant populations and host societies. Essentially formed by the logics of movement and memory, diasporas simultaneously illumine and recreate vectors of time and space. And as this book has been concerned with a postwar world, the time-space compression of the Indian diaspora has a special form that can be indexed to processes of globalization. Post-1947 Indianness in diaspora, then, inspires a broader reconsideration of history, place, the public, literature, and other genres of experience for a contemporary set of circumstances.

If there is a trajectory of Indian diaspora for our times, it has been motivated by the continued impulse to diversity. In the early years of Indian emigration to the United Kingdom and United States, in the late 1950s to early 1970s, an important preoccupation for new immigrant subjects was their visibility in broader landscapes of nationality and racial and ethnic formation. Yet as immigrants strove to constitute their own selves and their group, in relation both to local geography and communities in the homeland and elsewhere, they engaged in processes of representation that were necessarily contested and internally fissured. To be Indian was a necessary proposition in worlds where identities were created through origin, but it was a possibility that remained shot through with controversy, leading to endless questions: of what class? of what region? of what religion? of what space? And as Indian populations have grown in leaps and bounds since that period, contestations of what it means to be Indian have found multiple spheres of operation. Indian entrepreneurial and residential communities now exist all over England and the United States; books written by Indians about experiences of immigration appear frequently on bestseller and prize lists in both countries; and multiple histories of the group are claimed for a variety of political ends.

While sheer quantity, in the form of more people over time, has produced greater diversity within Indian diasporic formations, it would be a mistake to discount the synchronous developments in the apparati of the global system to provide new languages for understanding individuals and groups. Languages of self-recognition, around gender, sexuality, religion, and other kinds of "difference," have gained considerable purchase on the popular imagination, both because the identities that resulted have become more broadly accessible through technologies of travel and communication, and also because social movements have successfully pushed specific political interests into the public sphere. This is all to say, again, that the Indian diaspora has changed in time and space.

We might return to that rather basic presumption by contemplating diversity as it takes shape through one last problematic, of generations. Generation, I suggest, is one way of thinking through the new lives of diaspora. In this sense generation is both an actual social formation and a theoretical concept. Almost all meanings for generation carry some connotation of production, of concepts, things, or peoples. In each of these cases, there is the melding together of older elements to create something new, albeit with a relationship to the past. Even income is presumed to be the result of skills, willpower, and investment. And in that way, slippage between production and *re*production occurs.

Generations have described, in anthropological and sociological terms, groups of peoples who in their emergence become associated on the basis of some shared characteristics or interests, or consciousness. The timing of the life of those peoples and the processes by which they seek to express and thus create affinities, as well as disaffiliations, was what Karl Mannheim sought to capture in his famous essay, "The Problem of Generations."[1] Scholars in a number of disciplines have vigorously debated how to define and evoke generation.[2] It is the conflation between, on the one hand, age, and on the other, cohort, that some have found problematic in Mannheim's seminal work.[3] Perhaps another way of casting the conflation is in terms of convergence. For our purposes it seems that comprehending the creation of groups through the simultaneous processes of temporality and location may enable us to enter into the very social complexities of the postwar world that diasporas live in.

Mannheim has argued for seeing those two vectors of time and space, as they construct a generation, in broad but not endless complexity. Citing the influence of German historian Wilhelm Dilthey, he writes of the formative periodization: "The time-interval separating generations becomes subjectively experienceable time; and contemporaneity becomes a subjective condition of having been submitted to the same determining influences.[4] And so too does location exist not only with observable variables, but with a relativity: "Similarity of location can be defined only by specifying the structure within which and through which location groups emerged in historical-social reality."[5] While he notes that "membership in the same historical community, then, is the widest criterion of community of generation location," Mannheim also suggests that differentiated generational consciousness emerges through a "concrete bond." He identifies the former and broad experience with the term "generation" and the specific and subforms of affiliation, of a kind of convergent ideological expression, or, as he wonderfully puts it, an "identity of responses" in terms of "generational units."[6]

The bringing together of the temporal and the spatial, as well as the experienced and the expressive, that Mannheim's concept of generation invokes is central to understanding how new groups form out of and process Indian diasporic life. But an Indian diaspora is an international constellation that comprises diasporas, in the plural. As such, it contains multiple formations, or groups, that live in alternating "historical-social realities": local, national, and transnational. While these groups might at times establish mutually intelligible forms of seeing the world, and an "identity of responses" (as in the "generation-unit"), they continue to have their own trajectory of development that has a particular coherence: they emerge through different negotiations of time and space. What I mean to suggest is that because the field of diaspora is lateral rather than vertical, the successive formations cannot but be seen as in some sense autonomous from one another. With this in mind, it seems that generations, in the plural, may accentuate the relationship to diasporas, in the plural. That depth of relation is illuminated by the image of the fourth or fifth generation of Indians in Trinidad remixing bhangra produced by the children of Punjabi immigrants from the 1950s. The divergent memories of the social groups, as well as their contingencies in separate geographies, divide and connect, and create altogether different meanings for Indian diaspora.

Undeniably, postwar migration itself has made the question of generation more problematic. It is difficult to determine the timing and social location of those who have moved not only between nations, but also between narratives and experiences of history.[7] Identity for migrant groups is not just anchored by a sense of experience in the present but also by a constructed memory of the past. And in large part, the categories for change in the literature on immigration fit imperfectly with the new experiences of diaspora that I seek to comprehend with the term "generations," because many studies of immigration have employed the term primarily to connote succession and nationality. Scholars identify "first generation" or "second generation" as phases of the development of immigrant and then ethnic groups, whereby those who have immigrated are distinguished from those born and reared in host societies.[8] In this kind of work, much of it based in the United States, a new generation signifies most of all a transformed relationship to homeland and another land. The crucial shifts in such processes of becoming a generation occur in the sphere of nationality, and therefore necessarily conjure forth questions of assimilation and integration. Given the importance of ideas of integration for immigrants themselves and those who study them, it is not at all surprising that the concept of generation should be so thoroughly freighted with such meanings. And Philip Kasinitz has made the very interesting point that for the temporally delineated phase of "white ethnic" (Italian, Eastern European, Irish) immigration, from 1882 to 1922, there was a confluence of generation in the biological sense and generation in the historical sense, so that assimilation theory could have a certain explanatory power for those cases.[9] However, for the case of postwar migration, which has a decidedly continuous nature, the models need to be significantly reworked.

Integration, in fact, has been only one part of the complex cultural changes inherent in and symptomatized by the Indian diaspora that this book has elaborated. One argument has been that Indian migrant cultures function as part of the United States and Britain, but also autonomously in a more transnational set of arrangements, connected to India and to others around the world. That broader set of coordinates in space, however, cannot overcome the structuring impact of time on how the diaspora is constructed and lived, and the transitions in those productions. Maintaining the processual nature of generation creates stories of diaspora that move us away from origin, while the emergence of groups at any given moment still serves to illuminate identity, a central experience of diaspora.

Many transitions in the Indian diaspora have occurred through assertions of difference, not only in terms of youth but also gender, sexuality, class, race, and other categories. In suggesting that these modes of division produce contestations, it is important in the same breath to recall that the broader entity of diaspora is already fissured and continually negotiated. The emergence of a generation of diaspora may not, as in popular usage, signal the decline of another (previous) group of people, but may certainly make that previous group more complexly articulated to the whole. As Indians from the Caribbean, for example, become a new Indian diasporic population in the United States, they intervene in breaking apart an "Indianness" already open to contestation, though from a new direction. The "beginnings" or "ends" of Indian diasporas are thus difficult to identify. But in all the cultural formations explored in this chapter, there is an attempt to come to terms with changes of the Indian diaspora, articulated in time and location, through the concept of generation. It is not so much that these are diasporic generations, a set of groups newly constituted in diasporic time and space, but that they are *generations of diaspora*, groups created out of and marking shifts in the set of contradictions and complexities that have constituted diasporic communities.

New generations of any formation always seem to elicit the prospect of disappearance and loss, and this is certainly the case with new Indian diasporic cultures. A very old question, of what is Indian, less Indian, more Indian, and still Indian appears as the quality of Indianness becomes unmoored from nation, state, or any other mechanism of surveillance. Immigrants from India to the United States and United Kingdom lament that their children are not "Indian" anymore, precisely when youth express desires and longings that are distinct from those consolations of their parents. Likewise, when women suggest that the nuclear family must adapt to changed circumstances and gender arrangements of host societies, or when films spectacularize a relationship between an Indian woman and an African American or Afro-Caribbean man, the authoritative responses come in the form of a protection (and maintenance) of a mythical Indian culture. When difference comes into contact with sameness, the result is not always an elegant negotiation, but often a conflict in which all participant subjects mourn a loss, of self, of group, and of nation. In many ways this is but an inversion of Indian migrants' initial preoccupation with visibility in new lands. Tension between difference and sameness thematizes the challenges to the Indian diaspora as much as it is basic to the logic of the diaspora.

To Be Young, Indian, and Hip

By the 1980s, Indian youth cultures in both the United States and Britain had become organized and visible, particularly in the urban landscapes of New York and London.[10] This was due not only to the coming of age of the children of immigrants—because certainly those of English immigrants from the late 1950s to the early 1960s had matured earlier than the children of Indian immigrants to the United States in the late 1960s and early 1970s—but also to the simultaneity of the emergence of both generations, developed technologies of travel and expression, and the further development of languages for identity.[11]

And of course identity has been a major preoccupation for children of immigrants. The very different and to some extent public outlets for the processing of identity formation have made it seem like youths are more interested in questions of identity, but, as I have argued throughout this book, their parents necessarily have been located in processes by which their sense of self and relationship to groups were continually excavated and reconstructed as well. As youth are fond of suggesting, however, that was a different time and place. A need to describe themselves in terms intelligible to a range of communities continued to exist for children of Indians in the United States and United Kingdom, just as it was important to be located and differentiated within contemporary arrangements of race and ethnicity. Particularly in a post-1960s multicultural world, naming became a primary site for producing a kind of location for social groups.

Children of Indians in Britain came of expressive age earlier than Indian American children. An early group, in late 1960s and early 1970s England, began to develop a distinct sensibility at the same time as British racism was increasingly directed at nonwhite peoples. These youth groups constructed community as a response to and protection from a broader society; and global political movements provided an alternative language for identity and ideology in the service of that project. The complex of forces that we can see impacting youth in Southall at this critical moment, for example, is one early occasion of a new British Indian generation. New and old terms for identity—"blackness," "Indianness," "Asian-ness," and/or "Britishness"—created important points in maps for navigating the various intersections and divergences for these and other groups. The multiplicity of these signs for the experiences of Indian youth in places like Southall suggests a structuring problematic of new generations of any formation: that these cultures operate both within and against a whole range of authorities, not only in their parents' production of identity, but also through the racial and national arrangements in which they are located.[12] Being a "British black" subject, then, is to (simultaneously) contest the Indianness or Punjabi-ness of their parents, to challenge what is being proposed as British (read white), and also to align oneself with the antiracism of oppressed members of an Indian community, or with the emerging multicultural sensibility of a "new England."

Any category of identity has multiple and contradictory connotations, most especially so as a new generation takes a particular language out of an established context and imports it to its own. In this sense, Indianness, too, has been invested with different meanings, sometimes incongruous and sometimes quite pointedly literal, within youth cultures. Perhaps the most ironic use of Indianness is in the early 1990s rise of the musical phenomenon of Apache Indian in England and subsequently all over the world. Born in 1967, Steven Kapur grew up in Birmingham, an important site for the subsequent settlement of a range of Indian immigrants, including Punjabis, a group that Kapur belonged to, and Afro-Caribbean populations. As well as being quite ethnically diverse, Birmingham was also through the 1970s and 1980s a deindustrializing city that symptomatized many of the broader changes in urban life, including rising unemployment in vulnerable sectors like youth and minorities. It is in this context that Kapur chose the name Apache Indian to echo Jamaican reggae star Supercat, another kind of symbol of mixture, who had been nicknamed "Wild Apache" because of his half-Indian, half-African parentage. Apache Indian began to play a music that consciously mixed Caribbean, Indian, and African American sounds, at a time when something called "world music" was becoming ascendant in a global consumer economy.

Apache Indian's first album, *No Reservations* (1992), illuminates musically and textually what spoke to the complex desires of a new generation and the full extent of Kapur's self-appointment as a spokesperson for that set of concerns. While the music on the album incorporated a range of rhythms, from Indian bhangra to Bollywood and African rap and hip-hop, the overall sound remained West Indian dancehall reggae. Here Kapur exhibited an affinity not only with that music, but also with Afro-Caribbeans who had influenced him. The actual connections between the populations in question may be less important than the imagined coincidences of colonial history on the one hand and racial and economic dispossession in England on the other; Apache Indian's comparison might have been less about interaction than it was about allegory. In the context of early 1990s Britain, the gesture of an Indian toward another kind of blackness had specific political content.

The figuring of Apache Indian as a ragamuffin, in style and substance, created an essential challenge to a more authoritative Indianness positing financial and educational success as part of an ethnic profile, just as being another kind of Indian (an Apache) established an almost prior form of distantiation from that mainstream ethnicity. Here is a generation, Apache Indian seems to announce, that can take "Indianness" as play, treat it derisively, break it down, and eventually reconstruct it. And the intense self-consciousness at work is enabled by performance. In musical terms that became racial terms, Apache Indian could exist betwixt and between: not quite Caribbean because he was Indian, not quite Indian because he was a ragamuffin. In fact, the assumption of racialized music as a sign for subcultural identities has had a long history,[13] but it operated here in a specific and more local context as well, as Kapur himself noted recently upon reflection on his musical beginnings: "I was born in Handsworth in Birmingham in the UK. This is a multicultural city and is famous for reggae music. UB40 are from Birmingham and they are a white band that plays reggae and now I am an Indian that is involved with reggae."[14] Though Kapur utilized Indian rhythms, both bhangra and Hindi playback singing, he did so on this first album and with all his major hit songs through the early to middle 1990s as a subsidiary form to the basic reggae sound. And other musicians who participated in these recordings included mostly Caribbean reggae greats, like Maxi Priest, Sly from Sly and Robbie and Shaggy.

In fact, it is more in the lyrics, more broadly in the textual address that Kapur was making, that it is possible to read the cultural complexity of Apache Indian. In the song "Chok There," Apache Indian establishes broad contours for identification: "Chok There, Them a ball from Bombay city, Chok There, From the deepest parts of Delhi, Chok There, Fe the woman hitch up in a sari, Chok There, So me hear from Karachie,

New York, Kingston and London city."[15] In this, one of his biggest hits, Apache Indian creates a framework for the audience he seeks, through the worlds that Indian immigrants have occupied in South Asia, the Caribbean, England, and North America. He "speaks" directly to subjects in these spaces ("fe the woman hitch up in a sari"), and "hears" from them as well, evoking a flexible, participatory, call-and-response musical genre.

In this way Apache Indian, like Indianness itself, is a floating figure onto which desires can be projected, and through which needs can be expressed. Apache Indian utilizes travel as a mode for those processes. In several of his songs, Apache Indian entreats his listeners to move through space with him.[16] In "Come Follow Me," he outlines the borders of India, through the cities of Bombay and Calcutta, and also through more contentious areas like Kashmir and "Kalistania." But Apache Indian also suggests an "India" outside of the nation-state, by metaphorically moving through cultural producers and in fact another country: "So each and everyone go collect your rupee, Going fe take you fe a trip mon round me country. . . . Ravi Shanka the greatest sitar player, Who sing like a bird Lathomageska, History in-a me lon made by General Dya, Rajeev are the former Prime minister, And you no this ya youth go cross the border, Going fe pass one place called Sir-Lanka."[17] And in "Magic Carpet," Apache Indian uses an Orientalist image of the flying carpet to traverse continental space via his own identity-imaginary: "Beca me born a New Delhi but me live England, Fly way cross the sea reach the Caribbean. . . . Me love the curry goat dinner, Ackee and the dumplin, But me favorite place that a St. Catherine, Ca me find one shop a do the Balti-chicken."[18] Here the figure of Apache Indian appears amid not only otherness, but a mixture that includes an element of some kind of Indianness (balti-chicken), a landscape that is reminiscent, in fact, of the Birmingham where Steven Kapur grew up. While Kapur's stage persona is most conspicuously *Apache* Indian, oftentimes Apache Indian speaks of himself as Arawak, an "Indian" associated with the space of the West Indies.

The front and back cover images of the album *No Reservations* are interesting in this regard (figs. 12 and 13). On the front, Apache Indian appears in "rude boy" dress, signifying a tougher sound-system (as opposed to "roots and culture") reggae and African American hip-hop style, against a backdrop comprised of the flag of India that bleeds into a Rastafarian flag below. On the back are snapshot-images of Kapur as a young boy, his Indian parents, West Indian soccer players and music stars, international maps and currency. The effect of this visual presentation, within which the music has been packaged, is cultural pastiche.

Apache Indian posits identity as mobile and dynamic rather than fixed, in a world of multiple cultures and influences. He rose to prominence just as social formations in England and through the Indian diaspora were

Figures 12 and 13. Front and back covers of "No Reservations"
(courtesy Island Records & www.karmasound.com).

becoming more diverse in terms of generation, ethnicity, and class, as globalization's effects were felt in communities that traveled more, and as urban landscapes became spectacularly heterogeneous. Academic cultural theory, influenced by British cultural studies, conceptualized hybridity to intellectually and politically contest nationalisms that emerged as an answer to racism and the experienced shortcomings of multiculturalism. And Nestor Garcia Canclini has posited "hybrid cultures" as a response to and strategy for the melding of past and present that undergirds the demands of economic and social modernity.[19] Not surprisingly, scholars of those topics were drawn to figures like Apache Indian, just as audiences around the world were.[20]

As a genre, Apache Indian's music enables particular forms of identificatory circulation. Apache Indian exalts music and its cultures as having a special ability to bring all kinds of people together, and he works within a tradition of reggae artists who have made such claims for dancehall.[21] In "Feel it Fe Real," Apache Indian joins with popular reggae star Maxi Priest to promote the unifying qualities of this music: "Strange things happening on a Saturday night, I could almost feel excitement in the air. . . . Me say you take it from Apache Arawak Indian, Ca me feel reggae music and me feel well strong, From me soul-a-to me hear-a-no me heart can't wrong, From me head-a-to me back-a-no me foot them bottom, And over Canada and over Japan, And over India mon pass Pakistan, them a love a them there style mon every nation."[22] The traditional divisions, geographic and communalist (in the case of India and Pakistan), are transcended by rhythm, dance, and alternative communities that emerge in musical space. When Apache Indian and Maxi Priest sing, "Everybody do you feel what I feel for, Say we love this dance-hall music for real,"[23] dancehall is simultaneously a music, a place, and more broadly a cultural formation. In fact music as cultural formation, as a multiple set of expressions, contestations, and productions of identity, space and place that allow for *feeling*, is precisely what a second generation—in fact any generation that has precious few alternative spaces for understanding itself as part of a group—finds compelling. Music is often deployed as a means of creating communities as well as a tool in drawing distinctions between groups.[24] Rock-and-roll symbolized not only new musical trends, but also a new generation, just as acid rock, punk, or hip-hop have. In 1990s England, from a time and place, this mixed Indian-Caribbean-hip-hop music became the sign of a new generation of British Asians, and then of diasporic second-generation South Asians.

Youth cultures of the Indian diaspora were enabled, of course, by broader postwar developments that constructed new generations as "youth." Industrial (and post-industrial) capitalism in the West created culture industries that have profoundly shaped what it means to be a young person in this world. Those culture industries, and the sense of self that they imparted—as part of and participant in a global dialogue—have been central to young diasporic Indians' lives in the United States and United Kingdom, but certainly were never accessible to their parents at any time. And likewise, the centrality of consumption and identities based in that are a central feature of the "postwar" experience of *new* generations of diaspora that Apache Indian lays a claim to.

Apache Indian spoke to conventional cultural conflicts of this generation but was able to do so in ways that diverged from more mainstream or popular renderings, largely because he assumed the identity of being *from* the community. In one song he takes the archetypal clash between generations—marriage—as his subject. Arranged marriages, in particular, are central to the production of meaning of ethnic community in a variety of ways. Not only do they describe a basic form of reproduction of that community and retention of certain forms of membership, they also function as hyper-symptoms of misrecognition between East and West, that which continues to make immigrant communities, especially in Britain and the United States, unknowable, exotic, and mired in tradition. The western media easily latches onto the arranged marriage as descriptor of a struggle between the old and new worlds, the most sensational example of which was the 1992 case of two Yemeni girls from England who were forcibly sent back to Yemen by their father to marry men from his village for a dowry, subsequently described in the book *Sold*, which then was read on the BBC and became a *cause célèbre* for international feminist activists.[25]

In the song "Arranged Marriage,"[26] Apache Indian wrests control of the representation of culture, in a sense, from the exclusive hold of the West and remakes it as a site of complex desires. The beginning of the narrative is standard: "Well the time has come fe the original Indian to get married—And you done no, already when the Indian get married a pure, traditional business"; but there is a twist, as he continues: "So all the people that say them no too love the arrange marriage thing, catch this one here now," saying in effect that his story will not be easily captured by the stereotypical perception of an older Indian generation forcing arranged marriages on its children. In fact, Apache Indian wants an arranged marriage: "Now the time has come mon fe Apache, Fe find one gal and to get marry, But listen when me talk tell everybody, Me want me arranged marriage from me mum & daddy. . . . Me wan gal from Jullunder City, Men wan gal say a soorni curi, Me wan gal mon to look after me, Me won gal that say she love me." Though Apache Indian does make a nod to another set of experiences (remarking later, "About me arrange marriage me have a problem, When is the right time to tell me girlfriend!"), he returns to the desires expressed above, adding in the chorus, "Me wan gal dress up in a sari. . . . Me wan gal to make me roti." Running through Apache Indian's narrative are longings for a traditional Indianness, in the form of origin (a girl from "Jullunder City"). Asserted as wants or desires, this construction may assume a different edge than it would in a first-generation formation. And of course, there is the conception of love that is attached to the tradition of arranged marriage in a new way.

But Apache Indian's national romance has a gendered form. He seeks a Jalandhar girl who will "dress up in a sari" and "make roti," who in other words will be a partner in the reproduction of the traditional roles of man and wife. Interestingly, this patriarchal desire appears not only through a "homeland" of India, but also a homeland of indigenous peoples. Steven Kapur has chosen the Apaches, warriors of the U.S. southwest and symbols of virility, for his name. In one sense, Apache Indian's masculinity becomes doubly reconstituted by the symbolic nation. That the Apaches had a matrilineal social structure may be a fact that escaped Kapur.[27]

A complicated and contradictory desire for Indianness is essential to understanding the hopes and dreams of the children of immigrants. Stories of assimilation, and a presumed conflict between parents' homeland and youths' domicile, are unable to capture the profoundly diasporic sensibility that may recall India (or Punjab or other points abroad) among members of this generation. Such a sensibility, in its sometimes ethnicized, sometimes nationalist, and sometimes deeply gendered forms, is a building block for identity within worlds where individuals must be part of a group to belong. This seems important to recognize, particularly as hybridity and the radical political potential of spaces of racial mixture may be unwittingly valorized by critics and theorists.[28] While I do not mean to discount the important new and transgressive identities that emerge in and are expressed through music, I also want to explain that the extant investments in Indianness may both contradict fluidity and dynamism and operate in concert with mixture. In these examples, there are powerful resonances with the insights of Dick Hebdige's early work on subcultures, in which he suggested that youth culture does not simply depart from or contest an older generation, but in fact reproduces some of the contradictions that exist there, in our case around nation, race, gender, and ethnicity. An important question that may be left unanswered is whether certain identifications, Indianness for example, can be thoroughly remade.

It is within this complex field of signification that we might fully comprehend the prominence of bhangra in contemporary Asian youth cultures. A traditional folk and dance music from Punjab, in northern India and Pakistan, bhangra was in the background of celebrations of the harvest or the new year. And beginning in the mid-1980s, Punjabi Indian

British singers mixed bhangra with other contemporary musics to create a new meaning for bhangra writ large. In a symbol of a new generation, bhangra referred to music and, more broadly, to cultures of mixture. Bhangra became a catch-all category for musical production that did and did not primarily utilize Punjabi folk rhythms. Apache Indian, even though first associated musically with reggae, could be conferred membership in something called bhangra. But in some of the musics of popular artists of the earlier period, like Alaap, Bally Sagoo, or the Safri Brothers, the drum, or the dhol, produced fundamental rhythms, and the effect was a direct gesture toward the homeland genre.

The music that is most formally associated with bhangra rhythms has its own very interesting history that is part of the larger story told here.[29] The early male Punjabi and older part-time performers who popularized these musics at local social events in Punjabi immigrant communities seem rather different from the later artists who appealed to heterogeneous South Asian audiences through a more professionalized address. But instead of considering the transformations as from local and "pure" instances to more global and mixed forms, it may be more useful and in fact faithful to the genre to see them as dynamically continuous. Sabita Banerji and Gerd Baumann point out that bhangra emerges from Punjab, an area of the world that is astonishingly diverse in terms of religions and cultures and characterized very much by "cross-fertilization."[30]

Though this music had origins in Punjab and was first practiced in its new form in England by Punjabis, bhangra became simultaneously a sign for Punjabi-British, Indian-British, Asian-British, and then South Asian diasporic identity. An ability to shift registers, to move among those various categories, was the very special achievement of this cultural formation. Bhangra in this sense was an absorbent and flexible site; it could be projected upon and elicit participation to construct new forms of affiliation. Partly this had to do with form. When Bally Sagoo and other bhangra musicians mixed Nusrat Ali Fateh Khan's quaawali music into their own, drawing on and speaking to audiences of Muslim-Asian influence, they remade Indianness. And their Bollywood mixes that were transmitted throughout an Indian diaspora, including back "home," thoroughly destabilized any notion of authenticity.

Part of the flexible meanings of the music came from the cultures around bhangra. Beginning in the mid-1980s, disc jockeys and performers organized shows for young British Asians, including Punjabis, Indians, Pakistanis, and Bangladeshis. In accordance with the strict rules of the parents of this generation of youth, such as not going out at night (especially unaccompanied), many of the shows took place in the afternoon. Aside from dancing, these shows also became a space for youth to satisfy a series of longings, to be with people who were both like and unlike themselves.[31] Sometimes this was about heterosexual pairing, as the shows became a rare space for boys and girls to date; and sometimes ethnic tensions of the first generation were reproduced as Muslims, Hindus, and Sikhs fought for control over the turf. And sometimes loftier aims were achieved as a sense of community was lived and felt, a sense that assuaged the alienation produced by the hostile everyday arrangements of British race relations. As spaces to identify, transgress, and feel, bhangra shows operated very much like the idealized notion of the dance hall.[32]

Again, one can certainly see a multiplicity of effects of these cultures. In some cases, there were politically progressive ends to be served. In 1994 during a series of acrimonious negotiations around political representation and racial culture in the East End, particularly in the Tower Hamlets area, a show featuring Apache Indian and others was able to provide resources for Asian campaigns.[33] This brought together, politically, a range of Asian groups—Indian, Pakistani, and Bangladeshi—and infused those broader racial identifications, under the rubric of "Asian," with social meaning in a new historical context. And as Sanjay Sharma and others have pointed out, the category shifting of bhangra enabled alliances with other racial groups, like Afro-Caribbeans, that were more difficult to realize in the rather charged climate of 1980s England.[34] But oftentimes these musics remained within more clearly delineated boundaries of origin, in Punjabi Indian communities; bhangra therein was claimed as a specifically Punjabi form.

A special feature of music is its ability, indeed proclivity, to travel. In many respects, musical cultures are prototypical traveling cultures of the sort that James Clifford has theorized about.[35] They allow for relationships across time and space through forms in which a range of affiliations can be experienced. It is little surprise, then, that bhangra—the music and its forms of sociability—could become an exemplary diasporic formation. As the sign of a "new generation," bhangra music and styles launched in England quickly found multiple audiences in emerging youth generations of Indian communities in the United States and Canada. The melding together of Indian, other South Asian, and Caribbean rhythms created a language for cultural mixture in which the children of immigrants could find meaning. Themes in the texts themselves, like the conflicts over an arranged marriage that Apache Indian expressed, and relations elicited by actual participation in the physical spaces of bhangra, like the club or party, constituted new South Asian identities. A constancy of reference points elsewhere (London, Toronto, New York) made for a consciousness of participating in a culture that transcended the local-national context. Even though the production of the actual music continued to be located in England, its performative forms, in deejay mixes, and its consumption in public and private space, not only gave youth everywhere a kind of purchase on this culture but also created new possibilities for broad diasporic identities. Bhangra, Punjabi Indian though it might be, became a flexibly Asian (in the case of England) or South Asian (for the United States and Canada) cultural production for identity. Youth and others could find in the language of practices of bhangra their "Asianness" or "South Asianness" by participating in political formations around that construction, for example, or they could in fact develop acutely nationalist or regionalist sensibilities, like becoming more Indian or caste-bound in the relationships forged in spaces where bhangra was played. And though the music emanated from a set of fixed production sites, its consumption, mixing, and performance acquired the specificities of race and ethnicity in the United States or England when those identities were created. The travel of the musics and their special inventiveness produced broad and open scripts for identification to accommodate the multiple and unruly forces within which diasporic subjects were located. And even when affiliations from a past were rearticulated by bhangra, they necessarily were instantiated in the present, in the time-space of these generations, and therefore created cultures that were on some level new.

These are some of the dilemmas present in the appearance of bhangra within the broader framework of "world music." One can certainly read world music as a commercial instance of multiculturalism on a global scale: a garnering of profit through the representation of diversity. But the assertion of difference must also signify differential position within the whole. And so the power relations, between "whiteness" and "otherness" and between first- and third-world states, are manifested in even a cultural-commercial formation that seems to be organized under the sign of inclusion. The audience for "world music" largely comprises potential consumers in the first world, in North America and Europe, for whom places like Latin America, Africa, and Asia have come to be infused with a variety of cultural and political meanings. Those meanings might have been constructed through the experience of travel or political solidarities with groups in Latin America or South Africa fighting repression or imperialism, or simply from the reception of images of sites outside their own locales. That from elsewhere, outside of the first world, then, is the referent for the qualifier "world." In this production, music by the Beatles or the Rolling Stones cannot be "world" music, despite the evidence of its immense capability to travel around the world.

Contemporary bhangra, a first-world and highly technological sound expressing the conditions of life in largely urban centers and articulating the cultural ambivalences of a generation of new British and American citizens, raises a number of questions when it becomes enveloped in "world music," most of which remain unresolved. In part this is the incommensurabilty of the authentic and the syncretic despite the slippages that ethnicity strives to produce. Ashwani Sharma has pointed out that the marketing of world music creates a version of those slippages in touting "musical hybridity," while retaining origin as a sign of difference: "The national label is crucial in placing these global stars within particular imagined, but fixed ethnicities and so limiting the possibility of the artists being considered anteriorly as displaced, marginal or transcending their own cultural particularity, and permanently disrupting the binary logic of the centre-periphery."[36] But of course that "center-periphery" divide is transgressed in the name of profit when, as Sharma points out, major record labels like Sony sign up artists such as Bally Sagoo, whose music seems to have been borrowed from the West, and also record Bollywood film songs most certainly associated with the East, to address millions of potential consumers of this kind of Indian music, not only in the subcontinent but throughout the diaspora.[37] That some of this audience might be newly composed of youths and participants in a rather different set of cultures from recent immigrants' social events may not be fully accounted for in record companies' schematic marketing.

Confluences of different consumer audiences can be seen in the development of the originally Indian-owned record company Multitone, launched in the 1970s to provide British Indians with music from India. When bhangra was becoming a phenomenon in Britain, Multitone owners Pran and Jitesh Gohil began to record bands that could not gain a hearing from other companies. But then as bhangra grew in popularity, and as "world music" began to have broad and coherent markets, BMG acquired a large portion of Multitone. While many might have lamented the mainstream takeover of an "Asian-owned" business, the immigrant publication *Garavi Gujarat* reported this development within a positive frame of visibility: "And now, even the mass-market media . . . have caught on to the fact that young Asians are producing some of the most dynamic new music around."[38] In a mixture of ethnic pride and heightened sensitivity to the importance of financial and other kinds of support for culturalist products, the article very pragmatically noted that the company takeover "gives BMG a stake in the potentially lucrative Asian crossover market and injects Multitone with the resources to develop new acts." Tellingly, Multitone's next release after BMG's takeover was an album entitled "Culture Clash."

In their claims and assertions of bhangra as in some way "Indian," commercial capital, youth groups, musical producers, and performers, all in their own way, ascribe meanings to Indianness that transcend the nation-state. Indianness is remade as both diasporic and deeply global, even in its hybridity. This is not unlike the recent *National Geographic* spread on global culture that prominently featured Indian diasporic youth as a new kind of Indian national subject.[39] Through the Indianness constructed in new forms of diaspora culture, like that in bhangra, the boundaries between what is Indian or what is British and/or American become blurred. The generation of diaspora embodied in bhangra has created imperfect reproductions of what has come before, of older immigrants' experiences, and a fertile site of contestation and contradiction that most of all is defined by a rather different set of conceptual and geographic locations. Youth (and other) subjects who live a new sense of the nation and the world have found in bhangra a form of processing that transformed sensibility. And inasmuch as bhangra becomes a kind of broad discursive formation, it utilizes a range of vocabularies, including that of race and ethnicity.

Other fusion musics of Indian diasporas cast even wider nets for questions of identification than those of Apache Indian and Bally Sagoo. Talvin Singh became an important figure in the 1990s when he established a themed evening called "Anokha" ("unique" in Urdu) at Blue Note, a London club. Having gone to India to study tabla when he was a teenager, Singh was especially attuned to the possibility of combining Indian percussionist sounds with contemporary club musics, like acid house music and electronic jazz, and collaborated with non-Indian new jazz groups as well as the rock star Björk. His 1997 album, *Talvin Singh Presents Anokha: Soundz of the Asian Underground*, enjoyed considerable popularity and critical success, and his 1998 album, *O.K.*, won the mainstream Mercury Music Prize. Singh's music can certainly itself serve as an instance of genre-crossing, and he, like Apache Indian, engages in quite self-conscious explorations of identity as basic to his cultural production. Website promotional materials suggest as much in describing his œuvre: "[In] his Island debut 'Talvin Singh Presents Anokha' Singh revealed a collection of disconsolate sounds which worked their way into each other's grooves to create ambitious, memorable rhythms. 'O.K.' extends Singh's reach into the alienated space of transition where nothing really belongs yet everything is there. 'O.K.' comes from a floating world, music that captures the feeling of movement between identities, cultures, destinations, and languages. It could very well signal the globalism of the 21st century."[40] While bhangra artists like Apache Indian most utilized the language we might associate with hybridity as a preferred form of multiple identities, Talvin Singh found in cosmopolitanism, the travel that can be seen as transcending nation, a meaningful cultural and subjective model.[41] The "floating world" seems to envelop not only India but all nations as mythic places and, in fact, traces, that appear in a new musical genre; a certain ability to switch musics, to move geographically, is what is most celebrated.

Hybridity and cosmopolitanism, I would suggest, are rather different kinds of scripts for identity, though of course they might sometimes overlap. Where hybridity asserts multiplicity in the making of a new self, cosmopolitanism foregrounds mobility there. As new generations define themselves in these terms, various meanings then emerge for the diaspora with which they are associated. Steven Kapur, aka Apache Indian, and Talvin Singh are roughly the same age, have immigrant parents (in fact, both sets are Punjabi), and grew up in urban areas, Kapur in Birmingham and Singh in East London. Their apparent social location, then, is the means for membership in a "second" generation of Indian-British migration, and yet the languages in which they choose to render that "place" create different though certainly related maps for subjectivity: a hybrid diaspora and a cosmopolitan diaspora.

Within these constructions, India, contradictorily and paradoxically, appears. On some level, India is not necessarily a homeland, a stable place in the imagination to which this generation of Indians seeks return. Instead, India is a metaphor that can do all sorts of work in a conceptual space far removed from the nation-state. Desires for identity and belonging are projected onto this symbolic nation. Global capitalism and cultures have recreated India, and it is to that very contemporary space that Apache Indian, Bally Sagoo, and Talvin Singh have traveled; each of these artists has spent a good deal of time there, and Talvin Singh even maintains dual residences in London and Bombay.[42]

Apache Indian and Talvin Singh represent more broadly the diversity in this (youth) generation of the Indian diaspora and its pace of change. Within the field of the musics of British and U.S. Indians there are a variety of autonomous productions. Sheila Chandra mixes Hindu religious musics with western harmonies, saying of her song "Om Shanti Om," "I wanted to know what a blues guitar would sound like with a sacred chant."[43] And the *New Yorker* named as one of the best jazz albums of 2001 Indian American pianist Vijay Iyer's *Panoptic Modes*.[44]

The first song on Iyer's *Panoptic Modes* is entitled "Invocation," which Iyer describes as "a ritual for Rishi Maharaj," an Indian of Guyanese origin who was severely injured in a racial attack in Queens in 1998, and "his many fellow brown-skinned American victims of hatred and ignorance." While "Invocation" is marked by an insistent Vedic chant, not all tracks on *Panoptic Modes* employ Indian musical techniques. Iyer seems interested in producing a dialogue with traditions and innovations within the field of jazz music, but without suppressing multiple influences, rhythmic and social, as in the case of his obvious investment in questions of racial victimization. There is also a track, entitled "Numbers (for Mumia)," that is described as taking a stand on the death penalty.

Iyer, too, not only is cognizant of the complexities of his cultural production but is eager to develop a theory about it. In the beginning of the liner notes, he writes:

> In Chennai last summer, in the course of several long philosophical discussions, Madurai G. S. Mani exclaimed more than once, "You are nothing but memories, sir!" *Panoptic Modes* denotes the presence of multiple simultaneous levels of perception. In everyday life, we watch and listen analytically, processing detailed information as it comes in, but we also perceive and act synoptically—intuiting more ineffable qualities, seeing things all at once. . . . You can hear particular details of life experience encoded in music. . . . Continually, our improvisations index our individual and collective personal histories. The result is what I like to call an exploded narrative—fragments of storytelling refracted through shards of sound.

Iyer's understanding of narrative and perception might be compared to Edouard Glissant's notion of poetic relation, which strives to explicate experiences of the social world that contain traces of the past and produce an imagination from forms of contact with otherness and difference, and, ultimately that assert a new practice of reading and writing. This is another way to think of diaspora, in more fluid terms. And, like Glissant, Iyer finds the metaphor of the sea productive, in songs entitled "Atlantean Trope" and "Trident: 2001."[45]

Though it is tempting to organize the musics in a sequence, wherein bhangra with roots came first and other fusion and fluid forms, multiply located, came later, the fact is that several different musics began to emerge in the mid-1980s,[46] when many of the children of Indian immigrants to the United States and the United Kingdom came of age. Schema for the development of diasporic musics break down, too, upon deeper consideration of the projected and actual audiences for these productions. Youth clubs were not the only site for consuming bhangra or fusion; the music was also played and danced to at cross-generational weddings and other Indian events. Instead of simply becoming emblematic of a youth generation (or "second" generation) that rebelled against norms of early immigrants, bhangra in its most syncretic rendition became a sign for an "Indianness" expressed also at traditional rituals for the performance of cultural identity. And in the time-space compression of a diaspora with a past and present relationship to the Indian nation-state, bhangra is used in Bollywood films not necessarily to evoke India, but instead to signal a kind of modernity, sexualized and perhaps transgressive. The broad dispersal of these films themselves and their music, in Nigeria[47] Malaysia, and other places, reinscribes Indianness in a global setting with altogether different effects.[48]

Considering these musics as a symptom and embodiment of a generation of diaspora elicits the question, again, of how to most productively
cast changes in social formations of migrants. While on the one hand such
music's constitutive hybridity (and association with youth, a "second"
generation) might intimate evolution and a break with the past, on the
other hand, the prominence of traditions from the homeland as well as
the travel of new forms back to India suggest a kind of consolidation and
reproduction. And herein, too, lies the importance of the porousness of
the category of "youth" itself. Joe Austin and Michael Nevin Willard
have offered a succinct definition for youth as a "socially constructed and
multiple identity whose relations to other social formations are constantly
in flux and only definable temporarily and locally."[49] To see youth cultures
as contingent is to challenge the presumption of this site as an essential
vector for a necessary set of transformations: of citizenship, of nationality,
and of cultural identity. New generations produce musics filled with excesses—of style, rhythms, origins—and implicitly challenge narratives of
loss, as a logic of diaspora itself or as a lament of contemporary migrants
who fear cultural dissipation. And the self-articulated subjectivity of this
generation in diasporic terms can also make for a departure from immigrant stories, in which the children of immigrants would simply become
new nationals of the United States or United Kingdom.

To Be a Young Indian in America and Britain

The heterogeneous category of youth captures a range of associational
forms. What is evident from the discussion of musical cultures above and
in the multitude of Indian youth groups is the persistence of identificatory
longings: cultural, racial, political, and social. Those longings, of course,
only become clear through an understanding of location and contingency.
A large part of that location, for youths as well as for their parents, is in
the U.S. and British arrangements of racial and ethnic formation. A need
to belong to some nation (or religion), an urgency to contest forms of
social injustice, a wish to find cultural connections to others—all, I would
suggest, are responses, though rather different ones indeed, to the process
of racialization and the demands of ethnicization in both the United States
and Britain.

A newspaper editorial written by an Indian American high school student illustrates one identity strategy for life in the United States. Kiran
Patel's intention in "Other Holidays, Other Seasons" is to suggest that
Diwali, the Hindu new year, should be acknowledged within U.S. culture
through the establishment of an official school holiday. Patel's rationale
takes shape in an assertion of multiculturalism: "The . . . school [district]

views its diversity as an educational asset. Through programs like Human Relations, students are encouraged to embrace the culture of others. However students will not want to experience other cultures if they feel their own ethnicity is not respected."[50] Setting up a competitive model, Patel suggests that membership in a broader framework of multiplicity (and its attendant tolerance) can only be produced through a formal acknowledgment of ethnic identity. This is a sentiment echoed widely in Indian immigrant communities in the United States, around school holidays or parking regulations in New York. And here the slippage between Hinduness and Indianness is often made, just as it is in India proper and throughout formations of the Indian diaspora. Representation is essential to being American and also for those who might sense the possible loss of homeland affiliation, to being Indian; as Patel suggests: "Because Diwali is not acknowledged through a school holiday, Indian families find it more difficult to celebrate their own holy day adequately."

In emerging from a particular sense of locatedness, some youths seem to reject cosmopolitanism, and a certain fluidity of identity implied in that term, in favor of more stable reference points for the construction of self and group affiliation, not unlike what their parents have done. Various youths explicitly organize around being Indian, or, by extension, being Hindu, to simultaneously create for selves and groups a sense of identification and establish a categorical space within established social templates in the outside world.[51] On college campuses in the United States and United Kingdom, since the early 1980s and the rise of a "second" generation, there has been a huge increase in social organizations for Indian American or Indian British students.[52] This development coincides more generally in societies all around the world with the dominance of "identity politics" as a way of thinking about the place of groups within the whole, and as a form of addressing issues of inequality. Within a broad language of identity, these groups address, variously, social and cultural desires and political needs. The monikers—Indian, South Asian, Hindu, Asian—are a key to the specific content of ethnic identification, yet these too render open fields of signification. Hindu youth groups, be they apparently committed to the practice of religion or the maintenance of cultures from the subcontinent, often satisfy an exclusivist and nationalist understanding of Indian identity.[53] Religion here, as more generally in the diaspora, I would argue, is a language for nation.[54] Other religious articulations, as they might occur through Islam and Sikhism, which have active youth groups, too,[55] may be a counterpoint, even a challenge to India, by espousing other forms of nationalism. In all these cases, movements in the subcontinent reach out to their wayward sons, even if they are in a new generation and have a relatively abstracted relationship to the nation.[56]

In any discussion of the associational cultures of young Indians, one can hardly overlook or perhaps fully analyze the desire to be with others who are perceived to be similar, especially in terms of ethnicity. And at times that need operates in the service of more conventional understandings of community reproduction. In a group called the Network of Indian Professionals (NetIP), a largely North American organization, a variety of forms of affiliation coalesce. Originally started as an organization to promote professional development and networking among Indians living and working in the vicinity of local chapters, NetIP is also more broadly understood as a social space to meet other young Indians, and particularly dating and marriage prospects.[57] While the securing of a suitable mate of particular ancestry (religion, caste, linguistic, or regional group) has always been a concern for Indian immigrants invested in the maintenance of cultural traditions and the retention of homeland-derived forms of kinship,[58] here that desired literal reproduction of familial Indianness coincides with the reproduction of a professional class, of well-educated and credentialed, economically advantaged, to a certain extent Westernized individuals.[59]

But just as bhangra cultures found meaning in a set of ideas that transgressed the class and cultural values of a kind of mainstream Indianness, so too do a plethora of organizations and cultural formations of the youth generation create affiliations that pose a set of challenges to the focus on cultural retention. In the United States, many groups have used the category of "South Asian" to cut against national divisions in immigrant populations from the Indian subcontinent and address a range of social concerns around the difficulties of being a racialized immigrant. The construction of South Asian itself has a racial rather than national logic, and also bridges different waves of immigration: directly from India beginning in 1965, from the Caribbean after the mid-1970s, and credentialed and working-class populations later. South Asian Youth Action (SAYA!) is based in Elmhurst, Queens, and runs academic support programs, a summer camp to explore the city, sporting events, and girls' groups in an overall mission to "promote self-esteem, provide opportunities for growth and development, and build cultural, social and political awareness among South Asian youth."[60] Another group, Desi's Rising Up & Moving (DRUM), deploys the term "desi," a reference to the Hindi word for country, or homeland ("desh"), but here posited to imply a broader collection of peoples "who share a common history of colonization; people who have origins in the indian subcontinent: nepal, bhutan, sri lanka, bangladesh, pakistan, guyana, trinidad, india and the diaspora."[61] DRUM, which arose after the Rishi Maharaj incident, addresses itself directly to racial issues concerning working-class South Asian communities and is explicitly defined by social movement rhetoric rather than service-organization terms. Constituted in specific social and political terms, these groups may be seen to constitute their own new generation of diaspora. As a marker of that shift, perhaps, in May 2001, a one-day conference at New York University Law School entitled "Desis Organizing 2001" attracted twenty groups that broadly saw themselves within the rubric of "progressive politics." The British counterpart can be found in "Asian" groups that work in poorer (and largely Muslim) communities in urban areas like Brick Lane in London and Bradford and Oldham in northern England.

As much as racialization presents important challenges to diasporic Indianness, as I will describe shortly, it is a process that has a long history in being a topic of discussion and contemplation in migrant communities. Even when it is suppressed or repressed, race is a central feature of Indian life abroad. Race, in other words, has an ability to be narrativized within almost all renditions of Indian diasporas. This, I would argue, is not necessarily the case with gender and sexuality. Many scholars have suggested that gender deeply fissures nationalist constructions of India, both by developing alternative notions of the role of the state and undermining the patriarchal romance associated with independence.[62] And it is therefore not surprising that when Indian female immigrants have chosen to organize politically around questions of gender, in particular against domestic violence, in periods always after mainstream forms of associational culture have developed, they have done so by designating themselves as "South Asian" or "black." Assuming those broader (and racial) identities enables them, on the most practical level, to service emerging Bangladeshi, Pakistani, Sri Lankan, and other groups, and more conceptually, perhaps, to critique nuclear familial constructions glorified in contemporary recoveries of "Indian culture."[63] But for the most part, though these groups may be redefining what are important issues that have to do with being Indian in the United States and United Kingdom, they do not threaten other constructions, precisely because they tend to foreground their own service to women that experience familial violence, which, in almost all public articulations, remains indefensible.[64] Another important point here is that the membership of many South Asian women's organizations, like Sakhi for South Asian Women in New York, or Manavi in New Jersey, or Apna Ghar in Chicago, bridges conventional generation groups and includes women in their thirties, forties, and fifties who emigrated from the subcontinent some time ago, as well as younger women who were born and raised in the West. In this sense, age (or origin) is less a marker of this generation of diaspora than gender. And gender, too, may be taken up in a variety of forms, as some women may specifically describe the work they do as "feminist" and others may eschew that label.

Even more than gender, gay sexuality as a sign of difference and as an affective mode of experience truly disrupts and threatens mainstream constructions of diaspora. Gay and lesbian Indians (and other South Asians) draw simultaneously on diasporic understandings of community, often connecting to organizations in the subcontinent, and sexual identity, to create a sense of self and group. And there are determined efforts to trace gay sexuality and lesbianism back in time, through new readings of Indian cultural practice. Yet despite this seeming excess of reference points and connective possibilities, the diaspora that is created through sexuality is one that cannot be contained by conceptions of Indianness that rely on nation and family, precisely because queerness rethinks the ways that men relate to other men, and women to other women, to overhaul the entire concept of kinship.[65] And it seems also that part of the energy behind some established conceptions of diasporic production lies in its possibility of *re*-production; queer diasporas create different trajectories of development, that articulate not only to formations "back home," but also to other subjects of different origin. One obvious manifestation of the difficulties in incorporating alternative sexualities into diverse national-diasporic formations has been controversies around ethnic parades. While the St. Patrick's Day Parade, and the debate around including gay Irish marchers, has been most broadly publicized since the 1980s, conflicts since the early 1990s around the inclusion of the South Asian Gay and Lesbian Association (SALGA) at the India Day Parade in August have begun to achieve a canonical importance.[66]

The problematic of assimilation may appear to new generations of diaspora in forms other than becoming American or British. That paradigmatic question of whether Indianness is lost gets taken up with much fervor by some renderings of youth and rejected by others. And onto groups that cross age groups and rethink filiation, like those based in sexual identity, anxieties about disappearance are projected with much force, resulting in profound exclusions.

To Represent New Generations

Generation thematizes two films from the 1990s on the Indian diaspora, *Mississippi Masala* in the United States and *Bhaji on the Beach* in the United Kingdom. Not only is the topic of generation part of the content of the films themselves, generation also is central to how we might think of the production of a kind of cinematic Indianness in diaspora. These films, directed by Indian women who see themselves as part of a different age and social group than the first wave of Indians in Britain and the United States, were conceived as intervening in conventional productions of the story of immigration, with an eye to representation to a wider public (Indian and non-Indian), and they give diaspora a textual depth as well as a particular popularity.

Claims that the new cinematic subject is diasporic are by now taken as common truths in fields like film studies. Cultural producers as well as cultural critics have been eloquent about this new trend in the United States and Britain. The efflorescence of filmmaking in so-called first-world countries by those of Asian, African, and Latin American descent testifies to the accepted foregrounding of previously submerged identities within histories of colonialism, imperialism, and world capitalism.

There is, then, a community of cultural producers to which the directors of *Bhaji on the Beach* and *Mississippi Masala*, Gurinder Chadha and Mira Nair, belong. That community, including people like Isaac Julien and Pratibha Parmar on the more avant-garde (and British) side, and Wayne Wang in a more popular (and U.S.) vein, is one that has produced diverse discourses on race, ethnicity, and migration within which any production of diasporic Indianness must be situated. It is in the forces of those broad dialogues that I want to consider these films, which also coincide with other generational productions, like bhangra and nationalist and antinationalist youth associations.[67] If a diasporic generation has come of age in representations found in the music of Apache Indian and Talvin Singh, and through the Hindu Student Councils, then it has also done so in the cinema with these two films.

Bhaji on the Beach (1993) received mostly celebratory attention from the British media as well as bitter criticism from members of older immigrant communities in London. The film, about a group of Punjabi Indian women of several generations who come together for a day trip to Blackpool, showcases a wide array of characters—from teenage girls to a grandmother figure, from a divorced second-generation mother to longmarried immigrant women with grown children—and buttresses director Gurinder Chadha's claim about the diversity of the female Asian experience in Britain. The differences of experience within the group of women exalt converging and diverging ideologies; as these women are a part of one another, they are also apart from one another. The constitutive tensions of diaspora between difference and sameness are manifested in subcommunities, like those constituted through gender. The film seems to suggest that this generation of diaspora is not only different *from* the generation before or the generation being constituted in another site, it is also different *within*.

Cultural sameness is experienced through deep and abiding conflicts as the narratives of the film unfold. The recently divorced mother Ginder (Kim Vithana) has been the victim of physical and emotional abuse from her husband; this issue continues to complicate immigrant experience in the film as well as in Asian communities in Britain and the United States, and refers more specifically, I would suggest, to the pattern of feminist organizing within diasporic communities.[68] Hashida (played by Sarita Khajuria) has become pregnant in a relationship with an Afro-Caribbean man, the discovery of which by older members of the travel group leads to angry and painful ruptures.

A romantic liaison between an African American southerner and a Ugandan-Indian-American woman is one plot device of the 1992 film *Mississippi Masala*, set in Greenwood, Mississippi, the heart of the Deep South. Directed by Mira Nair, the film begins in Uganda in 1972 when Idi Amin's massive expulsion of Asians forces Jay (Roshan Seth), Kinnu (Sharmila Tagore), and their young daughter Mina (Sarita Chaudhari) to leave the land where generations of their family have lived. The comment that Jay's African friend Okelo (Konga Mbandu) makes a few minutes into the film—"Africa is for Africans, black Africans"—literally and figuratively resonates through a number of succeeding frames. Later settling in Mississippi with her family, the twenty-four-year-old Mina becomes involved with Demetrius (Denzel Washington), to the great consternation of her relatives who have rather uneasy connections to cultural difference and racial solidarity.

While both films discuss the Indian migrant, *Mississippi Masala* and *Bhaji on the Beach* give life to diverse conceptions of community and identity. *Mississippi Masala* sketches a picture of a community in transition, migrating through a number of different spaces and coming to rest in the United States, whereas *Bhaji on the Beach* portrays a community having migrated and squarely situated within the cultures of Britain. The diasporic nature of these films should not be confused with a more simplistic and free-floating formulation of "global culture," though they might indeed have been marketed within a rubric structured by local-global oppositions that are ultimately undone. These films were highly located even as they evoked movement, saying in effect that migration is not a unitary signifier because the cultures of immigrants and culture itself are a good deal more complex than the category of "Asian films" could possibly render.

At the outset of *Bhaji on the Beach*, the leader of the trip, Simi (Shaheen Khan), brings together the many characters of the film under the auspices of the Saheli Asian Women's Centre. As they are leaving the city limits, Simi delivers a short monologue on women's oppression and the development of alternative communities, concluding, "Have a female fun time." Meanwhile, the preceding scenes have illustrated the various conflicts that women on the bus are facing in their own lives and with regard to one another, and the construction of a community there seems very distant indeed. What is astonishing about this piece of work, however, is the way that it succeeds in convincing us that both a field of conflict and a sense of community can exist together. And perhaps differently from other evocations of idealized community, in theory and literature, here this very contemporary construction of a community gets produced through the exploration of dissent; in that way it is hardly determined by strict categories of "similarity" and "difference." In fact, a certain degree of open-endedness and flexibility characterizes all the important moments of the film.

The interracial relationship between the characters of Hashida and Oliver (Mo Sesay) speaks directly to questions of sexuality and race within the Punjabi Indian community. Hashida, discovering that she is pregnant by Oliver, faces a decision to have an abortion or jeopardize her plans to go to medical school. When other members of the trip inadvertently learn of this, they are effectively confronted with Hashida's sexuality and identity as a woman and also their own racial prejudices. The resulting fissures in the group climax in a scene where Hashida is so frustrated and upset that she throws hot tea in the lap of an older member of the group in a Blackpool coffee shop. A sense of frustration and anger produces a violent act that exists outside the realm of artificial resolutions that narrative accounts of ethnicity often trade in. It also brings to a crisis point, intragenerationally and intergenerationally, questions of race that are at the heart of constructions of the Indian diaspora.

In another major strand of the film, Ginder faces the disapproval and scorn of older members of the group for having left her husband. Initially, she is read as irresponsible for doing so even though the audience already knows that she has come from a shelter and has probably been battered. But as in other aspects of this film, the relationships here are complex; Ginder feels real sadness about taking her young son and leaving her husband. She also remarks at various points that her choices have been very difficult and that she has considered going back to her old life, not least because a certain degree of social legitimacy is important to her.

Popular representations of ethnic communities often focus on first-generation/second-generation conflicts and construct a set of very polarized choices, between tradition on the one hand and progress on the other. As Perminder Dhillon-Kashyap remarks, "Think of an Asian woman—what comes to mind? Arranged marriages? Domestic violence? Stuck between two cultures?" [69] Consider the U.S. television series *All-American Girl* and the British series *The Eastenders*, both of which were legitimately criticized for having rather flat Asian characters. Such representations have served to reify both "Eastern" and "Western" cultures and to deprive the subjects themselves of any agency. Most important, perhaps, such cultural moments close down the imaginative possibility of creating new cultures that are modeled on new experiences, particularly those of second- and third-generation American or British citizens.

In *Bhaji on the Beach*, the choices are more numerous and nuanced. Neither Ginder nor Hashida seriously considers leaving the world she lives in altogether; they both negotiate their conflicts within a broad web of relationships and identities. At one point, Ginder looks into the window of a beauty salon with envy; seeing this, Asha (Lalita Ahmed) passes her some money to get her hair done, despite the fact that their earlier conflict has not been resolved. Asha supports Ginder's husband in the dispute, but Ginder is still a young woman to Asha auntie and there can be love in their relationship even amid disagreement. Generational conflict is not the only way to understand this community, the film seems to suggest; *cross-generational* intimacy can be another field for the production of identity.

At the end of the film, all the women go back to their larger communities. This moment is happy and warm, but without an outward articulation of sameness or even complete settlement of the issues that emerged during the day. The moment of comprehension comes about through an appreciation of difference and a commitment to old and new communities. The social and cultural landscape of England is omnipresent in the film. Inasmuch as the communities that form there are socially constructed, so too is the landscape historically produced. At one point in the film the women stop at a rest area off the highway and come upon a group of white men who make unwanted, aggressive advances toward them. When the men are rejected, they become verbally abusive, resorting to a familiar racist discourse: "Go home where you came from." Later, Asha meets an older English man who mourns the passing of a more pristine British culture. He values in Asha exactly what is by this point in the film abundantly untrue, that is, the unchanged nature of Indian culture; he says that contemporary British culture is "not like you, you've kept hold of your traditions" and continually describes Asha as "exotic, exquisite, proud."

What is important about these scenes is the way they fill out and complicate a racial landscape that has been first signified in one of the opening scenes of the film by Indian shop owners washing racist graffiti off their front door. The men's anger over their sexual rejection emerges from a nexus of race, class, and gender, as does the old English man's fascination with Asha. Colonialism's effects include sexual oppression, migration, reification, and fetishization at various turns, and it is this background to Britain and Britishness that shapes Asian communities in England as well as a broader diaspora.

History differently informs *Mississippi Masala*. Uganda and particularly its racial world frame the entire film. Jay's nostalgia for a pre-African nationalist Kampala keeps his family in transition and not fully committed to or familiar with any one place; indeed, they are even separate from the recent Indian working-class community in Mississippi. But it is this very distance that accentuates the diversity in what might seem a homogeneous group of people: Indians owning and working in motels in the United States. The fact that Jay, Kinnu, and Mina are from Uganda broadens the international story of the Indian diaspora told here and shifts the terrain of identity production. Nair's interest in a diaspora constructed through double dislocation creates a repertoire of historical experiences and representations that disrupts Indianness as well as "Indian-Americanness."

Class positionality is also relatively uncharted territory in diasporic representation. The Indian immigrants who live and work in motels in small towns across the United States constitute a section of the Indian American population that is often left out of popular understandings. Well-credentialed and wealthy Indians who embody the "American dream" hold a large purchase on the popular imagination and the fact that "Indians in the United States" are becoming far more economically, socially, and culturally diverse is sometimes effectively denied by middle-class Indians themselves. Jay's despair about his family's occupations in the United States echoes the frustrations of other Asian and Latin American immigrants who may have had skilled jobs in their home countries but cannot do so in the "land of opportunity." The public accounting of such third-world immigrants in the United States has a scant recent history, particularly in the realm of popular cultural production.

Mina and Demetrius fall in love against and with reference to a larger narrative of race and immigration, specifically Mina's family history. This interracial relationship, like the one between Hashida and Oliver in *Bhaji on the Beach*, is crucial to the narrative. It is because Demetrius is African American and Mina is Indian that the boundaries of race are challenged both in black Southern communities, in Indian working-class communities, and, perhaps most important, in the viewers' expectations of who and what a racial subject is. Representing race as a site of desire and conflict central to the development of Indian diasporic identity brought to the surface a set of experiences occluded in popular accounts of ethnicity.

Mississippi Masala and *Bhaji on the Beach* reveal hybrid ethnicities of a new generation. Mina is not simply Indian, Ugandan, or American, nor is she a racialized subject in the same way that an African American is in the deep South—she is something else that she calls "masala." The characters in *Bhaji on the Beach* also carry multiple identities; they are Indian, Asian, black, and British at once because of the complicated nature of history itself. In some sense these films might be seen as responding to United States and British national stories of race and ethnicity with a counternarrative of hybridity. That they do so through a contemplation of generation suggests, all the same, a need to engage with historical context.

Migration and exile engender deep ambivalences, and the world of *Mississippi Masala* represents the association of some forms of diasporic identity with loss, but interestingly, the loss is not only associated with India. Jay's pain in leaving Uganda reflects the intersection of the histories of two continents and the political movements that have determined that history. It may be that Jay gives short shrift to the possibilities of African nationalism, but the moral seems less to be about the ethics of his claim to Uganda than about the difficulties in any transition, and in the accompanying identity shifts that take place, those that increasingly define new global frameworks.

In *Bhaji on the Beach*, Asha embodies a number of these processes of decentering. She owns a newspaper shop with her husband and has children from whom she feels more and more distant. As much as she creates her own world, she is also caught up in a larger process of cultural rearticulation and consequently has hallucinations that illustrate both her desires and her worst fears. Those forays into the phantasmic symbolize the anxiety of change and presence in a world where nothing is certain. For a time Asha does escape, courted by the elderly Englishman, but the departure finally proves illusory. Preferring the real, sometimes difficult, and sometimes joyful world of the women on the bus trip, she says with conviction: "I want to go back to my group."

The negotiation of such community solidarities and cultural differences in *Bhaji on the Beach* emblematically takes place in Blackpool. It is to the seaside and in fact to the border where all sorts of tourists go; it is a place where the cultural other can perhaps feel "at home." In *Mississippi Masala*, Mina and Demetrius also go to the shore to consummate their love and are discovered in bed there by her cousin and uncle, who see the world in more culturally absolute terms, inland. The ability to physically move in these films becomes annexed to other forms of imaginative freedom, not unlike the work that the trope of mobility does in the music of Apache Indian.

Though the revelation of the relationship between Mina and Demetrius has some transgressive potential, of course it is problematic that sexuality becomes a sign for "Westernness." Such a fabrication may uphold the East-West polarity and detract from other interesting questions that this kind of coming together might suggest. The romantic story supplants a number of important matters, though it seems to come out of a rather daring narrative impulse to connect racial bodies in the face of other essentialisms often endemic to desire in the contemporary social world. At one point in the film, Idi Amin appears on the television screen and says that Indians had remained in very closed communities in Uganda and not allowed their women to marry Africans. At the same time, viewers see an intense homosocial love between Okelo and Jay being challenged as Okelo encourages Jay to leave Uganda; Jay finally turns away from Okelo at what he perceives to be Okelo's rejection of him. At the beginning of her crush on Demetrius, when Mina asks her mother, "What happened between Daddy and Okelo?" she realizes that her situation revisits that other desire and that the desire is not free of race.[70]

But when Mina says to her mother that "nobody cares in America," the film traffics in myths of a multicultural romance of the United States. Mina falls for Demetrius, a black entrepreneur, not his brother who listens to rap music and displays a "street" black nationalism. The picture of race that Denzel Washington projects is a comforting one that can operate within a certain set of American ideologies, of hard work and achievement. As Mina distinguishes herself from her parents and their friends, she comes to emblematize a new subjectivity that is counterposed to essentialisms in the Ugandan and U.S. Indian communities. But this quixotic construction of America may play down questions of race, and in fact mirror more conventional self-representations of the Indian American immigrant community.

At the end of the film, Mina and Demetrius leave their respective communities to make their own lives and render their romance non-negotiable within the racial communities in which they live. Though there is the possibility of a new love, there is no allusion to a new community of subjects or interests. Symptomatically, however, in the very last scene of the film, Mina and Demetrius appear in "ethnic garb," she in Indian clothing and he in a scarf and hat of kinte cloth; in fact the actress, Sarita Chaudhari, is only dressed in Indian clothing in the scenes with Denzel Washington. These characters remain culturally ethnicized with regard to one another, and in that way the film stops short of really challenging some of the singular identities that have been presented so far. Likewise, when Mina says after spending time with Demetrius's family that "there's a real feeling of home there," she sees something authentic in that black Southern experience. The world that emerges, then, is constituted a bit by stereotypes as much as it is by forces for change.

Bhaji on the Beach emerges from a different set of cultural imperatives. A number of devices in the film convey disjuncture and difference rather than cohesion, and they are innovations that produce a different kind of content. Rather than rely on a linear narrative, Chadha chooses a more cut-and-paste style, a pastiche, where different moments of conflict and pleasure are juxtaposed to one another with coherence but not immediate sequence. The use of many kinds of music and genres, including bhangra and Bollywood drama, underscores the mixture of cultural styles and influences within an Indian community in Britain. Through an ingenious use of language, there are also different layers of meaning for a variety of consumers. At many points in the film, the characters speak in Punjabi, but unlike in *Mississippi Masala*, where the characters' spoken Gujarati is immediately translated into English, there is no translation in *Bhaji on the Beach*. Some viewers may understand perfectly, others who perhaps speak North Indian languages understand partly, and some may not catch the meaning of such lines at all; in every case, however, the viewers engage in a process of apprehension that has built into it a moment where they must pause and consider whether they do or do not understand and why.

In both *Bhaji on the Beach* and *Mississippi Masala,* the nation-state of India is absent. Mina says more than once that she has never been to India. In *Bhaji on the Beach*, when there is talk about Indian traditions and customs, a cousin from India continually asks the older immigrant women what India they are talking about and when they have last been back. These films actively eschew nationalistic affinities by an intense focus on the present. Even Jay's nostalgia for Uganda is shown to be embedded in a fantasy that is untenable in the world he comes to occupy. As much as immigrant communities have changed, say the directors, so too has the third world changed. The reference point is more temporally and spatially distant, and immigrant subjects may have less contact with that space, physically, though as diasporic subjects they create relationships of a symbolic nature.

As we consider the ways that ethnic and cultural identities get produced inside and outside of representation, we must also understand the discursive circumstances from which these forms of cultural production emerge. In other words, which languages "speak" these films? Though they are different because of subject matter and artistic direction, the divergences are also ordered by idioms of place and time. The contexts of the United States and Britain provide different and differently available symbolic systems of race, ethnicity, and nationhood. As the films articulate a set of identities with those other political and cultural formations, they produce an interesting narratival field of comparison.

British migrants work to examine particularities in that category of "race" through ethnicity and define themselves as "Black British," "Asian," and "Afro-Caribbean." The alliances evoked in the production of minority "blackness" come from an interpretation of the experiences of colonialism, patterns of worldwide settlement, and situatedness in postwar racial formation. This way of seeing the world has produced a generation of consciously affiliated cultural producers: Chadha and Hanif Kureishi at times describe themselves as "Black British"[71] and draw on the resources of prominent black intellectuals in Britain. Chadha notes: "I was reading *There Ain't No Black in the Union Jack* every time I reached a stumbling point with *I'm British But. . . .* Now what am I doing? How can I do this? And I would read it and everything would become clear. . . . It is the writings of people like Stuart Hall and Paul Gilroy that I read and which make sense to me. I had not read anything that an Asian person had written apart from Hanif [Kureishi]."[72]

The differences and divisions in black identity have been widely explored, particularly through critiques of nationalism and racial essentialism. That process of critiquing, exploring, expanding, and specifying racial and ethnic categories has resulted in the theorization of hybridity and multiple identities. Chadha herself speaks about the importance of particularities within broader categories of "black film": "*Bhaji* is about someone close to me being divorced and someone else close to me being married to an Afro-Caribbean guy, and the impact that had on my family, and my extended family and friends. . . . Looking back at it, I get this real sense of British-Asian history, from a very female, Punjabi, Southall point of view." In contemporary discussions about ethnicity in the United States, multiculturalism has maintained a dominant position. It is in this language, that of many discrete cultures composing what is the mosaic of the United States, that difference is described. The historical flexibility of the American rhetoric of inclusion for ethnic minorities other than those who are African American and poor (for whom an entirely different descriptive lexicon, for race, exists) produces the imperative to discuss ethnic difference in discrete terms. Ethnic and cultural identities get produced inside and outside representation, and also with regard to changes in the immigrant populations. The changing visibility of Indians in the United States has propelled a fixation by Indian ethnic organizations on a kind of assimilation that denies a process of racialization, as that has been the experience and strategy of other immigrant groups. This of course is different for the United Kingdom. The stories for ethnicity in these cultural occasions, then, are differently informed, in Britain by antiracism and in the United States by multiculturalism, and lead to very different senses of nationality and identity, in a contemporaneous set of representations. Having Mina become "American" lures Nair into a conceptual and political set of options that Chadha can avoid because being British and Asian is something altogether different.

Bhaji on the Beach and *Mississippi Masala* are also parts of a broader and more general category of diasporic cultural production, not because they necessarily express all the many and international aspects of an ethnic community, but because they leave that possibility open and because they provide important symbols. Diaspora is always incomplete, as is ethnicity here in these films; what is important to consider is the very process of construction. The films construct a dialogue between different groups of people who imagine some similarity of experience and in fact often organize for many different and varied purposes around such identities, be they "Indian," "South Asian," "Black," or "Female," or something else altogether. Most recently, *Bhaji on the Beach* was wildly popular in the United States, despite its "Britishness," not only because it was good enough to be able to speak to universal concerns but also because it was claimed by various groups as analogous to local issues. And the current political and cultural moment of a new kind of globalism has produced a shift to see race, ethnicity, and migration as international matters.

Mississippi Masala and *Bhaji on the Beach* make gender central to their narratives, and say in effect that the "new generation" is also female. Concerning young women and discussing the production of new forms of womanhood and gendered identities of the Indian diaspora, these films intimate that various communities of women that arise (as in *Bhaji on the Beach*) may be rather different from what is dictated by an older model of cultural feminism that is predicated on the prioritization of the abstract and unmediated figure of the woman. They also suggest that this female, Indian, diasporic generation may forcefully intervene in masculine productions of Indianness. Most especially, when the female generation is feminist and outlines different roles for women and expands the possibilities for their identity, it is rather different even from the masculinized generation that Apache Indian invokes in his desires for a girl to make him roti. These representational fields, of Apache Indian's address and of these films' stories, do not then cover the same space either conceptually or constitutively, in terms of who is included and why.

A significant aspect of the production of these films is in their transformation of the "popular" form; both films were widely viewed, not only on the art house circuit but also in big movie theaters in London, New York, and Boston. Gurinder Chadha won the British Film Institute prize for best newcomer and Mira Nair has her own salability within the U.S. context. They have not ceded the realm of public discourse to more traditional producers; indeed, their efforts to lay claim to that space have an effect on the dissemination of important cultural ideas within a general populace. This cultural production has a hand in rewriting what and who an Indian subject is in the popular imagination and more broadly who a migrant subject is.

Bhaji on the Beach and *Mississippi Masala* displayed a sensibility that speaks to a kind of class and cultural diversity, one that exists outside the cultural politics of essential difference. In that way, given their timing, they do operate in a kind of "third space" that Homi Bhabha speaks of, or one of "hybrid cultures" that Nestor Canclini has described for a rather different set of national circumstances. In both Britain and the United States, we have seen the growing influence of religious and cultural nationalist groups; middle-class Indians themselves expound on such traditionalist and politically conservative ideas in the name of cultural celebration. As these films revel in a more complicated and hybrid set of identities, they challenge those static definitions of community. Concerned as they are with the state of being ethnic in the United States and United Kingdom, these films rethink that possibility in terms of vital and dynamic cultures.

Coda: Generations Remake a Diaspora

In the years since Apache Indian's first album, the first Indian Students' Associations on U.S. and British college campuses, and the production of films like *Mississippi Masala*, the cultural and social work of new generations of the Indian diaspora has proceeded with an extraordinary pace and internal diversity. And of course the generations who began to critique the trajectory of migration in diasporic space in the early 1990s are no longer "new." The referent homeland, as well, cannot be held in a static position: India develops its own forms of culture that exceed the boundaries of the nation-state and reach out to its peoples abroad, making for a complex set of negotiations on the nature of identity, community, and history.

Perhaps the ironies are best understood in the popular Bollywood film *Lagaan* ("tax" in Hindi). Produced for an unprecedented 250 million rupees (or $5.32 million, partially funded from outside India), the film was specifically intended for a wide audience in the United States, United Kingdom, Canada, Malaysia, Hong Kong, South Africa, and the Middle East. And in fact, when it was shown in London during the summer of 2001, it appeared not only in the theaters on the outskirts of town, where middle-class Indians dwell, but also in the mainstream cinema in Piccadilly Circus. The British and Indian press made much of the fact that finally a Bollywood film could be seen at the center of an old colonial metropole.

Yet instead of spectacularizing life abroad, or even contemporary conditions in India, *Lagaan* created an anticolonial fable in the story of a small Indian village that rebels against the British cantonment's attempt to overtax in a drought year. The anti-British sentiment was understood to be a nationalist/anticolonial gesture of appeal, but in its location in the past it was also able to sidestep contemporary geopolitical tensions. As the producer, Aamir Khan, noted, "*Lagaan* is set in 1893, when India was undivided, so I think all South Asian audiences, including the diaspora, will relate to it. In fact, even a British audience will relate to it."[73] A story of the past, of an India before partition and all the divisions that resulted, then, becomes a way to live in the present. But in both the production and reception of the film, a collective space of performance, the self-conscious, complex making of a mythical history as a generation's history, is provisional. British Asians walked out of the theater not only to go home to a re-created space of India, but also to live in the contradictory multicultural world of London. Perhaps non-Indian viewers were also considered when the producers developed the film's central tension in a portrayal of a cricket match to resolve the dispute, which also worked as a metaphor to express the tensions of a developing empire.[74]

At a weekend showing of the film in Piccadilly Circus in June 2001, shortly after its release, the audience was almost entirely second- and third-generation South Asian men and women under fifty.[75] A frequent question to the ticket clerk was whether this Hindi film was subtitled, and if it was being shown in the "regular theater." Ten minutes after the film began, and the Bollywood style of the film had become evident (singing and dancing interspersing text), a group of white patrons left the theater, eliciting a round of incredulous laughter in the audience. And following that moment, the most active audience participation could be found in empathetic responses to the depiction of British racism toward the Indian villagers (gasps), and a resistance to the film's attempts to humanize the white British female character (laughter).

If this generation of the diaspora was present at the screening of *Lagaan* to partake in a familiar ritual of immigrant Indianness, of watching Bollywood films, it did so with a twist, with the benefit of translation: linguistic, spatial (in a central London theater), and cultural. And certainly there were points where, I would suggest, experience in diaspora was the bridging of time and space. Sentimentalized representations of British colonial prejudice may certainly have been apprehended through young Asians' experiences of racialization in contemporary England. And when the main Indian male character rejects the white English woman in favor of the loyal Indian woman, the gendered national fantasy constitutes an India not unlike the one that this audience has witnessed being constructed, say, in the music of Apache Indian. An Indian past, then, not only offers a language of nationalism to groups invested in transnational connection, but also vocabularies of hybridity to diasporic generations multiply located.

There has been a good deal of debate on whether the children of immigrants retain or lose the transnational orientations of their parents. Yet this question as it is formed, I have argued, cannot adequately account for the locational and temporal multiplicity that gives rise to the subjectivity of Indian American or Indian British youths or their elders, in fact. India is indeed present in the daily experiences and imaginings of those in the diaspora, and new generations rework that constitutive logic.

EPILOGUE

PRESENTS AND FUTURES

IN SEPTEMBER 1998, Rishi Maharaj, a nineteen-year-old Indian Guyanese man, was severely beaten and sustained near-fatal injuries in a racially motivated attack in Queens. During the summer of 2000, mostly Muslim Bangladeshi youths rioted all over northern England in response to renewed activity of British racist groups, structural unemployment, and other forms of cultural alienation. And after the September 11, 2001, attack on the World Trade Center by Muslim extremists, hundreds of incidents of racial bias against South Asians were recorded all over the United States, including the shooting death of a Sikh man in Texas. If Indians and other South Asians had any question about their continued racialization in the United States and England, these recent and much publicized incidents have removed that doubt once and for all.[1]

Here is one aspect of Indian diaspora's "changing same." Though its development proceeds at a breakneck pace, it cannot fully be unleashed from reference points in the past, such as legacies of postcolonialism and structuring and exclusionary frameworks of national citizenship. When Ford Motor Company closed an assembly plant in Dagenham, England, in which more than 40 percent of the workers were of Indian descent, and where there was a well-known problem of white foremen discriminating against and abusing Indian workers, an article in *India Abroad* ended with the observation that "it was the car industry in Britain that had recruited the early Indian migrants in large numbers when they first came to this country seeking a better life."[2] After decades of massive migration, and generations of Indians in Britain and the United States, Indian (and other South Asian) migrant subjects consistently repudiate the possibility of simply "melting in," though when Britain's favorite food is curry it makes things rather more complex. Impulses toward diversification meet with their *doppelganger*, a desire for stability and sameness.

Perhaps we can best see the development of Indian migrant populations in terms of their extremes. On the one hand, relatively recent Indian immigrant engineers now make up a significant portion of northern California millionaires, who created start-up companies in Silicon Valley and also veritable Indian residential neighborhoods, with concentrations of multi-million dollar houses or condominium apartments in area towns.[3] And then there are the Indian workers who in early 2002 were discovered to be locked up and detained against their will as a precondition for being brought to work at a company in Oklahoma.[4] That these two dramatically different experiences of living and working in the United States have "Indian" content may be of limited significance in the classed and racialized framework of such migrant subjects.

Dialogues between past and present Indian diasporas occur in surprising fashion for the most contemporary moments of Indian cultural formation. As in the last chapter, here new generations of diaspora engage in a set of negotiations of time and space. Many children of Indian immigrant budget motel owners in the United States now own or run large upscale hotel chains, and they often cite their childhood experiences, like working at the front desk, as well as their continued connections with communities of Indians, as influential in their careers. And more recent Indian immigrants to the United States from the Caribbean exhibit complexities around questions of nationality and belonging produced by "twice migration," very similar to those Indians who moved from East Africa to England in the early 1970s.

We return then to the questions of what it means to feel, to be Indian. And how does diaspora mark, if not rehearse, changes in that field of possibilities? If it makes little sense to reduce the catalysts for cultural transformation to the most contemporary rendition of globalization, if diaspora is embedded in the experience and representation of history, then there must be a necessary caution exercised in seeing the futures of Indian diaspora simply through the models of diversification and atomization widely celebrated and lamented by popular observers. The continual additive energy, of more and more migrants in more and more Indian communities around the world, operates in the service of change to give a rather different cast to Indianness, to open up its definitional boundaries, if not challenge them altogether, but we can never underestimate the power of national feeling in a world where nations are still dominant. The character of the grandmother in Amitav Ghosh's novel *The Shadow Lines* makes that complicated sensibility vivid, when she rails against her niece who seeks to forget India in England, in the only terms she knows: "She doesn't belong there. It took those people a long time to build that country. . . . Everyone who lives there has earned his right to be there with blood; with their brother's blood and their father's blood and their son's blood. They know they're a nation because they've drawn their borders with blood." And the narrator who defends his grandmother observes: "She was not a fascist. . . . All she wanted was a middle-class life in which . . . she would thrive believing in the unity of nationhood and territory, of self-respect and national power."[5] Ghosh's imagined dialogue about deeply felt nationality is in the midst of a novel that ultimately shows the impossibility of unities of nation in a world where displacement is the primary language of living.

In contemplating this more futurist dilemma, of how to see the relationship between the national and the global, almost every cultural occasion
of this book has something to offer. No figure or text in diaspora lives
outside of nationality, nor within a singular or stable nation. The very
state of India abroad is the state of multiplicity, of nations. And the multiplicity of the textual field, of Indianness in different sites in which meaning
is variously rendered, is one way of developing the nation's heterogeneity.
My attempt to produce narratives and a sense of historicity within the
chapters of this book, rather than simply a history that progresses
throughout, is a way of insisting on the disjunctural nature of forms of
organizing experience. It makes a difference whether we think of Indianness as formed through a notion of place or through a fictional narrative, and that difference gives us a special way of seeing. The collection
of sites is meant to provide one perspective on how to interpret Indian
diasporic cultures. New forms of representation, alternative sites of Indianness, like the internet or television, will give a rather different set of
possibilities to the density of subjectivity explored here.

Despite my commitment throughout this book to the idea that Indianness is internally contradictory and fissured, it seems important to reiterate in closing that Indianness, or India, is nowhere close to being transcended, even while those categories might be differently inhabited or
understood, or even when they might give rise to other possibilities. As
racialization proceeds in both the United States and England, as a variety
of migrant communities are subjected to that process, and as political
activists organize around shared experiences of the society and state, the
category of "South Asian" for the U.S. context and "Asian" for the British
acquire meaning again.[6] And important solidarities have emerged: for instance, when an African American congressman denounces as "racial pro-
filing" the recent practice of asking Sikh men to remove their turbans at
U.S. airports, it evidences the changing nature of race.[7] On college campuses and in professional groupings, "Asian American" as a category has
had greater purchase on a whole range of ethnic groups, including Indians.[8] But these instances do not overcome articulations of Indianness.
South Asianness and Indianness may exist side by side for different populations, and sometimes in different moments of identificatory expression
for the same people, just as "blackness" and "Indianness" and "Sikhness"
could simultaneously be expressed at given historical moments in Southall, London. And essential for a continued India abroad is the accumu-
lating power of a nation-state in its name. The Indian diaspora now has an
ambassador from the Indian nation-state to tend to its concerns, however
diverse.[9] This is testament to the force simultaneously of an Indian state
and an India abroad, in which an origin can never be fully determined.

In fact, diaspora and nation are increasingly familiar, perhaps even dominant, ways of being in the world. The apparent contradiction between those forms is continually negotiated in the cultures of migrants, without any impulse to resolution. Incredibly complex translations of living within and across plural nations in the diasporic cultures of Indianness refuse to answer to the anxieties expressed in the *National Geographic* series on global culture cited at the start of this book, though they may in fact increase them. And in the background, of course, is tremendous pressure to construct new unities, as war and ethnic strife violently and sometimes fatally reorganize the nation. Perhaps with the insights of diaspora, we can optimistically view those kinds of violence through their desperation and impossibility, rather than through any stable meanings. In that way, diaspora and displacement—of nation, of culture, of economy, and of the state—can no longer be the exclusive purview of migrants, but must belong to us all.

NOTES

INTRODUCTION
GEOGRAPHIES OF INDIANNESS

1. Joel L. Swerdlow, "Global Culture," *National Geographic*, August 1999, 2–33.

2. Catherine A. Lutz and Jane L. Collins have made a powerful case for seeing *National Geographic* as an expression of U.S. national preoccupations through time. *Reading National Geographic* (Chicago: University of Chicago Press, 1993).

3. Bill Allen, "From the Editor," *National Geographic*, August 1999, 1.

4. Liisa Malkki, in "National Geographic: The Rooting of Peoples and the Territorialization of National Identity among Scholars and Refugees," *Cultural Anthropology* 7 (1):24–44, takes the category of refugees to make a similar sort of critique of the correspondence between nation and identity.

5. Ranajit Guha, ed., *A Subaltern Studies Reader, 1986–1995* (Minneapolis: University of Minnesota Press, 1997).

6. Johanna Lessinger's very important work on Indian immigrants has elaborated these links in "Nonresident-Indian Investment and India's Drive for Industrial Modernization," in *Anthropology and the Global Factory, Studies of the New Industrialization in the Late Twentieth Century*, ed. Frances A. Rothstein and Michael L. Blim (New York: Bergin and Garvey, 1992); and *From the Ganges to the Hudson: Indian Immigrants in New York City* (Boston: Allyn and Bacon, 1995).

7. Mary Louise Pratt, *Imperial Eyes: Travel Writing and Transculturation* (London: Routledge Press, 1992).

8. U.S. Census Bureau 2000 figures. See also Suman Guha Mozumder, "Over a million India-born persons in the US," *India Abroad*, March 14, 2002, 32.

9. This is a 1998 estimate according to the Office for National Statistics (ONS); figures obtained from website *http://www.statistics.gov.uk*, accessed February 6, 2002.

10. Michael Hardt and Antonio Negri, *Empire* (Cambridge: Harvard University Press, 2000), 45. Arjun Appadurai, whom they reference, calls this the "production of locality" in *Modernity at Large: Cultural Dimensions of Globalization* (Minneapolis: University of Minnesota Press, 1996), 178–99.

11. The collection of essays entitled *Culture, Power, Place: Explorations in Critical Anthropology*, ed. Akhil Gupta and James Ferguson (Durham: Duke University Press, 1997), makes a significant intervention in this regard.

12. Gupta and Ferguson make similar kinds of critiques of ethnographic method in "Culture, Power, Place: Ethnography at the End of an Era," in ibid., 1–29.

13. For an interesting discussion on this topic, see M. Balasubramanian, *Nehru: A Study in Secularism* (New Delhi: Uppal Publishing House, 1980), especially Chapter 3, "Nehru on Minority Problem," 40–65.

14. Immanuel Wallerstein, "The Construction of Peoplehood: Racism, Nationalism, Ethnicity," in Etienne Balibar and Immanuel Wallerstein, *Race, Nation, Class: Ambiguous Identities* (London: Verso Press, 1991), 71–85.

15. Etienne Balibar, "The Nation Form: History and Ideology," in ibid., 86–106; quote appears on 94.

16. Ibid., 96.

17. Floya Anthias and Nira Yuval-Davis, *Racialized Boundaries* (London: Routledge, 1992). Also see Barnor Hesse's very good introduction on these debates in Britain in Barnor Hesse, ed., *Unsettled Multiculturalisms: Diasporas, Entanglements, Transruptions* (London: Zed Books, 2000). Other important works on multiculturalism include David Bennett, ed., *Multicultural States: Rethinking Difference and Identity* (London: Routledge, 1998); Avery Gordon and Christopher Newfield, eds., *Mapping Multiculturalism* (Minneapolis: University of Minnesota Press, 1996); Bhikhu Parekh, *Rethinking Multiculturalism: Cultural Diversity and Political Theory* (Hampshire: Palgrave, 2000); and Gregory Jay, *American Literature and the Culture Wars* (Ithaca: Cornell University Press, 1997).

18. Stuart Hall, "New Ethnicities," in *Stuart Hall: Critical Dialogues in Cultural Studies*, ed. David Morley and Kuan-Hsing Chen (London: Routledge, 1996), 446.

19. Even in the years that I have been working on this project, beginning in 1994, there has been a striking (and rapid) increase in the visibility of Indians in U.S. culture, in politics, on television, in the arts, and in influential sectors of the economy.

20. The show has an Indian convenience store owner, Apu, as a regular character. One recent episode portrayed him participating in an arranged marriage ceremony, to what turned out to be a very westernized Indian woman. "The Two Mrs. Nahasapeemapetilons," November 16, 1997, *The Simpsons*, Fox Television network.

21. Press conference by the president, February 16, 2000, the East Room (The White House Office of the Press Secretary, document on its website, http://www.pub.whitehouse.gov/uri-res/I2R. . .:pdi://oma.eop.gov.us/2000/2/17/10.text.1).

22. A number of anthropologists and cultural critics have emphasized this point in discussions of methodology. In addition to Appadurai, Akhil Gupta and James Ferguson consider local-global issues in a way that has been very influential for my work: "Discipline and Practice: 'The Field' as Site, Method, and Location in Anthropology," in *Anthropological Locations: Boundaries and Grounds of a Field Science*, ed. idem (Berkeley: University of California Press, 1997), 1–46.

23. Ania Loomba's *Colonialism/Postcolonialism* (London: Routledge, 1998) does a good job of surveying the field and its debates.

24. In a summer 2001 visit to London, almost every cultural producer mentioned to me the significance of numerous surveys in which Indian curry was named as the favorite British food. For a humorous commentary on globalization and cuisine, see Sunanda K. Datta-Ray, "Where Curry Rules the Roast: If Ersatz Indian Is Britain's National Dish, Asia's Must Be the Big Mac," *Time*, September 29, 1997.

25. Oscar Handlin, *The Uprooted: The Epic Story of the Great Migrations That Made the American People* (Boston: Little, Brown, 1951). See also his *Boston's Immigrants: A Study of Acculturation* (Cambridge: Harvard University Press, 1941).

26. Noel Ignatiev's *How the Irish Became White* (New York: Routledge, 1995) has been useful in discussions of this issue. And Matthew Frye Jacobson's recent book, *Whiteness of a Different Color: European Immigrants and the Alchemy of Race* (Cambridge: Harvard University Press, 1998), places the study of whiteness (and immigrants) in a theoretically nuanced discussion of racial formation.

27. John Bodnar, *The Transplanted: A History of Immigrants in Urban America* (Bloomington: Indiana University Press, 1985); Ronald Takaki, *Strangers from a Different Shore: A History of Asian Americans* (Boston: Little, Brown, 1989); Kerby A. Miller, *Emigrants and Exiles: Ireland and the Irish Exodus to North America* (New York: Oxford University Press, 1985); and Virginia Yans-McLaughlin, *Immigration Reconsidered: History, Sociology, and Politics* (New York: Oxford University Press, 1990).

28. See critiques of the push-pull hypothesis in Lucie Cheng and Edna Bonacich, eds., *Labor Immigration under Capitalism: Asian Workers in the United States before World War II* (Berkeley: University of California Press, 1984).

29. Nina Glick Schiller, Linda Basch, and Cristina Szanton Blanc have engaged in much collaborative work to theorize transnationalism, the result of which is a number of co-authored or co-edited works that include *Nations Unbound: Transnational Projects, Postcolonial Predicaments, and Deterritorialized Nation-States* (New York: Gordon and Breach, 1994); *Towards a Transnational Perspective on Migration: Race, Class, Ethnicity and Nationalism Reconsidered* (edited by Schiller, Basch and Blanc); and "From Immigrant to Transmigrant: Theorizing Transnational Migration," *Anthropological Quarterly* 68, no. 1 (1995). In the article, "Transmigrants and Nation-States; Something Old and Something New in the U.S. Immigrant Experience," in *American Becoming, Becoming American*, ed. Josh DeWind et al. (Washington, D.C.: Russell Sage Publications, 1999), Schiller lays out her various positions on the subject of transnationalism. Other works that I would broadly identify with this kind of project are Roger Rouse, "Mexican Migration and the Social Space of Postmodernism," *Diaspora* 1, no. 1 (1991), and "Thinking through Transnationalism: Notes on the Cultural Politics of Class Relations in the Contemporary United States," *Public Culture* 7, no. 2 (1995); and Aihwa Ong and Donald Nonini, eds., *Ungrounded Empires: The Cultural Politics of Modern Chinese Transnationalism* (New York: Routledge, 1997).

30. Schiller, Basch, and Blanc, *Nations Unbound*, 7.

31. Ibid, 22.

32. Nina Glick Schiller, "Transmigrants and Nation-States." In that article she limits the meanings of transnationalism more explicitly: "To utilize the concept transnational as a synonym for movement across international borders is to deprive it of any utility. Nor is it useful to equate transnational migration with the longings that immigrants may feel for home, if these sentiments are not translated into systematic participation in networks that cross borders."

33. Jawaharlal Nehru, "What Is Culture?" at the inauguration of the Indian Council for Cultural Relations, New Delhi, April 9, 1950 in *Jawaharlal Neh-*

ru's Speeches, 1949–1953 (Calcutta: S. N. Guha Ray at Sree Saraswathy Press Ltd., 1954).

34. Benedict Anderson, *Imagined Communities: Reflections on the Origin and Spread of Nationalism* (London: Verso, 1983); Partha Chatterjee, *The Nation and Its Fragments: Colonial and Postcolonial Histories* (Princeton: Princeton University Press, 1993), and *Nationalist Thought and the Colonial World* (London: Zed Books, 1986).

35. This is a term that Benedict Anderson has used in his recent work, *The Spectre of Comparisons: Nationalism, Southeast Asia and the World* (London: Verso, 1998).

36. For helpful discussions of these issues having to do with the definition of diaspora, see Khachig Tololyan, "The Nation-State and Its Others: In Lieu of a Preface," in *Diaspora* 1, no. 1 (Spring 1991), 3–7 and William Safran, "Diasporas in Modern Societies: Myth and Homeland and Return," in *Diaspora* 1, no. 1 (Spring 1991), 83–99. Also, more recently, Robin Cohen has provided a scheme for looking at different kinds of diasporas in *Global Diasporas: An Introduction* (Seattle: University of Washington Press, 1997). Cohen creates five categories of diaspora: victim, labor, trade, imperial, and cultural. While I appreciate his attempt to give some definitional coherence to a broad and sometimes amorphous term, it seems to me that the Indian diaspora of this book moves fluidly through those categories.

37. James Clifford, *Routes: Travel and Translation in the Late Twentieth Century* (Cambridge: Harvard University Press, 1997), 250.

38. Avtar Brah, *Cartographies of Diaspora: Contesting Identities* (London: Routledge, 1996), 183, 196. Though Brah's theorization of diaspora has been very influential on some of my thoughts here, I do not mean to employ the category of "diasporic space" in the manner that she does, as a specific kind of site that bridges the experiences of many "diasporic groups," to interrogate notions of who and what is "native" or not. In this book, diaspora space shall be used rather more generically, as the framework for negotiations of nationality and belonging.

39. Amitav Ghosh, "The Diaspora in Indian Culture," *Public Culture* 2, no. 1 (Fall 1989), 73–78.

40. Amitav Ghosh, *In an Antique Land* (New York: Vintage Books, 1992).

41. Ibid., 134.

42. See works by Jonathan Boyarin, including *Storm from Paradise The Politics of Jewish Memory* (Minneapolis: University of Minnesota, 1992) and *Polish Jews in Paris: The Ethnography of Memory* (Bloomington: Indiana University Press, 1991), and his edited volume *Remapping Memory: The Politics of Time-Space* (Minneapolis: University of Minnesota, 1994). While it is not my intention to posit strict similarities or equivalences between the Holocaust and British colonialism, I do want to suggest that we can consider these as analogues in terms of their diasporic constructions.

43. The character Dev in Anita Desai's *Bye-Bye Blackbird* (New Delhi: Orient Paperbacks, 1985) remarks, upon being introduced to Hyde Park and Rotten Row, "Of course . . . I have always known them . . . always. Ever since I could read" (64). And the narrator in Amitav Ghosh's novel *The Shadow Lines* (New Delhi: Oxford University Press, 1995), remarks upon his first visit to England:

"I've known the streets around here for a long time" (55). I will discuss these novels more fully in Chapter 3.

44. Here I follow from Walter D. Mignolo's points about a certain kind of cosmopolitanism emerging as a response to the "global designs" of colonialism, points that seem particularly well suited to the case of India and its peoples abroad. See his article "The Many Faces of Cosmo-polis: Border Thinking and Critical Cosmopolitanism," in *Public Culture* 12 (3), 721–48, as well as his *Local Histories/Global Designs: Coloniality, Subaltern Knowledges, and Border Thinking* (Princeton: Princeton University Press, 2000).

45. Hardt and Negri, *Empire*.

46. Ian Baucom has argued in a structurally similar way that Britishness was potentially unlimited, despite public discourses to the contrary, and evidences his point in the physical and symbolic expansions of empire, in *Out of Place: Englishness, Empire and the Locations of Identity* (Princeton: Princeton University Press, 1999). Though I will not treat the issue comparatively here, certainly the possibility arises about a more generalizable theory about national subjectivity and its lack of limits, particularly if we also consider the cultural consequences of American empire.

47. Celia W. Dugger, "India Offers Rights to Attract Its Offspring's Cash," *New York Times*, April 4, 1999, 12; P. Jayaram, "Government Launches PIO Card to Attract Diaspora," *India Abroad*, April 9, 1999, 4.

48. Homi Bhabha has used this term "third space" to develop an argument about the moment of enunciation that reveals an ambivalent relationship to the possibility of representation. While my arguments in this book are not psychoanalytically derived, they do follow from Bhabha's general points about the conceptual-discursive space (that for this book is diaspora) being one in which there is a working through of multiplicity, a process of translation. As he writes: "The theoretical recognition of the split-space of enunciation may open the way to conceptualizing an *inter*national culture, based not on the exoticism of multiculturalism or the *diversity* of cultures, but on the inscription and articulation of culture's *hybridity*." *The Location of Culture* (London: Routledge, 1994), 38.

49. Formative books on the "South Asian" diaspora that consider Indian, Pakistani, Bangladeshi, Sri Lankan, and other experiences include Peter van der Veer, ed., *Nation and Migration: The Politics of Space in the South Asian Diaspora* (Philadelphia: University of Pennsylvania Press, 1995); Colin Clarke, Ceri Peach, and Steven Vertovec, eds., *South Asians Overseas: Migration and Ethnicity* (Cambridge: Cambridge University Press, 1990); Carla Petievich, ed., *The Expanding Landscape: South Asians and the Diaspora* (New Delhi: Manohar, 1999); and Crispin Bates, ed., *Community, Empire and Migration: South Asians in Diaspora* (New York: Palgrave, 2001). Other books that identify a more specific purview, and with which mine is in dialogue, include Amitava Kumar, *Passport Photos* (Berkeley: University of California Press, 2000); Vijay Prashad, *The Karma of Brown Folk* (University of Minnesota Press, 2000); Sunaina Maira, *Desis in the House: Indian American Youth Culture in New York City* (Philadelphia: Temple University Press, 2002); and Brian Keith Axel, *The Nation's Tortured Body: Violence, Representation and the Formation of a "Sikh" Diaspora* (Durham: Duke University Press, 2001).

50. Though I shall periodically discuss religion, the full texture and importance of a religious diaspora is not explored here. It has been the subject of important work by other scholars. See Steven Vertovec, *The Hindu Diaspora: Comparative Patterns* (London: Routledge, 2000); and Harold Coward, John R. Hinnells, and Raymond Brady Williams, eds., *The South Asian Religious Diaspora in Britain, Canada and the United States* (Albany: State University of New York Press, 2000).

51. Benedict Anderson, *The Spectre of Comparisons: Nationalism, Southeast Asia and the World* (London: Verso, 1998). Also see a very good explanatory essay on Anderson's work: Pheng Cheah, "Grounds of Comparison," *diacritics* 29, no. 4 (Winter 1999), 3–18.

52. I thank Nancy Foner for a question at a recent presentation that forced me to clarify these points.

53. Thongchai Winichakul's *Siam Mapped: A History of the Geo-body of a Nation* (Honolulu: University of Hawaii Press, 1994) very interestingly considers the development of presumptive nationality, or "Thainess," as central to the project of the building of the Thai nation, particularly in the introductory chapter.

54. Arjun Appadurai, "Global Ethnoscapes," in *Modernity at Large: Cultural Dimensions of Globalization* (Minneapolis: University of Minnesota Press, 1996), 48–65; quotes appear on 55.

55. And in this avenue of inquiry, I am indebted to the work of Lisa Lowe, especially in *Immigrant Acts: On Asian American Cultural Politics* (Durham: Duke University Press, 1996), to see the United States anew from the perspective of Asian American cultural formations. While much of the material discussed in my book shows different things from Lowe's examples, I also appreciate Lowe's argument in structural terms, for I, too, understand the immigrant cultural space as one in which the nation is being reworked.

56. I see this book as participating in a project of more transnationally oriented studies of the United States. The Duke University Press series "New Americanists," the first book of which was the important *Cultures of United States Imperialism*, edited by Amy Kaplan and Donald E. Pease (Durham: Duke University Press, 1993), and recent American Studies Association conferences devoted to related themes (2000—"The World in American Studies/American Studies in the World; 1996—"Global Migration, American Cultures, and the State") suggest that this has become a trend in American studies. But while much recent work focuses on and comes out of literature and history, I would suggest that anthropology, and the questions being asked in that field about national formations and location, need also to be brought into the dialogue. The relative silences on this score thus far reflect many factors that include the underrepresentation of the social sciences within American studies, the identification of cultural studies with literature departments, and the more empirical orientation of those who work on North America within anthropology. I would argue that more recent theoretical and methodological developments in both American studies and anthropology might find surprising and productive complementarity; this book is the result of just such a produced convergence.

57. The "Indian," who is deeply internationalist and shaped by memories of colonialism across the Atlantic, also intervenes in the development of the interdisciplinary field of Asian American studies, which has largely focused on East Asian

Americans and fixated on the Pacific as the space through which cultural, political, and economic exchanges are processed.

58. Aihwa Ong, *Flexible Citizenship: The Cultural Logics of Transnationality* (Durham: Duke University Press, 1999), 6.

59. Partha Chatterjee, *The Nation and Its Fragments: Colonial and Postcolonial Histories* (Princeton: Princeton University Press, 1993).

60. Shilpa Dave et al., "De-privileging Positions, Indian Americans, South Asian Americans, and the Politics of Asian American Studies," *Journal of Asian American Studies* 3 (1), 67–100; Kamala Visweswaran and Ali Mir, "On the Politics of Community in South Asian American Studies," *Amerasia Journal* 25:3 (1999/2000), 97–108.

61. Paul Gilroy, *The Black Atlantic* (Cambridge: Harvard University Press, 1993), 101.

CHAPTER ONE
HISTORIES AND NATIONS

1. "Discover the Splendors of India," advertising supplement to the *New York Times*, July 14, 1991.

2. Closer to the time of the festival, this fact was realized and reported with much fanfare. Gitesh Pandya, "Indians Largest Asian Group in New Jersey," *News-India*, 23, no. 26 (June 25, 1993): 44. This continues to be true, as the Indian population in New Jersey grows in leaps and bounds. While Indian Americans numbered 79,440, or 1.03 percent of the general population of the state in 1990, their numbers grew to 169,180, or 2.01 percent of the total, in three years. (Figures are from the 2000 U.S. Census).

3. Veronica Horwell, "Jumbo-size, This Jewel in the Pally Patels' Crown," *London Times*, July 28, 1985, 7A.

4. Eric Hobsbawm and Terence Ranger, eds., *The Invention of Tradition* (Cambridge: Cambridge University Press, 1983), does not look at diasporic formations, but its collective theorization of history, nation, and empire is very useful for thinking through some questions that have to do with the formulations of nation in migrant culture.

5. Paul Veyne, *Writing History: Essay on Epistemology*, trans. Mina Moore-Rinvolucri (1971; reprint, Middletown, Conn.: Wesleyan University Press, 1984), 26.

6. Veyne's ideas influence a kind of historical methodology that underlies this chapter. He writes: "An event, whatever it is, implies a context because it has a meaning; it refers back to a plot of which it is one episode—or, rather, to an indefinite number of plots—conversely, one can always divide an event into smaller events" (*Writing History*, 34). As opposed to other critical accounts of history, Veyne's remains compelling and enabling to me because it does not completely dispense with the strategy of narrativity, though it certainly holds it up to scrutiny.

7. See Michel de Certeau, *The Writing of History*, trans. Tom Conley (1975; reprint, New York: Columbia University Press, 1988), especially the chapter entitled "The Production of Places."

8. My comments about the festivals arise from several visits to the U.S. festival in 1991; promotional literature about both the U.S. and U.K. festivals, and material from the BAPS website; conversations with U.S. and British participants in 1991 in Edison, New Jersey; and conversations in London in 1994 with those who had participated in the London production in 1985. The text of the exhibitions that I cite here is from the U.S. festival. While certainly the two festivals had some differences, most notably that Edison's festival was much larger, there is a certain convergence in the productions that enables us to see them together and in a continuum.

9. Interestingly, this "modern" part of the festival was the only one that I noticed to be unmentioned in the promotional brochure.

10. This chapter in part and this book as a whole rely on colonialism as a point of beginnings for India and the Indian diaspora. And yet colonialism should not be taken as forming the origins of India, or of migration, as I have commented upon in the introduction. Colonialism, however, has been central to the evolution of the modern nation-state of India, and as such, to the constitution of the Indian subject and its represented history, even when the limits of colonial power cannot be fully defined. See Nicholas Dirks, "History as a Sign of the Modern," *Public Culture* 2, no. 2 (Spring 1990): 25–32.

11. There have been a number of studies that discuss the economic, political, or cultural effects of colonialism; they include Ashis Nandy, *The Intimate Enemy: Loss and Recovery of Self under Colonialism* (Delhi: Oxford University Press, 1983); Partha Chatterjee, *The Nation and Its Fragments: Colonial and Postcolonial Histories* (Princeton: Princeton University Press, 1993), and studies by the Subaltern Studies Group, Ranajit Guha, ed., *Subaltern Studies: Writings on South Asian History and Society* (Delhi: Oxford University Press, 1993).

12. Robin Blackburn, *The Overthrow of Colonial Slavery 1776–1848* (London: Verso, 1988); David Brion Davis, *The Problem of Slavery in Western Culture* (Ithaca: Cornell University Press, 1966).

13. See Hugh Tinker, *A New System of Slavery: The Export of Indian Labour Overseas, 1830–1920* (1974; reprint, London: Hansib Publishing Limited, 1993), especially chapter 4, "Setting Up the New System," 61–115, for an in-depth discussion of the field of locations to which Indian indentured laborers were sent. Tinker also describes in this chapter how there was a significant emigration within India, from rural areas to tea plantations and to cities, from which there was further movement abroad. Changing patterns of production deeply influenced these shifts in population, locally in the development of British commercial ventures (tea, textiles) and internationally in British, Dutch, and French colonial systems of agriculture.

14. The difficulties and exploitation of indentured labor have been thoroughly explored in a number of important studies, and because the details are not central to this story, they are not recounted here. For more extensive histories of the system of indentured labor, the consequences of the system for Indian populations in plantation cultures, and the complex and variegated responses of British reformers and the Indian citizenry to the realities of the lives of Indian laborers abroad, see K. O. Laurence, *A Question of Labour: Indentured Immigration into Trinidad and British Guiana* (New York: St. Martin's Press, 1994); Madhavi Kale, *Fragments of Empire: Capital, Slavery, and Indian Indentured Labor Migration*

in the British Caribbean (Philadelphia: University of Pennsylvania Press, 1998); and David Northrup, *Indentured Labor in the Age of Imperialism 1838–1914* (Cambridge: Cambridge University Press, 1995).

15. G. S. Arora, *Indian Emigration* (New Delhi: Puja Publishers, 1991); Steven Vertovec, *Hindu Trinidad: Religion, Ethnicity and Socio-Economic Change* (London: Macmillan, 1992); Malcolm Cross, *The East Indians of Guyana and Trinidad* (London: Minority Rights Group, 1972); Bhikhu Parekh, "Some Reflections in the Hindu Diaspora," *New Community* 20, no. 4: 603–20; and Bhikhu Parekh, "The Indian Diaspora: Spreading Wings," *Little India* 4, no. 2: 30.

16. For an excellent description of the variations in the Indian population before 1947, see Rozina Visram, *Ayahs, Lascars and Princes: Indians in Britain 1700–1947* (London: Pluto Press, 1986).

17. Originally from the Hindi *lashkar*, for army or camp, used to describe Asian sailors in general, but especially those from India (*Webster's New World Dictionary of the American Language* [New York: Prentice Hall, 1986]).

18. Also see Peter Fryer, *Staying Power: The History of Black People in Britain* (London: Pluto Press, 1984), 232–33.

19. See Visram, *Ayahs, Lascars and Princes*, 29–30.

20. Joseph Salter's work as a Christian missionary exemplifies some of these efforts. See his written works, including *The Asiatic in England: Sketches of Sixteen Years' Work among Orientals* (London: Seely, Jackson and Halliday, 1873) and *The East in the West, or Work Among the Asiatics and Africans in London* (London: S. W. Partridge and Company, 1896). Also influential were groups like the Society for the Protection of Asiatic Sailors, the London City Mission, and the Strangers' Home. Visram, *Ayahs, Lascars and Princes*.

21. Salter, *Asiatic in England*, 24.

22. Ibid., 14.

23. Joan Jensen, *Passage from India* (New Haven: Yale University Press, 1988), 14–15; Carl T. Jackson, *The Oriental Religions and American Thought: Nineteenth Century Explorations* (Westport, Conn.: Greenwood Press, 1981); Wendell Thomas, *Hinduism Invades America* (Boston: Beacon Press, 1930).

24. Roger Daniels, "History of Indian Immigration to the United States: An Interpretive Essay," a paper presented to the conference "India in America: The Immigrant Experience," Asia Society, New York, April 17, 1989, 33.

25. This is an issue that roused passions not only in the North American West, but all over the United States and the world—everywhere, in fact, where Indians went to work and live. Indians, much like other immigrants have often been the target of critiques that they have taken jobs from other (native) peoples in a tight labor market. These debates achieved a particularly high pitch in places like Guyana, Kenya, and Uganda, and continue to rage on all over the diaspora.

26. In *Strangers from a Different Shore* (New York: Penguin, 1989), 296–97, Ronald Takaki discusses a number of articles published in the early 1900s that paint in broad strokes the perceived threat that Indian immigrants posed to the West, including Agnes Foster Buchanan, "The West and the Hindu Invasion," *Overland Monthly* 51, no. 4 (April 1908): 308–313; H. A. Millis, "East Indian Immigration to the Pacific Coast," *Survey*, 28, no. 9 (June 1912): 379; and Herman Scheffauer, "The Tide of Turbans," *Forum* 43 (June 1910): 616–18.

27. When I speak of a "remembered association," I refer to less material and non-literal renderings of memory that function as part of stories disseminated by a group about themselves, in the present and in the past. Jonathan Boyarin discusses these issues in "Space, Time and the Politics of Memory," in *Remapping Memory: The Politics of TimeSpace* (Minneapolis: University of Minnesota Press, 1994), 1–37.

28. For more in-depth narratives of the experiences of Asian Americans as a group unto themselves, see Takaki's *Strangers from a Different Shore* and Sucheng Chan, *Asian Americans: An Interpretive History* (Boston: Twayne Publishers, 1990).

29. This multiplicity of shaping historical frameworks is important to keep alive through a more globalized perspective on Indian migration. The relatively small numbers of Indians who came to the United States West between about 1900 and 1920 (6,400, according to Takaki, ibid., 294; 6,800, according to Karen Isaksen Leonard, *Making Ethnic Choices* [Philadelphia: Temple University Press, 1992], 24) have a much greater influence than their numbers would indicate, not only in terms of impacting the popular images of race and population changes in the area, but also in the scholarship on Indian Americans and Asian Americans more generally. For those who want to include studies of Indian Americans within the field of Asian American Studies, this early history provides important supporting material for the claim that the experiences of Indians in the West were structurally analogous to the experiences of other Asians in the area, and were indeed more similar to Asian immigrant experience than other white immigrant, African American, or other minority experiences. The writings on Indian immigrants in the United States are rather sparse, but two of the most important and widely cited monographs, *Making Ethnic Choices* (Leonard) and *Passage from India* (Jensen) concentrate on this early period of immigration. Some issues regarding the placement of the history of Indian immigrants within fields such as United States immigration history and Asian American studies will be discussed again in later chapters.

30. For historical background on this issue, see Romila Thapar, *A History of India: Volume One—From the Discovery of India to 1526* (New Delhi: Penguin Books, 1966).

31. Takaki, *Strangers from a Different Shore*, 208.

32. Jensen, *Passage from India*, 256–59; Chan, *Asian Americans*, 94; Daniels, *History of Indian Immigration to the United States*, 28.

33. Oriental and India Office Collections, Economic and Overseas Department File 2000 (1928); Subject "USA Immigration Act 1924—Entry of an Indian born European immigrant. Question of Quota in which he should be included."

34. Indu Prakas Bannerji, "Hindu Immigration, with special reference to the U.S. of America," *Modern Review* 17, no. 5 (May 1915): 608–16; quote appears on 609.

35. Bannerji notes: "While almost no Indian labor has been imported to Argentina, there is now a call for it on reasonable terms. Mr. M. A. Farias says that there is a fair field for Indian agricultural enterprise in the Argentine Republic." Ibid., 612.

36. Ibid., 616.

37. Ibid.

38. The contradictory impulses to see Indians who work and live abroad as freely moving and also as deserving of British protection can be seen in the work of a group called the Imperial Indian Citizenship Association. In S. S. Waiz, ed., *Indians Abroad* (Bombay: Imperial Indian Citizenship Association, 1927), histories of migrations are recounted alongside a report of the intense discrimination in places like South and East Africa and Fiji, "protectorates" of the British empire.

39. Visram, *Ayahs, Lascars and Princes*, 178, cites figures for Indian students studying at British universities that come from India Office Reports: in 1880 approximately 100 were counted; by 1910, over 700; and by 1931, 1,800.

40. For a highly romanticized and also pictorial description of upper-class Indians in Britain during the pre-independence period, see Kusoom Vadgama, *India in Britain: The Indian Contribution to the British Way of Life* (London: Robert Royce Limited, 1984).

41. Prior to 1960, British censuses did not include an ethnic origin question, and so all prominent historical sources on this period refrain from enumerating the number of Indians in England through the pre-independence period. The India Office did, as noted, keep records on the number of Indian students coming to British universities, but did not fully record how many stayed and how many returned; surveys of lascars and ayahs focused on communities and institutions (or boarding houses) and made no attempt to enumerate totals. Visram notes that the India National Congress estimated that there were 7,128 Indians living in England in 1931. N. V. Rajkumar, *Indians Outside India* (published by the Foreign Department of the India National Congress, All-India Congress Committee, New Delhi, 1951), statement I. Cited in Visram, *Ayahs, Lascars and Princes*, 190.

42. Dadabhai Naoroji was a Liberal Party member of the House of Commons beginning in 1892 (and the first black member of Parliament), and also the owner of a cotton concern who was never an outright advocate for Indian independence but who publicly argued against the detrimental effects of British exploitation of India's resources. See R. P. Masani, *Dadabhai Naoroji: The Grand Old Man of India* (London: George Allen and Unwin, 1939); Dadabhai Naoroji, *Poverty and Un-British Rule in India* (London: Swan Sonnenschein, 1901); and B. N. Ganguli, *Dadabhai Naoroji and the Drain Theory* (London: Asia Publishing House, 1965). Just as Naoroji lost his seat in 1895, a conservative Indian, Mancherjee Bhownagree, became a Tory member of Parliament for the district of Bethnal Green Northeast. Bhownagree's political inclinations diverged dramatically from Naoroji's; he was a staunch conservative who was supportive of British royalty and, mostly, British rule of India. See Visram, *Ayahs, Lascars and Princes*.

43. Robert Shaplen, "One-Man Lobby," *New Yorker*, March 24, 1951, 35–55.

44. Among others, see Partha Chatterjee, *Nationalist Thought and the Colonial World: A Derivative Discourse?* (London: Zed Books, 1986).

45. Harish K. Puri, *Ghadar Movement: Ideology, Organization and Strategy* (Amritsar: Garu Nanak Dev University, 1983). Puri also notes other accounts of the origin of the movement, including a meeting with Punjabi farm workers near Sacramento (73). Anil Baran Ganguly, *Ghadar Revolution in America* (New Delhi: Metropolitan Book Company, 1980), notes the formation of an Indian

Students Association at the University of Washington a bit earlier, in 1909, and the production of the journal *Free Hindusthan* from there. What seems clear is that a number of multipurpose Indian political groups arose within a span of a few years, responded to self-described "leaders" of the movement, such as Har Dayal, and eventually came to coordinate activities around Indian independence. See also L. P. Mathur, *Indian Revolutionary Movement in the United States* (New Delhi: Chand, 1970).

46. Puri, *Ghadar Movement*, 85.

47. Puri notes: "The Ghadarites were inspired by the revolutionary movements in Russia, China, Mexico, Ireland, Egypt, etc., and developed a sense of affinity with the revolutionaries of those countries, who were often described as fellow Ghadarites" (ibid., 179).

48. Peter Fryer, *Staying Power: The History of Black People in Britain* (London: Pluto Press, 1984), 265.

49. Ibid., 266.

50. Jensen's *Passage from India*, particularly chapter 8, "Students and Spies: Surveillance," 163–93, deals with these episodes in some detail. She also describes how several of these students traveled widely throughout their adult lives to further the cause of Indian independence, canvassing Indian exiles in Japan, moving through London and Paris, Puerto Rico, Canada, and New York, before reaching California. This testament to the wide reaches of the Indian independence movement as well as to the material, political, and social connections through the Indian immigrant diaspora during this early period is fascinating and deserving of more intensive research.

51. See Oriental and India Office Collections, folder no. 56 (Secret), "Indian Extremists in USA" (including letters from British consuls all over the Americas, 1939); folder entitled "Indian Extremists in America," Public and Judicial Department U.K. (letter P & J 3331/39).

52. Arun Coomer Bose, "Indian Nationalist Agitations in the U.S.A. and Canada till the arrival of Har Dayal in 1911," *Journal of Indian History* 43, part 1 (April 1965): 227–39.

53. Alan Raucher, "American Anti-Imperialists and the Pro-India Movement, 1900–1932," *Pacific Historical Review* 43, no. 1 (February 1974): 83–110. Also see Agnes Smedley, "Mother India," *The Modern Review* 42, no. 3 (September 1927): 296–99; J. T. Sunderland, "What Americans Say about Subject India," *Modern Review* 42, no. 2 (August, 1927): 153–57.

54. For background material on the pre-independence period, see Kharath R. Samras, letter to the editor, *Nation*, November 23, 1940, 516; Tarak Nath Das, "The Struggle of Indians to Attain Equal Rights in the United States of America," *Modern Review* 80 (October 1946): 263–66; Naeem Gul Rathore, "Indian Nationalist Agitation in the United States: A Study of Lala Lajpat Rai and the India Home Rule League of America, 1914–1920," Ph.D. diss., Columbia University, 1965; and articles in the *New York Times*, including "J. J. Singh Reports Progress on Trade Treaty," May 2, 1939; "To Mark Gandhi's Birthday," October 10, 1939; John Haynes Holmes, letter to the editor, October 15, 1940; "Nehru's Nieces Guests," July 10, 1943; "Speakers Demand Freedom for India," August 10, 1943; and "US Seeks to Aid India," October 30, 1943.

55. Shaplen, "One-Man Lobby"; J. J. Singh, letter to the editor, *Nation*, May 20, 1944, 607; "Mr. Singh Goes to Washington," *Time*, February 28, 1944, 19.

56. Leonard A. Gordon, "Bridging India and America: The Art and Politics of Kumar Goshal," *Amerasia* 15, no. 2 (1989): 68–88.

57. Kumar Goshal's columns appeared first under the heading "India's Views" and then "As an Indian Sees It" in the weekly *Pittsburgh Courier*, beginning on October 3, 1942, and ending, unceremoniously, on September 20, 1947. Many thanks to Jacquelyn Grey for her able research into this topic.

58. Kumar Goshal, "As an Indian Sees It," *Pittsburgh Courier*, October 17, 1942.

59. George Padmore, "Indian Pilots Train in Britain for Action," *Pittsburgh Courier*, May 8, 1943.

60. Penny Von Eschen, *Race Against Empire: Black Americans and Anticolonialism, 1937–57* (Ithaca: Cornell University Press, 1997).

61. Visram, *Ayahs, Lascars and Princes*, 192.

62. India Office Records, folder entitled "Rights of British Indians to U.S. Citizenship" (1939), includes material on the effort to extend citizenship rights to Indians, and letters from leading Indian activists for this issue, including Ramlal B. Bajpai, Mubarkek Ali Khan, and Godha Ram Chandan. Also in "Letters of Political Department," Records No. 1037, there is detailed information on the House of Representatives Bill 3517, and letters of correspondence from the Charge d'Affaires to Ernest Bevin, M.P., about this issue.

63. India Office Records, Political Department of Commonwealth Relations Office Correspondence, April 1, 1948: full copy of the Question and Answer for the meeting of the constituent assembly of India, asking questions about what would happen if the United States government amended the Immigration and Naturalization laws, and how many Indians actually gained admission in 1948.

64. In a 1948 letter to the *New York Times*, Singh protested Warren Austin's derogatory comment about the Soviet Union's political shifts around the issue of the atomic bomb as "an Oriental maneuver." Singh took issue with the statement as an Indian, and as a broader citizen of "the Orient" that included "not only Japan, China and Korea but also the Philippines, Indonesia, Malaya, Viet-Nam, Siam, Burma, India, Ceylon, Afghanistan and the Arab countries of the Near East. Why did Mr. Austin insult all the people of these countries—many of whom are members of the United Nations?" (*New York Times*, October 16, 1948).

65. For more detailed demographics throughout the pre-1947 period, see Daniels, *History of Indian Immigration to the United States*.

66. For a more in-depth discussion of the anti-denaturalization campaign among Indians, see Jensen, *Passage from India*, chapter 12, "Brown Is Not White: Naturalization and the Constitution," 246–69.

67. A significant number of those Indian men who stayed in rural southern California (in the Imperial Valley, to the east of San Diego) entered into domestic partnerships with Mexican immigrant women, and formed an interesting subcommunity that has been researched in some detail by anthropologist Karen Isaksen Leonard in *Making Ethnic Choices*. The three hundred or so of these marriages reflect a number of important developments in this immigrant population. First and perhaps most important, these Indians were clearly working toward establish-

ing themselves in a fairly permanent way in the United States; second, specific legal constraints on life and love brought these two nonwhite and non–East Asian groups together; and third, there were ways in which each group, Indians and Mexicans, recognized some cultural simpatico in the other and could in some form or another imagine hybridity composed of those parts. Finally, Leonard makes an excellent case for how a certain degree of ethnic flexibility was demonstrated by the choice and subsequent maintenance of discrete and syncretic cultures through time. Thus despite the small numbers of people involved, this case has important value for studying this period, and for understanding the building of local community in its various and perhaps untraditional forms. Those Indians married to Mexican women, and those who had been able to bring their wives to the United States, also formed small communities around religious rituals; they built Sikh temples, or *gurdwaras*, to provide more conventional forms of ethnic community.

68. The highly complex and widely divergent experiences of post-1947 immigrants from the subcontinent present a number of conceptual problems to scholars working to represent those histories. Because one of the effects of the many countries of the Indian subcontinent, including India, Pakistan, Bangladesh, Sri Lanka, Nepal, and the Bhutan, being all at one time considered "India" by the British colonial authorities, was a perceived suppression of cultural traditions and difference, and because in the post-independence period the Indian state has assumed a fairly aggressive role in the region, there is an understandable reluctance to continue using the term "Indian" to describe these many peoples, along with the actual political inaccuracy of such an umbrella category. The similarities of culture, of relationships to other areas in the world, and in representation among Westerners for all peoples of the subcontinent have motivated the use of the descriptive term "South Asian," however. This poses a set of paradoxes, and ultimately a dilemma to those trying to construct relatively cogent stories about the experiences of a group of people, or peoples; to categorize histories as "South Asian" threatens to flatten out the distinctly national expressions of specific groups of people, and to maintain the term "Indian" seems to restrict the study to nationalist boundaries that are in some respects arbitrarily drawn. My position in this chapter and in the ones that follow is that before 1947, the term "Indian" can and should be used to describe peoples that originated from the territories colonized by Britain as "India," and that after 1947, it should refer to those that have lived within the nation-state of India and/or have maintained some real or invented relationship to either the state or to the abstract representation of "India." That delineation occurs for both practical and conceptual reasons; on the one hand it is necessary to limit a study of this nature, and on the other hand I believe that national affiliations that are authorized by economic and political state units deeply structure how people see themselves in the world.

69. Anne Orde, *The Eclipse of Great Britain: The United States and British Imperial Decline, 1895–1956* (New York: St. Martin's Press, 1996), makes interesting arguments about how the rise and consolidation of the United States as a world power was linked to Britain's demise as an imperial power (160–92).

70. Zig Layton-Henry, *The Politics of Immigration* (Oxford: Blackwell Publishers, 1992), 10.

71. Henry Luce, "The American Century," in John K. Jessup, ed., *The Ideas of Henry Luce* (New York: Atheneum, 1969), 105–20.

72. Immigration and Naturalization Service data taken from Peter Xenos, Herbert Barringer, and Michael J. Levin, *Asian Indians in the United States: A 1980 Census Profile* (Honolulu: East-West Population Institute, July 1989), 15. The entire South Asian immigrant population migrating during this period was only slightly higher, 7,629, with the balance coming from available data for Pakistanis immigrating between 1954 and 1964.

73. D. S. Saund, *Congressman from India* (New York: E. P. Dutton and Company, 1960), 34.

74. For an interesting example of U.S. interest in the shape of the Indian economy, see the report of a visit by new Indian engineers to a steel company in West Virginia, in Don Wharton's "They Are Forging a New Link with India," *Reader's Digest*, February 1959, 167–72. The article ends with this line: "The Indians are taking home far more than steelmaking know-how, they come as ambassadors of their country; they go home as ambassadors of *our* country—keen, penetrating observers who as young captains of India's growing industry will tell their people the truth about private enterprise in America" (172). Apparent here is a sense that India could go either in the direction of socialism or capitalism, but that experience with America will show the benefits of the latter.

75. For an excellent history and analysis of these political formations, see A.W. Singham and Shirley Hune, *Non-Alignment in an Age of Alignments* (Westport, Conn.: Lawrence Hill and Co., 1986).

76. The Home Office figures for Indian immigration to England are as follows:

1955	5,800
1956	5,600
1957	6,600
1958	6,200
1959	2,950
1960	5,900
1961	23,750
1962 (Jan.–June)	19,050
1962 (July–Dec.)	3,050
1963	17,498
1964	15,513
1965	18,815
1966	18,402
1967	22,638
1968	28,340

Home Office-Immigration Statistics 1955–1968. Presented to Parliament by the Secretary of State for the Home Department by Command of Her Majesty (London: Her Majesty's Stationery Office, 1955–1968). These are the numbers used by all historians of the period, including Clifford Hill, *Immigration and Integration* (Oxford: Pergamon Press, 1970), and Sheila Patterson, *Immigration and Race Relations in Britain 1960–1967* (London: Oxford University Press, 1969). The numbers for other South Asians, particularly Pakistanis, are initially much smaller in comparison to Indian immigrant numbers but rise suddenly in 1961 and remain high but not as high as Indians (Patterson, *Immigration and Race Relations*, 3).

77. The West Indian immigrant figure peaks at 66,300 in 1961 and then falls precipitously, as the general character of immigration changes through the 1960s (to a more professional and credentialed group). Patterson, *Immigration and Race Relations*, 3.

78. Visram, *Ayahs, Lascars and Princes*.

79. David Owen explains this phenomenon for a more recent period: "Casual use of the term 'multicultural society' carries the implication that all parts of the country contain a range of ethnic groups. . . . However, the reality is of marked geographical separation between ethnic groups, since the bulk of people from minority ethnic groups live in a relatively small number of areas. In much of Britain, people from the white group may only occasionally come into contact with people from minority ethnic groups." ("Spatial Variations in Ethnic Minority Group Populations in Great Britain," *Population Trends* 178 (Winter 1994): 23–33; quote here from 23.

80. For a discussion of some of these issues, see Trevor R. Lee's study of West Indian immigrants, *Race and Residence: The Concentration and Dispersal of Immigrants in London* (Oxford: Clarendon Press, 1977).

81. Rashmi Desai, *Indian Immigrants in Britain* (London: Oxford University Press, 1963), 23.

82. See Roger Daniels, *Asian America: Chinese and Japanese in the United States since 1850* (Seattle: University of Washington Press, 1988), 21.

83. I shall discuss this in greater detail in later chapters.

84. Layton-Henry, *Politics of Immigration*, 74.

85. Amarjit Chandan, *Indians in Britain* (New Delhi: Sterling Publishers, 1986). Chandan comments that he has written a book about Indian immigrants for an audience in India, who retain fantasies about life in Britain; "but," he says, "the reality is different" (11) He goes on to describe strikes by Indian workers that went unsupported by the major trades unions and the Labour Party (42–43).

86. In *Nehru: The First Sixty Years*, ed. Dorothy Norman (New York: John Day, 1965), 322–23.

87. Takaki, *Strangers from a Different Shore*, 419.

88. Ibid., 418–19, and Chan, *Asian Americans*, 145.

89. See *Whom We Shall Welcome*, Report of the Presidential Commission on Immigration and Naturalization, Harry N. Rosenfield, Executive Director (Washington, D.C.: United States Government Printing Office, 1953), especially "America—A Land of Immigrants," 23–29, for formulations of American diversity that underpinned much of the impetus for changes in immigration laws.

90. Nathan Glazer and Daniel P. Moynihan, *Beyond the Melting Pot* (Cambridge: MIT Press, 1963); Milton Gordon, *Assimilation in American Life: The Role of Race, Religion and National Origin* (New York: Oxford University Press, 1964).

91. William E. Farrell, "The Song of India in Connecticut: Wesleyan Students Eat Curry While Marking Time," *New York Times*, February 21, 1966; Robert Shelton, "Indian Raga Music Gains in Popularity Across U.S.," *New York Times*, December 20, 1966; "Hinduism in New York: A Growing Religion," *New York Times*, November 2, 1967; and Elenore Lester, "Shankar, Unnerved by the Hippies' Adulation," *New York Times*, October 22, 1967. See also Gita Mehta's satirizing of this phenomenon in her *Karma Cola: Marketing the Mystic East* (New York: Simon and Schuster, 1979).

92. "That Guru Playing a Sitar May Be a New Yorker," *New York Times*, July 31, 1968.

93. United States census statistics enumerate the arrival of people who claim India as their originating point as follows:

1947	318
1948	198
1949	177
1950	107
1951	104
1952	130
1953	128
1954	159
1955	187
1956	202
1958	379
1959	302
1960	243
1961	352
1962	476
1963	975
1964	425
1965	549

United States Bureau of the Census, *Historical Statistics of the United States, Colonial Times to 1970* (Washington, D.C., 1975), 107–108.

94. The numbers from 1965 to 1974 are as follows:

1965	582
1966	2,458
1967	4,642
1968	4,682
1969	5,963
1970	10,114
1971	14,317
1972	16,929
1973	13,128
1974	12,795

Immigration and Naturalization Service data, cited in *Asian Indians in the United States: A 1980 Census Profile*, ed. Peter Xenos, Herbert Barringer and Michael J. Levin; Papers of the East-West Population Institute, Number 11, July 1989, p. 15. The numbers for Pakistani and other South Asian immigrants are not of the same magnitude for this decade, or even the next; by 1974 the figure is 2,570 and by 1984 the number of Pakistanis coming to the United States is 5,509 (compared to 24,964 for Indians, out of a total 31,925 for South Asians as a whole). Clearly Indians have made up the large majority of South Asian immigrants for many years now. More recently, in the last ten years, Pakistanis and Bangladeshi numbers have greatly increased, though not dislodged Indian dominance, a matter that will be taken up later in the work.

95. Anthropologist Maxine Fisher's *Indians of New York City* (Columbia, Mo.: South Asia Books, 1980) is one of the best early accounts of the post-1965 Indian immigrant community. There are various other studies on Indian immigrants that focus on particular aspects of identity or community formation: Sathi S. Dasgupta's *On the Trail of an Uncertain Dream* (New York: AMS Press, Inc., 1989) is based on case histories; likewise Parmatma Saran's *Asian Indian Experience in the United States* (Cambridge, Mass.: Schenkman Publishing Company, 1985) also recounts and analyzes a group of interviews; Arthur W. Helweg and Usha M. Helweg's *An Immigrant Success Story: East Indians in America* (London: Hurst and Company, 1990) is a more comprehensive history of Indian American immigration.

96. Helweg and Helweg, *An Immigrant Success Story*, 210.

97. Khalid H. Shah and Linda Shah, "Indians in New York," *Illustrated Weekly of India*, April 22, 1973, 19–22. Quote appears on 19.

98. Ibid., 19–20.

99. V. K. Puri and S. C. Malhotra, *Nabhi's Manual for Indian Residents Abroad* (New Delhi: Nabhi Publications, July 1987), 1.

100. See Maxine Fisher's description of this in *The Indians of New York City*, 68. Also V. Balasubramanian, *Indians Abroad: The NRI Syndrome* (Bombay: Business Book Publishing House, 1987); Chandrashekhar Sastry, *The Non-Resident Indian: From Non-Being to Being* (Bangalore: Panther Publishers, 1991); T. V. Ramachandran, *Non-Resident Indians; Investment Policy Guidelines and Procedures* (Bangalore: Puliani and Puliani, 1992); and Johanna Lessinger, "Nonresident-Indian Investment and India's Drive for Industrial Modernization," in *Anthropology and the Global Factory; Studies of the New Industrialization in the Late Twentieth Century*, ed. Frances Abrahamer Rothstein and Michael L. Blim (New York: Bergin and Garvey, 1992), 62–82. The economic impact of remittances from the 1970s until the present is the subject of Deepak Nayyar, *Migration, Remittances and Capital Flows: The Indian Experience* (Delhi: Oxford University Press, 1994). Nayyar also discusses remittances from Indian workers in the Middle East, an important part of this story that I do not have space to engage with here.

101. Steven R. Weisman, "Sikhs Here Trying to Mix Old and New," *New York Times*, August 8, 1971, Brooklyn/Queens/Long Island Supplementary Report, 67; Ian T. Macauley, "Today Is India Day in Valhalla," *New York Times*, September 11, 1977.

102. Fisher, *Indians of New York City*, chap. 7 and 8.

103. "A Brahmin in Brooklyn Performs Hindu Rites," *New York Times*, November 26, 1972; Richard F. Shepard, "The Ethnic Crackerbarrels of Queens," *New York Times*, February 20, 1972; Paul L. Montgomery, "Growing Sikh Community Celebrates 505th Anniversary of Founder's Birth," *New York Times*, December 2, 1974; Kim Lem, "Indians in Queens Reviving Heritage," *New York Times*, January 5, 1975.

104. When I spoke to a group of British Indian girls who were visiting the Cultural Festival in Edison, they expressed particular amusement and sarcasm about these exhibits.

105. See Layton-Henry, *Politics of Immigration*, as well as David Steel, *No Entry: The Background and Implications of the Commonwealth Immigrants Act, 1968* (London: C. Hurst and Co., 1969), 146–72.

106. Valerie Marett, *Immigrants Settling in the City* (Leicester: Leicester University Press, 1989); Thomas Patrick Melady and Margaret Badum Melady, *Uganda: The Asian Exiles* (Maryknoll, N.Y.: Orbis Books, 1978).

107. For an account of this period, see Mahmood Mamdani, *From Citizen to Refugee: Uganda Asians Come to Britain* (London: Frances Pinter Limited, 1973).

108. Marett, *Immigrants Settling in the City*, 13.

109. Helweg and Helweg, *An Immigrant Success Story*, 66.

110. For a portrayal of contemporary Asian communities in Leicester, see a special section in the February 3, 1995, issue of *India Abroad*, entitled "Leicester: A City of Many Cultures." Articles include Sanjay Suri, "Growth of a Home Away from Home is Fostered," "Many Corner Shops Doomed by Superstores," and "A Community that Remains Mostly Insulated."

111. I discuss some of these developments in greater detail in the next chapter.

112. A. Sivanandan, *A Different Hunger: Writings on Black Resistance* (London: Pluto Press, 1982); Philip Cohen and Harwant S. Bains, eds., *Multi-Racist Britain* (London: Macmillan, 1988).

113. I note this here particularly in response to some recent studies in which authors assert that the land of settlement has little to do with the internal logics of the diaspora. An example of this is Oivind Fuglerud's *Life on the Outside: The Tamil Diaspora and Long Distance Nationalism* (London: Pluto Press, 1999). See my upcoming review of this text in *International Migration Review*.

114. United States Immigration and Naturalization Service, 1978 Annual Report, in the 1980 *Statistical Abstract of the United States*.

115. Ranjan Borra, letter to the editor, *New York Times*, August 29, 1976.

116. Manoranjan Dutta, "Our Asian Indians," letter to the editor, *New York Times*, October 10, 1976.

117. J. Forbes Watson and John William Kaye, *The People of India; A Series of Photographic Illustrations of the Races and Tribes of Hindustan*, vol. 1–8, originally prepared under the authority of the government of India, and reproduced by order of the Secretary of State for India in council (London: India Museum, 1872).

118. Quoted in Bernard Cohn, "Representing Authority in Victorian India," in Eric Hobsbawm and Terence Ranger, eds., *The Invention of Tradition* (Cambridge: Cambridge University Press, 1983), 165–209.

119. Ibid.

120. Roger Ballard and Virinder Singh Kalra, *The Ethnic Dimensions of the 1991 Census: A Preliminary Report* (Manchester: Census Microdata Unit, University of Manchester, 1994), 32.

121. Paul Grimes, "Immigrants From India Find Problems in America," *New York Times*, August 2, 1977.

122. These ethnic niches have been widely reported since the late 1970s in the press as illustrations of the social changes of the new post-Fordist economy; see Ralph Blumenthal, "Indian Refugees Making a Living In the Subways," *New York Times*, February 14, 1977; Martin Gottlieb, "For South Asian Immigrants, News-

stands Fulfill a Dream," *New York Times*, January 3, 1986, 1; and Donatella Lorch, "An Ethnic Road to Riches: The Immigrant Job Specialty," *New York Times*, January 12, 1992, 1.

123. From the 1980 census (cited in Manorajan Dutta, "Asian Indian Americans: Search for an Economic Profile," in *From India to America: A Brief History of Immigration: Problems of Discrimination; Admission and Assimilation*, ed. S. Chandrasekhar [La Jolla, Calif.: Population Review Publications, 1982], 76–85). Asian Indian population in states with 20,000 or more:

> New York: 60,511
> California: 57,989
> Illinois: 35,711
> New Jersey: 29,507

124. On developing connections between Indian immigrants, see Lavina Melwani, "Desi Networks," *Little India*, February 28, 1994.

125. William Wei, *The Asian American Movement* (Philadelphia: Temple University Press, 1992), and Yen Le Espiritu, *Asian American Panethnicity* (Philadelphia: Temple University Press, 1992).

126. Johanna Lessinger, *From the Ganges to the Hudson: Indian Immigrants in New York City* (Boston: Allyn and Bacon, 1995), 139–42.

127. Melanie Warner, "The Indians of Silicon Valley," *Fortune Magazine*, May 15, 2000.

128. Sunil Garg, "Under My Skin," *New York Times*, September 7, 1996.

129. Ibid.

130. D'Souza refers to his background in public forums as well as in his writings; on an episode of *The MacNeil/Lehrer Newshour* (June 18, 1991, Tuesday, Transcript #4056), D'Souza comments: "I'm a native of India. I was raised in Bombay. I came to this country in 1978. I became a citizen last year. I'm a first generation immigrant to the United States. I think that America is becoming a multiracial society and the whole issue is transcending black and white." See also Dinesh D'Souza, *Illiberal Education: The Politics of Race and Sex on Campus* (New York: Free Press, 1991).

131. Despite the fact of no affiliation with any Indian ethnic or Hindu religious organization, I myself received a call in New Haven that spring asking if I would like to volunteer. While the caller certainly identified himself, his relationship to the Swaminarayan religious sect was not manifest, nor was the festival described as having any other than national-cultural content.

132. "Cultural Festival: Volunteerism Strong Amongst Youth," in *India-West*, August 2, 1991. This article notes that of 2,600 volunteers, 1,200 were youth.

133. Informal interviews conducted at the festival, August 5, 1991.

134. On two separate occasions, I sat on the lower ledge of an exhibit and was asked to move away within minutes.

135. Raymond Brady Williams, *A New Face of Hinduism: The Swaminarayan Religion* (Cambridge: Cambridge University Press, 1984), 201.

136. "Month-long Festival of India Planned by BSS," in *India-West*, February 16, 1990. The article notes the "prime purpose" as follows:

1. To give a comprehensive, authentic knowledge of Indian culture.
2. To encourage all other cultural groups to preserve their cultural roots and respect the culture of others.
3. To create understanding and cultural harmony, and bring humanity closer together.
4. To reveal the message of peaceful co-existence, and
5. To inspire one and all towards a better, fuller way of life through the humanitarian values of love, service, and purity.

The article goes on to describe in detail the planned exhibits, events, and decorations in quite accurate fashion, a year and a half before the actual event, which suggests quite tightly deliberated central planning.

137. "Cultural Festival of India"—a sixteen-page pamphlet put out in 1985 by the Swaminarayan Hindu Mission, London.

138. "Cultural Festival of India Concludes," *India-West*, August 23, 1991.

139. Ibid.

140. Veronica Horwell in the *London Times* refers to the large gateways and temple replicas as constructed "not to proselytise, but to inform near-assimilated Asians of their Hindu past." ("Jumbo-size, this jewel in the Pally Patels' crown," July 28, 1985; Brent Mitchell of the *Washington Post* writes: "While non-Indian faces are scattered through the crowd, the vast majority are people recapturing the feel of a country they left behind and trying to teach their children raised in North America" ("For Immigrants, Festival Captures Spirit of Home," August 6, 1991).

141. Rajen S. Anand, "CFI: Monumental Success," *India-West*, August 30, 1991. In an October 2000 interview (conducted by my research assistant Michele Moritis), a member of the BSS mandir in Flushing, Queens, who had volunteered at the 1991 festival made the following astonishing observation: "The Taj Mahal is not real Hindu culture. It is a beautiful edifice, but it has no cultural significance. "

142. Anasuya Prasad, quoted in Rajen S. Anand, "Cultural Festival of India: Hindu Saints Call for Unity," *India-West*, July 26, 1991. Also see Shiv Bakhshi, "Not Merely Crtiticism, Cultural Festival of India Organizers Need to be Debriefed," *News-India Times*, September 27, 1991; "Cultural Festival: Volunteerism Strong Amongst Youth," *India-West*, August 2, 1991; and Rajen Anand, "CFI: Monumental Success," *India-West*, August 30, 1991.

143. "Spirituality Abundant at CFI Convention," *India-West*, August 9, 1991.

144. Homi K. Bhabha, "DissemiNation: Time, Narrative and the Margins of the Modern Nation," in *Nation and Narration* (London: Routledge, 1990), 297.

145. Certeau, *The Writing of History*, 21.

146. "Cultural Festival of India Concludes," *India-West*, August 23, 1991.

CHAPTER TWO
LITTLE INDIAS, PLACES FOR INDIAN DIASPORAS

1. Prakash M. Swamy, "Super Star Aamir Khan Halts Traffic in New York," *News India*, June 8, 2001; Tanmaya Kumar Nanda, "Aamir Khan Causes Trafffic

Snarl in Big Apple," *India Abroad*, June 8, 2001. Bollywood is the popular name of the Indian Hollywood, located in Bombay.

2. I discuss this film in greater detail in Chapter 5.

3. Saskia Sassen, *The Global City: New York, London, Tokyo* (Princeton: Princeton University Press, 2001).

4. One could certainly make the argument that social and cultural experiences of the city have never been stable or consistent. Cities like New York have been especially marked by competing class, racial, and ethnic claims to space, political representation, and definitional authority. It is precisely that intense competition that has produced disciplinary discourses on what the city should and should not be. (For an earlier period, see for example Christine Stansell's *City of Women: Sex and Class in New York 1789–1860* [New York: Knopf, 1986].) But I would nonetheless maintain that the rise of third-world ethnicities, with particularly diasporic effects, has changed the character of cities like New York and London, creating an important shift that we can index to the late 1960s, after the Immigration and Naturalization Act in the U.S., for New York, and to the early 1960s, with decolonization, for the case of London. That this periodization roughly coincides with the rise of the "global city" that Sassen identifies is important, because it makes all these economic, cultural, and social changes codependent.

5. Susan Fainstein, Ian Gordon, and Michael Harloe, eds., *Divided Cities: New York and London in the Contemporary World* (Oxford: Blackwell, 1992). Also see Michael Keith and Steve Pile, eds., *Place and the Politics of Identity* (London: Routledge, 1993).

6. Victor G. Nee and Brett De Bary Nee, *Longtime Californ': A Documentary Study of an American Chinatown* (Boston: Houghton Mifflin, 1974); Peter Kwong, *The New Chinatown* (New York: Hill and Wang, 1987); and Min Zhou, *Chinatown: The Socioeconomic Potential of an Urban Enclave* (Philadelphia: Temple University Press, 1992). On Harlem, see Gilbert Osofsky, *Harlem, the Making of a Ghetto: A History of Negro New York, 1900–1920* (New York: Harper and Row, 1966).

7. Michel S. Laguerre, *Minoritized Space: An Inquiry into the Spatial Order of Things* (Berkeley, Calif.: Institute of Governmental Studies Press and the Institute of Urban and Regional Development, 1999).

8. Kay Anderson, "The Idea of Chinatown: The Power of Place and Institutional Practice in the Making of a Racial Category," *Annals of the Association of American Geographers* 77, no. 4 (1987): 580–98, and *Vancouver's Chinatown* (Montreal: McGill-Queen's University Press, 1991).

9. Anderson, "The Idea of Chinatown," 581.

10. Laguerre, *Minoritized Space*, 55.

11. See Jan Lin's very interesting book, *Reconstructing Chinatown: Ethnic Enclave, Global Change* (Minneapolis: University of Minnesota Press, 1998).

12. Henri Lefebvre, *The Production of Space*, trans. Donald Nicholson-Smith (1974; reprint, Oxford: Blackwell Publishers, 1991).

13. A number of writers have attempted to conceptualize the distinction and relationship between space and place outside of the obvious and, it seems, hasty ascription of abstraction to the former and materiality to the latter term. I think that Yi-Fu Tuan's simple and clear delineation actually gets at some of the com-

plexities: "What begins as undifferentiated space becomes place as we get to know it better and endow it with value. Architects talk about the spatial qualities of place; they can equally well speak of the locational (place) qualities of space. The ideas 'space' and 'place' require each other for definition. . . . Furthermore, if we think of space as that which allows movement, then place is pause; each pause in movement makes it possible for location to be transformed into place." From Yi-Fu Tuan, *Space and Place: The Perspective of Experience* (Minneapolis: University of Minnesota Press, 1977). Somewhat similarly, but more thoroughly, Michel de Certeau has explained:

> A place (*lieu*) is the order (of whatever kind) in accord with which elements are distributed in relationships of coexistence. It thus excludes the possibility of two things being in the same location (*place*). The law of the "proper" rules in the place: the elements taken into consideration are *beside* one another, each situated in its own "proper" and distinct location, a location it defines. A place is thus an instantaneous configuration of positions. It implies an indication of stability.
>
> A *space* exists when one takes into consideration vectors of direction, velocities, and time variables. Thus space is composed of intersections of mobile elements. It is in a sense actuated by the ensemble of movements deployed within it. Space occurs as the effect produced by the operations that orient it, situate it, temporalize it, and make it function in a polyvalent unity of conflictual programs or contractual proximities. . . .
>
> In short, *space is a practiced place.*

From *The Practice of Everyday Life* (Berkeley: University of California Press, 1984).It is in this sense that we can think of Jackson Heights or Southall as *places* for the Indian diasporas, of pause, of indication, while those diasporas continue to be *spaces* of dynamic (mobile) definition and narrativization.

14. Lefebvre, *Production of Space*, 41.

15. Ibid.

16. *Wild West*, dir. David Attwood, 1992.

17. For a concise description of this early history, see Paul Kirwan, *Southall: A Brief History* (London: London Borough of Ealing Library Service, March 1965).

18. Ibid., 33.

19. R. J. Meads, *Southall 1830–1982* (Tiverton, Devon: Maslands Ltd., 1983), *Growing-up with Southall from 1904* (Hounslow, Middlesex: Culprint, 1979).

20. A. R. Hope Moncrieff, *Middlesex* (London: Adam and Charles Black, 1907), 114–15.

21. See Martin S. Briggs, *Middlesex Old and New* (London: George Allen and Unwin Ltd., 1934). Briggs notes: "Southall shares with Hayes, Acton, Willesden and part of the Lea Valley the distinction of being a prominent industrial district of changing Middlesex. Regret for this change is quite futile; it has come to stay, and we must accept it. Its effects are not so disastrous as in some of the northern strongholds of nineteenth-century industrialism, because electric power has largely eliminated smoke, and most modern factories, designed to produce a large output from contented workers, are a great advance on those which made England prosperous fifty years ago" (232–33).

22. J. S. Cockburn and T.F.T. Butler, eds., *A History of the County of Middlesex* (London: Oxford University Press, 1971), 47–48.

23. For a detailed description of the early development of Jackson Heights, see Daniel Karatzas, *Jackson Heights: A Garden in the City; The History of America's First Garden and Cooperative Apartment Community* (New York: Jackson Heights Beautification Group, 1990).

24. There are various possible sources for this name. Some suggest that a Jackson family owned and lived on a portion of the 325 acres; others say that Jackson Avenue, which formed one of the borders of the parcel, was the source. Ibid., 19.

25. Ibid., 43.

26. *Jackson Heights News*, December 6, 1929.

27. Karatzas, *Jackson Heights*, 91.

28. "Queensboro Corporation Opens New Offices," pamphlet from the Queensboro Chamber of Commerce, May 1929.

29. *Souvenir Edition of the Jackson Heights News*, "Published upon the Opening of the New Executive Building of The Queensboro Corporation," May 1, 1929.

30. Ibid., 16.

31. *New York*, January 7, 1974, 34. The 1920s advertisements for various Jackson Heights apartment complexes all carry the proviso "Social and business references required." (Some of this material can be found in Vincent Seyfreid's *Queens: A Pictorial History* [Norfolk Donning Company, 1982].) While some area residents today readily concede the discrimination of a past age, they refrain from acknowledging more recent forms of housing exclusion. In 1990, two co-ops in Jackson Heights rejected apartment sales, first, to a white woman with two black children and then to an interracial couple, and were both cited for discrimination by the New York Human Rights Commission. Owen Fitzgerald, "Co-op Board Biased: City," *Daily News*, January 13, 1990 Edward Frost, "Co-op Charged in Bias," *Daily News*, February 8, 1990.

32. Karatzas, *Jackson Heights*, p.120–35. Though no documentation exists to this effect, it is presumably at this point, in the 1930s, that housing requirements became much less selective with reference to white ethnic minorities as well. Greek, Italian, and Jewish residents who came to comprise large parts of the Jackson Heights population started to come in after this time; prior discrimination was discreet and unstated, like the changes that occurred informally.

33. "Farmland to Thriving Community," in *Jackson Heights News*, April 1959, p.1

34. Karatzas, *Jackson Heights*, 159. In 1949, the president of the Jackson Heights Community Federation noted, "Average family incomes rank with the highest in the country. The working population is made up largely of business and professional men and women" ("Jackson Heights Looks to Its Futures: Report of the President of the Jackson Heights Community Federation," pamphlet, 1949, 4). For this period also see Helen Fuller Orton's "Jackson Heights: Its History and Growth," paper read before the Newtown Historical Society, January 17, 1950 (pamphlet at the Queensboro Library Long Island Division).

35. Of the changes, the Jackson Heights Community Federation wrote: "It is obvious even to the casual observer that Jackson Heights has changed since World War II—the golf courses and tennis courts are gone, almost all the vacant space

has been filled in with apartment houses, and the streets are more crowded. What is not so obvious, however, is whether the many newcomers are any different from the population already living here. Is the character of Jackson Heights as a community changing?" "Jackson Heights Takes Stock," publication of the Jackson Heights Community Federation, 1957).

36. Balwant Naik, *Petals of Roses* (Devon: Arthur H. Stockwell, 1982), 60. Naik was born in Gujarat and came to London via Kampala, Uganda; the poems in this collection were written in the years between 1972 and 1981.

37. Zig Layton-Henry, *The Politics of Immigration* (Oxford: Blackwell Press, 1992), 13. Kirwan, *Southall*, 49, cites another local story that suggests that the first Punjabi worker was an ex-soldier from the British army who upon arrival here sought work from the British rubber factory manager who had been his former officer. This tale, whether or not true, shifts the agency and responsibility, in terms of who needed whom, in a climate of hostility toward Indian immigrants.

38. Interview with Piara Khabra, London, June 9, 1995. The "network of spies" may be supposed, for example, in letters between officials of the British Foreign Office and various British consuls in the Americas, on the subject of "Indian extremists" in an earlier period, 1939. One set of correspondence includes a list of 252 people, of mostly Punjabi extraction, who were described as being ineligible for visas (Home Office Secret Folder No.26; Oriental and India Office Collection). The existence of this kind of material lends some weight to Khabra's accusations that elaborate mechanisms for government intelligence continued to exist through an early period of Indian immigration.

39. William H. Harlan, "Changes in the Sikh Community of Southall, London, 1963–85," South Asia Series Occasional Paper No. 39 in "Punjab Perspectives," ed. Surjit Dulai and Arthur Helweg (East Lansing: Michigan State University, Asian Studies Center, 1991).

40. Ibid., 136.

41. Layton-Henry, *Politics of Immigration* 76.

42. Meads, *Southall 830–1982* 81.

43. West Indian immigrants were also to be found in those places that had large manufacturing sectors. See Margaret Byron, *Post-War Caribbean Migration to Britain* (Aldershot, England: Avebury, 1994).

44. Select Committee on Race Relations and Immigration Session 1972–73, Education Section, Minutes of Evidence from Wednesday 9th May 1973 (London: Her Majesty's Stationery Office, 1973), 345. According to this report, the policy commenced just as immigrants began to arrive into Southall and continued through Southall's incorporation into the Borough of Ealing. It is around this later period, during the mid-1960s, however, when the policy began to be formulated and institutionalized within formalized languages for assimilation.

45. Informal interview, London, April 20, 1994.

46. See Ione Malloy, *Southie Won't Go: A Teacher's Diary of the Desegregation of South Boston High School* (Urbana: University of Illinois Press, 1986); Bernard Schwartz, *Swann's Way: The School Busing Case and the Supreme Court* (New York: Oxford University Press, 1986); "Milliken v. Bradley—The Implications for Metropolitan Desegregation," Conference before the United States Com-

mission on Civil Rights (Washington, D.C.: United States Government Printing Office, 1975).

47. Select Committee on Race Relations, 353.

48. Ibid.

49. One might presume that this is why the *Times of India* covered the issue ("Southall busing system may end soon," June 2, 1976).

50. From informal discussions and more formal interviews with various Southall political activists and residents.

51. For a broader discussion of some of these issues, see Bob Carter and Ian Grosvenor, *The Apostles of Purity: Black Immigration and Education Policy in Post-War Britain* (Birmingham: AFFOR, 1992).

52. Edward Pilkington, *Beyond the Mother Country: West Indians and the Notting Hill White Riots* (London: Tauris, 1988).

53. "What Mr. Enoch Powell Said at the Luncheon," *Middlesex County Times and West Middlesex Gazette*, Southall edition, November 6, 1971.

54. Ibid.

55. "'Immigrants Flow Must End': Tories," *Middlesex County Times and West Middlesex Gazette*, Ealing edition, August 11, 1972.

56. "'Southall Can Take No More Migrants'—M.P.," *Middlesex County Times and West Middlesex Gazette*, Ealing edition, August 11, 1972.

57. Sidney Bidwell, *Red, White and Black: Race Relations in Britain* (London: Gordon Cremonesi Ltd., 1976), 172.

58. Valerie Marett, *Immigrants Settling in the City* (Leicester: Leicester University Press, 1989), 62.

59. See Ibid. and Parminder Bhachu, *Twice Migrants: East African Sikh Settlers in Britain* (London: Tavistock, 1985).

60. *Middlesex County Times and West Middlesex Gazette*, August 3, 1972.

61. Manohar Singh Gill, "Southall Revisited," *Illustrated Weekly of India*, July 11, 1976.

62. Ibid.

63. Ibid.

64. Campaign Against Racism and Fascism (CARF)/Southall Rights, *Southall: The Birth of a Black Community* (London: Institute of Race Relations, 1981), 30–31.

65. For a more in-depth discussion of the development of Asian business in this veritable enclave, see Charu Shahane's "Southall Means Big Business," *Asian Enterprise and the Regeneration of Britain, by the Gujarat Samachar* (London: New Life, 1989). While Shahane details the existence of a number of Asian businesses by the early 1970s (pp.45–49), a 1977 publication of the Southall Chamber of Commerce ("The Southall Chamber of Commerce, 1902–1977," pamphlet compiled by Evelyn M. Barrett and Harold G. Hallett, Central Ealing Library, London) curiously has no mention of Asian business nor any officers or participants pictured who are not white.

66. As well as being referred to as a "Little India," the Southall area has also been called Chota Punjab or "Little Punjab," according to Marie Gillespie in her *Television, Ethnicity and Cultural Change* (London: Routledge, 1995), 35.

67. Laguerre, *Minoritized Space*.

68. CARF, *Southall*, 51.

69. *India Weekly*, June 10, 1976.

70. This event also received prominent coverage in the Indian press. See "Asian Stabbed to Death by Whites," *Times of India*, June 6, 1976; J. D. Singh, "Tension running high in Southall," *Times of India*, June 7, 1976; J. D. Singh, "Uneasy calm prevails in Southall," *Times of India*, June 8, 1976. Also on June 9, 1976, *Times of India* ran a main editorial entitled "Dark Deeds" on its opinion page. J. D. Singh, who seems to be the main reporter for immigrant issues in England, expresses ambivalence about the representativeness of the Chaggar murder and the killings of two other foreign students in "Racial Tensions in Britain: Anti Immigrant Feeling Being Whipped Up," *Times of India*, June 8, 1976: "It will be wrong for anyone in India to assume from the murder of three foreign students in Woodford and Southall that the great mass of White population in Britain is busy hounding the Asians out of their homes, of knife and dagger in hand, chasing them on the streets. Nothing can be further from the truth." And, in August 1976, the cover story of *India Today*, a news magazine in India, was about racism in England (Chottu Karadia, "British Racialism Creates Immigrants Dilemma," August 15, 1976.)

71. The Indian Workers Association is a name applied to a number of organizations around Britain; the original one was formed in Coventry in 1938 in order to support the cause of Indian independence from colonial rule. Since then a number of processes of centralization and consolidation have occurred, most notably in 1958 under the umbrella group of the IWA (GB). John DeWitt Jr. discusses some of this history in his *Indian Workers' Associations in Britain* (London: Oxford University Press, 1969). Accounts of the Southall IWA's relationship with the IWA (GB) vary widely, with some IWA-Southall leaders saying that theirs has always been an autonomous organization and other written accounts suggesting quite a bit of cooperation (and implied affiliation) between 1958 and 1962. It does seem clear, however, that some kind of split took place around 1962, having to do with politics in the Indian subcontinent as well as ideological directions of the organization, the IWA (GB) being more interested in class politics and the IWA-Southall directing itself to "community service." For an excellent discussion of the various political and cultural issues in this history of the organizations, with more current analytical emphasis than DeWitt's seminal book, see Sasha Josephides, "Towards a History of the Indian Workers' Association," Research Paper in Ethnic Relations Number 18 (Coventry: Centre for Research in Ethnic Relations, December 1991).

72. IWA, "History of the Indian Workers' Association Southall," 1991.

73. More detailed information on these strikes can be found in CARF, *Southall* 11–22. Also, for an in-depth analysis of the Woolf's strike, see Peter Marsh, "Appendix VIII, Area Report-Southall, Part III," in *Immigration and Race Relations in Britain, 1960–1967*, ed. Sheila Patterson (London: Oxford University Press, 1969), 423–30.

74. Harlan, *Changes in the Sikh Community* 142.

75. CARF, *Southall* 52.

76. Oral sources.

77. Interview with Suresh Grover, London, May 13, 1994.

78. For more on the relationship between race and policing during this period, see Stuart Hall et al., *Policing the Crisis* (London: Macmillan, 1978); *Policing*

Against Black People (London: Institute of Race Relations, 1987); and for an examination of some of these issues for a more contemporary period, see Michael Keith, *Race, Riots and Policing* (London: UCL Press, 1993). The construction of the young black male as criminal has its counterpart in the United States, but that attended solely to African American men, and most usually did not include other minorities, neither Asian nor even Latino.

79. *Southall 23 April 1979: The Report of the Unofficial Committee of Enquiry* (Nottingham: National Council for Civil Liberties, 1980), 24.

80. Ibid, 27.

81. The National Council for Civil Liberties report (30–66) has one account of events, an account that many people in the community felt particularly identified with. The story I tell here, in large part, derives from that understanding of the moment precisely because it is one that has become so central to the discourse of community in Southall among those to whom I spoke.

82. All told, 2,756 men of the Special Patrol Group and mounted police were deployed in Southall that day, according to the group Southall Rights in *23rd April 1979: A Report by Southall Rights* (Southall: Southall Rights, January 1980), 4.

83. "The Southall Tragedy," *Asian Post*, June 1979.

84. In the *Times of India*: B. K. Joshi, "One killed in Southall clashes," April 25, 1979; B. K. Joshi, "Asians' fear of more Southalls," April 26, 1979, 1; "Rajya Sabha concern at Southall incidents," April 26, 1979; "India asks UK to probe Southall clashes," April 27, 1979; "Gov't 'deep concern' at Southall episode," April 28, 1979; A. Vanaik, "Police and Black People in UK," May 2, 1979, and May 3, 1979, series of articles on editorial pages; "Immigrants in for a tougher time," May 5, 1979; B. K. Joshi, "Grave consequences of Tory win," May 6, 1979; and "UK assures India of race harmony," May 13, 1979. In the *Hindustan Times*: Rakshat Puri, "Asians in Bloody London Riots," April 25, 1979, and "Southall rally again," April 26, 1979.

85. "British racism to be raised at C'wealth," *Hindustan Times*, April 25, 1979.

86. See for example Gill's article, "Southall Revisited."

87. This insight is based on a range of comments from Indians that I have interviewed in the United States.

88. Lee Dembart, "The Old Neighborhood," *New York Post Daily Magazine*, December 29, 1969. See also Fred Powledge, "Mason-Dixon Line in Queens," *New York Times Magazine*, May 10, 1964.

89. C. Gerald Fraser, "In Jackson Heights Now, Se Habla Mucho Espanol," *New York Times*, January 25, 1975; Murray Schumach, "Enterprising Hispanic Merchants Revive a Block in Jackson Heights," *New York Times*, May 6, 1976; Randall Sullivan and Miguel Perez, "Cocaine Capital of U.S.: Cocaine People and Their Turf," *New York Newsday*, four parts beginning November 19, 1978.

90. Mort Peters, publisher of the twenty-eight-year-old weekly, the *Jackson Heights Record*, quoted in Fraser, "In Jackson Heights Now, Se Habla Much Espanol."

91. Quoted in Deborah Orin, "Jackson Heights: Will It Be Decay or Renaissance," *Long Island Press*, April 7, 1975.

92. See Chapter 1 for more details on this group of migrants.

93. For an excellent discussion of these developments, see Madhulika S. Khandelwal, "Indian Immigrants in Queens, New York City: Patterns of Spatial Concentration and Distribution, 1965–1990," in *Nation and Migration*, ed. Steven Vertovec (Philadelphia: University of Pennsylvania Press, 1994), 178–96.

94. Ibid., 180–81.

95. Interview with Subhas Ghai, New York, July 14, 1995.

96. Figures from 2000 United States Census.

97. Emi Endo, "Surge in LI's Asians: Indians lead 58% rise in population," *Newsday*, May 23, 2001.

98. See a variety of articles by Indian Americans on the website *http://www.sulekha.com* that include "New York Indians," by Rohini B. Ramanathan; and on *http://www.rediff.com*, an article about the filmmaker Piyush Dinker Pandya, who made the feature film *American Desi* (2001), describes trips to Jackson Heights as formative:

> Pandya grew up in an Indian household on Long Island in the 1970s, at a time when there were hardly any South Asian faces in the neighborhood. A high point for the family was the occasional jaunt to Jackson Heights (a predominantly Indian locality) in Queens, New York, to stock up on Indian groceries. "I remember the trips to Jackson Heights for Indian groceries were a huge event," recalls Pandya who now lives in New Jersey. "I mean it was a big deal just to do grocery shopping and it was so far away. Jackson Heights had a few grocery stores and there was nothing anywhere else." On one such trip to Jackson Heights the Pandya family saw Raj Kapoor's movie *Bobby*.

99. Steven Lee Myers, "Bazaar With the Feel of Bombay, Right in Queens," *New York Times*, January 4, 1993, and George Vecsey, "India Casts Its Subtle Spell on Queens," *New York Times*, August 19, 1994.

100. Many shop owners have kept their doors locked during business hours and installed doorbells to "screen" potential shoppers. This practice is widely considered to be racist in other contexts (see Patricia Williams's discussion of Benetton in Manhattan in *Alchemy of Race and Rights* [Cambridge: Harvard University Press, 1992]).

101. Much of the information in this section comes from a group of interviews conducted in 1995 in New York.

102. Interview with William Gandhi, July 14, 1995.

103. Interview with Subhas Ghai, New York, July 12, 1995.

104. See *Jackson Heights Merchants Association Newsletter*, January 1990.

105. See "Dinkins Joins in Celebration," *New York Times*, October 11, 1992.

106. In the late 1970s, Indian shopowners in the Lexington Avenue and 27th–30th Street area of Manhattan also lobbied for the official designation of "Little India." See Pavan Sahgal, "N.Y.C. Mayor Seeks Help of Indians to Revitalize Dying Neighborhoods," *India Abroad*, June 15, 1979, and "Board No. 5 Approves Little India Festival," *India Abroad*, December 14, 1979.

107. Interview with William Gandhi.

108. Saskia Sassen, *The Global City: New York, London, Tokyo* (Princeton: Princeton University Press, 1991).

109. Oral sources.

110. Karatzas, *Jackson Heights*, 169.

111. Informal interview with Daniel Karatzas, New York, July 30, 1995.

112. In an afterword to Karatzas's book, Frederich B. Fox Jr. writes: "In response to the rapid deterioration of the environment of Jackson Heights over the past several years, the Jackson Heights Beautification Group was formed in early 1988 by its founder and president, Michael J. Crowley" (*Jackson Heights*, 171).

113. Oral sources.

114. *All in the Family* was a television sitcom popular in the 1970s set in Queens, about a racist patriarch, Archie Bunker (the reference of the Jackson Heights resident's comment) who engaged in debates about political issues with his liberal son-in-law. *All in the Family* was based on a British program called *Till Death Do Us Part*.

115. For a discussion of formations of Sikh diaspora in Southall, see Brian Keith Axel, *The Nation's Tortured Body: Violence, Representation and the Formation of a Sikh Diaspora* (Durham: Duke University Press, 2000).

116. *Against the Grain: A Celebration of Survival and Struggle*, ed. the Southall Black Sisters Collective (Southall, Middlesex: Southall Black Sisters, 1990), 7, 10.

117. Ibid. 16.

118. Avtar Brah, "A Journey to Nairobi," in *Charting the Journey: Writings by Black and Third World Women*, ed. Shabnam Grewal (London: Sheba Feminist Publishers, 1988), 74–88. Also see a careful study of a 1979 cultural performance produced by the Southall Black Sisters in Paula Richman, "A Diaspora Ramayana in Southall, Greater London," *Journal of the American Academy of Religion* 67, no. 1 (1999): 33–57.

119. During interviews conducted in 1995 with members and staff of South Asian women's organizations like Sakhi for South Asian Women in New York and Manavi in New Jersey, many women spoke admiringly of the Southall Black Sisters when I mentioned that I was doing work on England.

120. Interview with Suresh Grover, London, July 11, 2001.

121. Oral sources.

122. In my own visits to the IWA offices in 1994, almost all meetings that I witnessed seemed to concern citizenship and immigration regulations, particularly with regard to bringing family members to England.

123. Interview with Piara Khabra, London, June 9, 1995.

124. Interview with Balraj Purewal, London, May 9, 1994.

125. The emergence of gangs as a response to political and social pressures in an ethnic community is a worldwide phenomenon, and a more comparative study remains to be done. In the United States, African American, Latino, and increasingly Asian communities have all witnessed with a mixture of alarm and sympathy the tendency for gangs to form when other political options seem limited. See the following literature on this issue: Martin Sanchez Jankowski, *Islands in the Street: Gangs and American Urban Society* (Berkeley: University of California Press, 1991); C. Ronald Huff, ed., *Gangs in America* (Newbury Park, Calif.: Sage Publications, 1990); and Felix Padilla, *The Gang as an American Enterprise* (New Brunswick, N.J.: Rutgers University Press, 1992).

126. See Pragna Patel "Southall Boys," in *Against the Grain*, 43–54, and "Gangs: Myth, Reality and Youth under Pressure," in *Southall Review*, Spring 1989, 3–4, 12.

127. "Gangs: Myth, Reality, and Youth Under Pressure."

128. Axel, *Nation's Tortured Body*.

129. See Yasmin Alibhai-Brown, "Fear and Loathing in Southall" *Independent*, June 6, 1995. Obviously, recent events show how the development of radical Islamic fundamentalism in the diaspora has been one effect of a variety of forms of alienation in places like Britain

130. One local activist intimated that his group would work with leaders of the Somalian population but would not assume responsibility for organizing them, that his interests remained with the Indian community

131. For more on Somalis in the diaspora, see Rima Berns McGown, *Muslims in the Diaspora: The Somali Communities of London and Toronto* (Toronto: University of Toronto Press, 1999).

132. Insights in this section come from recent follow-up fieldwork in June and July 2001.

133. It is notable, however, that in several interviews with a variety of residents and political leaders, and those from various generations, I did not once hear a racist denigration of Somalis as black. Here, as always, it seems possible that my status as a researcher prevented entree into a more private world where certain forms of racism would be articulated. I did, however, hear negative comments on Muslims more generally, particularly among Hindu and Sikh women; perhaps my own Hindu background was presumed to make me sympathetic to that form of prejudice.

134. Interviews and observations from July 2001.

135. A recent murder in Southall of a Pakistani restaurant owner suggests that "Asian" harmony, too, is fictional. An article in *India Abroad* reported that the victim, Imitiaz Husain Syed, had been having trouble with Sri Lankan Tamil and Sikh male customers, and implied as well that tensions arose when a war between India and Pakistan was mentioned. Area Minister of Parliament Piara Khabra, perhaps anxious to downplay for a broader public ethnic tensions within Southall, is quoted as saying: "The town is quiet and community relations are very good." Shyam Bhatia, "Pakistan restaurateur's murder raises concerns in London," *India Abroad*, February 2, 2002.

136. For a discussion of community formation and diversification in Southall, see Gerd Baumann, *Contesting Culture: Discourses of Identity in Multi-Ethnic London* (Cambridge: Cambridge University Press, 1996).

137. My own observations of the difference in Southall, even in 1994–95 when I first went there for fieldwork and in 2001 when I completed follow-up interviews, confirm residents' perceptions of the change. One small indication of how Southall has fallen off the radar of national consciousness may be the fact that when in 1994–95 I bought British rail tickets from Paddington to Southall, the desk attendants were knowledgeable about where Southall was and how much it would cost to travel there. On more than one occasion in 2001, attendants seemed confused by my destination, having to look it up on the map to figure out in which zone Southall was located.

138. Tania Anand, "Blending business with culture," *India Worldwide*, September 30, 1995.

139. Ashok Easwaran, "Bye Devon Avenue, We Have Moved On," *India Abroad*, August 24, 2000.

140. "March to raise awareness of domestic violence," *India Abroad*, June 22, 2001.

141. Jyotirmoy Datta, "Diwali Festival by Jackson Heights Merchants Association," *India Abroad*, October 22, 1999.

142. Ibid.

143. J. S. Furnivall, *Colonial Policy and Practice* (New York: New York University Press, 1956), 308.

144. The merchants interviewed were all very apt to describe their successes through U.S. ideologies of capitalist success, to say that working hard does pay off, and that any immigrant can succeed. To a large extent, this has been true for these people, many of whom had very few resources at the outset.

145. Jennifer Morrill, "A Sari Situation on 74th Street; The Traditional Indian Dress is Going Out of Style with Immigrants," *Newsday*, September 15, 2000. Ramesh Navani, the president of the Jackson Heights Merchants Association and manager of the India Sari Palace, notes: "When the children grow up, you also hope they will be your customer. . . . Most of the sari merchants, this is what they know how to do. . . . It would be hard to try something else."

CHAPTER THREE
AFFILIATIONS AND ASCENDANCY OF DIASPORIC LITERATURE

1. Rohinton Mistry, *A Fine Balance* (New York: Knopf, 1996).

2. Arvind Kumar, "'Good' Books," *India Currents*, October 2000, 1.

3. Salman Rushdie, "Damme, This is the Oriental Scene for You!" *New Yorker*, June 23 and 30, 1997, 50.

4. One could argue that all of Rushdie's fiction, with the possible exception of *The Jaguar Smile*, employs the tropes of hybridity and mobility to create an imaginary Indianness. See *Midnight's Children* (New York: Avon, 1982); *The Ground Beneath Her Feet* (New York: Henry Holt, 1999); *The Moor's Last Sigh* (New York: Pantheon, 1996); and *The Satanic Verses* (New York: Viking, 1988).

5. Here there are clear resonances with both psychoanalytic languages for stages in the production of the self (the Imaginary) and Marxist understandings of group formation (Ideology). Many writers have found either or both languages, and theorists associated with such concepts such as Jacques Lacan and Louis Althusser, to be of use in exploring the processes of psychic identification and colonial power, most notably Homi K. Bhabha, *The Location of Culture* (London: Routledge, 1994); Michael Sprinker, *Imaginary Relations: Ideology and Cultural Production* (London: Verso, 1987); Terry Eagleton, *Ideology: An Introduction* (London: Verso, 1991); and Mary N. Layoun, *Travels of a Genre: The Modern Novel and Ideology* (Princeton: Princeton University Press, 1990).

6. Building on Stuart Hall's important essay "Signification, Representation, Ideology: Althusser and the Post-Structuralist Debates," in *Critical Studies in Mass Communication* 2, no. 2 (1985): 91–114, and Gayatri Chakravorty Spivak's *In Other Worlds: Essays in Cultural Politics* (New York: Methuen Press, 1987), Mary Layoun in *Travels of a Genre* discusses the importance of bridging concerns

of individual and collective subjectivity for a nuanced conceptualization of ideology (15–20) for her project of geographically decentering the development of the modern novel. Though in the end she creates theoretical possibilities through a recasting of the term "ideology" within the space of the novel, my own discussion of the "imagination" bridges the individual/collective divide by moving among genres of the novel, autobiography, and letters. It nonetheless owes a great deal to Layoun's clear and careful formulations.

7. Included in this body of literature are many different kinds of work, such as Sara Suleri, *The Rhetoric of English India* (Chicago: University of Chicago Press, 1992); Christopher L. Miller, *Blank Darkness* (Chicago: University of Chicago Press, 1985); Rob Nixon, *London Calling: V. S. Naipaul, Postcolonial Mandarin* (New York: Oxford University Press, 1992); Jenny Sharpe, *Allegories of Empire* (Minneapolis: University of Minnesota Press, 1993); Michael Gorra, *After Empire: Scott, Naipaul, Rushdie* (Chicago: University of Chicago Press, 1997); and Inderpal Grewal, *Home and Harem: Nation, Gender, Empire and the Cultures of Travel* (Durham, N.C.: Duke University Press, 1996). While I am more explicitly concerned here with the postcolonial critics who work on texts about India, there is also much postcolonial work on Africa and the Caribbean, and I would suggest that these points hold for those cases as well.

8. Scholars in the field of Asian American literature in particular have begun to approach Indian American or South Asian American writers with a focus on their immigrant status. See, for example, Susan Koshy, "The Geography of Female Subjectivity: Ethnicity, Gender and Diaspora in Mukherjee's Fiction," *Diaspora* 3, no. 1 (1994): 69–84; Arvindra Sant-Wade and Karen Marguerite Radell, "Refashioning the Self: Immigrant Women in Bharati Mukherjee's New World," *Studies in Short Fiction* 29, no. 1 (Winter 1992): 11–18; and B. A. St. Andrews, "Cowanderers Kogawa and Mukherjee: New Immigrant Writers," *World Literature Today* 66, no. 1 (Winter 1992): 56–59. Also see essays in Deepika Bahri and Mary Vasudeva, eds., *Between the Lines: South Asians and Postcoloniality* (Philadelphia: Temple University Press, 1996).

9. Mukherjee has herself commented widely on immigrant writing; see "Immigrant Writing: Give Us Your Maximalists!" *New York Times Book Review*, August 28, 1988.

10. Rudyard Kipling, "The Ballad of East and West" (1889), in *Rudyard Kipling, Complete Verse* (New York: Doubleday, 1989).

11. Those who are oriented to psychoanalytic theory might find clear resonances of this construction with the language of Jacques Lacan. Here, to use Lacan's terminology, a certain opposition between the Imaginary and the Symbolic may be cast as a movement between comprehension and articulation. Lacan, *Ecrits: A Selection* (New York: Norton, 1977); *The Four Fundamental Concepts of Psycho-Analysis* (New York and London: Norton, 1977). Translator Alan Sheridan quite lucidly explains the relationship between the terms "imaginary" and "symbolic" in *The Four Fundamental Concepts of Psycho-Analysis*: "It is the symbolic, not the imaginary, that is seen to be the determining order of the subject, and its effects are radical: the subject, in Lacan's sense, is himself an effect of the symbolic" (279). Mary Layoun, in *Travels of a Genre* (156–58) discusses these concepts to illuminate how a new kind of symbolic order might be developed, in the novel, to challenge the always and already formed nature of, and the subject's unconscious participation in, the symbolic-linguistic realm. More to the point,

Homi Bhabha has noted: "The Imaginary is the transformation that takes place in the subject at the formative mirror-phase, when it assumes a *discrete* image which allows it to postulate a series of equivalences, samenesses, identities, between the objects of the surrounding world. However, this positioning is itself problematic, for the subject finds or recognizes itself through an image which is simultaneously alienating and hence potentially confrontational. It is precisely these two forms of identification that constitute the dominant strategy of colonial power exercised in relation to the stereotype which, as a form of multiple and contradictory belief, gives knowledge of difference and simultaneously disavows or masks it" (Location of Culture, 77). The diasporic imagination, formed by transnational (not colonial or immigrant) strategies, may be a space in which it is possible to enunciate and confront the alienation that the lines from Kipling evoke, precisely by continually returning to that discursive space, in classically psychoanalytic form.

12. The March to the Sea, or the Salt March, which began on March 12, 1930, and ended with Gandhi taking salt from the sea, was organized to protest the British colonial government's monopoly control over the production and distribution of salt in India, a peninsular region.

13. James Robert Payne, "Introduction," in *Multicultural Autobiography: American Lives* (Knoxville: University of Tennessee Press, 1992), xi–xxix. On broad questions having to do with autobiography, also see Diane Bjorklund, *Interpreting the Self: Two Hundred Years of American Autobiography* (Chicago: University of Chicago Press, 1998); and James Olney, *Metaphors of Self: The Meaning of Autobiography* (Princeton: Princeton University Press, 1972).

14. Krishnalal Shridharani, *My India, My America* (New York: Duell, Sloan and Pearce, 1941), 59. Further references to this book are in the text.

15. Randolph Bourne, "Trans-national America," in *The Radical Will: Selected Writings, 1911–1918* (New York: Urizen Books, 1972), 259–60.

16. William I. Thomas, *Old World Traits Transplanted* (New York: Harper and Brothers, 1921); Robert E. Park, *The Immigrant Press and Its Control* (New York: Harper Brothers, 1922).

17. The 1940s were a time when concepts of ethnicity began to be theorized with regard to both white immigrants and African Americans (see note 12 in the Introduction), and Shridharani's formulations here, though not yet named as "ethnicity," nonetheless illustrate certain intellectual trends of the time.

18. Interestingly, Saund does not explain his ability to immigrate to the United States amid very tight restrictions on the entry of Asians during this period.

19. Despite Saund's status as not only the first Indian American congressman, but also the first Asian American congressman, he has not been claimed in Asian American history in ways that other less public figures have. This is somewhat surprising, especially given his location, on the West Coast, where a kind of representative Asianness has been asserted, and what I will go on to argue is his relative consciousness of being Asian and categorizable with East Asians, like Chinese and Japanese Americans. Largely, this has to do with the constitution of the field of Asian American studies by East Asians in the late 1960s and the recent nature of population significance and political assertions by Indian Americans as part of the broader category of Asian American. Post-1980s formulations of the field of Asian American studies, in conferences, anthologies and university courses, have begun to assert with much consistency that Indian American experiences are integral to

the broader discipline; Saund's status as a "first" may therefore be claimed in the future.

20. D. S. Saund, *Congressman from India* (New York: E. P. Dutton, 1960) v. Further references to this book are in the text.

21. And this is one reason, among many, why he and this work have not been incorporated into a broader canon of Asian American studies.

22. Anzia Yezierska's works come to mind here. See *Arrogant Beggar* (Garden City, N.Y.: Doubleday, Page and Co., 1927) and *Bread Givers* (1925; New York: Persea Books, 1999).

23. See Karen Leonard's *Making Ethnic Choices*, on Indian farmers in Imperial Valley, as well as Ronald Takaki's *Strangers from a Different Shore*.

24. He recounts having said in Japan, in answer to questions about Little Rock: "My friends, no matter where we may live, whether it be in Japan, in India, or the United States of America, there exists in one form or another injustice of man toward man. They are trying to do the best they can, and I shall urge to my friends in Japan, and to people wherever I go, to try to understand this difficult problem of the people of the United States, just as they would want other people to study and understand their problems" (157).

25. Bourne, "Trans-National America," 260.

26. Amitav Ghosh, *The Shadow Lines* (New Delhi: Ravi Dayal, 1988). Further references to this book are in the text.

27. Ghosh himself is an anthropologist and has written a number of non-fictional pieces on how to conceptualize diaspora and belonging, including "The Diaspora in Indian Culture," *Public Culture* 2, no. 1: 73–78.

28. See note 5.

29. See my discussion of these issues in the previous chapter.

30. Anita Desai, *Bye-Bye Blackbird* (New Delhi: Orient Paperbacks, 1985). Further references to this book are in the text.

31. To this end, Inderpal Grewal's *Home and Harem: Nation, Gender, Empire and the Cultures of Travel*, while discussing nineteenth-century texts of travel, nonetheless brings up questions of national community that are relevant to the points made here.

32. Harriet Tytler, *An Englishwoman in India: The Memoirs of Harriet Tytler, 1828–1858*, ed. Anthony Sattin (New York: Oxford University Press, 1986); Fanny Parks, *Wanderings of a Pilgrim in Search of the Picturesque*, 2 vols. (London: Pelham Richardson, 1850). See Sara Suleri's discussion of these writers in *The Rhetoric of English India*, chapter 4.

33. Caren Kaplan very interestingly discusses some of these issues in *Questions of Travel: Postmodern Discourses of Displacement* (Durham, N.C.: Duke University Press, 1996), 3–5 in particular.

34. *Complete Verse of Rudyard Kipling*, 233.

35. Meena Alexander, *The Shock of Arrival: Reflections on Postcolonial Experience* (Boston: South End Press, 1996); and Gita Mehta's *Snakes and Ladders: Glimpses of India* (London: Becker and Warburg, 1997), though more about India than migration.

36. These authors, most of them relatively recent, appearing in the 1970s to 1980s, include Bharati Mukherjee, Chitra Banjerjee Divakaruni, and Meena Alexander.

37. Bharati Mukherjee, *Wife* (1975; Ontario: Penguin Books Canada, 1987), 45. Further references are in the text.

38. Mukherjee examines these issues in "Two Ways to Belong in America," *New York Times*, Sept. 22, 1996.

39. They give life to, in particular, Maxine Fisher's study of Indians, *The Indians of New York City*.

40. Part of this perception comes from the fact that all dramatic tension in the novel involves Dimple's relationship with Amit: her marriage to him, her increasing dissatisfaction with his professional status, her betrayal of him, and finally her murder of him.

41. Mukherjee, "Two ways to belong in America."

42. Ibid.

43. Ibid.

44. Ahmad notes: "The vast majority of immigrants and visitors who go from 'the peripheries' to the 'Western centre' in the United States either take no part in politics and scholarly endeavour or turn out to be right-wing people, well represented in the field of literature by Bharati Mukherjee." *In Theory* (London: Verso, 1992), 207–8.

45. Tina Chen and S. X. Goudie, "Holders of the Word: An Interview with Bharati Mukherjee," *Jouvert: A journal of Postcolonial Studies*, no. 1 (section 66), 14 (electronic journal).

46. Ibid. (section 6), 3.

47. Ibid. (section 5), 3.

48. Ibid. (58), 12.

49. Ibid. (74), 16.

50. Abraham Verghese, *My Own Country* (New York: Vintage Books, 1995), 16. Further references are in the text.

51. James Agee and Walker Evans, *Let Us Now Praise Famous Men* (Boston: Houghton Mifflin, 1941).

52. "The Long Voyage" is from Malcolm Cowley's *Blue Juniata: A Life*. It is interesting that Verghese should pay an intellectual debt to Cowley, who in the late 1950s wrote an article celebrating the quintessential American poet Walt Whitman for his spiritual journey east in the piece "Passage to India." Cowley, "The Guru, the Beatnik and the Good Gray Poet," *New Republic*, October 26, 1959, 17–19. Marc Dolan, in *Modern Lives: A Cultural Re-Reading of "The Lost Generation"* (West Lafayette, Indiana: Purdue University Press, 1996), makes interesting points about Cowley's impulse to American assimilation and the broad inclusionary possibilities of that project, particularly in the book *Exile's Return* (1934; New York: Viking Press, 1951). See Dolan, chapter 3, "Becoming an American: Modern(ized) Life and *Exile's Return*," 87–116.

53. Urmila Mohapatra, *With Love, from Britain* (Mumbai: Bharatiya Vidya Bhavan, 1999). Further references to this book are in the text.

54. Those novels about the United States are *The Ground Beneath Her Feet* (New York: Henry Holt, 1996) and *Fury* (New York: Random House, 2001). Rushdie has also physically moved to, and makes much of his transition to America.

55. Jhumpa Lahiri, "The Third and Final Continent," in *Interpreter of Maladies* (Boston: Houghton Mifflin, 1999), 198.

56. "Sir Vidia loses his temper," *India Abroad*, March 1, 2002.

57. Tanmaya Kumar Nanda, "Indians have a lot to thank Saund for," *India Abroad*, January 4, 2002; Arthur J. Pais's story "They quit India too," *India Abroad*, August 24, 2001, on independence fighters in the U.S., prominently, and somewhat inexplicably, features a picture of Saund shaking hands with John F. Kennedy; Tanmaya Kumar Nanda, "Large turnout for banquet in memory of Congressman Dalip Singh Saund," *India Abroad*, January 25, 2002.

CHAPTER FOUR
INDIA IN PRINT, INDIA ABROAD

1. Benedict Anderson, *Imagined Communities: Reflections on the Origin and Spread of Nationalism* (London: Verso, 1983).

2. Jürgen Habermas, *The Structural Transformation of the Public Sphere* (Cambridge: MIT Press, 1989). For a broad discussion of debates on the public sphere, see Craig Calhoun, *Critical Social Theory* (Oxford: Blackwell, 1995), especially 240–48.

3. Robert E. Park, *The Immigrant Press and Its Control* (New York: Harper and Brothers, 1922), 87. Park also made the important point that national identity at that time had a great deal to do with language, which is why he focused on the foreign-language press. In the postwar period, and for Indian middle-class migrants especially, the questions must be framed somewhat differently, to describe what I suggest is the broad impact that an English language press has had. However, foreign-language papers have emerged in both Indian American and Indian British communities, and might be explored in another study that builds on the insights of Park and others with regard to this more recent phenomenon.

4. Anderson, *Imagined Communities*, 37.

5. Anderson takes this formulation from Walter Benjamin, writing that "homogeneous, empty time" is an idea "in which simultaneity is, as it were, transverse, cross-time, marked not by prefiguring and fulfilment, but by temporal coincidence, and measured by clock and calendar" (30). By way of example, he notes: "The date at the top of the newspaper, the single most important emblem on it, provides the essential connection—the steady onward clocking of homogeneous, empty time." (37).

6. I take the wonderful phrase "ethnicity entrepreneur" from Philip Kasinitz, *Caribbean New York: Black Immigrants and the Politics of Race* (Ithaca: Cornell University Press, 1992). And I am thinking of Antonio Gramsci's use of the term "organic intellectual," but with obviously very different political interpretations. See Quentin Hoare and Geoffrey Nowell Smith, ed. and trans., *Selections from the Prison Notebooks of Antonio Gramsci* (New York: International Publishers, 1972).

7. *India News Service of the Friends of Freedom for India*, published weekly, beginning probably in 1919. The first issue at the Library of Congress is for July 17, 1920, and appears as vol. 2, no. 5.

8. *India News Service of the Friends of Freedom for India*, July 17, 1920.

9. "Boycotting the Briton," in *India News Service of the Friends of Freedom for India*, August 7, 1920.

10. This quote has the diction of self-translation, with misplaced articles. "Our Aims," *Independent Hindustan*, September 1920, 1.

11. Ibid., September 1920, 12–13.

12. Ibid., 29.

13. *India Bulletin*, published monthly by Friends of India, London, February 1932 to July/August 1939.

14. "Our Object," *India Bulletin*, February 1, 1932, 1.

15. Ibid.

16. See for example Atma S. Kamlani, "The Communal Question in India," *India Bulletin*, September 1932, 1.

17. *India News*, published by the Public Relations Department of the High Commissioner for India; India House; Aldwych, London, from January 1949 to February 23, 1974.

18. *India News* acknowledged these changes in its 1974 issue: "*India News*, which first appeared as a printed publication in January 1949, will cease publication with the issue of February 23, 1974. During these years, the journal has met the informational needs of our British friends and the Indian community. Happily now a large number of journals are published in Britain in various Indian languages as well as in English" (*India News*, February 16, 1974). While the stated reason is the multitude of new publications, it seems also that there is a marked and perceived shift in the types of issues relevant to a migrant Indian community very different from the one whose cultural activities had been reported by *India News* in the period immediately following Indian independence.

19. *India Weekly*, published in London by Ashoka Publications, from December 3, 1964, to the present.

20. "To Introduce Ourselves," *India Weekly*, December 3, 1964, 1.

21. "Unity in Diversity," *India Weekly*, January 21, 1965, 1.

22. Interview with Peter Pendsay, current editor of *India Weekly*, London, May 14, 1994.

23. Many of these publications were in existence for small periods of time and addressed a range of specific and general issues. For example, one paper, *India Review* (G. D. Publishers Ltd., London), was in existence for less than two years in the mid-1960s, and structured its editorial content around a pro-Kashmir stance; while it discussed other issues, its main intention seemed to be to influence Indian immigrants' perspectives on Kashmir.

24. As I have discussed in previous chapters, some Indians also used the term "black" to identify themselves as well as express solidarity both with resident Afro-Caribbean populations and the international struggles of black peoples. This political identity that the term "black" signifies was limited to particular communities, mostly younger Indians and largely second-generation Indian British who had lived with and waged political struggles in more leftist terms. Those constituencies neither had many financial resources at their disposal, nor necessarily assumed the role of representing the Indian community in the way that middle-class, first-generation British Indians did. Unsurprisingly, then, I was not able to find immigrant newspapers that primarily saw themselves in terms of the identification of "blackness." Some newspapers did use the term "black" to describe Indian experiences, as I discuss in relation to the paper *Asian Times*, but not with a primary black identity.

25. I discuss this more extensively in chapter 2.

26. "Responsibilities after the Southall murder," *India Weekly,* June 10, 1976, 1.

27. "Appeals for calm follow death of Indian student" and "The importance of equal opportunity—An interview with Mrs. Margaret Thatcher by Mrs. Kailash Puri," in *India Weekly,* June 10, 1976, 1–2.

28. There were a couple of publications, from 1979 through 1984, called the *Asian Post.* The one I am describing here was published in magazine style by Janata Publications and assumed a militant stance toward issues of racism. Another, begun in 1983, according to earliest editions found at the British Library, was published by a group called Asian Publishing, Ltd. It discussed racism and also included more mainstream issues like international policies and trade.

29. Anand Naidoo, "What we want is Asian Power," *Asian Post,* December 1979, 1.

30. This new incarnation of *India News* was published from June 1, 1978, to March 18, 1982, by the High Commission. It inexplicably ceased publication, only saying in its last issue that it "bids its readers good-by" (*India News,* March 18, 1982, 12).

31. N. G. Goray, "Our Objective," *India News,* June 1, 1978, 1.

32. Indian American newspapers like *India Abroad* and *News-India* also follow closely the activities of Bharatiya Vidya Bhavan.

33. "Bharatiya Vidya Bhavan: U.K. Centre," *India News,* July 20, 1978, 12.

34. "Bharatiya Vidya Bhavan's New Premises Opened," *India News,* July 27, 1978, 12.

35. "Statement on Southall Incident," *India News,* May 3, 1979, 1.

36. Ibid.

37. Frustrations among immigrants are evidenced in an editorial in the *Asian Post* entitled "Act of commission": "The CRE has failed to deliver the promise embodied in its name. . . . The Commission as it stands now, does not enjoy the confidence of the people it was expected to serve. Its links with the ethnic minorities are poor. . . . Surely far more needs to be done, specially in the sphere of indirect discrimination, than has been undertaken by the Commission" (April 16, 1983, 1). For a more in-depth treatment of some of these issues, see *Racism and Equal Opportunity Policies in the 1980s,* ed. Richard Jenkins and John Solomos (Cambridge: Cambridge University Press, 1987).

38. Interview with Gopal Raju, New York, February 13, 1995.

39. In early years, the classified advertisements appeared under a column titled "Chhota Bazaar." And one could track the development and diversification of Indian migrant communities by the listing of social events, which, in the early 1970s, occupied just a short column and were mostly those held in public schools and at Columbia University. Of the latter, many immigrants of the early to late 1960s recall Columbia as the one place for Indian activities in New York City. Today, of course, the "Calendar of Events" is extensive and categorized by regions and types (arts, religion, television).

40. Kailash Vajpeyi, "Mexico, Another Indian Counterpart," *India Abroad,* October 4, 1974, 5.

41. Rita Fawaz, "India Still Needs the United States," *India Abroad,* November 1, 1974, 2.

42. J. J. Bannerji, "Problems of Unity in Nonaligned Movement," *India Abroad*, May 25, 1979, 2; Francois Duriaud, "Cuban Leadership of Nonaligned Is at Issue," *India Abroad*, June 29, 1979.

43. "Nonaligned Group to Meet," *India Abroad*, February 29, 1980, 6.

44. Jane Chandra, "Up the Corporate Ladder," *India Abroad*, May 25, 1979, 15.

45. Pavan Sahgal, "N.Y.C. Mayor Seeks Help of Indians to Revitalize Dying Neighborhoods," *India Abroad*, June 15, 1979, 1. Note also how this language about Indian Americans is not necessarily bounded by historical moment; as I noted in the Introduction, President Bill Clinton remarked: "I think we forget that among all the some-200 ethnic groups . . . Indian Americans . . . have been among the most successful in terms of education level and income level. They have worked and succeeded stunningly well" (press conference, February 16, 2000).

46. Satya Sheel Pachori, "Letters to the Editor," *India Abroad*, August 10, 1979, 18.

47. S. N. Rao, "Letters to the Editor," *India Abroad*, June 15, 1979, 18.

48. See the 1976 letter to the *New York Times* from Ranjan Borra on "denying racial heritage," which evokes similar specters, discussed in chapter 1.

49. Vishnu V. Patel, "Letters to the Editor," *India Abroad*, June 29, 1979, 18.

50. Jagdish Desai, "Letters to the Editor," *India Abroad*, June 29, 1979, 18. See also letters in the July 6, 1979, issue of *India Abroad*.

51. Gopal Raju, "Letter from the Publisher," *India Abroad*, June 29, 1979, 1.

52. "Indian Scientist in US Discusses Ways to Help India Meet Her Needs," *India Abroad*, November 9, 1974, 5; Pavan Sahgal, "India Gives Foreign Investors High Returns; Conditions Are Misrepresented by Press Here," *India Abroad*, December 6, 1974, 5; "How to Invest Funds in India," *India Abroad*, June 20, 1975, 4. See also "Indians Abroad Remit More," From a Correspondent, *India Abroad*, August 10, 1979, 12; Abraham Thariath, "India Seeking Help From Natives Abroad," *India Abroad*, February 29, 1980, 1.

53. Jagannath J. Desai, "Reorientation Program Urged for Indians," *India Abroad*, December 7, 1979, 9.

54. Nandita Mukherjee, "Letters to the Editor," *India Abroad*, November 16, 1979, 18. Mukherjee comments: "I wish the Indian associations in America . . . would get their priorities straight. Instead of being preoccupied with entertaining visiting dignitaries . . . they should involve themselves with Indians who are in dire need of help. The recent spurt of harassments to which the residents of Hoboken have been subjected is a case in point."

55. "Race Tension in U.K. in Wake of Poll" (*India Abroad*, May 4, 1979, 3), for example, describes India's Minister of State for External Affairs Samrendra Kundu's comments about the violence in Southall.

56. The original incarnation of the newspaper was the monthly publication *Asian Digest*, which operated for three years, beginning in 1980, before being transformed into the 1983 newspaper *Asian Times*. The shift indicates both the perceived audience for a weekly newspaper of this kind (and the scarcity of "Asian papers") and also the goal of the newspaper owner, Arif Ali, to have a new kind of role in an emerging cultural politics; the existence of weekly immigrant newspapers is central to the development of self-conscious community formation.

57. "Where We Stand," *Asian Times*, January 28, 1983, 1.

58. "Lord Avebury's *Asian Post* supports apartheid," *Asian Times*, January 28, 1983, 5.

59. Progressive Indians at home in India were hard at work developing allegiances with groups in other parts of the subcontinent, to develop an alternative to the aggressive nationalism of the Indian state. In fact, the term South Asian emerged from those efforts. Indians in places like Britain were contending with nationalist, caste, and religious divisions as well. The term "Asian" was very much like the term "South Asian" back home, in its perceived ability to cut against divisions and also mediate class antagonisms, in England especially, between Indian middle classes and poorer Bangladeshi and Pakistani groups. As "Asian" also foregrounded race in Britain as central to the formation of a range of groups, it also made some reference to progressive developments back home.

60. See Chapter 1 for some elaboration of this trend, which is general (relating to per capita incomes and levels of educational achievement) and does not of course explain specific and numerous examples of poorer Indian communities and wealthy Pakistanis and Bangladeshis.

61. Books published by Hansib over the years include yearly editions of *Third World Impact*, edited by Arif Ali, a reference book on racial minorities in Britain and the politics of their places of origin, a reprint of Cheddi Jagan's *Story of British Guiana*, and books on Indian indentured labor, Marcus Garvey, cricket, and racism. This fact and other observations in this section come from interviews I conducted with him and members of his staff.

62. More recently he has noted that Hansib continues to send papers to Ministers of Parliament and has always been conscious of constantly shifting political opinions: "We see ourselves as a family paper. . . . Fathers and daughters can read it. . . . We try to avoid articles that are too contentious while remaining a little radically minded." (Interview with Arif Ali, London, May 18, 1994.)

63. The first issue of *India Mail* was published in October 1989, out of Wembley, in London. It is owned by an Indian company, Business India, which also owns the magazine *Business India*.

64. Interview with Shiv Sharma, London, March 31, 1994.

65. Shiv Sharma, *Dimly Before Dawn* (Essex: Asian Observer Publication, 1990).

66. Interview with Anil Tandon, London, March 31, 1994.

67. Ibid.

68. This need not imply the absence of cultural myths, particularly with regard to the financial success of Indians in Britain. Tandon and, presumably, other editorial and writing staff at the paper believe heartily that family values and a work ethnic contribute to an understanding of Indian fortune relative to that of other immigrants.

69. "Alarm as police reports increase in race crimes," " 'Most racist city in Britain,' " "New race bias shock for Asian doctors," by Sumeet Desai, "Churches in fight against racism," and "Fire chief's short reply on jobs for minorities," *India Mail*, April 7–13, 1994, 2–3. Note that these were five out of a total of fourteen on two "UK News" pages.

70. Sharma remarks: "These classifications have been forced on us. . . . Afro-Caribbeans, Asians, etc. are all lumped together as 'blacks' . . . because in this

country, unfortunately, people do not know the difference between Indians and Pakistanis and East Africans." (Interview with Sharma.) Note here how the existence of British racism explains and justifies a return to roots, and the ascription of complexity to the field of ethnicity, and a kind of simplicity to race or racial identity.

71. Interview with Pendsay.

72. Ibid.

73. And though *Asian Times* does not keep figures on the ethnic background of its readership, we can infer that other "twice-migrants" (Indians from the Caribbean and East Africa, particularly) might find in the paper a more comfortable set of perspectives.

74. Interview with Raju.

75. Interview with Venugopal Naidu, owner and editor of *India Monitor*, New York, February 20, 1995.

76. Interview with Raju.

77. Interview with John Perry, New York, February 15, 1995.

78. Ibid.

79. Ibid.

80. Imtiaz Ahmad, ed., *Caste and Social Stratification among Muslims in India* (New Delhi: Manohar, 1978).

81. Interview with Perry.

82. Interview with Naidu. This anti-Pakistan remark can be a code for outright opposition to the territorial disputes between Muslims and Hindus in Kashmir.

83. Krishan Ralleigh, "Managing Editor writes . . . Raison d'etre of 'India Link International,' " *India Link*, November 14, 1993.

84. In the several years that I have done research on Indian diasporic communities, from 1994 to 2001, I have only seen *India Link* in London, usually in the shops of Southall.

85. "Fund Raising Dinner for the Conservative candidate in Ealing," *India Link*, June/July 2001, 34; Tim Jones and Mark Evans, "Satpal Ram," in *India Link International*, June/July 2001.

86. Interview with Tandon.

87. Interview with Mujibul Islam, managing editor of *Eastern Eye*, July 5, 2001, London.

88. Shyam Bhatia, "$425 million bonanza for British Indian publisher," *India Abroad*, November 10, 2000, 30.

89. Even *Asian Times*, which had had very specific political inclinations under the editor-ownership of Arif Ali, was becoming more broadly popular in its address. As current editor Gary Khangura noted in 2001: "*Asian Times* is undergoing quite a big change at the moment. Traditionally it's been regarded as a slightly more mature paper. . . . We are beginning to cover a lot more U.K. news, we are beginning to encroach on territory which is traditionally more easternized, part of this easternized area. . . . We're trying to get more features writers, bring more personalities to the paper" (Interview with Khangura, July 5, 2001, London, transcribed by Michele Moritis).

90. Interview with Shihab Salim, London, July 4, 2001.

91. Typical comments from letters include: "I was hoping that being launched in the new millennium, AW&B would differ from other publications when it came

to projecting stereotypical images of what is considered beautiful and what isn't. I looked hopefully through the magazine to find a model that resembled me in terms of skin colour—no luck" (letter from Nisha Shukla, via e-mail, *Asian Woman & Bride*, Autumn 2000, 17).

92. Bala Murali Krishna, "*India Abroad* enhances on-line features," *India Abroad*, July 16, 1999, 30.

93. Rediff.com India Ltd. has its headquarters in Mumbai, and has offices is New Delhi, Chicago, and New York. It has holdings in telecommunications and also has online retail services. ("Rediff.com Re-launches India Abroad Weekly Publication," limited press release, August 1, 2001, newswire: http://investor.rediff.com/releases31.html.)

94. Som Chivukula, "Nicole Narain is *Playboy's* Playmate of the Month," *India Abroad*, February 1, 2002; and Som Chivukula, "Skin and deeper," *India Abroad*, November 30, 2001. This latter piece, on Sunny Leone, was the cover story of the magazine section of the newspapers. Chivukula comments on Leone's background (Punjabi) and national orientation with a string of cliches: "Sunny would tell you that she is 100 percent Indian—it says so on her Web site. And she'd also tell you that today she's as American as apple pie."

95. Robert E. Park, *The Immigrant Press and Its Control* (New York: Harper and Brothers, 1922), 359–60.

CHAPTER FIVE
GENERATIONS OF INDIAN DIASPORA

1. Karl Mannheim, "The Problem of Generations" (1952), in *From Karl Mannheim*, ed. Kurt H. Wolff (New Brunswick, N.J.: Transaction Publishers, 1993), 351–95. I thank Paul Silverstein for a useful and interesting conversation on diaspora and generation that caused me to pick up Mannheim's essay.

2. Three important pieces that lay out different perspectives on the issue of generations are David I. Kertzer, "Generation as a Sociological Problem," in *Annual Reviews of Sociology* 9 (1983): 125–49; Julian Marias and Marvin Rintala, "Generations" in *International Encyclopedia of the Social Sciences*, ed. David L. Sills (New York: Crowell Collier and Macmillan, 1968); Alan B. Spitzer, "The Historical Problem of Generations," in *The American Historical Review* 78, no. 5 (December 1973): 1353–85. Also see various essays in David I. Kertzer and Jennie Keith, eds., *Age and Anthropological Theory* (Ithaca: Cornell University Press, 1984).

3. David I. Kertzer is particularly critical of this tendency. He notes: "Were the term 'generation' used simply as a popular synonym for cohort the matter would not be of great importance. The problem is that when authors use the term in this sense they often retain the notion of genealogical relationships. In this way independent variables are confounded" ("Generation as a Sociological Problem." Largely we can see the different views on the topic in terms of conceptual-disciplinary inclinations. Mannheim's interest in the category is more philosophical, as a broad field of possibility for being, I would suggest, while Kertzer's interest in material effects of social structure produces a desire for "generation" to *quantitatively* measure change. We might construct Mannheim's response to Kertzer through his praise of Wilhelm Dilthey's work: "The relative novelty of Dilthey's

work consists in just this distinction which he made between the qualitative and quantitative concept of time. Dilthey is interested in the problem of generations primarily because, as he puts it, the adoption of the 'generation' as a temporal unit of the history of intellectual evolution makes it possible to replace such purely external units as hours, months, years, decades, etc., by a concept of measure operating from within" (357). Mannheim thus seems particularly invested in the qualitative changes experienced by a generation.

4. Ibid.

5. Ibid., 365.

6. Ibid., 378–79; the term "identity of responses" appears on 381.

7. This point is particularly well-argued by Kertzer, "Generation as a Sociological Problem," (141), though he makes no attempt to recover the term for migrant formations, as I seek to do here.

8. An example of this tendency can be found in V. C. Nahirny, J. A. Fisherman, "American Immigrant Groups: Ethnic Identification and the Problem of Generations," in *Sociological Review* 13, no. 3, 311–26. Other works on the "second generation" include Pyong Gap Min, "A Comparison of Post-1965 and Turn-of-the-Century Immigrants in Intergenerational Mobility and Cultural Transmission," *Journal of American Ethnic History* 18, no. 3: 65–94; Alejandro Portes and Dag MacLeod, "What Shall I Call Myself? Hispanic Identity Formation in the Second Generation," *Ethnic and Racial Studies* 19, no. 3: 523–47 (July 1996); Shamita Das Dasgupta, "Gender Roles and Cultural Continuity in the Asian Indian Immigrant Community in the U.S.," *Sex Roles* 38, nos. 11/12 (1998): 953–74; "Second Generation—Asian Americans' Ethnic Identity," special issue of *Amerasia Journal* 25, no. 1 (Spring 1999), guest editors Pyong Gap Min and Kyeyoung Park; and *Ethnicities: Children of Immigrants in America*, ed. Ruben C. Rumbaut and Alejandro Portes (Berkeley: University of California Press, 2001).

9. Philip Kasinitz, public lecture, Barnard College, New York, December 6, 2001.

10. This is the title of an interesting article by Somini Sengupta in *New York Times*, June 30, 1996, 1.

11. And Indian youth cultures were quite visible in Toronto as well, but I do not have space to consider that here.

12. Dick Hebdige has made this point for his subject matter in *Subculture: The Meaning of Style* (London: Routledge, 1979). I am not primarily concerned here with terming new generations of diaspora "subcultures," largely because I do not want to create the impression of one broad and hegemonic formation and smaller resistant groups within that; instead my aim is suggest the continually contesting nature of the new diasporic formations. In this way a "generation of diaspora" is different from a subculture, largely because diaspora itself does not function as hegemonic. Nonetheless, I do think that much of Hebdige's theorization, occasioned only very casually by his example of white working-class (punk) cultures, can be of great use to us in understanding the form and content of many of the illustrations of this chapter.

13. Hebdige outlines this kind of move quite convincingly with a different set of examples.

14. "Music Has No Colour, No Barriers," August 1, 2001, group interview with Steven Kapur, posted on www.rediff.com.

15. Apache Indian, "Chok There" copyright 1991 MCA Music Publishing.

16. This is not unlike the music of the group Soul to Soul, which includes the song "Keep On Moving" that Paul Gilroy has described in *The Black Atlantic: Modernity and Double Consciousness* (Cambridge: Harvard University Press, 1993), 15–16.

17. Apache Indian, "Come Follow Me," copyright 1993, MCA Music Publishing.

18. Apache Indian, "Magic Carpet," copyright 1992, MCA Music Publishing.

19. Nestor Garcia Canclini, *Hybrid Cultures: Strategies for Entering and Leaving Modernity*, foreword by Renato Rosaldo, translated by Christopher L. Chiappari and Silvia L. Lopez (Minneapolis: University of Minnesota Press, 1995).

20. Les Back writes very interestingly about the cultural crossroads of Apache Indian's music in "X Amount of Sat Siri Akal! Apache Indian Reggae Music and the Cultural Intermezzo," *New Formations* 27 (1996): 128.

21. Stephen King and Richard J. Jensen, "Bob Marley's 'Redemption Song': The Rhetoric of Reggae and Rastafari," *Journal of Popular Culture* 29, no. 3 (1998): 17.

22. Apache Indian and Maxi Priest, "Feel it Fe Real," copyright 1992, MCA Music Publishing.

23. Ibid.

24. George Lipsitz, *Dangerous Crossroads: Popular Music, Postmodernism and the Poetics of Place* (London: Verso, 1994).

25. Zana Muhsen with Andrew Crofts, *Sold: A Story of Modern-Day Slavery* (London: Warner, 1994). Also see Vron Ware, "Moments of Danger: Race, Gender and Memories of Empire," *History and Theory* 31, no. 4 (December 1992): 116.

26. Apache Indian, "Arranged Marriage," copyright 1992, MCA Music Publishing.

27. Louise Lamphere very helpfully pointed this out.

28. See Homi K. Bhabha, *The Location of Culture* (London: Routledge, 1994); essays in *Performing Hybridity*, eds. May Joseph and Jennifer Natalya Fink (Minneapolis: University of Minnesota Press, 1999).

29. See Sabita Banerji and Gerd Baumann, "Bhangra 1984–8: Fusion and Professionalization in a Genre of South Asian Dance Music," in *Black Music in Britain: Essays in the Afro-Asian Contributions to Popular Music*, ed. Paul Oliver (Birmingham: Open University Press, 1990), 137–52; also various articles in Sanjay Sharma, John Hutnyk, and Ashwani Sharma, *Dis-Orienting Rhythms: The Politics of the New Asian Dance Music* (London: Zed Books, 1996). My intention here is not to detail the development of bhangra, but to use its formation as an instance of new generational formation, the topic under consideration.

30. Sabita Banerji and Gerd Baumann, "Bhangra 1984–8: Fusion and Professionalization in a Genre of South Asian Dance Music," in *Black Music in Britain: Essays in the Afro-Asian Contributions to Popular Music*, ed. Paul Oliver (Birmingham: Open University Press, 1990), 137–52 (the section that I refer to here is on 137–38).

31. For more on these youth cultural spaces in New York, see Sunaina Maira, *Desis in the House: Indian American Youth Culture in New York* City (Philadelphia: Temple University Press, 2002). And for a perspective on the cultures of these musics in Canada, see Jacqueline Warwick, "'Make Way for the Indian': Bhangra Music and South Asian Presence in Toronto," *Popular Music and Society* 24, part 2 (2000): 25–44.

32. See, for example, Rachel Salazar Parrenas, "Legacies/Identity—'White Trash' Meets the 'Little Brown Monkeys': The Taxi Dance Hall as a Site of Interracial and Gender Alliances between White Working Class Women and Filipino Immigrant Men in the 1920s and 30s," *Amerasia Journal* 24, no. 2 (1998): 115–35.

33. The show was entitled "No Justice, No Peace: Tower Hamlets 9 Defence Campaign," with Apache Indian, JC001, Urban Species, Hustlers convention and other top DJs. (March 4, 1994, north London).

34. See various essays in Sharma, Hutnyk, and Sharma, *Dis-Orienting Rhythms*.

35. James Clifford, *Routes: Travel and Translation in the Late Twentieth Century* (Cambridge: Harvard University Press, 1997), chapter 1.

36. Ashwani Sharma, "Sounds Oriental: The (Im)Possibility of Theorizing Asian Musical Cultures," in *Dis-Orienting Rhythms*, ed. Sharma, Hutnyk, and Sharma, p. 24. See also John Hutnyk, "Adorno and Womad: South Asian Crossovers and the Limits of Hybridity-Talk," in *Postcolonial Studies* 1, no. 3 (1998): 401–26.

37. See Sharma, "Sounds Oriental," 25–26.

38. "Music Mahal," in *Garavi Gujarat*, September 11, 1993, 8.

39. Joel L. Swerdlow, "Global Culture," 2–6 and Erla Zwingle, "A World Together," 6–33, in *National Geographic*, August 1999. See my analysis of this text in the introduction.

40. *http://imusic.artistdirect.com/showcase/club/talvinsingh.html*.

41. Timothy Brennan, *At Home in the World: Cosmopolitanism Now* (Cambridge: Harvard University Press, 1997); Walter D. Mignolo, "The Many Faces of Cosmo-polis: Border Thinking and Critical Cosmopolitanism," *Public Culture* 12, no. 3: 721–48.

42. See *The U.K. Telegraph*, February 15, 2001, for an interesting description of Singh's recent activities, which include his romance with Shyla Lopez, a former Miss India.

43. Liner notes to Sheila Chandra, *The Struggle*, Indipop Records, copyright 1985, 2001.

44. Steve Futterman, "All This Jazz: Best Jazz Albums of 2001," *New Yorker*, January 14, 2002, 12. Vijay Iyer, *Panoptic Modes*, Red Giant Records, copyright 2001.

45. Edouard Glissant, *Poetics of Relation*, trans. Betsy Wing (Ann Arbor: University of Michigan Press, 1997).

46. Sheila Chandra's first album was released in 1985.

47. See Brian Larkin's very interesting work on the reception and consumption of Indian films in Nigeria: "Indian Films and Nigerian Lovers: Media and the Creation of Parallel Modernities," *Africa* 67, no. 3 (1997): 406–41.

48. Also consider here how in 2001–2, after the U.S. government deposed the Taliban political regime in Afghanistan, a form of experiencing "liberation" from

Islamic religious law and cultural surveillance was the mass release, again, of Indian films and the passing around of Indian female movie star cards (like baseball cards). Arthur J. Pais, "Of Dharmatma and chai in Kandahar," *India Abroad*, November 23, 2001, 3; Syed Firdaus Ashraf, "Bollywood Set to Return to Afghanistan's Big Screens," *India Abroad*, November 30, 2001, 1.

49. Joe Austin and Michael Nevin Willard, "Introduction: Angels of History, Demons of Culture," in *Generations of Youth: Youth Culture and History in Twentieth-Century America*, eds. Austin and Willard (New York: New York University Press, 1998), 3.

50. Kiran Patel, "Other Holidays, Other Seasons," *New York Times*, December 28, 1997.

51. This is roughly in line with what some social scientists have identified as "political generations" ("Generations," section 2: Political Generations, in *International Encyclopedia of the Social Sciences*, ed. David Sills, 92).

52. Prior to this time, loosely organized Indian associations catered mostly to students from India who regularly gathered to cook Indian food and attend performances. Those who attended university in the early to middle 1980s speak of conscious efforts of identity production, in the form of new organizations to distinguish between those from India and those who grew up in the United States or England, or a second generation. Also it is important to consider how college or university is an important time for the production of identity. Indian Americans, especially, note that it was during those four years of their lives when they developed a sense of being an "ethnic." A recent letter from Mona Kaleem in *India Abroad* makes this point quite succinctly: "As the American-born daughter of Indian immigrants, I rarely interacted with people of Pakistani or Bangladeshi origin or heard the words 'South Asian' until I went to college" (*India Abroad*, February 8, 2002). Ms. Kaleem make this point in the service of "South Asian" unity: "We should attempt to come together as 'American Desis'—another term that surmises the characteristics of all people from the Indian subcontinent," but the identity experience and consciousness can take a variety of forms.

53. See my discussion of this trend in Chapter 1. It is also true, however, that the address that many Hindu youth formations make, most especially in the contemporary period, studiously avoids references to Indian nationalism. For example, the web page of the National Hindu Students Forum UK (*www.nhsf.org.uk*) focuses on "better understanding of the Hindu Dharma." Yet in conversations with those who are involved with such activities, the relationship between religion and nation, and the political implications of that, in exclusions of non-Hindus from the ideal of India, are manifest. In an article on the 2001 Hindu Youth Festival in London, third- and fourth-generation British Indians are described to sustain minimal relationships to the Indian nation (presumably physical travel), but bear attachments to "vedic India, ancient India" (Rashmee Z. Ahmed, "UK Hindu youths' quest to find roots," *The Times of India News Service*).

54. Steven Vertovec, "Three Meanings of 'Diaspora,' Exemplified Among South Asian Religions," *Diaspora* 7, no. 2 (1999). Also see his *The Hindu Diaspora: Comparative Patterns* (London: Routledge, 2000).

55. See Laurie Goodstein, "At Camps, Young U.S. Sikhs Cling to Heritage," *New York Times*, July 18, 1998. One interesting point in the article is that this

Sikh summer camp, Lohgarh Retreat, which actively urges against assimilation, actually transformed a space in southern Pennsylvania, in the Poconos, that had been a Jewish camp. This fact fits neatly into the classic succession model, in which ethnic groups come to replace one another as they move along the trajectory to becoming American; it also resonates with many Indian migrants' explicitly articulated admiration and emulation of Jewish Americans.

56. Sumar Guha Mozumdar, "RSS Chief Wary About Young Hindus Losing Their Identity," August 3, 2001, *India Abroad*.

57. From interviews with New York–area Indian Americans.

58. A large section of all immigrant newspapers, even in early 1970s *India Abroad*, has been the matrimonial advertisements, most of which are quite specific in their requirements for background of prospects. And more recently there are dating personals in some of the glossy fashion magazines discussed in Chapter 3.

59. Precisely because dating is such a Western phenomenon, these activities could not occur within more traditional Indian social functions, nor, presumably, with those who do not experience or want to partake in mainstream social life in the U.S. or U.K.

60. Mission statement on organization newsletters entitled "SAYA! Today" (South Asian Youth Action, Elmhurst, New York).

61. DRUM homepage: *http://www.drumnation.org/drum.html*.

62. Rajeswari Sunder Rajan, *Real and Imagined Women: Gender, Culture and Postcolonialism* (London: Routledge, 1993); Sangeeta Ray, *En-gendering India: Women and Nation in Colonial and Postcolonial Narratives* (Durham, N.C.: Duke University Press, 2000).

63. Sandhya Shukla, "Feminisms of the Diaspora Both Local and Global; The Politics of South Asian Women Against Domestic Violence," in *Women Transforming Politics*, ed. Cathy Cohen, Kathleen Jones, and Joan Tronto (New York: New York University Press, 1997).

64. Because these women's groups do provide an important service to South Asian communities, they elicit a good deal of respect. However, gender stereotyping certainly occurs within more mainstream (and private) representations of these groups. In almost all conversations that I have had with leaders of Indian cultural associations in the United States, when asked about *Sakhi for South Asian Women*, subjects respond that "they do good work, but are aggressive in their approach." Likewise, in Southall, male members of liberal Indian service organizations describe their own differences with the Southall Black Sisters sometimes in terms of liberal-left political poles, but also at times with respect to more elusive questions of "style" and "oppositionality" that seem highly gendered.

65. This is a point that was very powerfully made at a panel on queer diasporas at the 2001 annual meeting of the Association of Asian American Studies in Toronto. Members of that panel included Gayatri Gopinath and Martin Manalansan.

66. See a more detailed discussion of this issue in "Feminisms of the Diaspora."

67. It seems clear that in artistic terms, *Bhaji on the Beach* is a far superior film to *Mississippi Masala*, but I want to sidestep, if possible, the tedious debates on merit and value that have colonized a good deal of space in current discussions of "Third World Art." The question "Are these films really good?" often short-

circuits the more interesting issue of what it means for other cultural producers, different audiences, new arrangements of power, and communities in question to become subjects of our analysis. I would also suggest categories of merit and value, and arguing on that terrain, leads us back to rather uncritical and finally futile notions of multiculturalism that present little real opposition to the prevailing political and cultural order.

68. Here Chadha gestures at actual feminist movements, like those that created the Southall Black Sisters, and with which she has been in dialogue. In fact, the Southall Black Sisters oversaw a fundraiser with the film as showpiece just as it was released. And there is also a framework of interaction and conversation, between Asian feminist activists, filmmakers, and other cultural producers that the representations of this film are embedded in.

69. Perminder Dhillon-Kashyap, "Locating the Asian Experience," in *Screen*, 29, no. 4 (Autumn 1988), "The Last 'Special Issue' on Race?"

70. The questions of desire and race are complicated and deserve further treatment than they receive here. The question of how to represent desire without resorting to simplistic notions continues to perplex cultural producers. One outstanding example seems to be *Young Soul Rebels* (1991), directed by Issac Julien, where arguably there is love, desire, and the mixing of racial bodies in a way that does not utilize stereotypes. But *Young Soul Rebels* is also utopian and may suggest that the very model of utopia enables such representation.

71. Lawrence Chua, "What does it mean to be black and European?" *Bomb*, Summer 1994.

72. Gargi Bhattacharya and John Gabriel, "Gurinder Chadha and the Apna Generation: Black British Film in the 1990s," *Third Text* 27 (Summer 1994), 57–58.

73. Interview with Tanmaya Kumar Nanda, in *India Abroad*, June 8, 2001, 45.

74. There is a long history of using sport to do this narrative work, a wonderful example of which is Trinidadian writer C.L.R. James's 1963 text *Beyond a Boundary* (Durham, N.C.: Duke University Press, 1993).

75. Observations in this section emerged from my own participation in this event.

EPILOGUE
PRESENTS AND FUTURES

1. Immigrant newspapers, like *India Abroad* and *News-India* have been filled with articles about hate crimes against Indians and other South Asians. Jeet Thayil, "Hate Crimes are now a way of life," *India Abroad*, February 8, 2002; Somini Sengupta and Vivian S. Toy, "United Ethnically, and by an Assault," *New York Times*, October 7, 1998; Sukhjit Purewal, "Star-spangled turban doesn't save Sikh from attack," *India Abroad*, December 21, 2001. Focusing on Britain, see Shyam Bhatia, "Attempts to defuse backlash against South Asians," *India Abroad*, September 28, 2001. For riots in Britain in 2000, see Shyam Bhatia, "Bradford burning," *India Abroad*, July 20, 2001; and Arun Khandhani, "From Oldham to Bradford: The Violence of the Violated," in report of the Institute of Race Relations entitled "The three faces of British racism," October 2001, Lon-

don. See also Gary Younge, "Bradford needs hope, not teargas," *Guardian*, July 10, 2001.

2. Sanjay Suri, "British Indians hit by Ford's decision to shut down plant," *India Abroad*, May 26, 2001. Britain is now also actively seeking nurses from India, another sign of the historical resonances of the contemporary moment with both early experiences of Indian migration and also other migrant histories, like the United States's active solicitation of Philippine medical professionals ("Indian nurses in demand," *India Abroad News Service*, February 23, 2001).

3. Melanie Warner, "The Indians of Silicon Valley," in *Fortune* 141, no. 10, May 15, 2000; Arvind Padmanabhan, "Khosla named top venture capitalist by *Forbes*," *India Abroad*, February 23, 2001; Aziz Haniffa, "Being Indian is seen as a plus in Silicon Valley," *India Abroad*, December 17, 1999.

4. George Joseph, "Indian 'slaves' file suit against Tulsa company," *India Abroad*, March 1, 2002; George Joseph, "'Slave' workers overwhelmed by community support," *India Abroad*, March 8, 2002; George Joseph, "53 Indians rescued from 'slavery' in Oklahoma," *India Abroad*, February 22, 2002.

5. Amitav Ghosh, *The Shadow Lines* (New Delhi: Ravi Dayal, 1988), 77, 78.

6. See a very interesting piece on this debate by S. Ali, entitled "'I would like to be known as an Indian,'" *India Abroad*, January 11, 2002.

7. Aziz Haniffa, "African-American lawmaker slams airport staff for targeting turbaned Sikhs," *India Abroad*, November 30, 2001.

8. Arthur J. Pais, "Asian American journalists urged to speak out against prejudice," *India Abroad*, August 17, 2001.

9. Ravi Adhikari, "Agnihotri discusses his plans for NRIs across the globe," *News India-Times*, October 19, 2001. While one might certainly expect this new position to be devoted to the interests of financially successful NRIs, there are indications that the Indian government is also concerned about the conditions of less affluent Indian workers abroad; see P. Jayaram, "Yadav says Gulf workers need protection," *News-India Times*, October 19, 2001.

ACKNOWLEDGMENTS

I welcome the opportunity to reflect on the rich networks that have sustained me. I must first thank those who have had the most to do with this book's origins. I benefited greatly from the (still) unmatched critical insight and consistent advice of Jean-Christophe Agnew, Michael Denning, and Hazel Carby. These extraordinarily generous scholars and teachers form a point of reference for all of my work in the academy. I can only hope that this book captures some of the depth of their influence and attention.

I have learned so much from Paul Gilroy and his work and feel tremendously lucky to have had him as an inspiration in both New Haven and London. Dominick LaCapra made ideas seem exciting when I was still an undergraduate; it seems only fitting that I should have revisited that energy while finishing up this book at the Society for the Humanities at Cornell University. Henry Louis Gates, Jr., first encouraged me to go to graduate school. Don Nakanishi and Enrique de la Cruz facilitated a productive year at the Asian American Studies Center at UCLA. Gary Okihiro has given me unqualified support as a senior scholar in Asian American Studies. And I thank E. Valentine Daniel and Nicholas Dirks for bringing me into the field of anthropology.

Support for this book has included a grant from the Yale Center for International and Area Studies and summer faculty development grants from Columbia University. I had valuable research assistance and input from many students, including Jacquelyn Grey, Seema Rizvi, Serguei Oushakine, Krista Hegburg, Kristen Drybread, Vishnupad Misra, Patrick Gallagher, Michele Moritis, and Nadia Loan. An anonymous and very insightful reader of the manuscript helped a great deal in structuring its revisions. I am grateful to Mary Murrell at Princeton University Press for getting behind this project and for her understated but powerful interpretive style.

This book, like most, owes much to other people's work. I thank all those in London and New York who spoke to me about what they do, briefly or at length, and inspired me to translate that for others. In London, that group includes Suresh Grover, Sukh Sandher, Piara Khabra, Gurinder Chadha, Arif Ali, A. Sivanandan, and Kala Vasani. In New York, I thank Gopal Raju, John Perry, Daniel Karatzas, Prema Vohra, numerous merchants and shoppers in Jackson Heights, and others too numerous to name.

Many of the ideas in this book took shape in presentations at the history department of the University of California, Irvine, Wesleyan University's Center for the Americas, City of New York Graduate Center's Sawyer Seminar, and various conferences, including those of the American Studies

Association, the Association of Asian American Studies, the American Historical Association, and the American Anthropological Association. I thank all who patiently listened to me speak in those venues. Though this project changed so profoundly over the years, it drew something from each and every conversation along the way, such as those with Gerald Jaynes, Robert Stepto, Patricia Pessar, Sara Suleri Goodyear, Dan Pillay, Adam Green, Barbara Savage, Nikhil Singh, David Waldstreicher, Pamela Haag, Jonathan Holloway, Yen Le Espiritu, Shirley Hune, Shu-mei Shih, Karen Leonard, and Claire Potter. I thank Brian Axel for reading and commenting at length on my work. I enjoyed reflecting on race and nationality in London with Stephanie Smallwood, Mark Harding, Cristobal Marín, Gopal Balakrishnan, and especially Anne-Marie Fortier. Closer to home, only Michelle Stephens knows how deeply she has helped me with this project. And I am very grateful to Matthew Frye Jacobson for reading the entire manuscript and being supportive at critical junctures.

I have never felt on my own with the daily work of this book. Rachel Adams, Julie Crawford, and Kristina Milnor generously discussed several of these chapters with me over good food and wine. I continue to enjoy the camaraderie of a writing group in the New York area that has included Sanda Lwin, Mary Lui, Mae Ngai, Lok Siu, Julianna Chang, Shirley Lim, Evelyn Chien, Cynthia Tolentino, and Lisa Yun. Sujatha Subramanian provided empathic insight while this book was in its latter stages. Colleagues at Columbia, like Sherry Ortner, Casey Blake, David Eng, Nicholas DeGenova, and Nicole Marwell have shown kind interest in me and my work. Brian Larkin and Paul Silverstein continually engage me in exciting dialogues about our shared interests. I also thank Roz Morris for being an excellent colleague and a dear friend. I hope that Dorothy Miller, Daniel Klubock, and Katharine Klubock understand how important their encouragement has been to me over the years. And crucial to all of my pursuits is the remarkable friendship and intellectual companionship of Emily Bernard, Vilashini Cooppan, Miranda Massie, Carol Jennings, Michelle Stephens, and Heidi Tinsman. I thank my father, Rajendra Shukla, for having always hoped for daughters and for believing that they could do anything they wanted. My mother, Ranjana Shukla, made that lofty aim a reality. My sister Sobha Shukla provides a special form of understanding that extends in many directions. It needs to be said that a lifetime of conversations with members of my family, all of whom have their own rich perspectives on what it means to be a citizen of the world, has given this project a substance that lies beyond the reach of any archive. And they have made it possible for me to write about it.

Last, and first, Thomas Klubock helps me process the complicated pleasures and disappointments of every single day into a reckless optimism for the next. He has lived with and profoundly shaped this book. For that and more, he has my very deepest gratitude and love.

INDEX

Adhikari, Ravi, 302n.9

African Times, 195

Afro-Caribbeans, 217, 218, 226, 244

Agee, James, 288n.51

Ahmad, Aijaz, 288n.44

Ahmad, Imtiaz, 294n.80

Ahmed, Rashmee Z., 300n.53

AIA (Association of Indians in America), 60, 66

Alaap, 225

Alexander, Meena, 288n.35

Alexandra Palace (New York), 26

Ali, Arif, 195, 198, 293n.61

Ali, S., 302n.6

Alibhai-Brown, Yasmin, 283n.129

All-American Girl (TV show), 239

Allen, Bill, 253n.3

All in the Family (TV show), 118

Amalgamated Engineering Union (England), 103

"American Century," 46

Americanization: *India Abroad* debate over assimilation and, 189–90, 202; newly gendered stories of self-identificatory move toward, 160–67; as overlaying productions of Indian subjectivity, 171–72; political/social analysis of, 140. *See also* assimilation; modern Indianness

"Americanization Studies" series (Carnegie Corporation-funded), 176

Amin, Idi, 98, 238

Anand, Rajen S., 273n.141, n.142

Anand, Tania, 284n.138

Anderson, Benedict, 13, 18, 175, 176, 177, 256 nn.34 and 35, 258n.51, 289 nn.1, 4 and 5

Anderson, Kay, 80, 274 nn.8 and 9

Andrews, Naveen, 129

Anthias, Floya, 254n.17

Apache Indian (Steven Kapur), 218–24, 225, 226, 229, 230, 246, 248

Appadurai, Arjun, 253n.10, 258n.54

Arora, G.S., 261n.15

"Arranged Marriage" (Apache Indian), 223–24

"Aryan" immigrants, 36

Ashraf, Syed Firdaus, 299n.48

Asian Americans: comparing number of Indian immigrants with, 65–66; questioning identity of, 22–23

Asian Digest (English newspaper), 293n.56

Asian identity: bhangra music as youth expression of, 224–29, 231; immigration to England (1970s) and adoption of, 193; "Indian" (1980s) as descriptive tool instead of, 193–99; Indian racial consciousness as, 184; international reference points associated with, 185; questioning, 22–23; South Asian vs., 71, 293n.59. *See also* identity; South Asians

Asian Monitor (New York), 200

Asian Post (English newspaper), 106, 185, 194, 291n.28

Asian Times (English newspaper), 5, 177, 193, 194, 195, 198, 205, 206

Asian Woman magazine (London), 207–8, 211

The Asiatic in England (Salter), 32

assimilation: as applicable to "white ethnic" immigration (1882–1922), 216; changes in perspective of postwar world, 12–13; literary use of marriage as symbol for, 145, 155–56; which denies process of racialization, 245. *See also* Americanization

"Atlantean Trope" (Iyer), 231

Austin, Joe, 232, 299n.49

Axel, Brian Keith, 257n.49, 282n.115, 283n.128

Back, Les, 297n.20

Bahri, Deepika, 285n.8

Bains, Harwant S., 271n.112

Bakhshi, Shiv, 273n.142

Balasubramanian, M., 253n.13

Balibar, Etienne, 6, 7, 254n.14, n.15

"Ballad of East and West" (Kipling), 160

Ballard, Roger, 271n.120

Balusubramanian, V., 270n.100

Banerji, Sabita, 225, 298n.29

Bannerji, Indu Prakas, 37–38, 262n.34, 263n.35

Bannerji, J. J., 292n.42